THE INVENTION OF

THE AMERICAN POLITICAL PARTIES

THE
INVENTION
OF THE
AMERICAN
POLITICAL PARTIES

BY

Roy F. Nichols

THE FREE PRESS, NEW YORK

COLLIER-MACMILLAN LIMITED, LONDON

Library of Congress Catalog Card Number: 67-12797

First Free Press Paperback Edition 1972

The Macmillan Company, New York
Collier-Macmillan Canada Ltd., Toronto, Ontario

The Invention of the American Political Parties
by Roy F. Nichols
was first published in hard cover edition by
The Macmillan Company

Printed in the United States of America

printing number

1 2 3 4 5 6 7 8 9 10

TO THE RISING GENERATION OF POLITICAL HISTORIANS
WHO HAVE GIVEN NEW MEANING
TO THE AMERICAN CHARACTER
BY MORE ACCURATELY DEFINING
ITS BEHAVIOR PATTERNS.

ACKNOWLEDGMENTS

I am particularly indebted to my secretary, Mrs. Anna B. Shirley, to the staff of the University of Pennsylvania library and to my advisers in the offices of The Macmillan Company.

CONTENTS

PREFACE

The system of self-government called American democracy is Anglo-American in origin and history. It was never completely planned nor projected, and even in the laws and constitutions which have been its charters, it was never fully described. Certain of its chief elements were neither designed nor authorized, while some of its most effective instruments of operation have been unspecified improvisations and adaptations. Therefore, discovering the process of such improvisation and adaptation is the key to an understanding of this democracy's operating mechanism.

The United States of America from the beginning, not only of their existence as a federal government, but for two centuries before as a series of dependent communities on the far shores of the Atlantic, were dedicated to some form of self-government. Numerous of their inhabitants were participants in the process of choosing representatives and in some instance of electing the executive. From their forebears in the British Isles they had inherited, in significant part, the customs devised for registering their choices, and they proceeded to cultivate this capacity on the shores of America.

As this Atlantic democracy involved the behavior of many people, intricate mechanisms have been needed to bring the various individuals and groups into political cooperation. In order to achieve the necessary machinery of politics, many men have had to be ingenious and resourceful and to contrive much. American politics has had to be adjusted constantly to the many changes which the mounting rate of growth has required, so art has been constantly brought into play to supply ever more intricate devices to meet the needs of a self-governing community becoming increasingly complex.

One of the most elaborate of these inventions has been a unique instrument, the American political party machine. Its design was long in the making, and not until the mid-nineteenth century was it, for all intents and purposes, completed in the form of an organized and institutionalized two-party system, a device which enabled the community to carry on the periodic contests for power which are one of the chief features of the practice of self-government. Interestingly enough, this instrument was conceived and developed without any statutory or constitutional authorization.

Such a political machine was created to mobilize citizens in the efficient expression of their choices, in popular elections, of those whom they wished to bear rule over them. The history of its assembling was long; some of its elements were a millennium in the making. Its description has also been complicated by semantic confusions in which different elements have been called by the same name, and terms fitting in one era have been projected backward in time and applied to institutional stages of growth for which they are not appropriate. As F. W. Maitland describes it, "Too often we allow ourselves to suppose that, could we but get back to the beginning, we should find that all was intelligible and should then be able to watch the process whereby simple ideas were smothered under subtleties and technicalities. But it is not so. Simplicity is the outcome of technical subtlety; it is the goal, not the starting point. As we go backward the familiar outlines become blurred; the ideas become fluid, and instead of the simple we find the indefinite."[1] This the curious inquirer finds to be true, for the organism was an unplanned, folk construct of long and devious evolution, with its seed, like that of the government itself, sprouted beyond the seas and then transplanted to the American shore.

1. Robert Livingston Schuyler, "Frederick William Maitland, Historian," *Domesday Book and Beyond* (Berkeley, 1960), p. 95.

THE INVENTION OF

THE AMERICAN POLITICAL PARTIES

CENTURIES OF EVOLUTION

*O*N A May morning in 1848 the Honorable Andrew Stevenson of Virginia for a second time assumed the chair at a Democratic National Convention. In 1835, while he was speaker of the national House of Representatives, he had taken this place in a day when such gatherings were in the experimental stage. The experience in the three presidential campaigns in the years intervening had perfected the party organization which had been evolving. National conventions and other partisan instruments had proved their worth, and Stevenson who on his first experience had expressed a hope could now announce its fulfillment. He proclaimed in his opening remarks, that national conventions to nominate presidential candidates "springing immediately from the people have become the only practicable mode of uniting and giving effect to the popular will." They were the mechanism needed to make self-government work.

When a few days later the record of these deliberations was completed by Samuel Treat of Missouri and his colleagues in the convention secretariat, they dispatched it to the political printers, Blair and Rives, so that it could be run off and distributed broadcast among the citizens of the republic. Whether they realized it is very doubtful, but they were completing a record long in the making.

It was now the responsibility of a new functionary in the American political hierarchy to take over and perform his duties. This was a rotund figure, Benjamin Franklin Hallett of Massachusetts. The son of an evangelist to sailors, Hallett had a desire to convert the Democratic party in Massachusetts into a winning combination and to confound Daniel Webster. He was an only son with thirteen sisters and thus took naturally to political organization. He was now to become the first national party chairman and mobilizer to assume any but a temporary responsibility. His appointment marked the practical completion of the essential machinery of the Democratic party, one of the most ingenious devices invented to make efficient the practice of self-government and destined to promote the art of politics.

The completion of this political machine brought to a very undramatic climax a process that had been centuries in evolution. Some of the parts of this machine were very old, for they had been conceived originally in England almost a millennium before the great migration. They had been developed on the island of Great Britain and then borne across the Atlantic by the American settlers. Scattered evidences of their origin and shadowy early history can be gleaned from the oldest sources of British history.

A thousand years or so before Mr. Hallett's elevation, some industrious monks of King Alfred's day began compiling the *Anglo-Saxon Chronicle*, but they lacked certain skills which are today taken for granted. They were not learned in the methods much later refined by historians; their techniques, like their motives, were in fact rather simple. There was a good deal of interesting tradition and folklore floating about which they thought ought to be recorded. The king was interested, the Church was well staffed with scribes, let these annals be gathered and arranged in some chronology to glorify God and to honor the king.

As they labored, these religious compilers scattered through the pages certain items that suggest the antiquity of various patterns of self-government. Within the cumulated miscellany that intrigued them, they included some significant political observations. Then, as now, politics was a machine, a contrivance to insure the continuity of government. Strikingly enough, despite the fact that it was so long ago, there had already evolved in England a species of self-government with a politics all its own, though its kingdoms were functioning uneasily on the periphery of a continental society seemingly dominated by various absolutisms. The chroniclers present neither a complete story nor a connected narrative, but their compilation suggests an epic, the saga of a great development in human history. A selection from these monkish sentences stirs the historical imagination, suggesting as they do some precedents for the election of the executive:

"In this year [A.D. 757] Cynewulf and the councilers of the West Saxons deprived Sigeberht, his kinsman, of his kingdom because of his unjust acts." A little later follows another entry: "In this year [774] the Northumbrians drove their king Alhred from York at Easter, and took as their lord Ethelred, Moll's son, and he reigned for four years." A century later appeared another notation referring to the city of York: "And there was great civil strife going on in that people, and they deposed their king Osbert and taken a king with no hereditary right." In 924 it was recorded: "And Athelstan was chosen by the Mercians as king, and consecrated at Kingston."

In 1014 when Swein died and Cnut was elected king by the Danish fleet, the record states that "all the councillors who were in England, ecclesiastical and lay, determined to send for King Ethelred, and they said that no lord was dearer to them than their natural lord if he would govern them more justly than he did before." He sent his son with messages to tell them he would "reform all the things which they all hated." But Ethelred died, so "all the councillors who were in London and the citizens chose Edmund as king, and he stoutly defended his kingdom while life lasted." When Cnut died, "there was an assembly of all the councillors at Oxford. And Earl Leofric and almost all the thegns north of the Thames and the shipmen in London chose Harold to the regency of all England, for himself and for his brother Hardacnut, who was then in Denmark." In 1042 when Hardacnut died, "before he was buried, all the people chose Edward as king, in London."

The Conquest itself by no means erased the idea of election in choosing the monarch. After the battle of Hastings, William the Conqueror paid some heed to it. King Harold had been killed and immediately "Archbishop Aldred and the citizens of London wanted to have Edgar [Atheling] as king, as was his proper due." William did not go on to London to take over the kingdom but "went back to Hastings and waited there to see whether submission would be made to him." When the English did not come immediately, William went inland and began ravaging. This led the archbishop and Edgar and "all the chief men from London" to approach. "They gave hostages and swore oaths to him, and he promised them that he would be a gracious liege host. All went to London and there he was crowned, but not until he had sworn that he would rule all this people as well as the best of the kings before him, if they would be loyal to him." Then the Conqueror was elected by customary acclamation and swore the traditional oath to the Church and the law.

William II seems to have followed his father and to have been crowned as a matter of course. But when he became the first of the Anglo-Norman kings to have his reign and his life ended violently, his astute younger brother, Henry so-called Beauclerc, had to persuade the notables that they should accept him rather than his elder brother

Robert. This they did and he shortly issued the Constitution of 1101 in which he undertook to promise to make reforms and to right wrongs which had come to flourish, particularly in the last reign. At Henry's death there was a period of anarchy. He had tried to insure the succession of his daughter Matilda by agreement of the notables. Stephen, another heir, contested this, and like monarchs in a previous era, he was acclaimed by the Londoners, who sent for the archbishop to crown him.

Intermittent civil war followed, which resulted finally in an agreement to let Stephen occupy the throne and to accept Matilda's son, Count Henry, as his heir by agreement of the "Archbishop and the wise men," an agreement which the "king [Stephen], the count [Henry], the bishop and the earls and powerful men all swore to keep." Interestingly enough, the agreement was honored, despite the fact that Henry was in his French dominions at the time of Stephen's death. The *Chronicle* says that "nobody dared to anything but good to another because they were in such great awe of [Henry II]."

As a result of this agreement a dynasty was created, and for more than a century the succession was hereditary, though anything but peaceful. Henry II was plagued by intrigues and revolts fomented by his queen and their sons. When John, his younger son, became king, he was eventually forced to grant Magna Carta. At his death shortly thereafter, a group of nobles elevated his nine-year-old son, Henry III, to the throne. The latter ruled from 1216 until 1272, and during this long reign the Great Council of nobles, which replaced the Witenagemot, began to assume the functions of a parliament. When Henry III died, his heir, Edward I, was in the Holy Land, but his throne waited for him during the two years that it took him to return. In this distinguished reign, 1272–1307, Parliament was finally established, including representatives of the commons, and it grew in power. In 1327 Edward's son, Edward II, was deposed and his son chosen king by Parliament as Edward III. The latter's grandson, Richard II, was likewise deposed in 1399, and Parliament then changed the dynasty by electing Henry IV of Lancaster as king.

Thus, during long experiences stretching over centuries in which Anglo-Saxons, Danes, and Normans shaped the emerging English political system, they had produced a cumulation of precedents involving on occasion the election of the executive.

The machinery of electing lawmakers was later in origin and more clearly recorded. Prior to the thirteenth century the bodies which preceded the English Parliament, namely the Anglo-Saxon Witena-gemot and the Great Council of the Normans and Plantagenets, had been assemblies of notables, advisers to the king often acting as a court of law, in which no element of election seemed present. But in that century the increasing complexity of government and especially its mounting expense aroused the English kings to sense of a new need. They began to realize that the feudal sources of revenue were not adequate. They then saw the necessity for turning to the growing number of men of wealth, particularly to men in commerce who had ready money. They found that "consultation" with representatives of this group during meetings of the Council generally produced acquiescence in taxes. From this situation arose parliamentary elections.

From the days of Edward I two knights were elected from each shire, and from "each town or city" in each shire, two or more "of the more discreet burghers or citizens, capable of work," were dispatched to the metropolis "with full and sufficient power for themselves and for their respective communities to do and consent to those things which in . . . parliament shall be ordained, lest for lack of this power these matters should remain unaccomplished." For many years there met in the Great Hall of the king's palace at Westminster some seven hundred men, presided over by the king himself. Those present were the king's intimate council, the great nobles, the archbishops and bishops, and seated behind them, the knights of the shires, and at the rear the burgesses and citizens. This was the Parliament of the realm with the three estates—nobles, churchmen, and commons—who were to set the precedents for lawmaking bodies in which popularly elected representatives of the people would participate. By slow process, what was originally a court and an administrative council became a tax-consenting and a lawmaking body, although at about the time American colonization was getting started, Parliament had only begun to assume the form and functions recognized today. During the course of this evolution, there had of necessity grown up a system of election much more definite and periodic than the shadowy element in the choice of kings. The knights from the shires and the burgesses from the boroughs were selected by a series of methods which were to pattern the elections that became so central a technique in the operation of American democracy.

The method of parliamentary election in Elizabeth's time was still simple. The shire representatives had been elected since 1430 by those males who possessed a forty-shilling freehold; at the call of the sheriff they came together at the shire hall in the county town and there voted viva voce. As a matter of fact, local noblemen and country gentlemen generally nominated these "knights of the shire," there was seldom a contest, and all an election amounted to was a shout of approval by a few freeholders.

On the rare occasions when there was a contest, it generally arose from local rivalry among the country gentry. Then, as in feudal days, the freeholders would rally around rival family standards as contesting landholders, who felt that the family honor was at stake, made their appeals. Such contests were often the expression of ancient feuds.

Some embryonic political methods had been developed. Although there was a prejudice against open canvassing, there was some discreet letter writing. Upon occasion a committee might be formed which would seek to enlist the interest of various men of standing and influence. Some candidates had friends and agents who went among the freeholders, threatening dispossession of their houses if they did not vote as they should. Outsiders could be brought in; a gentleman from a neighboring shire might come over with his followers. Then, too, voters could be made by giving individuals small parcels of land on the understanding that they would relinquish them after the day of the election.

The climax of such politics came on election day. Since voting was done only in the shire town, freeholders had to come in to the shire hall, where the election was held, at eight in the morning. Because of the early hour, it was necessary at times to find lodging and board for those who must come far, and a wise candidate would hire an inn to see that his retainers had a place to eat and sleep. If the agent of one could secure all the inn accommodations, he had a great advantage. That shire halls were generally small presented another hazard. On election day each side tried to secure possession of its limited space; when the sheriff put the names, the viva voce response for the one controlling the hall would be overwhelming. Again, if the sheriff was favorable to a candidate, his influence might be the deciding factor, for when the result appeared to be close, the sheriff was supposed to poll the crowd. Each man had to give his name, his vote, and if challenged, swear that he was worth at least forty shillings. Sheriffs were even known to adjourn elections and reconvene them in unexpected locations or to falsify returns. This sort of politics was not typical, for contests were rare, but such things did happen.

Election procedures in the shires were not duplicated in the boroughs. Custom, in fact, varied from borough to borough, and any description which implies uniformity is misleading. There was not even any common definition of a voter. The democratic procedures which seemed to be emerging in some boroughs during the later Middle Ages had quite generally given way to oligarchic control. The borough government, composed of local magistrates sitting usually as two houses, frequently chose the members of Parliament. These councils, which had originally been elected either by popular assemblies or by the trade guilds, had for the most part become closed corporations which filled vacancies as they occurred. It had therefore become the custom in many such towns for the mayor and council to choose the members of Parliament without reference to popular will. On occasion their procedure might be complex. In one borough, for instance, the mayor named four burgesses. These four named four more, and the eight then named an additional four. In turn, these twelve men—six aldermen and six members from the lower house—chose two members of Parliament, usually from among the members of the borough council. Thus the choice of members of Parliament rested largely in the hands of local magnates either in country or town.

In the course of the centuries of evolution of the election machinery, the rudimentary form of another pattern of political mechanism becomes visible. Traces of party organization begin to appear, but here again the early indications are vague and elusive. They are determined by the fact that for the first millennium of the Christian Era England had been subject to invasion. Even before the Christian Era the Romans attacked the island and eventually conquered parts of it, setting a pattern for Angles, Saxons, Danes, and finally Normans in the centuries to follow. Each time, there was a conquest; those of the Romans and Danes were but temporary, but the Angles, Saxons, and Normans came to stay. Thus from 55 B.C. to A.D. 1066 the inhabitants of the island became familiar with the concept of two population groups and interests as a recurring phenomenon. These were Romans and natives, Anglo-Saxons and natives, Danes and natives, Normans and natives. Each force of invaders played the role of conqueror and undertook to rule.

In the organization of government after the conquests, the conquerors had to deal with the local leaders and the populace in general. Over long periods of time, therefore, there was a natural, unplanned two-party grouping engaged in working out governmental policy. The existence of this division in the patterns of political behavior over so long a period of time may well have produced a tendency to expect society to be organized in two groups, and this expectation could have served as a conditioner for the two-party system which was to develop so much later.

This tendency for society and politics to divide into two forces was further accentuated by conditions arising out of the close relations between Church and State in the sixteenth century, on the eve of the American migration. The primary units, religious and political, in England were the parishes, each with its church which served not only as a place of worship but of popular assembly and association as well. The parish was the fundamental instrument both of ecclesiastical polity and of civil government. In the rural districts it could be a seat of government. There the vestry met and there some of the local taxes were assessed. Closely associated religious institutions—the priories, monasteries, chantries, and guilds—were also integral parts of the civic life of the people. Charity was often dispensed, sickness cared for, and recreation provided by these agencies; people looked to them so long for so much.

By 1540 basic changes, stemming from the Reformation, were in process. Monasteries, chantries, and guilds had been disbanded. The Church had been nationalized. There were new ideas about the forms of the religious service. Many people were no longer interested in adoring mysteries and blindly obeying priestly injunctions: they had begun reading the Bible, now available in English; they wanted to hear expository preaching. All told, there was much to talk about, and much of it was controversial. Naturally, it was to be in the parish that the greater part of this controversy was to take place. Politics began to appear in the vestry.

The subject of the most active controversy was the nature of the church service. Should the images be torn out, should candles and incense be abandoned? Should the altar become a communion table and be placed in the center of the church? Should the rood and screen be pulled down and the crucifix laid aside? Should the priests abandon vestments? Should they preach more? All these questions produced differences of opinion, and when it came time to choose the churchwardens, there might well be disputes dictated by such divergences of view.

It must not be forgotten that the questions of who should direct vestry policy and who should be churchwardens were coming to mean more in community life just about this time. Originally, vestries had merely managed the minutiae of keeping the church in repair, of providing proper vestments and supplies for the service. For these expenses the churchwardens had levied rates or taxes, but now new functions were added. When the monasteries and charitable guilds were eliminated by the government, those who had taken care of the poor were deprived of their means. Furthermore, such economic policies as enclosing small farms to make sheep pasture and debasing the coinage had caused unemployment, higher prices, and more poverty. Some new provision had to be made for poor relief, and in Elizabeth's reign this responsibility was assigned to the parishes. The churchwardens and the justices of the peace were now required to support the unfortunate by assessment. The parishes were also given the new obligation of maintaining highways. Thus the churchwardens and vestrymen became economically as well as religiously responsible, and ambitions for securing these offices may have become more active.

The center of parish discussion and often its leader was, of course, the clergyman. A number of parish priests sought to lead their parishioners in new ways. Some of them abandoned vestments and used the new Geneva prayer book. Such activities were encouraged during the 1560's when a number of French Huguenots and Dutch Protestants fled from the Continent and brought their experiences to various English parishes. There was likewise a growing determination to increase the activity of laymen in parish government. The civil magistrates, well aware of this trend, realized that the new popular interest in government was a force to be reckoned with. They themselves in many instances were endeavoring to take over functions which had hitherto belonged to ecclesiastical courts. Some of the perquisites also brought them into close association with church vestries, since the magistrates, as local gentry, often possessed the right to appoint priests to local parishes.

Parish independence and increased lay participation in management and discussion were encouraged by a new feature appearing in this troubled time. The lack of educated clergy had led certain of the authorities in cathedrals and large town parishes to organize discussion groups to which the less-educated clergy and interested laymen might come for information, scriptural interpretation, or religious doctrine. This activity was called "prophesying." Frequently, on some weekdays, large groups of interested people from the surrounding region would come in to listen or to ask questions. These prophesyings strengthened the Puritan tendency to manage parish affairs locally, upon occasion in defiance of central authority.

But local enterprise went further than this. Groups who were dissatisfied with local parish conditions seceded, and Elizabeth had been only seven years on the throne when independent organization began. The custom during the Marian terror of meeting in private houses or secular buildings was resumed; people formed their own organizations, elected their officers, chose their pastors, and drafted covenants or constitutions. Such clandestine groups were illegal and invited punishment, but their members were not afraid of being sent to jail. "Separatism," with its congregational form of government, was spreading.

By the close of the sixteenth century, the century of Reformation, the political implications of the parish system had become very clear. The growth of Protestant opposition to the Church of Rome had infinite repercussions. Because many clung tenaciously to the old forms and Roman loyalties, two religious parties arose, Catholic and Protestant. This fact cut deep because the identity of Church and State meant that refusal to conform could be construed as treason and such punishments as the block and the stake might be decreed. Also, the individualistic tendency of the day and the awakening of individual thinking produced a variety of religious ideas and interpretations. Each parish was a potential seat of controversy in which religion and politics were thoroughly intermingled.

The emergence of the variant groups—Puritans, Presbyterians, Separatists—precipitated a political contest for control of the ecclesiastical organization and doctrinal formulation in the English Church. These contests anticipated various modern political behavior patterns. Those who wished to make the Church more scriptural in its doctrine, less ritualistic in its form, and more presbyterian or otherwise independent, i.e. congregational, in its organization, waged war, not only against liturgical service forms, but also against the rule of the bishops, which, of course, meant proposing to limit the power of the queen. They realized they must work through Parliament and hence through politics. So they began to run candidates for Parliament, and when they won, the new members began to work together. There was much of this politics in shire, borough, and parish, and an organized opposition reflected it in Westminster. Queen Elizabeth became adept at dealing with it. Laws were passed against the most radical who would defy the crown and leave the Church—a few were hanged at Tyburn; some, under compulsion, abjured the realm—but in the main Elizabeth managed well without invoking penalties. Thus these religious differences, more vividly than the conditions during the millennium of invasions and still more firmly, fixed a pattern of twofold division foreshadowing the two-party system of a later age.

Finally, there had developed a politics which had origin in the world of commerce. A new set of patterns had been designed, not in hall or in church, but in the "general courts" of business corporations when the managers and stockholders began to create commercial depots outside the realm. In the thirteenth century adventurous merchants began to unite their capital and enterprise in combinations formed to trade, first on the Continent and then, within three centuries, all over the known world. Politically, these promoters were ingenious. They organized companies of stockholders who were governed by officials chosen by them at the general courts. These companies in turn negotiated outposts on the Continent where they were granted the privilege of establishing compounds in foreign cities, where they would be free to govern their concerns.

In the 1570's and 1580's when England was first confronted with the problem of sending Englishmen to America to set up some sort of permanent establishment, management and government made decisions which started the weaving of other patterns of American politics. The enterprising promoters of the sixteenth century made use of English experience with experiments which had been in progress for these centuries, during which a pattern of self-governing trading stations had been created outside the realm. During Elizabeth's reign this idea was tried in America by such adventurous spirits as Martin Frobisher, Humphrey Gilbert, and Walter Raleigh. Efforts in Greenland, Newfoundland, and Virginia brought dearly won experience and scarcely any success, but they had charted a course across the Atlantic.

These doubtful ventures were steps in the direction of creating an American polity. The British crown found that it was not able to undertake empire-building directly or at its own expense; the donation of a few hundred pounds was all that the government would give. But it could encourage private enterprise to establish outposts by granting charters or patents to individual enterprisers authorizing them to create societies in the form of trading posts designed to be governed as English municipalities and placing land at their disposal with which to encourage settlement and possible speculation. The government would withhold for itself a share of all treasure discovered, but it was the individual enterpriser who was to assume the burden of the great venture and to be creative in adapting or inventing such political institutions as would be necessary for management and governance.

When finally English colonists were ready to undertake the creation of new societies across the Atlantic, there was already a national tradition of popular elections and of the politics that accompanied them. There were significant precedents, and those venturing across the seas in the seventeenth century were well aware of these lessons learned at Westminster, in the shire halls, in parish vestries, in congregational meetings, and in general courts of chartered companies. Would the transatlantic migrants find soil which would nourish the stock about to be transplanted? The first to discover such soil were those who managed the London Company, which undertook to establish posts in Walter Raleigh's ill-fated Virginia.

·◦§ II §◦·

VIRGINIAN ORIGINS

*P*OLITICS CAME over to America on the ships with the English migrants. Not that it was so intended, for the promoters were more mindful of economic gain or social experiment than of political operation. No English politicians ever sat down to plan a miniature political stage in America where understudies would speak well-known lines. In fact government seems to have been too little thought of. Yet it can be said that American political behavior began on shipboard as the first colonists of the London Company of Virginia ploughed their slow way across the Atlantic. On the decks and in the cabins of the *Sarah Constant* and her two consorts, which set sail from Blackwall on the Thames on December 20, 1606, began some of the processes of political behavior which, involved as they were in the education in self-government and the struggle for power, were to be such important patterns in the American democratic design.

For it was in 1606 that certain London and Plymouth merchants and other adventurers undertook to follow the chartered-company routine of the previous century in new efforts to develop commercial outposts in America. The Plymouth Company failed during a disastrous winter on the Maine coast, but the London group, returning to Virginia to the north of Raleigh's failure, were to achieve permanence.

They chartered three small vessels, the largest of only one hundred tons burden, enlisted one hundred men and four boys, and sent them forth to explore and report on the possibilities. During the voyage the three ship captains were to command, but on arriving in America they were to open sealed instructions which would give the details of future government and operation.

The voyage was long and difficult and the leading personalities proved possessed of degrees of incompatibility. Two in particular had gotten on each other's nerves. Edward Maria Wingfield, a veteran of England's wars, a man of good family, and one of the incorporators of the London Company, entered into violent quarrels with a garrulous and boastful venturer, the redoubtable John Smith, who had joined the expedition fresh from exploits in the Near East. Before long Wingfield charged Smith with mutiny and caused the ship captains to put him in irons. This personal feud was to have political implications which were to play an important part in the venture. For Wingfield represented the vested interests of the company and his associates among the shareholders, while Smith represented adventurous actionists. This was a fundamental political division which was to appear and reappear so frequently in the American centuries to follow.

The implications of this feud were all the more important because of the nature of the government. Just before sailing, the Council for Virginia, which represented royal authority, though made up largely of the stockholders of the company, had made decisions as to who was to rule and what the program should be. Following a practice developed by the British East India Company and the terms of the charter, they had appointed a commission of seven to carry out Operation Virginia. But of men and plans they gave the expedition no clue. In the meantime, Admiral Newport had in his possession the box containing sealed packages of orders which were not to be opened until America was reached.

When, on an April evening, the storm-tossed ships came to anchor in the quiet waters of the Chesapeake, the seals were broken and a governing septemvirate was revealed. The instructions produced a "nice" situation, for Smith, who was named to the committee, was in irons. As Wingfield and the three captains in the employ of the company made up a majority, there was no difficulty in coming to two decisions: Wingfield should be president of this Virginia council and Smith should be excluded from its deliberations. With these decisions made, the expedition explored the region and hit upon a narrow, swamp-infested peninsula as the site of their new post, Jamestown.

Newport, unfortunately, was scheduled to leave early in the summer. He was an experienced man, and as he soon saw that Wingfield and his council were weak and indecisive governors, he took thought. The colony needed some decisive leadership, and Smith, despite his romancing tendencies, seemed to have some executive capacity and energy. Newport already had found the council unpopular among the settlers and had been called upon to strain his powers of conciliation. So as his day of departure approached, he probably urged that Smith be admitted to his place on the council. This was reluctantly conceded, and Newport and his fleet set sail for home, leaving to his associates the difficult task of ruling.

Wingfield now had to preside over a council from which the conciliatory Newport had departed and in which Captain John Smith could very readily take the part of leader of the opposition. Conditions were growing worse: food was short, Indians were hostile, summer was hot, mosquitoes were present in clouds, and there were no signs of gold deposits discoverable. Some of the colonists began to sicken of malaria and die, and the Indians murdered others. It was dangerous to leave the triangular fort; and the tents, the wooden shacks, and the dirt caves gave little comfort. The council was most plagued with discord. George Kendall, kinsman to Sir Edwin Sandys of the company, was very outspoken in his complaints and dissents. So in a few short weeks his fellows expelled him on the charge of fomenting discontent among the wretched settlers. In August Captain Gosnold died of the fever.

Thus only four were left and Wingfield was ever more incompetent and lacking in popular confidence. Then Smith saw his chance. Smith and Captain John Martin, who represented the anticompany party, approached Captain Ratcliffe. They pointed out Wingfield's "obvious" incompetence and impressed Ratcliffe with the need of more vigorous leadership such as he could provide. They proposed that the three of them depose Wingfield and make Ratcliffe president. The latter was not hard to convince.

Wingfield was therefore surprised one morning when his colleagues came to his tent and gravely presented him with a warrant bearing their signatures. They charged him with stealing, with feasting upon company stores while others starved, with being an atheist, and with treasonable efforts to escape with the colony's one sailing vessel in order to combine with the Spaniards to destroy the colony. They declared "him very unworthy to be either President or of the Council, and therefore discharged him of both." With Wingfield thus deposed, the new triumvirate set themselves up as a court and ordered him to stand trial before them on these charges. He, however, demanded a hearing before the king and they dared not refuse. So they locked him up on board their one boat to hold him prisoner until he could be sent home.

Ratcliffe proved to be no particular improvement over Wingfield. He even got into a brawl with one of the colonists, who struck him.

This affront to majesty was about to be avenged by death when the culprit confessed a plot to destroy the colony involving Kendall, so Kendall was hanged instead.

Food became so short that Smith undertook a prolonged foraging expedition, and during his absence Ratcliffe and Martin admitted Gabriel Archer, one of Smith's enemies, to the deliberations of the council. He was eager to cast off company ties altogether and set up a popularly elected governing body, the first suggestion of democracy in America.

What might have happened had not Smith come back, we shall never know. However, he and Archer got into a dispute, and as two of Smith's men had been killed on the expedition, Archer indicted him as responsible for their deaths, citing Leviticus. Ratcliffe, Martin, and Archer thereupon undertook to try him, and he might have met the same fate as Kendall had not Newport returned in January 1608 with supplies from England. Newport, always the conciliator, persuaded the council to drop the charges. He also brought a new councilor commissioned from London in the person of Matthew Scrivener. As Archer and Martin decided to go back to England, the council was now again one of three—Ratcliffe, Smith, and Scrivener—but it was no more harmonious.

During the summer, while Smith again went exploring, Ratcliffe became so unpopular, particularly because he made the reduced and ailing population work on a mansion for himself, that there was a mutiny, and Scrivener was called upon to take the presidency for the balance of Ratcliffe's one-year term. When it expired in September 1608, Smith was back in Jamestown, and it was agreed that he should succeed. Newport returned again in December and Ratcliffe shortly accompanied him back to England. Richard Waldo and Peter Wynne were placed on the council—but not for long. In January 1609, Scrivener and Waldo were drowned and Wynne died shortly thereafter. Smith at last was in undisputed control—he was the government, it might be said, by default. But there were still malaria, starvation, and death, and despite a certain amount of success which Smith claimed in Indian relations, via Pocahontas, the life of the colony was precarious. No gold had been found and the surly population had little enterprise, subsisting as best they might from the company's store. Likewise, the cape merchant was dead and Smith assumed his job. He set to work with a will but ill fortune dogged his footsteps during the year of his rule, 1608–9. In August his old associates, Ratcliffe, Martin, and Archer, returned with word that a new charter and a new governor were on the way. Smith expected to serve out his term, but quarrels developed, and when Smith, though incapacitated by an explosion of gunpowder, refused to surrender his authority, the former councilors, Martin, Archer, and Ratcliffe, took his office from him and bestowed it upon George Percy. Such was the febrile origin of the politics of self-government in America.

American politics thus had been born of novelty and bewilderment. Those who stood first on American soil found it strange. As they looked around, there were no familiar landmarks, only a strange shore, their own strained faces, their stained clothing, and the torturing ship which had almost literally disgorged them on this unknown strand. All else too was dismaying. In such surroundings, theirs was to be a task supremely taxing to their powers of adjustment and control.

Word of these troubles plus a disturbing lack of profits led the London Company to prescribe reorganization. They abandoned the idea of agency by committee, substituted government by a single agent with more power, made provision for local government, and assigned a good deal of independence to the new communities. The governor who took the place of the ineffective committee was assisted by a council of representative men from the colony, a pattern copied from the company organization in London. This "able and absolute" governor was to be under instruction from the company, and the colonists were guaranteed the "Liberties, Franchises and Immunities of Englishmen." He and his council served as the judiciary of the colony in what was to become a quarterly court.

Under this stronger leadership there was greater growth, and more "planters" and stockholders came out. They were to be assigned allotments of land which they were to work for seven years for the common cause. At the end of this period they would receive land in fee simple. In the meantime, protection against the Indians and the extending of settlement made necessary the creation of local government.

As on the Continent and in Raleigh's venture, the model which the English expected to use was the municipal corporation, and four boroughs were established. But it was soon apparent that Virginia was not to be primarily commercial or industrial and that cities were not to play a part. Virginia was to be an agricultural community whose citizens were to be planters with their tenants and indentured servants.

By 1616, when the seven-year trial period of organization was ended and grants of land were made, the form of local organization adapted to American conditions was the hundred, or organization of planters in a locality similar to the English rural hundreds. These hundreds became administrative and judicial divisions managed by the leading planters. In fact, associations of adventurers were invited to bring tenants and establish themselves in communities which would be given the privileges of self-government, largely independent of the government of Jamestown.

Each of the hundreds had an officer nominated by the proprietor and commissioned by the governor as commander. He was to be both military officer, responsible for defense and order, and civil magistrate. In some hundreds this officer appears to have had a group of associates with functions something like the county court in England. As the colony grew and it was no longer feasible to take all court business to Jamestown, this officer and his associates, when he had them, would meet periodically, perhaps once a month. Later these monthly courts met at different points under their jurisdiction, submitting their records to the quarter courts sitting at Jamestown. These officials were instructed to copy as far as possible the methods of the English justices of the peace at quarter sessions.

All these developments were pointing in one direction, namely toward the introduction of the English county. In 1634 eight were created, and they became the most important units of local administration. They were presided over by the members of the county courts, or county commissioners, as they were sometimes called. Their executive officer was the sheriff, appointed by the governor on their recommendation. Closely associated with the English county organizations were the parish officials, but in America the parish did not become the significant local unit that it was in the home country. In Virginia, parishes were much larger, occasionally having the same boundaries as the counties.

Another element in the emerging pattern of American political behavior was the civil-religious function of the parish. This English unit of civil and religious life was transplanted to Virginia, but as so often was the case in America the circumstances were quite different. The same men oftentimes were the justices of the county courts and members of the vestry, and they administered courts and parish matters without much distinction between them. Also, there were to be no ecclesiastical courts, so the parish officers, in making presentments for violation of public morals and in keeping vital statistics and probate records, were acting with and for the county courts. Church-wardens, vestrymen, and county justices were generally of the same small class of the responsible planters who bore the burden of local government in Virginia. There were no bishops in America, the parishes chose their own priests, and as they often did not present them to the Bishop of London, they were in effect independent con-gregations ruling themselves.

Thus in Virginia the county-parish system rather than the munic-ipal corporation system of self-government developed. Neither of these patterns proved very suitable. They operated much the same as the corresponding institutional pattern in England, but there were significant differences dictated by American conditions. The system itself was not introduced ready-made but grew up out of American experience piece by piece.

In fact the venture turned out very differently from the way it had been planned in London. It was not to be a trading and industrial outpost operated for the profit of the stockholders and those who ventured overseas. It was not to be a series of boroughs. A group of ambitious smalltime people had re-created what they knew best and most admired at home: a British squirearchy, county in form and government, with themselves as the squires. It was not what London planned but what the experience and dreams of the migrants, together with the environment, had enforced. Thus was demonstrated a basic fact peculiar to North American political development—namely that emigrants from England, conditioned by their *past* experience, by their dreams for the *future*, and by the rigorous dictation of their *present* environment, were establishing in the New World those in-struments of local self-government based on English practice which they could adapt to their new environment.

In their first permanent colony the Virginians, during their initial, turbulent dozen years of experience, had organized their area into four boroughs and seven hundreds, each with some measure of self-government. This policy of creating local, self-governing units was accompanied by an even more significant contribution to the demo-cratic idea. This contribution came from a rather unexpected source —no less than the London Company stockholders themselves! To the end that more planters and settlers might be expected to migrate if their right to participate in the government was even more positively recognized, the London Company voted in a stockholders' meeting November 28, 1618, to establish a House of Burgesses in Virginia to make laws and to serve as a court, and orders were dispatched to carry out the plan. The legislature was to be summoned from the four boroughs and seven hundreds in which the now one thousand Virginians dwelt. The governor sent messengers to the commanders of these outlying settlements instructing them to call their people together to select two representatives to repair to Jamestown. He likewise summoned the members of the council. So the captains assembled the men in their districts to make the choices in general meeting. Factions appeared; some planters were bitter against the company, others were willing to support its new regime in hopes of better things. Personal rivalries of course appeared and local quarrels were reflected. Voting seems to have been viva voce, and in due course twenty-two men were chosen.

They assembled at Jamestown on the day set, July 30, 1619, and a hot and miserable day it was. The marshy lowlands were steaming and mosquitoes were out in force. The House of Burgesses was to meet in the wooden church which had been somewhat refurbished for the occasion. The governor marched to the place of worship followed by his council and the House. He sat in his chair within the choir with his council to the right and left of him. The secretary of the colony, John Pory, had been designated speaker, and he sat before the governor with his clerk, John Twine, on one hand and the sergeant at arms, Thomas Pierce, standing at the bar. The burgesses also sat within the choir. The Reverend Mr. Richard Burke, Oxford graduate and parish priest, opened the proceedings with prayer. Then the House of Burgesses was requested to retire to the body of the church. The speaker called the roll, and twenty returned to the choir. The names of two were not called: Thomas Davis and Robert Stacy who came from Captain John Martin's plantation were excluded on the ground that under the captain's patent he was declared independent of the colony. The new legislature now adopted a protest against such a patent and announced their determination not to accept any representative from Martin's settlement until that provision was deleted.

The twenty burgesses then took the oath of supremacy, "none staggering at it," and the first legislature in America was thus constituted. The speaker, "who a long time had been extreame sickly, and therefore not able to passe through long harangues, delivered in briefe to the whole assembly the occasions of their meeting." He read to them the charter and the "lawes" which Governor George Yeardley had brought from the company. These laws he had arranged in four "books," and he divided the burgesses into four committees to consider them. Two of these committees brought in petitions for amendments which were to be sent to London. The other two committees found no changes desirable. This finished, the assembly gave their assent and applause to the laws. Then they debated "such instructions given by the Counsell in England to several Governors as might be converted into laws." A number of these they enacted. Next on the agenda was a third sort of laws, "such as might proceed out of every man's private concept." These were referred to two committees and, upon recommendation, voted the next day. The final duty of the legislature was to sit as a court on two cases. These disposed of, "being constrained by the intemperance of the weather and the falling sick of diverse of the Burgesses"—in fact one had died—they broke up abruptly at the end of the fifth day, "before they had so much as put their laws to engrossing, this they wholly committed to the fidelity of their speaker." American representative democracy had begun to function, albeit under difficulty.

As the colony slowly grew and its population extended in sprawling fashion into the wilderness, it had continuous need for government and defense, for relations with the aboriginal inhabitants were never secure. With the numerous indentured servants inclined to be unruly, it was necessary to have some system of law enforcement. At first the governor and his council sitting at Jamestown had been sufficient for magistracy and defense, and then the plan was to develop municipal corporations such as the colonists had known in England. Where stockholders had migrated to operate their own landholdings, plantations, or hundreds with tenants, feudal institutions were to be the order.

The pattern of political action thus begun was to facilitate the development of political pathways. Hereafter, at intervals the colonists were to gather at plantation houses or churches and to give to the commanders viva voce their choices for legislators. The men of their choice were to go to Jamestown to join with the governor and his council in hearing petitions, approving laws prepared in England, initiating legislation, and rendering judicial opinions.

The voters in the boroughs and on the plantations and the legislators in Jamestown were to develop differences of opinion and to counsel policies at variance one with another. During these years of improvisation and adaptation of political institutions, controversy and contest flourished. The clash of personalities which had characterized the feud for power in the first council next developed on a broader scale. John Smith's associate in opposition, Captain John Martin, continued his role. He disliked the rule of the company and on occasion opposed its policies as administered by its governors. He had influential friends in England, and as he returned home occasionally, he kept these ties warm. When the distribution of land to the stockholders took place, he demanded more and used his influence in England to secure a special patent for Martin's Hundred, which was to be free from "any commaunde of the colony." The first legislature, because of this special privilege, had refused admission to the burgesses from Martin's patent. He was, in fact, forced to get a new patent. This made him no more cooperative and he seized various opportunities to foment opposition to the governors. It is likely that he had a part in the efforts being made to have the English government oust the company and take over the colony.

The corporation was, in fact, in grave financial difficulties, burdened with a debt that it probably never could pay, and it is not strange that the crown took notice. In 1623 the Privy Council sent over a commission of five men, all but one of whom had lived in the colony. The House of Burgesses cooperated reasonably with the commissioners but on some points refused to do what was requested. In particular, they refused to submit drafts of some papers they were sending to England. When the commissioners obtained these papers by bribery, the venal clerk was condemned to stand in the pillory and have his ears cut off. Martin and his following claimed this was an affront to the king. He also declared that he expected to see Governor Francis Wyatt and members of his council in this same pillory and prophesied that there would soon be a change in government. Wyatt finally lost patience with him and suspended him from his council.

Martin, however, seemed to know what he was talking about, for even before the commissioners had reported, the crown had sought court action against the company, and it had been dissolved by judicial order. Thereupon the king undertook to govern. He continued Wyatt as governor, at the same time appointing a new council. Then he died. The king's death in 1625 deprived Wyatt of his commission. He was now left with no power to call a House of Burgesses, yet he felt that colonial opinion must be mobilized. The last House had sent over recommendations and petitions regarding the government they hoped the king would create, but their messenger had died and there was no knowing whether their views had ever been presented. So the governor called a "convention" to meet May 10, 1625, to send a new appeal to the crown, continue the House of Burgesses, and grant them freedom from monopoly control of tobacco marketing. Martin attacked this body as without standing and continued his policy of opposition to Wyatt.

Thus dissolution of the company had turned out to be a development which advanced the colony on the road to self-government. For they were given no new charter. In fact, they were left without much direction of any kind. It became apparent over the years that the crown was not going to undertake the direction of their behavior which the company had always attempted. The king, indeed, sent governors, but in general they did not have very definite instructions. Although no specific authorization of yearly meetings of the legislature was sent over, the governors now and then called them for consultation.

The colonial leaders were disturbed a good deal by this uncertainty as to their share in the government. This was not conducive to calm rule, and conflict was likely to occur sooner or later between the colonists and the king's governor. In 1628 John Harvey was appointed governor. He had been much in the colony and should have known its temper. However, he seemed more interested in working out policies desired in London, so he heeded little the resentments around him. The colonists were particularly disturbed over attempts by the crown to make the tobacco trade a monopoly for government benefit and also, in 1632, by the king's gift of part of Virginia to Lord Baltimore, who thus became the Catholic proprietor of a new colony to be known as Maryland. Governor Harvey openly approved both of these policies. Besides, he had grown arbitrary, acted independently of his council, and even attempted to lay taxes.

Now the secretary of the colony, William Claiborne, whose property on a Chesapeake island had been turned over to Baltimore, took Martin's place as leader of the opposition. Harvey finally removed Claiborne from office in 1634 and appointed a friend of Baltimore's. Also, he pocketed a petition of the House of Burgesses against the tobacco monopoly and approved an assault upon Claiborne's traders made by Baltimore's agents.

The result was the first American revolt. Harvey's enemies met at the home of William Warren at York in April 1635 to draw up a vigorous protest. Harvey had them arrested and brought before the council. When the council refused to punish, he flew into a towering rage and began to hurl charges of treason, particularly at one of his councilors, George Menifie. Samuel Mathews hurled these charges back and accused the governor of the same crime. Council thereupon arrested the governor, elected a new executive themselves in the person of Captain John West, and sent Harvey back to England in the custody of two members of the House of Burgesses. The council next called an assembly which ratified these actions. The king attempted to repress this self-governing tendency by summoning some of the council to England and by sending Harvey back. But he accepted councilors opposed to Harvey, and that officer did not remain long in his restored position.

Political contest was activated not only by differences between executive and the responsible elite, but it was also to gain pattern from the appearance of groups with variant and conflicting ideas. The prevailing differences between king and Parliament over religious matters, which were so vital a characteristic of English politics in the 1640's, traveled overseas. A Puritan group began to be discernible, particularly in Nansemond County in the seashore area of southeastern Virginia. These men felt the need of more spiritual comfort, and Richard Bennett and some like-minded men in 1642 determined to take steps to secede from the Church of England. In consequence, they sent to New England for ministers and three came in response. This schismatic evidence disturbed the governor and House of Burgesses, who in 1643 passed harsh measures against nonconformity. Though the new ministers were soon driven out under warrant of this law, the influence grew no less. In fact, an Indian massacre which followed hard upon this persecution was taken by some to be a punishment from heaven, and the governor's chaplain was converted to Puritanism. He became the minister of Bennett's church in Nansemond. Until 1648, the new governor, William Berkeley, withheld his hand, but in that year the Reverend Mr. Thomas Harrison had to go, and with him migrated nearly one thousand to nearby Maryland, where they created a settlement and a faction.

All this occurred as the Puritan revolution in England was being climaxed by the Civil War. In due time, Charles was dethroned and superseded by the Commonwealth government. The Puritan influence was sufficiently strong in Virginia, together with the influence of those mindful of economic advantage, that when representatives of the Parliament appeared in Virginia, Bennett and Claiborne took the lead in persuading Governor Berkeley, who would have liked to resist, to make an agreement to surrender.

The commissioners, of whom Claiborne was one, called a new House of Burgesses chosen by such voters as would take an oath to support the Commonwealth. This assembly met with the commissioners and together they formed a convention which created a government for the colony. The House of Burgesses was now assigned the power to elect the governor and his council and a secretary of state. The House was definitely to be the government. This scheme was sent to England for approval, but in the meantime it was put into operation by electing Bennett and Claiborne governor and secretary of state. Thus, on April 30, 1652, another step toward self-government was taken. The English government, the Protectorate, never came to any conclusion on the plan, so there was no interference in its operation. Virginia now was, for all intents and purposes, an independent republic. The Puritan party was in the ascendant and for the time being Berkeley and his supporters were in eclipse.

With the advent of this independence, there developed yet another phase of political conflict in which were involved personal factionalism and probably religious differences. The colony was not very prosperous, the new Navigation Law disturbed the trade of the colony, and there was the continued concentration on tobacco. Naturally, these difficulties were reflected in the current politics. Bennett the Puritan was succeeded by Mathews of the Anglican–Governor Berkeley faction, and he undertook to curb the House of Burgesses, finally dissolving them. They refused to accept this order and deposed the governor. Mathews finally gave in, acknowledged the authority of the House, and was then reinstated. When word came that the Commonwealth was over, former Governor Berkeley was elected by the legislature, and in due time he went to England where he was recommissioned by King Charles II's government. He came back charged with establishing the Church of England, with recognizing the House of Burgesses as the source of law, with diversifying agriculture, and with promoting town organization.

Thus, in its half century of troubled existence, the colony of Virginia had demonstrated an aptitude for political improvisation, always in the direction of more independent self-government, which was typical of American experience. An outpost, planned to be operated by the agents of a commercial company, under the challenge of peril and hardship had taken the English political behavior patterns which they knew and improvised therefrom the necessary institutions to maintain their community. In so doing, they had become a body politic which was capable of self-government and versed in the fine art of politics.

WILDERNESS ZIONS

*R*ELIGIOUS POLITICS, so influential in England, was to have a mighty influence on American migration and the new political plantations. The controversies of the English Reformation, which so divided the people of the realm, had their American repercussions at the founding of the seventeenth-century colonies. Less than a score of years after the outset of Virginia experiments by the varied adventurers, there began a series of settlements by those whose religious views deeply colored their ideas of social order and governance.

First to come was a party led by a nucleus of the most radical group, the Separatists, who had seceded from the Church of England and established independent congregations. This smacked of treason under English law, and at various times the government sought to bring these independents to book. In face of threatened prosecution in the last years of Elizabeth, the last decade of the sixteenth century, a London congregation fled to Holland where there was religious tolerance, and in the next decade others from the north of England followed. They found freedom in Amsterdam and Leyden, but Holland was not England, and as time went on these exiles, themselves not really prosperous, were distressed to see their children growing up in a strange land, adopting strange customs, and speaking a strange tongue. The settlement in Virginia stirred their imaginations and stimulated in them a desire to create a community of their own ordering which would be, as they so earnestly desired, on English soil.

They sent agents back to London to seek both authorization and capital to establish such a settlement within the bounds of the London Company's grant. At length, at the close of some discouraging and complicated negotiations, the agents, John Carver and Robert Cushman, brought back a contract which bound these "Pilgrims," who were now to cross the seas, to work for their London backers for the first seven years. On these terms the money needed for transportation and equipment was obtained. This contract was approved at congregational meetings in Leyden, and preparations were concluded. However, when the final steps had been completed, it became apparent that only a minority of the Leyden congregation was willing or able to go, thirty-five out of two hundred. Thereupon, the pastor, the Reverend John Robinson, decided to remain in Holland with the larger part of his congregation, while his associate, Elder William Brewster, would be the spiritual guide of the new venture, with Carver its executive head. After discouraging mishaps and delays, the Pilgrim ship, The *Mayflower*, in September 1620 at last set out across the Atlantic.

Like the Virginia migrants, the Pilgrims had perforce to consider political organization during the tedious, tempestuous voyage. During these wearing two months on the sea, certain facts had to be faced. When the move was originally planned, it had been a congregational project, and the usual congregational government had been taken for granted. But the fact that so small a number of the Leyden church finally would consent to go meant that recruits had to be obtained in England, so that out of the 101 who sailed, 66 were not of the congregation. Rather, they were bent on a business venture. Translated into political terms, there were 41 responsible citizens of whom but a minority, 19, were of the Leyden congregation. Experience on the voyage indicated elements of dissension and danger because of the variety of opinions among the adventurers. Those who had joined the Leyden congregational element were not of their way of life and probably not much in sympathy with it. In fact, some of the recruits had plainly declared that, once on shore, they would be beholden to no one but "would use their owne libertie."

This spirit was disconcerting to Carver and Brewster who were well aware of the hazards of their informal status. They were bound by a contract, but they had no charter nor any formal document prescribing the organization, rules, and discipline necessary to fulfill it. Therefore, drawing upon their own experience in which the church covenant was an effective and revered form, the leaders made a significant decision. When land was finally sighted, they drew up such a covenant, and before anyone landed, it was signed by the responsible males, of whom nineteen were from Leyden, sixteen were from England, four are described as servants, and two were members of the crew who had decided to stay. In their own words:

In the Name of God, Amen. We whose names are underwritten, the loyal subjects of our dread sovereign Lord, King James, by the grace of God, of Great Britain, France and Ireland, King, Defender of the Faith, etc.,

Having undertaken, for the glory of God, and advancement of the Christian faith and honor of our King and Country, a voyage to plant the first colony in the northern parts of Virginia, do by these presents solemnly and mutually in the presence of God, and one of another, covenant and combine ourselves together into a civil body politic, for our better ordering and preservation and furtherance of the ends aforesaid; and by virtue hereof to enact, constitute and frame such just and equal laws, ordinances, acts, constitutions and offices, from time to time, as shall be thought most meet and convenient for the general good of the Colony: Unto which we promise all due submission and obedience. In witness whereof we have hereunder subscribed our names at Cape Cod the 11 of November, in the year of the reign of our sovereign Lord, King James of England, France and Ireland the eighteenth, and of Scotland the fifty-fourth. Ano. Dom. 1620.

Carver was then either elected or confirmed as governor, Isaac Allerton was designated "Assistant," and the little group undertook to function subject to the rules made in community meeting.

The Leyden congregation had been remarkable for its peacefulness and quiet ordering and for a season this calm seemed to continue its influence. Despite hardship and death—half the signers of the compact died during the next few months—the church leaders continued to command public support. When Governor Carver succumbed during the second year, William Bradford took his place. A board of assistants of five was created in 1624 and enlarged to seven in 1633. Bradford and his board carried on the government with occasional reference of matters to the community meeting, or General Court as it came to be called, using the term then common to describe stockholders' meetings in chartered companies. There was an annual election of governor, and Bradford was elected thirty times.

The General Court was composed of the "freemen" who were such responsible citizens as the court admitted. There was no stated church membership qualification but the privilege was not conferred freely. By 1643 there were only 230 freemen, or voters. When other settlements were founded in the Cape Cod region, Plymouth continued to be the center and the freemen must come there to the "Courts." In 1638, however, the principle of representation was adopted, and thereafter the towns sent two each, except Plymouth, which was entitled to four. Two years before, the Court adopted a code of laws, establishing the strict ideas of conduct which they felt necessary to govern a morally superior community.

Though they sought a charter, the Plymouth colony never obtained one. However, when it transpired that they had settled, not in the Virginia domain of the London Company where they had expected to establish themselves, but within the jurisdiction of the Council for New England, the successor of the Plymouth Company, they did secure various permits culminating with the Pierce patent of January 13, 1630, which provided for them and their successors the "liberty" to frame and make orders, ordinances, and constitutions.

Thus, this little congregation from Leyden had shown the capacity to undertake two migrations, to maintain independent self-government, to create institutions whenever necessary, to handle difficult situations, to absorb alien groups, to develop an orderly and prosperous society, and to keep the reins of power within their own hands. The necessary contention was kept at a minimum. "They governed according to the free liberties of a free people." It was a masterpiece of improvisation.

This community, intent as it was on perfecting a socioreligious experiment of an improved community, at length suffered from internal division, like its Virginia sister which it had hoped to join. The fact that the promoters had been forced to seek recruits and to accept those who had little sympathy with their lofty objectives eventually made trouble. This factionalism which had appeared on board the *Mayflower* had been quelled for a time by the hardships of settlement and the frequent visitation of death during the first months. Newcomers, however, were constantly appearing, and in 1623 John Oldham, a natural factional leader, arrived together with a lecherous clergyman, the Reverend John Lyford. They found things not to their liking, even though Lyford, as befitted his clerical calling, was admitted to the inner governing circle. He and Oldham began encouraging those not in sympathy with the rule of the elders and organized something like a party. Oldham's intrigues and Lyford's too frequent amorous conquests at length led the ruling group to banish them, and a measure of concord was restored. But it had been demonstrated that politics could be troublesome even in a wilderness Zion.

This Separatist project was but the first which stemmed from the Puritan-Presbyterian movement. After some experiment with fishing and commercial outposts in the vicinity of Salem in what is now Massachusetts, a distinguished group of Puritan men of means in England, disturbed by contemporary political, social, and economic situations which threatened their status and their happiness, organized themselves into a chartered corporation and planned to migrate in a body, taking their charter with them, to establish a "commonwealth" in America.

A group of them met at Cambridge and on August 26, 1629, signed an agreement to migrate, provided that "the whole government together with the patent for the said plantation be first legally transferred and established to remain with us and others which shall inhabite" New England. Three days later, at a stockholders' meeting in London, this was agreed to. At the next quarterly meeting of the corporation in great and general court a Puritan gentleman of landed estate, John Winthrop, friend and relative of some of the principal stockholders, was chosen governor. So efficient and expeditious was the management, so impressive its proposition that by June 1630 fourteen ships with over a thousand colonists were on their way.

Arriving at Salem, the leaders undertook to explore and counsel together. Eventually the thousand colonists scattered in a dozen settlements on Boston harbor and in the valleys of the Mystic and the Charles with headquarters at Boston. Governor Winthrop and his board of assistants held their first formal meeting in America on August 23 under a tree in Charlestown, and on October 19 the first General Court of the stockholders was held at Boston. They reelected Governor Winthrop and the assistants. Under the charter, only freemen or stockholders could vote, a group few in number and all on the board of assistants. However, the "people" had been invited to this General Court and propositions had been presented them which they approved by the "erection of hands." Furthermore, an invitation was issued to all those who wished to assume the responsibilities of freemen to hand in their names. Over a hundred made such application and a number were accepted, even some who were not church members. This latitude was short-lived, however, for in 1631 it was decided to confine the privilege of being a freeman only to those who took an oath of fidelity and were members of the various town churches.

A new spirit was moving in the churches. A number of those who had dared the mighty deep to create a wilderness Zion wanted it a Zion indeed. Hardly had some of these new churches been established than they and their pastors undertook to see that those who were to become members were men and women who could demonstrate that they had experienced a change, that they had been converted and had been saved and freed from sin. In some of these Massachusetts churches, those desiring the sacraments and admission to the church were required to relate in convincing fashion the experience which had demonstrated that they possessed a saving faith and were of the elect. Only after producing such a proof could they become members in full communion and vote for the officers of the town. Thus, within a year, the charter of the Massachusetts Bay Company had been violated in letter and spirit to the end that a Puritan theocracy had been created, and a government chosen by the church members was effectually in the hands of their leaders. The goal of this theocracy was centralization, but the settlers had to be reckoned with, and from time to time governor and assistants must yield reluctantly some segments of the complete authority which they craved.

Therefore, side by side with this central government, there developed an increasingly independent number of local units, the famous New England towns. These were at first scattered along the Massachusetts coast, but they soon began to be established inland. In them the instrument of government was the town meeting. Here the freemen—church members for the time being, though eventually all men of mature years who had taken an oath of fidelity, which omitted any mention of the king—were admitted to participate in the discussion of town affairs.

The New England town was a masterpiece of improvisation. Its founders had much to choose from as there was no uniformity at home in the pattern or customs of English local communities. Some were villages with group farming on the ancient open-field system, others were little communities with independent farmers operating each his own enclosed acreage. Some migrants came from borough governments, from municipalities. In various of the New England settlements, men and women from all of these types might find themselves sharing the responsibility for creating a new "town." The result was a blend of forms, a prime example of adaptation by consensus. The founders generally abandoned the courts-baron where the tenants had gathered to make their agricultural arrangements and settlements, the parishes where churchwardens and vestries had fixed rates, and the borough governments with their mayors and councils. Instead, they created a more or less uniform system of towns where the "free townsmen," all male adult citizens who had been admitted by the meeting, gathered together and managed both civil and religious matters. They defined their "liberties" and in their exercise they were to choose and judge. This New England town was something of their own invention, like nothing in England. They had abolished feudal rank and tenure, and parish and borough government as well, and had created their own instrument of self-government. These builders of their new Zion even reduced the civil power of their pastors almost to the vanishing point. They could influence by preaching and example, but they could not even perform marriage ceremonies.

At the annual town meetings taxes were fixed and boards of select men were chosen to govern, together with numerous other officials charged with collecting taxes, keeping the peace, maintaining health and orderly civic behavior; there were tax collectors, constables, hogreeves, fence viewers, and the like. While only freemen could vote for governor and only freemen and church members could hold office, it appeared that many were reluctant to assume the responsibility of becoming freemen because they did not want to be liable to hold office. Many who were in opposition to the theocracy refused to seek "freemanship" but stayed outside the ranks in order more effectively, they thought, to express opposition.

These towns were determined not only to govern themselves but to play an active part in the government of the colony. Within three years, the exercise of the taxing power by the assistants and the General Court had brought objection from the various towns, notably from Watertown as early as 1631, where there was a protest voiced against taxation without representation. The town meetings insisted that they could not journey to Boston to the General Courts, and they demanded a representative system. On May 14, 1634, their pleas were heeded. The General Court hereafter was to be made up of representatives of the towns. Thus the charter was now completely abandoned. A representative legislature had been established to take its place along with the Virginia House of Burgesses. A second improvised political creation was to the credit of the American colony.

The original process of choosing the governor likewise was further modified. When the decision was made to admit as freemen only those who were church members and had taken the oath, the leaders felt they might widen the privilege of election somewhat, and again by a show of hands it was agreed that the governor and deputy governor, formerly chosen only by the assistants, as well as the assistants, should be chosen by the body of freemen, though as before, from among the assistants. Again, after the principle of representation had been accepted and deputies representing the towns began to attend the General Court in the place of the body of freemen, the election procedure was still further altered. In the town meetings which chose the deputies, the freemen hereafter were to vote (give their proxies) for governor and deputy governor, then their proxies were to be carried to the General Court. At its spring meeting, the Court counted them and announced the result. Then the officials thus elected were sworn in. Thus was inaugurated a procedure that was to be the order in much of New England for two hundred years. Though this power of election had been yielded, the theocracy hoped that it would be exercised only *pro forma*. Magistrates, they felt, should be reelected annually as long as they were willing to serve, and the Reverend Mr. John Cotton so expressed himself in an eloquent sermon. But the freemen were not so minded, and the very next year, 1634, they elected the deputy governor, Thomas Dudley, governor in the place of John Winthrop, much to the latter's surprise.

The magistrates, namely their governor and his assistants, with their exalted ideas of mission still could see little need of popular participation in government, and they undertook to guide the choice of the top officials as much as they could. But they were dealing with enterprising men who were willing and able to have their own opinions and not averse to expressing them. Nor did they wish to be observed. So, in 1635, they insisted on using paper ballots.

In this system of election the element of political conflict was, in fact, present from the beginning. It was a contentious time in the new Protestantism, and there was an unusually large number of active clergymen for the size of the community. There was bound to be strife within the theocracy. Then, too, it was a fast-growing, very fluid community, a great variety of newcomers were constantly arriving, and, as in Plymouth, they were frequently people with little knowledge of, or even sympathy with, the objectives of the magistrates. Conflict was inevitable and conflict came. And as in England in the previous century, ecclesiastical verbiage confused the understanding of these political struggles for the modern.

In 1631 a most attractive young clergyman arrived in Boston, Reverend Mr. Roger Williams. Immediately, the Boston church wished his services, but he refused, telling them that they had not the courage to declare themselves separate from the Church of England. Likewise, he charged that the magistrates arrogated to themselves too much power. So he went to Salem, then to Plymouth, and back again to Salem, in each place taking a leading vocative role in the Church. As he proceeded, his political ideas became more radical: he advanced the striking notion that the Indians owned the land and the king had no right to dispose of it. In 1635 the magistrates cracked down on him. He was arrested, tried, and banished, just as Plymouth had banished their dissidents.

So far, the differences in Massachusetts had been more associated with individuals, but there next developed a political issue of wider significance which caused the forming of faction. Ostensibly, the point at issue was the religious position taken by Mrs. Anne Hutchinson, a talented and charitable parishioner of John Cotton's who was a natural leader. She and a clerical brother-in-law, Reverend John Wheelwright, and, to some extent, the Reverend Mr. Cotton were dissatisfied with the harsh theology of those who believed in God the Awful Judge who demanded abject obedience of predestined man to his inflexible law. Mrs. Hutchinson was antinomian. The antinomians believed in free will. To them God was a God of grace, a God of love who manifested himself to his creation by inward sweet communion, who soothed, comforted, and inspired even as he sometimes punished. Those who enjoyed this sanctification needed no evidence of works to prove their salvation.

This doctrinal difference was accentuated by personality complications which had political overtones. There were factions in the Boston church and one of them used Mrs. Hutchinson's views as political ammunition. The most severe theologians opposed her liberal views, probably also resenting the intrusion of a woman into their man's world. Then, too, her brother-in-law, Wheelwright, was being pushed by some for membership in the Boston ministry. Governor Winthrop's policy, too, added to the strife. He was a mild man who sought to rule by lenience, avoiding drastic action. The more strict and orthodox were impatient with his easy way and protested against it. Their opposition added bitterness to the schism.

In the fall of 1635 an attractive young gentleman, one of the few men of title to migrate, arrived in Boston in the person of Sir Harry Vane, son of a member of the king's government. He was religious, emotional, and somewhat naive. He saw Governor Winthrop's difficulty and presided over a harmony conference which failed. This effort on his part, together with his rank and English connections, resulted in his election as governor in 1636.

Upon assuming office he almost immediately espoused Mrs. Hutchinson's cause. This aroused the more rigid theologians, and in what appears to be the first political election campaign in America, they marshaled their forces, moved the election to Newtown where there was less antinomianism, and after a sharp political battle in 1637, defeated Vane and put Winthrop back into the chair. The theocracy, now restored to power, proceeded to banish Wheelwright and Mrs. Hutchinson.

Within six years of the formal founding, Massachusetts had almost forgotten the charter. The colonists had created what was to all intents an independent republic. They made their own laws in town meeting and legislature, levied taxes, and chose their officials in regularly constituted elections. Self-government was practiced on two levels, local and colony. Factions formed and elections were conducted in which spirited contests were most prominent. A Puritan community had been created. It was a *tour de force* of improvising and demonstrated the flexible character of colonial political ideas.

The political behavior developed in Massachusetts and the large influx of migrants joined together to develop another typical pattern in the American system. This was a repetition of the creation of bodies politic, of the use of the force which had just been operating to cause so many to leave England and cross the seas to found new communities. The pattern of moving on to greener pastures did not stop when the migrants disembarked. After they had founded the colony with its towns, perfect satisfaction did not always prevail. Newcomers kept constantly arriving. Sometimes they found the good land divided and distributed. They and younger children now growing up found too little resource available for them. Rather than demand reallotment they could meet their needs by moving. An appeal to the General Court might and did on occasions secure another townsite to the westward. Then there would be a new migration and the process repeated. Soon there were groups leaving Massachusetts to create for themselves. Theirs was not so great daring, nor was their journey so far, but their motivation was similar.

Massachusetts was not a happy place for those who did not see eye to eye with the theocratic rulers. Those who were banished had to seek new homes. Also, there was not too much desirable land in the Bay region or along the coast, and people soon learned of the fertile Connecticut Valley. Interest in this region had begun in Plymouth where the Pilgrims, earnest to secure the money to free them from debt, had been seeking the means to earn it. They had explored the Massachusetts and Maine coasts for sites for fishing and trading posts and had penetrated to the Connecticut Valley to Windsor, where they established a trading post in 1633, offering a half interest to the Massachusetts Bay authorities, which they refused. Likewise, the successors to the original Plymouth Company of 1606 were thinking of a possible settlement in the Connecticut region and from the Bay colony came evidence of similar interest. Some of the Massachusetts towns were none too happy. Either they were dissatisfied with the quality and quantity of the land at their disposal or they disliked the rule of the magistrates on either political or doctrinal grounds. So, in 1634, a group from Watertown had migrated to Wethersfield, and in 1635 preparations began in Dorchester and, particularly, in Newtown to seek greener pastures in the vicinity of Hartford. The agent of the old Plymouth Company of 1606, John Winthrop, Jr., came to Boston to plan for a Connecticut settlement. He was to set up a post under grant from the Earl of Warwick who expected to receive authority from the successor corporation to make a settlement at the mouth of the Connecticut to be called Saybrooke after Viscount Say and Sele and Lord Brooke.

Winthrop found on his arrival in Boston that these various groups had already settled or were planning to settle at Windsor, Wethersfield, and Hartford. These locations were within the Warwick claims, and so the younger Winthrop found it necessary to protest the right of Massachusetts people to settle in a region outside the jurisdiction of that colony. A series of conferences were held, generally in a friendly spirit, for Winthrop wanted settlers, and the Massachusetts men needed a place to settle. The result was that the prospective colonists and the agents of Warwick drew up a plan of government. Warwick's agents had no power to establish a self-governing community of emigrants. They therefore sought the nearest official body, which was the Massachusetts General Court, and asked that body to act as a go-between to give some official sanction to this agreement. On March 3, 1636, the Court issued a commission containing this agreement as made by them and John Winthrop, Jr., on behalf of the Massachusetts citizens who wished to settle in the Connecticut River Valley.

This commission recited the fact that "where there are a people to sit down and inhabite there will follow upon occasion some cause of difference"; consequently, the General Court granted eight men powers of government in this new region such as were necessary to ensure "the peaceable and quiett ordering of the affairs of the said plantation," and they were authorized "to convene the said inhabitants [of the settlements] to any convenient place that they shall think meete, in a legal and open manner, by way of court, to procede in executing the power and authority aforesaid."

The vanguard of these settlers took immediate advantage of this commission and, on April 26, five of these eight men met at Hartford to form the first governmental body. They made some rules and commissioned constables for Windsor, Wethersfield, and Hartford. John Winthrop, Jr., was recognized as governor. In 1637, when the Pequot War was impending, the first elections were held, and a legislature came together to meet the emergency.

The politics of Connecticut, like that of Massachusetts, was to be ecclesiastical. The colony was a confederation of scattered congregation towns, each distant enough from the others to be practically independent. Each unit was a world of its own, self-reliant and self-contained. The nature of this confederation was set down simply in the Fundamental Orders of 1639, adopted by the General Court January 14 of that year. The government was to be in the hands of the "freemen," men chosen by the General Court or designated by magistrates as worthy to bear the responsibility. Such freemen chose the magistrates and the governor and only freemen could hold such offices. Within the towns the number of those who could attend town meetings, vote for deputies to the General Court, and share in local government was generally three times as large as the number of freemen. These local voters were the "admitted inhabitants," men of "good conversation" and "religious carriage" who could take an oath such as only Trinitarian Christians could subscribe to. The town meetings passed upon the qualifications of those "admitted inhabitants" and could dismiss as well as admit them. This was not democracy but rule by the responsible, by carefully chosen men who would conform to God's will. However, it was broader than the Massachusetts system. There was no metropolis, no center of the elders. The magistrates who sat with the governor in the General Court could not negate the voice of the deputies from the towns. Never was there the rule of the elders; rather was there the independent rule of the towns. Connecticut politics started in the town meetings where local personalities and small issues generally supplied the basis of group divisions and the conflicts of local politics. Quite frequently these divisive questions were religious: questions of personal conduct and interpretation of religious dogma.

The deputies to the General Court were chosen in the spring town meetings. The Court met twice a year. In April it held an election meeting. Here candidates from among the freemen for governor and magistrates were voted upon by as many of the whole body of freemen as could manage to come to Hartford. Those to be voted on for governor must be church members and magistrates. The deputies from the towns had nominated such as were "fitt to be chosen" at a previous session, and from among these nominees the freemen made their choice. In the fall, a second session was held in which the business was legislative and judicial. After 1645, the legislature was divided into two houses. The governor and magistrates composed one and the deputies from the towns the other.

So a confederation of self-governing towns was established under a scheme of their own framing, initially without reference to England, though later confirmed by royal charter. In most respects it was like that of Massachusetts, save that there never was the oligarchal rule of the Boston elders. Political power was exercised in the towns and there minister and elders exercised great influence, but each head of a family and householder, unless he was of bad character, had a part in the town's affairs and could play at its politics.

Rhode Island was founded by a series of "independent" groups made up of individualists who were even more unhappy in Massachusetts than the founders of Connecticut had been and who had been so vocal in their unhappiness that some of them had been banished by the Bay Colony theocracy. Roger Williams was the first of these. Driven forth into the bitter New England winter, he had taken refuge with some Indians in what was to be Rhode Island, in January 1636. He was joined by certain others of like mind, and they concluded a purchase agreement with the Indians for the site of Providence. Williams and his companions formed an association of heads of families which met once every fortnight and to which later young unmarried men were admitted. They adopted a social compact somewhat resembling the *Mayflower* agreement and agreed to submit to the will of the majority, but "only in civil things"—each was to be his own authority in religious matters. Mrs. Hutchinson and her family joined them.

Two years after the founding of Providence, another free spirit, William Coddington, an antinomian friend of Williams, organized a company in Boston, which they incorporated as a body politic in the presence of the great Jehovah, and proceeded to Providence. In the year following, they settled at Portsmouth. However, these high individualists had great difficulty in living together, and there was a series of secessions which resulted in the forming of settlements at Newport, Pawtucket, and Warwick.

Williams' enterprise persisted despite the difficulty of organization, and in 1643 he proceeded to England where he was able to secure a patent authorizing a government over these colonists on the lands they had purchased from the Indians. Under this patent, Williams contrived the union of the various towns as the colony of Rhode Island and Providence Plantations. Their government was somewhat similar to that of Connecticut, and a General Assembly was organized in 1647 which made the laws. The people annually cast votes by proxy for governor in the towns, and these proxies were sent to the legislature where they were counted and the election of governor declared. The legislature enacted one of the earliest of the colonial law codes, "the first to embody in all its parts, the precedents set by the laws and statutes of England." Organization and statutes, however, did not quell the varieties of individualism. Williams found himself constantly combating opposition, particularly from one of his earliest associates, Harris. Rhode Island was truly the home of the "otherwise-minded" and thrived on controversy. In this the Rhode Island towns presented a decided contrast to the Connecticut towns who on their part developed a peaceful, even commonplace, measure of self-government.

Shortly after the Connecticut and Rhode Island towns began their active life, a third enterprise developed, this also dominated by religious enthusiasm for an ideal community. Certain English Puritans, parishioners of St. Stephen's Church in London, of a straighter sect even than the Massachusetts Bay, sought the new world. They were moved by a desire to avoid Archbishop Laud's tyrannies and migrated to Boston in 1636. However, upon arrival, they found no choice of land nor any harbor site; furthermore, the antinomian controversy, they believed, had weakened strict orthodoxy, so they would go elsewhere. On the north shore of Long Island Sound, west of the Connecticut River, they found a site for what they termed their New Haven. They purchased it from the Indians and without legal sanction undertook to create a biblical community. Much influenced by Cotton's code, "Moses, his judicials," they organized a church which was to rule the settlement with no law save the Bible. Those coming with them consented to this at a general meeting by a show of hands in June 1639. A committee of twelve was chosen by these, and they chose seven men to organize the theocracy. They provided that the freemen, all of whom were church members, should elect a governor and four assistants. To these five men, elected annually, was given the full responsibility for administering the government according to the Bible.

In the course of a few years, other towns—Guilford, Milford, and Stamford—were formed, and at length, in 1643, Indian troubles caused these towns to federate with New Haven. They then agreed upon a constitution and created a judicial system, without trial by jury as there was no sanction for such in the Bible, and a General Court consisting of the governor, assistants, and two deputies from each of the four towns. These latter were to make laws and annually elect the governor and assistants. In the course of time two more towns on the shore and one on Long Island joined the New Haven confederacy. These towns, however, were not contiguous, and it was hardly a closely knit league.

These several wilderness Zions were by their independence able to proceed in another direction. Not only did the settlement of Plymouth, Massachusetts Bay, Connecticut, Rhode Island, and New Haven illustrate the tendency toward constant expansion, the proliferation of independent bodies politic which was such a characteristic of American democratic behavior, but they also first demonstrated a capacity for union and for federation.

The New England colonies from the first were beset by dangers. The Indians were in many instances hostile, and a frightening war with the Pequots broke out in the Connecticut Valley in 1637. Furthermore, to the west and north of these settlements were operations of the Dutch and French. Trade rivalry and religious and boundary controversies were constantly inviting hostility. The Dutch wished to control the trading opportunities in this region and claimed that the New England colonists were encroaching upon their domain. The French were Catholic and thus there was religious tension as well as rivalry for control of the Indians. Furthermore, the French claimed most of New England and upon occasion interfered with English ventures. The colonists truly were surrounded by hostile forces.

This common danger started efforts during the Pequot War to organize to present a common front. Negotiations went on for several years, particularly between Connecticut and Massachusetts Bay, but they generally broke down because of Massachusetts' inclination as the larger and stronger to play a dominating role. At length, on May 10, 1643, agreement was signed forming the "United Colonies of New England," usually referred to as the New England Confederation. Four colonies—Massachusetts, Connecticut, Plymouth, and

New Haven—agreed to accept each other as equal confederates, but they refused to include the settlements in New Hampshire, Maine, or Rhode Island. This was to be a union of the theocratic colonies and they would have no association with the otherwise-minded. Each of these four colonies was to appoint two commissioners, "all in church-fellowship with us." These eight men were to have annual meetings and to plan the external security of the colonists. Measures could be carried by six votes, and the commissioners had the power to conduct war, make peace, and levy for funds. These taxes were to be apportioned according to the number of people in each colony between the ages of sixteen and sixty. This union was to have no authority over the domestic concerns of its members except to guarantee their boundaries and local independence.

This initial step toward colonial union continued in existence for some thirty years but its effectiveness was not great. It had no executive authority, no control over individuals, no way of enforcing its decisions. Massachusetts, much the largest of the members, sought to dominate and on occasion disregarded the provisions of the agreement. It was still functioning in the troubled days of King Philip's War, 1675–76, but after that, new conditions in England and in America were working to undermine the independence of the New England colonies and to bring them under closer control by the mother country. In these new difficulties, the union declined into nothingness.

The settlements in this second series thus had presented something of a contrast to those in Virginia. The Virginia enterprise was a business venture, projected by a corporation, and originally the corporation had expected to manage and profit from the enterprise. The New England settlements on the other hand were the work of religiously minded individuals and groups who thought primarily of a social experiment where religious people might find a happier dwelling place. They came mostly without sanction from the crown and proceeded to create their own order of governing. In this their experience was in reality very similar to that of the Virginia colonists who, despite their difference in original motivation, found that wilderness necessities meant that they too should be practically self-governing. In all these colonies there was constant improvisation. Everywhere they built upon what they knew with a minimum of innovation. The mold of their creation was to a great degree the English experience of themselves and their ancestors. They had thereupon erected a structure of improvisation, expansion, and union which foretold much of the future.

·•⊰[IV]⊱•·

FEUDAL ADAPTATION

A THIRD group of English colonial projects in America
came into being because of the mighty force of individual
enterprise. American democracy owes much to the imagination and
daring of the adventurous men who followed the pattern laid down
by Gilbert and Raleigh, men who labored, not in companies or congregations, but alone as proprietors.

Such men were Sir Ferdinando Gorges, Captain John Mason, and
Sir George Calvert. Their imaginations were kindled by dreams not
merely of wealth but of feudal grandeur. They could talk in the
terms of the market place, but their thoughts were shaped by ambitions for landed estates and baronial privilege, perhaps patents of
nobility.

Sir Ferdinando Gorges, an adventurous soldier, had long been governor of the port of Plymouth in England and there was no limit to
his enterprise, his imagination, and his bad luck. He had been the
principal figure in the Plymouth Company, and after the failure of its
Maine settlement, 1606–7, he had done his best to promote other
activity to the north of Virginia. He had even hired Captain John
Smith to explore and had published a book. He was associated with
another man of action, Captain John Mason, a resident of Hampshire
who had been governor of Newfoundland, the Raleigh-Gilbert enterprise. Here he had surveyed the island and gained an interest in the
region to the south.

After more than ten years of frustration, Gorges and his associates
undertook to improve their fortunes by reorganizing their means of
operation. The original Plymouth Company was renamed the "Council established at Plymouth in the County of Devon for the Planting,
Ruling and Governing of New England in America," thereafter usually referred to as the Council for New England. This change was

consummated while the Pilgrims were planning and achieving their settlement, and one of the council's early acts was to give the Pierce patent to these colonists. Likewise, they assigned a series of grants to Gorges and Mason in 1622–23, authorizing them to exercise feudal, proprietary, and trading post rights and privileges in what are now Massachusetts, New Hampshire, and Maine.

These new proprietors proceeded at once to recruit leaders and colonists and to send them out to develop their interests as their employees, somewhat in the early Virginia manner. Sir Ferdinando's son Robert was sent over in 1623 as governor of New England, together with the Reverend William Morell who was to establish the Church of England. They spent a winter in what is now Weymouth, Massachusetts, but could not exercise any more authority than Captain West who at the same time had been appointed admiral of New England and was presumed to collect license fees from fishermen. They all failed in their assignments.

More definite results came from less ambitious activities of the Mason-Gorges interest. Christopher Levitt, one of Robert Gorges' associates, did establish a permanent settlement on Monhegan Island in Maine that year, and at the same time agents of Mason had some success in New Hampshire. Here, under the direction of Mason's men, posts were established at Rye, Portsmouth, and Dover, where the few settlers struggled along without much help from the proprietor. And after his death in 1635, they were left almost completely to their own devices, for his heirs were for years indifferent.

Even before his death, Mason had begun to sell his assets, and in 1633 he had sold Dover, or Cocheco, to the same lords, Saye and Sele and Brooke, who had been operating in Connecticut. Their ownership made the young settlement attractive to a number of Puritans, and thither a company went. These people were of a mind to transform the makeshift government of Mason's agents into a Congregational establishment. However, the Mason settlers resisted this so strongly that the Puritan enterprisers moved on and in 1638 created a settlement, also in New Hampshire, which they named Exeter. The leader of this venture was none other than the Reverend Mr. Wheelwright, Mrs. Hutchinson's brother-in-law, and under his inspiration, the new community, on October 4, 1639, adopted a "plantation covenant," resembling the type used previously in Plymouth and Connecticut, containing these few simple words:

Whereas it hath pleased the Lord to move the heart of our dread sovereign Charles, by the grace of God, king, &c., to grant licence libertye to sundry of his subjects to plant themselves in the westerne parts of America. We, his loyal subjects, brethren of the church in Exeter, situate and lying upon the river Piscataqua, with other inhabitants there, considering with ourselves the holy will of God and our necessity, that we should not live without wholesom lawes and civil government among us, of which we are altogether destitute; do, in the name of Christ and the sight of God, combine ourselves together to erect and set up among us, such government as shall be, to our best discerning, agreeable to the will of God, professing ourselves subjects to our sovereign lord King Charles, according to the libertyes of our English colony of Massachusetts, and binding ourselves solemnly by the grace and help of Christ, and in his name and fear, to submit ourselves to such godly and christian lawes as are established in the realm of England, to our best knowledge, and to all other such laws which shall, upon good grounds, be made and enacted among us, according to God, that we may live quietly and peaceably together, in all godliness and honesty.

Within two years Dover adopted a similar government and so presumably did Portsmouth, which had likewise become the property of Lord Saye and Sele and Lord Brooke.

Massachusetts had been watching these Puritan associates making their homes in New Hampshire, and they became to the Bay Colony a sort of Naboth's vineyard. They undertook to lay claim to them as within the territory granted to them in their charter. In 1641, better to buttress their claim, they "planted" a town, which was called Hampton, in the New Hampshire region. The Puritan settlers of Exeter and the noble Puritan proprietors of Dover and Portsmouth were not unsympathetic to Massachusetts' pretensions. In fact, the latter preferred her established government to the local weakness of their scattered towns. So, in the same year, Dover and Portsmouth accepted the Bay Colony's protection, and two years later Exeter did likewise. Massachusetts guaranteed the towns the liberties described in their covenants and included them within her county of Norfolk. Forthwith they sent deputies to the Great and General Court meeting in Boston.

While these New Hampshire settlements were struggling in Mason's domain, there was more activity in Maine, where Sir Ferdinando Gorges held sway. He had all the will in the world to develop the region and he and the Council for New England gave out a most complicated series of grants from 1623 to 1635. Upon occasion he sent over members of his numerous family as agents and governors and his grantees did the same. Settlements were gradually planted in six principal regions along the Maine coast. Then in 1635, when the council finally went out of business, the doughty knight saw his chance, and in 1637 he secured from Charles I a charter granting him the same rights from New Hampshire to the Kennebec which Sir George Calvert secured in Maryland, the rights of the Bishop of Durham in his county palatine. Once more Gorges' imagination soared. He would have a lieutenant governor, a chancellor, a marshal, a treasurer, an admiral, a master of ordinance, and a secretary who were likewise to serve him as a council of state. He selected the little collection of huts known as Agamenticus (York) and renamed it Gorgeana. This would be his capital with a municipal charter of his granting, thus making it the first city in the English colonies, and he provided for the rule of the 250 inhabitants thereof some twoscore officials.

Little of these feudal, regal, metropolitan trappings survived, but in the various settlements the beginnings of self-government and the orderly administration of justice soon appeared. After Sir Ferdinando's death, in 1647, the portion of Maine nearest New Hampshire with the towns of York, Wells, and Kittery held meetings at one of these, and at Wells in 1649 Gorges' agent Edward Godfrey was elected as their governor. As it was apparent that Massachusetts was interested in absorbing them, as she had taken over Mason's province in 1641, the inhabitants then met at York and declared themselves a body politic.

The Maine men were right about Massachusetts' intentions. The Puritan commonwealth could and did maintain that Maine lay within the bounds of her charter as Massachusetts interpreted them. After Sir Ferdinando died, and while the English Civil War was being fought, Massachusetts began to covet Maine most actively. She sent commissioners with warnings to resurvey. In the face of this militant action, the Gorges settlers yielded and entered the Massachusetts system as the County of York. A few settlers north of these Gorges outposts held out for a few years hoping for aid from Cromwell, but when this failed they capitulated, and by 1658 Massachusetts had all of Maine as well as New Hampshire.

The plans that had been so ambitiously mapped out by Gorges and Mason had brought no satisfaction to these adventurers, nor had any of them been carried out as their designers had planned. They had, on the other hand, produced a series of experiments in self-government, and they had demonstrated further the capacity of colonials for such government and for independent enterprise. The growth of Massachusetts as she absorbed these experiments in independence was another demonstration of a latent capacity for expansion and integration which was to prove so significant a mark of the later development of the American republic.

Among these early proprietors, Sir George Calvert, a Catholic gentleman, alone achieved success. He, like Gorges, was filled with the idea of a feudal domain, at the same time to be a Catholic refuge. He had already tried unsuccessfully to establish one in Newfoundland and, not discouraged, was determined to try again. In 1632 Calvert's son, Cecil secured from Charles I a feudal charter giving him powers such as were enjoyed by the Bishop of Durham in his border province, powers within his realm such as the king enjoyed elsewhere in England. The younger Calvert, having succeeded his father as Lord Baltimore, then proceeded to establish the colony of Maryland in 1632 under this feudal charter.

Feudalism, however, was not destined to be strong in America. Calvert sent over his brother Leonard to rule with the aid of a small council, and local manors were apportioned to landholders who were to establish tenants upon their broad acres. These manor holders were presumed to hold manorial courts as in feudal England and to be responsible for local order and justice. Where population was somewhat more concentrated, hundreds were established, also on the old English model, presided over by a high constable. In the charter, it was provided that Baltimore was to enjoy "free, full, and absolute power" to make the laws "with the advice assent and approbation of the freemen." The proprietor initially interpreted this to mean that he could draft the laws in England and then send them to Maryland where the colonists would be called together in a general meeting to give their assent to his program. Their power, he conceived, was purely one of suggestion.

Few of these feudal proprietary plans were to survive very long in the form in which they had been projected. The manors soon proved to be farms; baronies and the baronial manor courts were little used. Nor did the hundreds become a significant element in local government. Rather, as in Virginia, the scattered population of farmers found the country system, with its justices of the peace and sheriffs, more fitted to their needs.

In the lawmaking process, the democratic spirit early asserted itself. The legislature as first conceived by the proprietor's governor was to be an advisory body which had the power to assent to the laws which he proposed. He could call them and prorogue them at will. But the representatives would have none of this. They wished to initiate legislation and not to be prorogued save with their own consent. They secured the right to initiate legislation and undertook to model their procedure very much after Parliament. They succeeded in maintaining their dignity and power. At first, the members and the governor and his council met in one body, but the members of the lower house were insistent upon their independence, and after 1650 it was recognized. At first, representation was made up of delegates from the hundreds, the lords of the manors who served as councilors, and, for a while, any freeman who wished to come in person or send a proxy. In fact, legislation was dominated by the proprietor who had enough proxies to control. After 1654, however, the lower house was made up solely of representatives from the recently organized counties.

In these legislative sessions, there was a good deal of controversy. The proprietor always had opponents, sometimes encouraged by William Claiborne of Virginia who had been driven off of Kent Island. He encouraged faction in Maryland and fanned the natural antagonism that sprang up between Catholics and Protestants. When the Civil War broke out in England, Claiborne saw to it that it had repercussions in Maryland. In the name of Protestantism and the parliamentary cause, he, together with another trader, Richard Ingle, sought to harass Baltimore's representative. In 1644 Claiborne took over Kent Island, Ingle invaded Maryland and captured the little capital city. Baltimore had to flee into Virginia. For two years there was chaos until Governor Berkeley helped Baltimore regain his province. The latter then tried to allay religious hatred by his Act Concerning Religion which restated the proprietary policy existing from the beginning, giving freedom of worship to all Trinitarian Christians.

However, the fires of religious controversy were kept bright by the coming of the Virginia Puritans in 1648, invited by Governor William Stone, first Protestant governor of the province. They settled at Providence, near present-day Annapolis, and governed themselves. They sent a bloc of seven to the legislature, where one of their number became speaker in 1650. This religious factionalism was complicated by an attempt of the Jesuit order to obtain land so that they might set up a realm of their own, answerable only to the Pope.

Baltimore joined with the Protestants in opposing this, and finally the Jesuit superiors in Rome ordered an end to the project.

The contest with the proprietor came to a climax after the execution of Charles I when the Commonwealth government appointed commissioners to receive the submission of Maryland as well as Virginia. The two principal commissioners, Claiborne and Richard Bennett, leader of the Maryland Protestant party, came over to St. Mary's and expelled Baltimore's governor, planning to take over the government themselves. The Maryland citizens wanted none of this and protested so strongly that the governor was restored until they could hear from London. When no news arrived except new demands for recognition of his authority by the proprietor, Claiborne and Bennett went back to Maryland, again deposed the governor and appointed a Puritan in his place whom they ordered to call an assembly. This body annulled the proprietor's authority and set up a Puritan act concerning religion. Baltimore's governor resisted and a civil war developed in 1655 which the Puritans won. Meanwhile, Baltimore was fighting his battle in London and so successfully that he was recognized and given back his power on condition that he forget the past and treat alike all who sought land. He thereupon re-enacted the Act Concerning Religion, but this procedure did not prevent more trouble. Not until Charles II was restored and Baltimore had appointed his half brother governor did there develop a semblance of peace. During this contest the assembly had gained in resourcefulness and power, the idea of a Puritan commonwealth had been defeated, and the principle of toleration had been reinforced. Maryland was not a feudal barony nor Baltimore a feudal lord; rather he was a proprietor, quite uncertain of the nature of his authority over a vigorously independent colony.

The period of the Puritan Revolution and the Commonwealth (1640–60) briefly interrupted the series of proprietary ventures. Yet, even in these troubled times, Cromwell and his associates projected a program of expanding interest in America called the Western Design. The one tangible achievement under this plan was the capture of the West Indian Island of Jamaica, which was reduced by an expedition under Admiral William Penn, whose son was to play a notable part in later American ventures.

The restoration of the Stuarts, however, was followed by a series of new projects for American settlement and expansion. Charles II had regained his throne with the aid of a group of promoters, the chief of whom were General George Monk (soon to be the Duke of Albemarle) and Lord Clarendon. This group also included Craven, Sir George Carteret, and Lord Berkeley of the Lords of Trade, Sir William Berkeley, Governor of Virginia, Anthony Ashley Cooper (Lord Ashley), and John Colleton (soon to be Sir John); these latter had been active in the West Indies, particularly Barbados. The king's brother James, Duke of York, lost no time in associating with them and their projects, and his cousin, Prince Rupert, was likewise of this interest. As early as 1660, a number of these men organized the Company of Royal Adventurers to Africa who were to promote slavery in the colonies by trading in these human chattels. Somewhat later, they secured a new Bahama Grant and in 1670 formed the Hudson Bay Company to discover the Northwest Passage.

These men had in mind their own profit, their own power, the defense of England against her enemies, and the extension of the interests of the new English empire. They were much interested in America, and two points on which they would naturally focus were the land south of Virginia, which ought to be developed to keep the Spanish out, and the Hudson and Delaware River valleys, occupied by the Dutch, which separated New England from Maryland and Virginia.

A group of pressures was at work to promote speedy action. The Ashley-Colleton interest from the West Indies was anxious to get action south of Virginia where Sir William Berkeley as governor of the Old Dominion was likewise interested. The Maryland and New England colonies were actively hostile to the Dutch; Lord Baltimore was nervous about them, and there was constant friction between New England and New Amsterdam. A Bostonian, Samuel Maverick, was a correspondent of Clarendon's, and at the time of the return of Charles II, he was in England and in touch with the earl. Furthermore, there were many English in New Netherlands, among whom was George Baxter, Peter Stuyvesant's secretary. There were also a dozen or more English towns on Long Island, and just recently men like Baxter and Captain John Scott had been fomenting revolts and planning to proclaim English rule in the city of New Amsterdam itself. It seemed obvious that the time was ripe to move.

These promoters thereupon made plans and pressured Charles II. The king authorized an association of eight of them—Clarendon, Albemarle, Craven, Carteret, Ashley, Colleton, and the two Berkeleys —to develop the region south of Virginia as the Proprietary of Carolina, and he and they planned to take over New Netherlands from the

Dutch by force. This latter was to be the project of James, Duke of York, the king's brother, soon to be Clarendon's son-in-law and now Lord High Admiral. An armed expedition was placed at his disposal and with it was to go a civil governor and a commission to examine the New England situation.

These promoters were planning to use the proprietary idea, particularly as developed by Baltimore. They would set up governments with authority, such as was exercised by the Bishops of Durham in their frontier county and would invite a colonial elite to cooperate. Colonel Richard Nicolls was commissioned by the Duke of York to establish such an order after he had captured Dutch New Amsterdam. The reduction was easily accomplished in 1664, but the task of setting up a government as planned proved complex.

Nicolls found himself called upon to take charge of a colony numbering some eight thousand souls. A babel of tongues showed what a polyglot group of settlements it was, for not only were there people from the Netherlands but also from the British Isles, Scandinavia, Germany, Poland, Bohemia, France, Portugal, and Italy. These settlements had been established by the Dutch West India Company and theoretically had been ruled absolutely by the company's governors and their few advisers. Municipalities had been erected and had been ruled by self-perpetuating oligarchies of schout and schepens (sheriff and aldermen). However, just as in the English colonies, there had been a good deal of improvisation.

The Dutch colonies had been governed under a Charter of Freedoms and Exemptions, twice revised, which provided that new towns might be established by groups of settlers. Under these provisions, various English parties had come in, mostly from New England, and settled a series of towns on eastern Long Island. These towns were practically as much self-governing as were their New England contemporaries, save that the Dutch governors made appointments from panels chosen by the townsmen and appeals could be taken from the local magistrates to the governor. Even among the Dutch the rule of the governors was not as absolute as the letter of the West India Company's regulations would indicate. The troubled state of Indian relations during the 1640's had more or less compelled the none-too-competent governors to call for elections by the heads of families of boards of advisers to help them conduct the Indian wars and to provide money for mobilization and defense. One of these boards had attempted to make permanent arrangements for calling such councils and had prepared a petition and remonstrance which was sent to

Holland. This step produced immediately only rebuff and persecution for its initiators, but it did lead to a provision for municipal elections of officials and judges in 1653. These officials took up the battle for greater participation in government.

In the last decade of Dutch power, growing difficulties with their English and Indian neighbors produced at least two elected assemblies and a further remonstrance to Holland. In fact, all during Dutch rule it is apparent that public opinion had a potent effect upon even the most autocratic of governors and oligarchic of councils, and on various occasions the colonists participated very actively in the direction of public concerns. The authoritarian tendencies of the Dutch businessmen were no more effective in binding the colonists than were those of the English.

Governor Nicolls, in negotiating the surrender of the Dutch, gave terms which included a guarantee to the city of the choice of deputies with "free voyces in all publique affaires." In the meantime, most civil officers and judges were to keep their positions until the next election. Freedom of religion was promised and previous legal acts and judgments were to be respected. Nicolls, then, acting as the agent for the Duke of York, began to adjust the government and otherwise promote the duke's interest.

He accepted Dutch law and government, which meant a conveniently autocratic form. He and a council of his own appointing became the government. In the course of the next few months, he began replacing certain Dutch civic arrangements, notably by creating a new government for New York City. He likewise gave attention to the suburbs: Staten Island, Long Island, and the region just north of Manhattan. These he formed into a county called Yorkshire, and for them he prepared a law code, the Duke of York's laws, drawn for the most part from the laws of Massachusetts and New Haven. Then he called an assemblage made up of deputies chosen by the taxpayers of Yorkshire, and to this body, meeting at Hempstead, Long Island, in March 1665, he presented these proposed statutes and promulgated them in their presence. For some years they did not apply to New York City. The deputies acquiesced, settled some boundaries, and acknowledged their allegiance to the Duke of York. Then they went home, conscious perhaps that the proprietor's governor had conceded no political rights to them.

While in the process of adjusting the governmental machinery, Nicolls was endeavoring to induce settlers from the older colonies to settle the duke's vacant lands. When he had left England, he had been advised that the duke's boundaries included what are now not only New York but also New Jersey and Delaware. He undertook first to seek settlers for the west shore of the Hudson near Kingston, New York, but in his proclamation he offered to entertain propositions for other locations.

The plan was to let associations purchase land from the Indians upon warrant from Nicolls. The associates could then lay out a town free from taxation for five years. The associates should have liberty of conscience, but they were obliged to support a clergyman elected by a "major part of the Householders." These towns were to have "liberty to make their peculiar laws" and to decide "all small causes within themselves." They were to have "the free choice of all their officers, both Civil and Military." All could be esteemed freemen and vote who had taken the oath of allegiance to his Majesty and who were "admitted to enjoy Town-lotts," i.e., such as were not servants or day laborers.

Nicolls promoted the Duke of York's interests in New Jersey by confirming the Dutch settlers in Bergen and making two large grants of land to settlers on Long Island. One of these was the Elizabeth-town grant to a group of men at Jamaica, Long Island, and the other, the Monmouth Grant, to a group from Gravesend, Long Island. These grantees were authorized to establish towns and villages and to create town governments composed of selectmen elected "by the major part of the inhabitants." These governments could make laws and try cases of "debt and trespass."

All this was enlightened promotion, but a complication soon developed which was to condition this region permanently to a unique experience in politics. Even before Nicolls had reached America, James had given what was to be hereafter New Jersey to two of the promoting group, Sir George Carteret and Lord John Berkeley, and these gentlemen assumed quite illegally the power of the Bishop of Durham over both land and government. The Duke of York had no right to give them this power, only the crown could have done it. However, they went ahead and appointed a governor, Philip Carteret, a cousin to Sir George, who arrived in the summer of 1665.

But by this time Nicolls' grants had been consummated and settlers were making homes in what were to be called Elizabeth and Monmouth. When Carteret arrived, he began to operate in real estate for the proprietors in such a way that there developed conflicting concepts of title in which the relative validity of the grants of Nicolls, acting for the Duke of York, and Carteret, acting for grantees of the duke, clashed. This conflict was never resolved judicially, and for a century this doubt as to land titles created much uncertainty and insecurity and encouraged attitudes toward government which were fruitful of political use. To add to this confusion, Carteret and Berkeley did not operate together long, and within twenty years each sold his interest to different purchasers. In so doing, they divided what is now New Jersey into what were known as East New Jersey and West New Jersey. Each for a time had different government, different policies of operation, and different types of settlers. Here again was the basis for division of opinion, conflicting attitudes, and partisan strife.

The proprietors, whether Carteret or Berkeley or those to whom they disposed of their proprietorships, were eager to get settlers to buy the land and to pay quitrents. So Governor Philip Carteret had brought a series of concessions and agreements, largely copied from one prepared for the Carolina proprietors. In these, Carteret offered a government and a popularly elected house representing the freeholders.

Carteret also undertook an extensive advertising campaign. As things were difficult in New Hampshire, which had been absorbed by Massachusetts, and in New Haven, which was being absorbed by Connecticut, he was able to interest people to migrate from those areas to East Jersey. Some interesting phenomena developed, most notable of which was the migration of a congregation from New Haven which set up a New England town in East Jersey which they called Newark. By 1668 Carteret called an election, and the first assembly met, to which each of the towns sent "two able men that are freeholders," though after three sessions there met no other for seven years. In the meantime, there had been developments in West Jersey. Here there were scattered settlements of Dutch, Swedes, and Finns in the Delaware Valley, and one of Nicolls' fellow commissioners, Sir Robert Carr, was sent to take charge of these Delaware districts. When Nicolls retired, and Francis Lovelace, the Duke of York's governor of New York, took over, he set up a civil government consisting of a governor and council and began the collection of taxes. Despite this separate jurisdiction, the Delaware settlements sent two deputies to a session of the first East Jersey legislature.

The situation was further confused politically when in 1674 Berkeley sold his part of the Jerseys to the Quaker John Fenwick in trust for another Friend, Edward Byllynge, and ran a boundary between East and West Jersey, proclaimed July 1, 1676. A Quaker settlement was made on the Delaware at Salem in 1675 before the boundary was finally concluded. This was challenged by the New York authorities, and Fenwick was arrested and charged with unauthorized settlement. In the meantime, Byllynge, who had put up the larger part of the capital and thus owned the larger part of West Jersey, went into bankruptcy, and his creditors turned his estate over to their fellow Quaker William Penn and two associates for settlement of claims. These arbitrators allotted to Fenwick one-tenth of the purchase and undertook to develop the rest in Byllynge's interest. In March 1677 they issued concessions and agreements similar to those of East Jersey and established their headquarters at a settlement called Burlington. They would not recognize Fenwick's pretensions to rule, nor did the governor of New York, now Edmund Andros, wish to give up his jurisdiction over the Delaware. Likewise, Andros began to assert claims in the Duke of York's name over East Jersey. Just as soon as he heard of Sir George Carteret's death, he arrested Governor Carteret in 1680 and took him to New York. Though a jury refused to convict Carteret, Andros continued to exercise jurisdiction over both the Jerseys.

At this point, Penn stepped in, and he and Byllynge prepared a Grand Remonstrance defending their title and secured a favorable decision from English legal authority. This decision and the duke's friendship for Penn plus political difficulties in England because of James' Catholicism caused him to recognize the independence of the Jerseys from New York. Penn thereupon bought out most of Fenwick's holding, thus gaining control of West Jersey, and with eleven others he bought Carteret's East Jersey. These twelve men immediately sold one half to twelve others. Thus, East Jersey was the property of twenty-four Proprietors, largely Quakers. By 1682, Jersey, still divided, was in the hands of a group predominantly Quaker but with an important Scotch element in the East Jersey control.

The establishment of self-government in Quaker West Jersey was slower in getting started; not until 1681 did any assembly meet and begin to work with Byllynge's deputy governor, Samuel Jennings. In both East and West Jersey the operation of self-government was just as stormy and confused as the complex of proprietary rights and the conglomeration of peoples could make it, and that is saying a good deal. Groups and factions were virulent from the start, and the assemblies were constantly quarreling with governors who themselves had to serve so many proprietary masters. The early trend in East

Jersey was Puritan and strict, while in West Jersey the Quaker influence was more individualist and liberal. Here was the basis of the widest diversity.

This confusion and controversy, this clamor of many voices and conflicting interests, stimulated William Penn to another and independent venture in the vicinity. The Society of Friends had been interested in an American colony as a place where they might find the opportunity of establishing a society of their own planning where they would be free to worship as their consciences advised. Their efforts in New Jersey had been disappointing because of the people of other minds who were not sympathetic with Quaker ideals. Therefore, William Penn, to whom Charles II owed a large debt for money which his father, Admiral Penn, had loaned the Stuarts, undertook to secure a large grant from the monarch in settlement. He was successful and in 1681 secured a vast estate between Maryland and New York which included what is now the state of Delaware, all to be known as Pennsylvania.

This region was not without inhabitants. Dutch, Swedish, and English had settled within its limits, and in 1681 they numbered about a thousand, half in present Pennsylvania and half in present Delaware. Most of these colonists themselves or their parents or grandparents had come in under the Swedish and Dutch rule. Some one hundred probably had come in since the Duke of York had taken over in 1664. There were two small centers of population in Pennsylvania, one at Upland (present Chester) and the other in present Philadelphia, where Swedish and Dutch forts and settlements had been established; some English were in present Bucks County as well. In Delaware there were centers at present Wilmington, New Castle, and at Hoornkill in the South. The English had established courts at Upland, New Castle, and Hoornkill, the duke's laws had been administered, and grants and land titles were being made and confirmed by these courts under the general jurisdiction of the Duke of York's governor of New York.

William Penn immediately made plans for a holy experiment, sent over a governor to prepare the way, and himself arrived at Chester in 1682. Penn was both a philanthropist and a promoter. He wanted to create an ideal community and to operate a real estate development. So he offered two kinds of inducement: liberty and land. Like so many of the seventeenth-century promoters, he was addicted to paper plans and elaborate sets of rules. He was a sincere believer in liberty and toleration, and he wished to build a state upon those principles—but it was also his property and he wished to enjoy it and profit from it. He prepared four documents. One of these, *Some Account of the Province of Pennsylvania*, was an advertising leaflet; the others were more formal documents. These were *Certain Conditions or Concessions*, the *Frame of Government*, and *Laws Agreed upon in England*. The first was a contract to be made with land purchasers which ensured the proprietor a large share of the lands and a considerable portion of profits from land sale in general. The second was a constitution. The third was in fact a series of laws covering all of the required restraints upon human conduct.

Penn, upon his arrival in America in October 1682, called the freemen to elect seven representatives from each county to meet him in Chester, as he now called Upland, and presented to them the *Great Law*, or code of laws, which was there adopted. He then began to set his ideas of government and real estate promotion to work.

He discussed his *Frame of Government* with many of the citizens and as a result made such a number of changes that it was really a different document that was presented to a second general assembly. This constitution was approved and a permanent government thus came into being. It was to be a government with the proprietor or his deputy sitting with a council consisting of three members from each county. They were to have the power of rule and should also prepare the agenda for the assembly. The voters were those who held land, regularly one hundred acres, though freed servants needed but fifty, while in the towns artificers who paid taxes could vote.

Penn's first assembly naturalized the Dutch and Swedes. The proprietor required all land titles to be submitted and confirmed, and likewise he laid out his own city of Philadelphia, here requiring any landholders whose holdings did not fit into his plan to take an equivalent which did. He was anxious to sell land in large tracts and looked forward to being associated with a number of very substantial landholders.

Penn himself was not able to remain very long in his new province; he was forced to return to England to defend his title to the southern portion of his grant against Baltimore. He left his colony in charge of the council and soon sent over a deputy governor. But this all spelled trouble—politics had an early start in Pennsylvania.

The variety of population—Dutch, Swedes, Welsh, English—the religious differences among the Quakers and the variety of other creeds, and the succession of ruling powers and elites, these elements of confusion must shape a confused politics. Then Penn placed Thomas Lloyd in charge. He was a very active Quaker but so little able to manage that Penn, after trying a government by committees of the council, sent over a governor from England in 1688. He was not a Quaker and developed a capacity to rouse the opposition of Lloyd. The result was that the assembly, which was largely Quaker, began to see things differently from the governor and thus a Quaker and a proprietary party began forming. Likewise the three "lower counties" drew away from their "upper" neighbors, and this produced political differences which eventually resulted in a separate legislature for the "lower counties," or Delaware, as the district came to be called. Here too was an improvisation not according to the proprietor's planning.

While the middle colonies were being actively promoted by the "American group" close to the crown and by the Quakers, the former also had interests afoot farther south. Even before the New York project was officially launched, documents relating to the southern move had passed the seals. In 1663 Charles II granted to eight of this group—Clarendon, Albemarle, Craven, Lord John Berkeley, Ashley, Carteret, Sir William Berkeley, and Sir John Colleton—a charter for Carolina, located south of Virginia. This enterprise was to have two points of operation.

The region immediately south of Virginia, until then thought of as part of Virginia, had been the object of the latter's interest in one slight way or another for forty years. Since about 1650 a few settlers had been going there under Virginia authorization, so there were, in 1663, a number of settlers along the Chowan River in what was to be known as the Albemarle region. So the proprietors need now only develop this locality further. Their second point of operation was to be in the region which was to be known later as South Carolina, where the Barbadian members of the proprietary group hoped to establish a new enterprise.

The settlers in the Albemarle, or North Carolina, region who had been functioning under the slight ministrations of Virginia were now given a government of their own. In 1663 Sir William Berkeley, governor of Virginia, who was one of the Carolina proprietors, was charged with the responsibility of setting up a government for the Chowan planters. He was to appoint a governor with a council of six and an assembly which was to consist probably of all the planters. This was done. The government began functioning in 1664 and within a year the first assembly was summoned. As might be expected, the chief interest of the planters was to petition for a more liberal land policy. The proprietors consented and at the same time revised the government, enlarging the council and providing a representative assembly of twelve. But of its operation little is known as the record is slight.

The projects in the southern part of the grant were doomed to move slowly and the first efforts were not successful. One of the difficulties, Lord Ashley believed, was that there was no comprehensive plan to follow, so he turned to the political philosopher John Locke, who prepared the famous Fundamental Constitutions of 1669, one of the most remarkable documents produced in this century of colonial projects.

Carolina was to be a county palatine. The eldest of the lords proprietors was to be the palatine, to be succeeded when he died by the next eldest; the remaining proprietors should be the admiral, chamberlain, chancellor, constable, chief justice, high steward, and treasurer. The province was to be divided into counties, each county with eight seignories, eight baronies, and four precincts, each precinct into six colonies. Each proprietor should have a seignory in each county. In addition, there was to be an order of nobility made up of landgraves, one for each county, and twice as many caciques. The proprietors, landgraves, and caciques were to have 40 percent of the land. There was to be a grand council consisting of the eight proprietors and forty-two councilors representing the courts of the seven proprietors other than the palatine, who was viceroy and president of the proprietors sitting in a supreme court. This council was to prepare the agenda and originate all matters which were to be presented to the Parliament. The Parliament was to meet biennially and to consist of the proprietors, the nobility, and one freeholder from every precinct to be elected by the freeholders. Suffice it to say here that the project was completely unworkable and the labors of those seeking to govern were marked by constant improvisation.

Under this pretentious authorization, a settlement was finally successfully planted in March 1670 on the Ashley River and named Charles Town. In the planting of this settlement, a series of accidents began a succession of quick improvisations. The governor designated by the proprietors went only as far as Bermuda where he decided not to continue and appointed as his substitute William Sayle, an elderly Bermuda Puritan whose health was none too good and whose ability was mediocre. According to instruction, Sayle put the process of self-government in operation, not by calling an assembly, because there were not enough qualified people to serve, but by having five councilors elected at Port Royal by the settlers to join him and the five deputies of the proprietors in ruling. However, as there was dissatisfaction, particularly about some of the governor's Puritan ideas, he called a public meeting at Charles Town on July 4, 1670. Here there arose a spokesman for popular rule, William Owen, who cited Magna Carta and the Petition of Right and persuaded the meeting to elect delegates to a "parliament." This irregular body did nothing of consequence. Shortly thereafter, the governor died. In anticipation he had designated his successor, and the council elected him as Sayle had wished. Charles Town was completely self-governing for the time being and even possessed of a leader of the opposition in the person of Owen.

Already there was division. There were two natural groups: those who had come from Barbados with a good deal of colonial experience already and knew something of the score; then there were the colonists straight from England, who were largely ignorant of colonial problems. To add to the possibility of division was the fact that the officers were confronted with the obligation to carry out the Fundamental Constitutions, which on their face were impossible. Yet here they were, and any colonists wishing to be strict constructionist, exhibitionist, or just plain mean could always indict the authorities for failure in the trust. As baiting those in authority is a human trait which adds much to the technique of the politician, the South Carolina situation gave it full play.

On July 8, 1671, the first parliamentary election was held to choose the twenty men who were to be the lower house. They were to pass the necessary laws and also to elect five members of the council to serve with the governor and the proprietors' deputies in the upper house. In this government, the Barbadians, headed by Sir John Yeamans, who made a specialty of bearing titles and abandoning settlements and responsibilities, joined with Owen and his friends in opposing the governor. Sir John even tried to seize the governorship for himself.

In the meantime, South Carolina was on the way to developing a unique political structure. The plan of organizing a series of towns did not work out, nor did the creation of three counties lead to the evolution of a county type of government. Rather the inhabitants tended to concentrate first at the original Charles Town founded in 1670 and later in the new Charles Town, created ten years later at the union of the Ashley and Cooper rivers on the shore of a fine harbor. From these towns settlers went out to select favorable plantation lands upon which they started extensive agricultural operations and, after failure with other staples, began to specialize in rice. The authority of government never scattered like the settlers. It was a unique feature of South Carolina's political experience that government continued to be located almost exclusively in the new Charles Town (Charleston after 1783). All government officials and records were concentrated there. All elections were held there and all court sittings. In fact, hardly any government business was transacted anywhere else. Anyone with such concern must go there. The government, so developed, would be in the hands of a group of townsmen and planters who spent much of their time in town houses in the metropolis on the sea with occasional sojourns on their plantations. In this fashion, they could maintain themselves in the semitropical climate.

Thus the Carolinas were established. North Carolina was a series of widely scattered settlements and lonely farmsteads where government was at a minimum and individual independence most pronounced. A proprietary governor with a scattered council and a shadowy legislature went through certain forms of rule without much influence. In South Carolina, settlement and government were concentrated in the port of Charleston. A planting elite organized in parishes was gradually spreading out from Charleston but with little independence. The growing number of magnates met in true oligarchic style in Charleston to receive and quarrel with the proprietors' ideas, as reported by their agents, to take such steps toward defense against Spaniards and Indians as their wisdom and the exigencies of the times indicated, and to plan for their welfare as they visioned it. There was as much politics in Charleston as there was ignorance of it in North Carolina.

In these later proprietary enterprises the concept of a proprietor's plan and direction was still maintained, but it was ever more clearly understood that the settlers, particularly elites, must be taken into some form of cooperation and encouraged to assume a share of responsibility. Nowhere was there too much official concern with political privileges for lesser men, but there were not wanting signs that the individual settlers of whatever degree were assuming an independence partly, at least, required by the hazards of outpost fortunes.

In these proprietary ventures, as in the Virginia and New England experiments, improvised self-government triumphed even over the form and spirit of feudalism. English colonies, no matter by whom planned or by what interest ordered, ended up as active, self-governing, politically minded communities with a gift of improvisation and an ever developing capacity for independent political behavior but with a respect for certain families and traditions and a tendency to accord them deference.

·▸[V]◂·

PORTENTS OF INDEPENDENCE

*I*N THE last quarter of the seventeenth century, even before the final colonial experiments in self-government were well established, a novel phase in the political experience of the New World communities began to manifest itself. In each there was an attempt to hurry on the process of evolution with varying degrees of precipitation, and crystallization of political behavior assumed various forms in the several colonies.

A number of influences were at work to produce these altered patterns. One was the process of internal development in the American societies, and the other, the combination of external influences in a new period of revolution in England and of British war experience in Europe and America. These were prime influences contributing to a wave of political change, some of it following the time-tested English tradition of overthrowing government by force. In almost every instance the innovations occurred just about fifty years after the founding.

During this first half century of American experience, the patterns of self-government had been taking shape amid primitive surroundings. The new political mechanisms had been put in operation in primitive dwellings, in meeting houses, in rude churches, in makeshift court houses, in lonely dwellings, and out in the open air. Here issues were debated, officers elected, laws enacted. Natural leaders had appeared, elite groups had become established, opposition factions had emerged, reformers had made their pleas. Factors most effective in determining this political behavior were the changes in their ways of living; the ill-health suffered by the colonists; the novelty of experience; the undeveloped resources which stirred them to seek government aid; the scarcity, particularly of money; the emotional instability due to loneliness and fear; the tensions of religious difference; the antagonism of race; the contrast between town and country, tidewater and back country; quarrels over power; rivalries between colonies; threats by foreign neighbors. These were truly an imposing array of confusing forces. They all united to produce hostilities, tensions, and quarrels which strained the still not fully developed capacities for self-governing. Seventeenth-century confusion in England was to cap the climax and set off a chain reaction in the final years of the 1600's.

Evidence of the overseas transit of political violence became manifest before the English Revolution of 1688. In fact, it appeared in Virginia as early as the 1670's. Conditions with which the government of the Old Dominion had to cope were most difficult, and they served to make too obvious certain governmental inadequacy.

Virginia, the oldest colony, was now almost seventy years of age. Gone were the original settlers and those hardier souls who had later built up a tobacco-planting society in the tidewater region. As time passed the rude strength such as these men of fortitude possessed was no longer needed. A new group followed them, a group who knew only remotely the problems of the founding and serving of the colony. This new generation too was coming over from England. Many of them were of better social standing than their predecessors, and they came to create estates, to enjoy membership in an elite, to establish family prestige and continuity. They flourished under Governor Berkeley and held office under him; some of them had been appointed justices of the county courts, some were his sheriffs. They associated with him as members of his council and made up a Jamestown social set. When the Navigation Acts went into effect, some became collectors of the customs. The basis of tidewater gentility was established.

The expanding frontier on the other hand was pushed out by a new influx of population who found themselves less favored and felt frustrated. The tidewater gentlemen had little interest in satisfying the land hunger of the newcomers nor in disturbing the peaceful Indians with whom trade could be profitable; this ran counter to the interests of the border men who wanted the Indians out of their land so they could dwell in safety. Virginia was an expanding society. Colonists were ever pushing westward and seeking new lands in Indian country, in part inhabited by friendly tribes. The aborigines resented this penetration of their hunting grounds and undertook reprisals. The frontier demanded forts, arms, military leadership, and the removal of the so-called friendly Indians, but government was slow to heed these demands. Also, the enmity of the Spanish and

Dutch toward the English had colonial repercussions which pointed to local defensive measures by the Virginians.

Virginia's government was not coping with its complex problems very actively. The colony suffered because it had put most of its economic eggs in one basket; almost everyone was raising tobacco and their prosperity and sense of well-being depended on whether the price of this leaf was good. It was depressed by a series of situations which, wherever they appeared, were to prove weakening to government. The governor, Sir William Berkeley, was old, infirm, conservative, and arbitrary. He had been long in power. He had come to the colony in 1642, and since 1662, after the Restoration of the Stuarts, he had been making himself more and more powerful. He and a group of wealthy planters composed a ring that ruled Virginia as they saw fit. A legislature had been elected in 1662 on limited suffrage, but Berkeley prorogued it from time to time for some fourteen years without another election. He also chose his own councilors, and he and this ring appointed the county officers. The House of Burgesses, more and more under the sway of the ring, levied few taxes and those designed to favor the wealthy planters. They spared on protection and almost left the frontier defenseless, depending on the good offices of the "friendly" Indians. The officials of this ring, so long unchecked in the enjoyment of power, were set in their ways, oppressive, and accused of corruption. Offices were bought, it was charged, justice sold, and those in debt persecuted. Tax money stuck, so it was alleged, in the pockets of the collectors.

These grievances were exaggerated as they were passed on from tongue to ear in the isolated farmsteads and plantation houses, in churchyards and taverns on court days and Sundays or as planters enjoyed each other's hospitality. At this point it is essential that attention be given to certain types of people universal in a democracy whose names have not survived but whose activity has always been significant and will ever continue to be so. They were the first contrivers of the democratic machine. One type is the nameless political operator who spends his time mainly in talking politics. He may be called Alpha, for agitator. This is the man who in the tavern, on the street, in the churchyard, at the entrance of the town hall, wherever he meets anyone, talks politics. He is interested particularly in governmental gossip, he scents grievances, and seems to secure satisfaction in spreading scandal. He can and does embroider facts, his imagination initiates rumor of abuse and distress. When Alpha meets people, he communicates to them ideas and so-called facts which may well arouse the interest in spreading further what he has told them and in stirring up emotion which can lead to action. At this point his talk was all the more effective because the price of tobacco was down, and the British system of navigation laws, operating according to mercantilistic principles, was taxing tobacco, restricting its export, and reducing the price while encouraging the Dutch and French to grow their own. Debt to London merchant monopolists, who fixed prices, further kept the planters uneasy and frustrated.

Protests against the abuses and dangers were of little avail, partly because of the arbitrary and unresponsive character of the governor and council and partly because of Beta, the bureaucrat, who by nature encouraged the ring in their course. Beta, like his Alpha contemporary, is generally unknown to history. He is the clerk, the office convenience, the bureaucrat of long standing. He is the one who often controls who sees the responsible officials and what papers come before them. He briefs his superiors. He can keep information from them, he can hold papers back, he can prevent people from seeing the chiefs. He can manipulate matters so that he frequently controls and shapes policy. Unseen, he pulls certain hidden strings and nobody knows it.

In 1675–76 hard times and a series of Indian difficulties aroused the pioneering planters to the westward, and they sent urgent pleas to Jamestown for help. Berkeley showed his indifference by delaying, working ineffectively, and then getting angry and resentful when the efforts of government came to nothing. Finally, word was sent to the west that the governor wanted no more petitions.

In the meantime, as almost inevitably happens when there is community apprehension and governmental inadequacy, or lack of faith in government, a new leader appears. He quite frequently can be typed: he is enterprising, courageous, somewhat inclined to exhibitionism and demagoguery, yet sincerely interested and willing to take chances, to endure hardship, and even to risk his life to lead in finding a solution. Such a one was Nathaniel Bacon, a scapegrace son of a good family who had come to America to "start over again" as so many have done before and since.

He undertook to "defend" the frontier by driving out the Indians and forced the governor to call an election for the first time in fourteen years. The governor made an agreement with Bacon promising him military command, a promise which, it was charged, he did not carry out. Bacon, claiming he had been double-crossed, undertook to get rid of the governor, captured and burned Jamestown, and then died of fever contracted from exposure.

The crown sent troops, removed Berkeley, and attempted an amnesty, but not until Berkeley had executed some dozen in a fit of vengeance. Continued economic difficulties, border war, and Stuart political ineptitude kept the fires of discontent smoldering for some twenty years in Virginia after this ill-starred effort at reform by force of arms.

This episode in the Old Dominion seemingly was by way of prelude, although it turned out to be an isolated incident. The situation which developed in New England was markedly different and more inti-mately connected with the revolutionary politics of England. The independence which the Massachusetts theocracy had maintained and expanded had received no check during the Puritan Revolution; on the contrary, it had been viewed with a certain sympathy by Crom-well. But a basic change had occurred within the polity.

In the first decade the Massachusetts congregations had deter-mined to reach a state of sanctification more satisfying to their desire for holiness. They would accept for church membership only those who could convince the congregations that they had had a religious experience which evidenced saving faith. However, this generation was dying out and the younger people had not shared in this conver-sion. Was the test still going to be required and, if so, could member-ship ranks be kept filled? The Puritans might be visionary but they were also practical. Some new way must be found. So in 1662 at a general synod, it had been agreed to accept a Half-Way Covenant whereby the churches would grant congregational affiliation, if not full membership, to baptized worshipers even though they would claim no conversion. This was a difficult decision to reach and many were shaken by its necessity. Interestingly, it was taken shortly after the Stuarts returned to the throne.

The situation was soon fraught with danger. Charles II was a notorious liver, and he could have little sympathy with Puritanism. Also, the New England theocracy was facing other enemies. The Mason heirs had not been reconciled to the loss of New Hampshire to Massachusetts, and those of Sir Ferdinando Gorges wished to regain Maine. Urged by their importunities, the crown began an investiga-tion of Massachusetts and undertook a series of moves to curtail very decidedly the independence and power of the Bay Colony. The theocracy was ordered to stop executing Quakers and to grant tolerance to Anglicans. Connecticut and Rhode Island were finally given charters and their boundaries defined, in part because of a desire on the part of the home government to prevent Massachusetts from reaching southward. New Hampshire was detached from the Bay Colony and the claims of the Mason heirs to property rights recognized, although the government of New Hampshire was assumed by the crown. The claims of the Gorges heirs were also recognized, and Massachusetts bought them up, thus retaining control of Maine. The more the home government investigated Massachusetts, the less it liked what it found, and toward the end of Charles II's reign, court action was begun which annulled the Bay Colony's charter, October 13, 1684.

The death of Charles II almost immediately thereafter brought his brother, the Duke of York, to the throne. He already owned New York and had once possessed the Jerseys. He now undertook a major reorganization which involved the creation of a Dominion of New England which would include New Hampshire, Massachusetts, Connecticut, Rhode Island, New York, and New Jersey. He sent over as his governor Sir Edmund Andros who easily took over Massachusetts, including Plymouth, and New Hampshire and received the submission of Rhode Island and Connecticut, which were being proceeded against in the English courts for the annulment of their charters. In 1688 James II assumed jurisdiction over New York and New Jersey.

Thus Massachusetts stood deprived of her self-government, with the king's governor bearing rule over her, levying taxes unhampered by the critical watchfulness of a colonial legislature. Simultaneously came threats challenging the land titles of the Massachusetts colonists. The theocracy had never issued legal titles, and now the crown was obviously going to question land ownership and perhaps make new grants necessary. Fees would be charged for these grants, and hereafter payment of quitrents would be required. The governor would also have charge of granting the remaining frontier lands. Finally, Andros was ordered to enforce religious toleration and to establish the Anglican Church.

Every one of these items was found to arouse fear, resentment, and, of course, opposition among a church membership somewhat shaken by disillusionment. The theocratic leaders immediately began to counsel as how best they could restore their power. They sent Increase Mather to England to labor with James II and his government. Furthermore, they began to collect evidence of the "corruption and tyranny" which Massachusetts must now endure and to plot the overthrow of Andros.

Resistance began in the counties. Up in Essex, at a town meeting in Ipswich, the cry of "taxation without representation" was sounded as it had been in Watertown in 1631. The rights and liberties of Englishmen had been violated. A number refused to pay taxes and when jailed were unable to invoke the privilege of the writ of habeas corpus. Border difficulties added to the confusion. Indian warfare broke out and gave opportunity for a rumor that Andros was going to surrender to the French. James II was a Catholic and in sympathy with the French king and his religion. New England was threatened by popery and Indian massacres.

While the theocratic leaders were creating plans and propaganda to hasten their return, word came in March 1689 that the Revolution of 1688 was bringing William of Orange to the English throne. This gave the theocracy the opportunity they sought. Their plan was sprung. Organized crowds seized various officials and set up a new government headed by a Bradstreet, a Winthrop, and their associates. Almost immediately these revolutionaries proclaimed a formidable series of reasons for their actions designed to show that they were protecting liberty, religion, and property against tyrants, foreigners, and the "Scarlet Whore." Then the leaders issued another statement accepting the new responsibility, although they claimed ignorance of its origin.

The promoters of the revolt invited twenty-two others to join them in establishing a "Council for the safety of the people and conservation of the peace" and called a convention to consider what the permanent government should be. This group came to no very definite conclusion, so another was assembled representing fifty-four towns. Both of these gatherings showed vigorous opposition to going back to the old charter which had bolstered the theocracy, so a compromise was adopted which called back the officials chosen in the last charter election before the late consolidation. Meanwhile, Rhode Island, Connecticut, and Plymouth just faded out of James' Dominion.

The new government carried on though beset by the difficulties of a divided populace, many of whom wanted no more of the theocracy, and those supplied by the world war which had broken out in 1689. Their efforts at warmaking were not very successful and proved so burdensome that the new government embarked on the issue of paper money. In the meantime, Mather was in England negotiating for the reissue of the old charter, but the government of William and Mary was not so minded. A new charter was issued which, while it restored the assembly, provided a royal governor and altered suffrage so that property holding, not church membership, was to be the necessary qualification. The theocracy was defeated but in its last gasp of power-grasping sought compensation in a witch hunt—the Salem witchcraft trials.[1]

Between 1676 and 1729 something like a cycle of behavior had been completed. In all of the colonies save the self-governing colonies of Connecticut and Rhode Island, some basic change in government had taken place. These changes were frequently accompanied by violence, and almost all of the colonies showed a variety of examples of independent action and enterprise which illustrated vividly the growth of a capacity for self-government.

The eighteenth-century colonial experience, ushered in as it was by such an almost universal turbulence, was to demonstrate an institutional crystallization which gave convincing evidence of the increasing maturity of colonial political behavior. Each colony was developing a stability and an independence of political action which in the various societies were similar, although in most instances marked by unique characteristics.

The developing democratic behavior patterns, while continuing to be shaped by traditional forms, were responding more and more to environmental influences and to the dynamics of social change. The resulting models were taking on the complex local, regional, and continental characteristics which were dictated by their creation as separate entities, their location in three physiographic regions, and their common allegiance to the British crown.

During the seventeenth century, individual systems of politics had taken form in each of the colonies; in the early eighteenth it became apparent that part of their design was being shaped by their regional

---

1. Similar situations developed in most of the colonies. In Maryland religious antagonisms served to create tensions. Anti-Catholic prejudices gave certain Protestant agitators their cue, and at the time of the Glorious Revolution, a Protestant protective association drove out Lord Baltimore's agents. In New York there was the operation known as Leisler's rebellion. The same revolution of 1688 was the occasion of such confusion in the Jerseys that in 1689–92 and from 1700 to 1703 there was no real government in these communities and the proprietors surrendered their rights to the crown. Difficulties were less marked in Penn's domain, but even there Delaware secured its own legislature, and Penn gave Pennsylvania the Charter of Privileges of 1701. Somewhat later the Carolinas proved so unruly that the proprietors were willing to sell their rights to the crown.

location. There emerged three groups: southern, New England, and middle colonies, each with characteristic political folkways.

The southern tier of colonies consisted of social organisms in which the population was scattered in rural environments with a minimum number of towns. The predominant economic interest was agricultural. The leaders of the society were men of the English squire type. The population, though in a sense polyglot, was predominantly English in origin or descent and in tradition. Virginia, Maryland, the Carolinas, and Georgia were developing common interests and behavior patterns which were dominant in politics as well as in life in general.

Virginia, the Old Dominion, much the oldest, had reached a political maturity and position of influence which were to become basic factors in American politics for another hundred years and more. This colony was practically entirely rural. Its inhabitants were almost exclusively engaged in agriculture. Most of them dwelt within convenient reach of riverside landing places. Up and down the numerous streams cargo boats from Europe delivered goods and collected tobacco. There was thus no need for trading centers, and there was scarce a good-sized village in the colony. Williamsburg had succeeded Jamestown as the capital but it was little more than a village. At widely scattered crossroads could be found an occasional little brick courthouse with a small cluster of structures and in each of the widely separated parishes, a church. Most of the inhabitants lived lives devoted to local concerns, traveling little save for the often not inconsiderable distances to courthouse and church.

The early pattern of local government by county squires, stemming from England, had become well established. The early groundbreaking planters, living rude, hard-working lives, often under threat of Indian danger, had done their work, and their bodies lay moldering in consecrated corners of their plantations. The new group, many of them recently migrated from England, were perfecting the society so sturdily started by their predecessors. They had known neither the toil nor the rude hardships of the previous century. Close to English patterns, these planters had now built mansion houses, imported English furniture and books, and lived in a style reminiscent of English squires, building up an aristocratic family tradition with the novelty of Negro slave labor. Characteristically American features of this culture, known not at all in England, were tobacco farming, Negro slaves, and the absence of towns or cities.

Some of the planters, as did the English squires, bore commissions as justices of the peace and, sitting together as the county court, had the responsibility for local government in the county units. Likewise, they commanded the militia and organized for defense. They shared other governmental responsibilities with the local vestries of the parishes. As vestrymen, they were charged with encouraging morality, having powers similar to those of a grand jury; with caring for orphans and illegitimate children; and with helping those in dire poverty or distress. For such purposes, they had the power of assessing and collecting "rates," or taxes, and the parish budgets were on occasion larger than those of the county. The churches, though Episcopal and Anglican, had no bishops or central organization and were largely independent congregations under the shadowy jurisdiction of a commissary.

As in England, this local squirearchy took the lead in all these agencies of government; the same men frequently were justices of the peace, vestrymen, and militia officers. Members of this elite were likewise usually the members of the colonial legislature. In this legislature, the lower branch, the House of Burgesses, in the eighteenth century was an assembly of 104 members, 2 from each county and one each from Jamestown, Williamsburg, Norfolk, and the College of William and Mary. Its members were chosen at frequent elections. In these contests the planters and small farmers mingled, generally to choose from two or more of the gentry.

Elections were quite literally outdoor sports in which almost everyone joined. The body of the voters, often humble people, relished the fact that theirs was the choice—they had the numbers that counted. The elections were held at the courthouses, generally in the open air. The election officers, who were the sheriff and the clerks, one for each candidate, received the voters on the courthouse green in the presence of the candidates and recorded the votes as they were given viva voce. The body of freeholders could look on and even keep score. The candidates often would thank those voting for them individually and immediately. Many of them had refreshments on hand which were liberally dispensed—in fact, treating was essential. The alcoholic excitement generally increased as the day advanced, and the atmosphere of convivial holiday-making was very obvious.

All the freeholders could vote who were possessed of twenty-five acres with a house, one hundred acres of unsettled land or who leased a property to tenants or who owned a house and lot or a house and part of a lot in one of the few towns. Many rode far to exercise their franchise and to enjoy the fun. Land was plentiful, and few, save indentured servants and slaves, were denied the privilege; it was open to the former when they had served their time. Few, save the utterly incompetent, were without the prospect of political participation.

The burgesses thus elected assembled once or twice a year and were fined if they did not attend. While in session they received thirty shillings a day. Although they were predominantly of the tidewater elite, there were others elected on occasion, "persons of mean figure and character," representing the "mob." There was increasing pressure to enlarge the number of representatives admitted from the western frontier settlements. As the burgesses gathered at the little capital in Williamsburg, they found they must deal with the royal governor who dwelt in some state at the "palace." He had associated with him his council, appointed by the crown on his nomination. These councilors, who formed an upper house of the legislature, were usually magnates or "ruling oligarchs," men of large estate and of provincial prominence, leaders of society, frequently closely connected by blood or marriage. These councilors met constantly with the governor and might or might not see eye to eye with him.

The governor in his turn must deal with both the council and the House, and as the council and the burgesses were predominantly of the elite, he would find that theirs was the controlling voice. He, however, might have instructions from the home government, unpopular with the squires, or he might find himself temperamentally at odds with them. In either case he must seek to win over such of the House of Burgesses as he could to his support. His relations with them involved hospitality, patronage, and promises of influence.

In his contests with the local gentry, particularly in the House of Burgesses, the governor found himself in some difficulties when it came to building up support. The governor had some appointive power, mainly customs collectors and tobacco inspectors. But the burgesses had limited his capacity to build up any political machine with them. These appointees could not vote, nor even be present at the polls. When they relinquished their offices they could not be elected to the House for two years afterward. Nor were the burgesses eligible for office-holding. The governor was not to build up a civil service politically useful to him.

Some governors undertook primitive electioneering and found the necessity distasteful. They must vie with the large landholders. Electioneering in this event could be vigorous, as Governor Spottswood reported home. His opponents "upon an approaching election, set themselves to inventing most false and malicious stories and spread them about the county to poison the minds of the people and prejudice them against such candidates as should seem most worthy in the eye of the government, and as they are the familiar companions of the common planters, they have continued opportunities to propagate the scandalous reports and absurd notions among the vulgar."

Some years of experience showed, however, that the odds were against a governor who depended upon factional aid and patronage support among the burgesses or who appealed to the voters. He was indeed not in a very strong position. However, in Virginia, in contrast to most of the royal colonies, the governor had a settled salary and was therefore not dependent upon the will of succeeding legislatures; financially, at least, he could be independent. On the whole there was not much bitter contest, and the government of Virginia settled down by 1720 to a comfortable relationship between governor and the oligarchic council, who worked together to see to it that the House of Burgesses kept reasonably well in line. It was a government of wealthy planters, the Church, and a bureaucracy, headed, but not always led, by the royal governor. It was almost like a club; discussion, not oratory or political speeches, prevailed.

The controlling social-kinship grouping had, in fact, a closely knit political machine. They even had a peculiarly convenient financial resource. The economy was one of great wealth but little money. Most of the planters had to operate on credit with London factors who marketed their crops and bought their imports from England on the proceeds. But the planters had need of cash in Virginia, in some part for land purchase. A convenient source was adopted. The speaker of the House of Burgesses was also treasurer of the colony. For many years John Robinson, kinsman and friend to so many of the planters, had held this dual office. He was willing to accommodate his friends with loans from the treasury. When he died suddenly, it appeared that he had loaned £100,000 of public funds, not an inconsiderable fund which sustained the gentry in their pretension to power.

This government of the elite, held together by ties of kinship and mutual interest as it gathered around its dining tables or lounged in the comfortable legislative chambers, dealt, it would seem, almost casually with problems, even those of moment. The question of taxation was complicated by the fluctuating price of the leading commodity, tobacco. Likewise, the colonial government must try to satisfy the almost insatiable land hunger that arose from the soil-destroying properties of tobacco culture. Defense likewise was still a problem; need for an adequate supply of money raised the paper money issue. The back country was clamorous for the organization of new political units and for a greater share of representation in the House of Burgesses. These problems roused much political agitation.

Most of these controversies were carried on by the Alphas by word of mouth, and change was resisted or directed by the burgeoning bureaucracy (Betas). But a new engine was at hand. Governor Berkeley had boasted three-quarters of a century after the founding that there was no printing press in Virginia, but finally, by 1730, William Parks, a Maryland printer, brought in a press and in 1736 appeared the *Virginia Gazette*. At last there was the possibility of more frequent and regular circulation of the printed word.

Yet within the compass of this field of controversy there seems to have been little if anything resembling party organization or function. The society created in the Old Dominion did not encourage it. The population was homogeneous, the rule of the elite very tolerable, the opportunity for those of lower degree to improve their status was ample. Even the type of royal governor who on arriving might seek to increase the prerogative and build up his own power was lacking. In Spottswood's time, conflict between governor and the planters had roused each to seek to influence the electorate and to organize the House of Burgesses, but for most of the eighteenth century governors like Sir William Gooch had been in the palace, men who were content to work with the predominant group in both council and House of Burgesses and to adopt their way of thinking. However, elements of possible factionalism were present, for new population was coming in which was different in social and religious background, being in part German, Scotch-Irish, and dissenter. Also, these newcomers were settling in the more remote regions and were developing the frontiersmen's sense of neglect which was to lay the foundation for that "sectional politics" destined to play so important a part in the workings of Virginia's partisanship.

But, by and large, despite foreign wars, social expansion, and economic difficulty, Virginia by 1760 had experienced nearly a half century of the smooth operation of a government in which planter influence was dominant, supported by a loyal electorate in a fashion dictated by a social unity, a survival of feudal loyalty plus confidence in opportunity to improve one's status. The planting oligarchs were ruling like gentlemen, with due respect for crown and Church but it must be a crown served by complacent governors and a Church without bishops, in the hands of the local vestries which, to all intents and purposes, were ordering independent congregations. This closely knit government was self-sufficient, respectful, yet undoubtedly independent and jealous of its self-defined prerogatives. Any interference or violation would be taken amiss.[2]

In this fashion the southern colonies had developed a way of life characterized by slave-operated plantations and a politics adapted to the needs and inclinations of such a society. By and large, with certain exceptions, these were homogeneous populations, content with a certain fluid feudalism. Here the leadership of the landholders was accepted, but most everyone with ambition could look forward to entering that class, and in the meantime they had complete freedom of expression and usually a part in the choice of their representatives in the lawmaking bodies.

A second regional type of political behavior was developing in New England where there was a completely different environment. In the four colonies of Massachusetts, New Hampshire, Connecticut, and Rhode Island, people dwelt in towns, and there were a few cities, notably Boston. People lived more frequently as urban or village neighbors rather than in scattered rural isolation. Commerce and industry were as important as agriculture, or more so. Fishing and fur-trading, shipbuilding, and storekeeping engaged many. Town meeting and Congregational Church services were the gathering places rather than the county court and the Anglican parish meetings of the southern colonies. These were the centers of government and politics.

Of the four New England colonies, Massachusetts had reached the point of political sophistication in advance of the others, just as Virginia had among the southern colonies. After enjoying sixty years of practical political independence, the citizens were beginning in the eighteenth century the process of adjusting to their new status as residents in a royal colony under a governor appointed by the crown.

In making up their specifications for governmental change, the British government had left much unaltered. The Massachusetts towns were practically untouched. They were still full of politics and independence. The householders continued to meet periodically in

2. Virginia's northern neighbor, Maryland, and her southern associates, the Carolinas, together with the last colony, Georgia, established in 1732, produced politics of a similar order. A local squirearchy or a ring of officeholders was operating a politics of their own.

town meeting. Here they chose a moderator and clerk to conduct the sessions and a group of men, usually seven, to act as selectmen and to administer the town's affairs. Besides, a great variety of local responsibilities were assigned to individuals, and there was a multiplicity of titles, such as hogreeve, fence-viewer, and the like.

Likewise, the Great and General Court, or legislature, continued to exercise its lawmaking functions. The lower house was undisturbed in its composition and organization. It was chosen by voters who had real estate valued at forty pounds or who paid forty shilings a year tax. The upper house was also to be chosen by the lower house in the first instance, but after it was organized, both the houses filled the vacancies in the upper. The legislature continued to choose most of the colonial officials, and it remained the source of the law.

The powers of the royal governor, in comparison to those of most of his colleagues, were limited. His council was chosen for him, and though he could refuse to accept those designated, he did not have the freedom in creating his advisory group that would have been most satisfying. Likewise, he could comfort himself with a belief that he could veto the choice of a speaker of the lower house, but he had little patronage and was dependent upon the General Court for his salary. The governor therefore was in a weak position to withstand the legislative leaders, but as he often had instructions from the government to attempt unpopular measures, he must try to organize some political support.

The politically minded in Massachusetts, however, had had a long experience with independence, so that the governors found experienced legislative leaders, well trained in free operation, who were difficult, if not impossible, to overawe. These men marshaled the representatives of the towns, chosen in town meeting by popular voice and often carefully instructed. They no longer represented the old theocratic interest, for now Massachusetts was secularized. They rather represented people who were thinking perhaps more narrowly in terms of the needs of the towns and the colony than in terms of a unit in God's Great Zion. They had their own leaders, notably Elisha Cooke who led the "country party" and undertook to serve as tactician in the frequent contests with the governor and his "court party."

The contests between the governor and the legislative leaders often gained their vocabulary and their substance from the problems of the day. This was particularly true during the French and Indian War, particularly at the times when Massachusetts troops were actively engaged in the campaigns in hand. The inefficiencies of the

British, the inexperience of the colonials, and the accidents of warfare all contributed to casualties and disappointments despite some notable victories. Likewise, in times of peace, in periods of enterprise, there were demands for governmental action which caused contests.

These policy questions often involved the distribution of the lands still unused or ungranted. Massachusetts communities had been more or less continuously feeling the urge to seek other pastures. Many of the citizens wanted to move into new settlements where there would be greater opportunity; others wished to profit from speculation on this possibility. Therefore there was demand for the grant of new townships to various sets of "proprietors." The allotment of land and the profit made from it by speculating promoters caused rivalry for securing grants and grievance over lost profit or over too great gain. These grievances could and did take the form of protest against favoritism or resentment of the poor against the rich.

The question of land was closely associated with that of lumber. The English government saw many masts for his Majesty's walls of oak in the tall pines of New England's forests and therefore sought to prevent the woodsman's axe from felling them by marking them with the King's Broad Arrow and making it unlawful to touch them. This hindered or might have hindered, had the command been obeyed, the lumber business of the colonies and presented another grievance against the government.

Development of the frontier, of course, created new communities and more politics. These new towns had to be fitted into the legislature, although some towns were indifferent about assuming the responsibility of sending representatives. But whether sending deputies or not, these towns were new and to the east of them were the old, the seats of experience and power. These older settlements thought of themselves as the more significant and entitled to be recognized as such. This was not easy for the new towns to accept. There was to be a natural cleavage in the legislature between the old and the new.

Then there were the necessary relations with the outside world. Massachusetts, without sufficient fertile soil to be a thriving self-sustaining society, must trade. Under English mercantilistic regulations and under the defense conditions that prevailed during so much of their warlike period, the Massachusetts traders were presumably denied their most lucrative commercial opportunities by the prohibition of business with the French West Indies. Shortage of money also meant that dealings with Britain had to be on the basis of long-term credit, and often British merchants found it hard to collect their debts. The British officials in Massachusetts, from the governor down, were involved in enforcing unpopular trade restrictions and laws to aid in the collection of debts. These duties made it easy for colonial legislative leaders to invoke popular support in their struggles with the governors over pay and prerogative.

Most useful, however, as a teacher in the school of partisan organization and operation was a simple economic fact. There was not enough actual money in the colony to meet its needs. The expenditures during the two wars, 1689–1713, and the adverse balance of trade had caused a draining off of the silver and gold and the substitution of paper. During the wars, Massachusetts had begun the issue of paper money and the practice had proved very exciting to the colonials: it was such a convenient solution to so many problems. When in trouble, print your way out of it. Also, the neighbors were doing it. So the people in the town meetings were for it and the legislators in Colony House. But creditors, those who were better acquainted with the hazards of inflation, those who feared high prices and devalued debts, those whose morals shrank from default and the easy way were opposed. So were British governors under instruction from the crown, which had London mercantile interests at heart. So the leaders of the "popular," "people's," or "country" party, headed by Cooke, whose speculative instincts welcomed the panacea, now had an issue which had even more appeal.

In these political controversies a rising press played a modest part. There had been a paper in Boston since 1704 when John Campbell launched the Boston *News Letter*. Then came the *New England Courant* founded by James Franklin and later immortalized by his brother Benjamin in his *Autobiography*. These sheets were joined by others, and by 1760 the *New England Weekly Journal*, the Boston *Evening Post*, the Boston *Gazette*, and the Boston *Post Boy* had made their appearance and occasionally opened their columns to political news and controversy.

Despite these controversies, there was as yet little that resembled political organization, no mechanism of continuing activity, nor any colony-wide propaganda. During legislative sessions "popular" and "court" members saw each other daily, fraternized in taverns, had some meals together. In this group of politicians there were various attitudes, conflicting personalities, rasping emotions arising from differences of opinion and antagonisms of will. The issues debated showed differences of view and interest: frontier vs. seaboard, country vs. city, poor vs. rich, crown vs. colony. All these were useful in legislative maneuvers, in their arguments with the governor, in their rivalries among themselves. But they were symptoms of something deeper, verbalizations of more fundamental emotional conflicts. The fact was that there was a divided assignment of power. There was a numerous body of legislators, men often of necessarily limited horizons, dedicated to the concept of a self-governing colony. On the other hand, there was the royal governor, responsible to the crown but dependent for salary upon the legislature and without much patronage. In between were the members of the council elected by the legislature to advise the governor, men generally substantial and secure, men of responsibility who must see and try to harmonize the interests and duties of both crown and colony. The division encouraged politics.[3]

Thus in New England there had evolved a second general pattern of political behavior. Here a relatively homogeneous population had developed the art of self-government, not in the fashion of a gentlemen's club, but in the manner of local townsmen meeting frequently in a community place of assembly to transact their own business and to instruct their representatives. This type of government was generally not much broader than the town and was distinctly local in its outlook.

3. Connecticut and Rhode Island contributed to the New England pattern in unique fashion. They were the two colonies of the thirteen which during the entire period of colonial existence were almost independent. Their connection with the crown was of the slightest. Upon occasion they reported to the Board of Trade in London and recognized some obligation to operate within the framework of the imperial customs service. On the whole, however, they enjoyed a political experience of their own ordering.

Thus in Connecticut there had emerged a vivid politics, part sectional, part religious, part economic. The colony was falling into a two-party pattern and partisan contests began to develop in the elections of governors. Here, as elsewhere, there were few indications of partisan organization or the creation of party caucuses, but the basic two-party pattern was there and bound eventually to flourish. On the eve of the Revolution the conservatives were still in control, but the strength of their opponents was growing and seemed within sight of victory.

Rhode Island, though self-governing in many respects, was a decided contrast to Connecticut. In fact it was unique, ever the home of the otherwise-minded. Here there was freedom of religious opinion and hence no ecclesiastical dominance, as in Connecticut. Nor did the towns have the significance in the structure of this colony. Rather the ports of Newport and Providence were centers of politics because commerce was more important and agriculture less so.

Isolated in a New England niche was New Hampshire, until recently part of Massachusettts and now a somewhat blurred copy of the larger commonwealth. It had been erected politically, like Massachusetts, on the town meeting pattern. But since it had been separated from the Bay Colony, it had been administered by a royal governor, for a time usually the same man as "ruled" Boston. But it now had its own legislature and enjoyed its own politics.

In these self-governing colonies it must be noted that certain elements of balance had been recognized. The lower houses of the legislature were chosen by a large number of voters, but there was in these societies a psychological state described at the time as "fear, reverence, respect and awe." This meant that some in society—clergy, elders, sometimes men of wealth, wise men of experience—were looked up to and their words heeded. These in New England were something of an aristocracy, though one of different components than the southern elite.

The third regional group of colonies was situated geographically between the southern and New England units. These middle colonies had more lately been established as segments of the British Empire and had been settled by more heterogeneous populations than most of the other thirteen. They were especially versatile and dynamic, and their politics was to be unique. As compared with their southern and New England neighbors, who were rather set types, the middle colonies developed flexibility, practicality, and a capacity for discovering the expedient course, which were to be characteristic of them in ever greater degree. In them developed patterns of organized contest, of machine politics, of composing differences, and a complex variety of interests. Their role has been most significant but it has never attracted the attention that those of the South and New England have, and the part they played, particularly in the formative years of American democracy, is not too well understood.

New York, from the standpoint of social complexity, was probably the most intricate of all the colonies. During the period of Dutch rule it had attracted people from all sections of Europe, and its port, New York City, was truly a polyglot community. The British conquest was followed by extensive immigration of inhabitants of the British Isles, France, and the German Rhineland. Thus there was a variety of national groups with different speech and varying capacities for misunderstanding. These differences were reflected in multiplying religious organizations—Dutch Reformed, Congregational, Presbyterian, Anglican, Roman Catholic, Huguenot, and others. Finally the basic cleavage caused by the succession of British to Dutch control persisted.

The complexity of New York interests arose furthermore from the great size and geographical diversification of the colony. There was not only the port of New York, but there were the communities on Long Island, the settlements in Westchester County, the Hudson River towns, and the city of Albany, center of the fur trade with the

Indians. Stretched along the Hudson were the estates of the Dutch patroons and the manors of the English grantees. Beyond to the north were large areas for land speculators, Indian country, and the water routes to the Great Lakes and Canada, trading paths for the French. Similar diversity was found in New Jersey and Pennsylvania, particularly the latter. In all three of the colonies, therefore, the evolving patterns of self-government would have to be based on the fact that these variations spelled potential conflict and that the political leaders must be skilled in ways of coping with such disharmony. The middle colonies, therefore, provided laboratories for experimenting in practical politics not found in the simpler societies elsewhere.

The confusion of groups, interests, attitudes, and politically active individuals found in New York produced a complex politics which was to be characteristic throughout the history of the colony and state. So much depended on who ruled. New York was potentially so rich and largely undeveloped, it had so extensive an exposed frontier, and such a variety of communities. It was therefore obvious that the responsibilities of government would provide great opportunity and great differences of opinion. The bringing of such a variety into consensus would be difficult. This complex was to place a pressure upon political management, upon the practice of the art of politics.

The center of this politics was to be the legislature. Practice in the operation of this institution did not begin until 1691. After that year those with forty pounds worth of property were to vote for its members. The number of voters was small. Elections, particularly in the rural areas, were held at places inconvenient for most voters. The sheriff presided, the candidates and a few voters were present, and the result was presumed to be ascertained from a show of hands. If the decision was challenged, each voter was sworn and his vote publicly announced. Nominations were generally made by leading landholders or businessmen, but in New York City public meetings began to be arranged in the eighteenth century where nominations were made and then published in the *Gazette*.

The assembly had to make a place for itself in a government hitherto carried on exclusively by the governor and his council. In order to wrest from the governor due recognition, they concentrated on working through their control of taxation and appropriations, maintaining that the assembly's powers were like unto those of Parliament. It was an uphill fight, but after twenty years the leaders of the legislature had so far succeeded that the governor felt it necessary to build up a political organization strong enough to elect his supporters to the legislature in sufficient numbers so that his political lieutenants would be able to marshal sufficient assemblymen in the governor's interest to pass the measures he desired. The early examples of this type of political management were arrangements which Governor Robert Hunter made through his manager, Lewis Morris, whereby the governor agreed to sign certain bills paying claims and facilitating naturalization in return for long-term appropriations for his support. In succeeding years Governor Hunter and his successors made use of patronage and favors in the customhouse, the admiralty court, and the attorney general's office to build up their political support, and they found their power to make land grants helpful. In one instance, at least, Governor Hunter campaigned in a legislative election.

These political operations on the part of the governors were naturally matched by similar efforts in the assembly. The assembly's leaders became politically skillful, aided as they were on occasion by the bad conduct, unwisdom, and even corruption of certain of the governors. At one time or another certain executive policies regarding the Indian trade stirred up vested interests, but most notable in arousing popular antagonism and promoting interest in democracy was the Zenger case. In 1733 Governor William Cosby was infuriated by some articles attacking him published by Peter Zenger in the New York *Weekly Journal*. The governor had Zenger arrested and indicted on a charge of false and scandalous libel. Certain leaders of the assembly party secured the services of an eminent Philadelphia lawyer, Andrew Hamilton, to defend him. The normal procedure in those days, which the governor expected to be followed, was to submit to a jury the mere fact of publication. If the jury found that the matter in question had been published, the judge, an appointee of the governor, would decide whether the writing in question was libelous. Hamilton, however, pleaded the cause of the liberty of the press so eloquently that the jury in their verdict found the matter true and Zenger therefore not guilty of libel. Out of the burgeoning of New York politics thus came a great precedent safeguarding the liberty of the press.

During this contest also appeared the first colony-wide political machine. Leadership in the assembly's political organization came into the hands of James De Lancey, a member of a prominent New York mercantile family, allied by marriage with some of the great Hudson Valley landlords. De Lancey and his associates worked with a steering committee in the legislature. It met secretly and in association with certain lawyers, who did not even bother to seek seats in the legislature, managed legislation. This coterie had little difficulty in persuading the legislators, many of whom were small farmers of limited outlook, to take their advice in making laws. It was a strong and wise governor who could thereafter take over the management of the legislature.

The climax of political management came when De Lancy became lieutenant governor and thereby frequently acting governor. By clever politics in the 1750's he combined his executive duties with his leadership of the assembly. Not only did he have the support of commercial associates and landholders but, in a period of wartime paper money prosperity, he won favor with small businessmen and artisans by policies of *laissez faire* and free trade.

During the extended life of the De Lancey power, this organization naturally made enemies, and as a consequence, a third development emerged in the evolution of practical politics. It is almost an axiom of politics that in any long period of power rulers disappoint and frustrate, and the disappointed and the frustrated develop cumulative resentments. Also, such an organization can hardly help finding in its ranks some who take profit for themselves or make it possible for others to do so. During long stretches of control, climates of opinion are also bound to change, particularly if basic alterations in community attitudes occur, such as are produced by the coming of peace or the decline of prosperity. These changes are often accompanied by hardship and dissatisfaction and the causes can be attributed to those in power.

In the middle of the eighteenth century some of the Hudson River manor proprietors fell out with the De Lanceys. These magnates felt that the party in power was dominated by the merchants' interests in New York City and was careless of the needs of the landlords. Revenue was raised by land taxes rather than by tariffs, and there was no protection of the great estates from squatter invasion. The government, it was charged, failed to make war against the French with sufficient vigor. Many who were opposed to the Anglican Church resented colonial support for King's College, which had no use for dissenters as students. Finally, the De Lancey party was accused of graft and gross favoritism.

This resentment culminated in the 1750's when one of the powerful Hudson River manorial families, the Livingstons—the three brothers, William, Peter, and Philip, together with their cousins, Robert R. and Robert R., Jr.—broke with their erstwhile allies, the De Lanceys. They rallied their tenants and through their legal practice in New York City they worked up support among the embryo urban proletariat.

Ever since the hectic efforts of Governor Cosby to stifle criticism, a growing number of liberals had been active, opposing the crown's pretensions and supporting the cause of self-government and freedom. They spent their evenings on occasion in taverns and coffee shops and could be thought of later as forerunners of the Sons of Liberty. John Morin Scott, William Peartree Smith, William Smith, Jr., James Duane, John Jay, and, notably, William Livingston and his younger cousin Robert R. Livingston, Jr., were of this group. The Livingstons gained allies from their Hudson Valley manorial kinsfolk among the Van Rensselaers, the Schuylers, and later the Van Cortlandts. They also had associates among the Quakers in Queens County on Long Island. Their strength grew until in 1758 they captured the legislature.

Thus in New York political action had developed along an independent line. Here were two organizations, both American, fighting for control of the government. This was not the crown vs. country party typical of other colonies; it was rather an American two-party system, one conservative and the other liberal, yet both led by men of essentially similar ideas and background, two groups of followers rallying to leadership predominantly aristocratic and impressive. Three basic concepts of self-government had been achieved. The representatives of the people had gained control of taxation and expenditure. The right of freedom of the press had been vindicated in the Zenger trial. The existence and operation of organized opposition to the colonial and royal authority had become an accepted pattern of political behavior.

New York's achievement was unique. Her government was not a club of wealthy landholders sitting conversationally around a groaning board as in Virginia. Nor was it a series of rural town meetings sending representatives from the meeting houses to the Colony House in Boston to fight it out if necessary with the king's governor. Here were two fluctuating groups representing various interests, attitudes, and prejudices but with something like independent organizations seeking to promote autonomous self-government within the Empire.[4]

4. Pennsylvania, Delaware, and New Jersey also developed politics of their own. Both Pennsylvania and New Jersey had built-in partisanship. New Jersey was divided into East and West Jersey and developed a delightful incompatibility between the sections. Pennsylvania was the property of the proprietary family, and they were soon at odds with significant segments of the colonists, particularly when the Penns became Anglicans. Quakers, various German sects, Pietistic and otherwise, Scotch-Irish Presbyterians, Anglicans all developed religious and cultural differences which made political causes. And then Pennsylvania developed a master politician, Benjamin Franklin, who functioned notably when Quaker pacifism had to meet the challenge of world war and foreign invasion.

Thus the eighteenth century had witnessed the achievement of a political maturity and a dedication to self-government which was universal in the Atlantic seaboard colonies. Now developing in three regional groups—South, New England, and middle colonies—there was a corresponding number of general types of political behavior. In the South the squires were the dominant group, in New England were the town meeting leaders, while in the middle colonies there were appearing practical operating politicians who were adept at flexible and expedient management and who eventually were to set the political pace of American democratic behavior.

VI

POLITICS OF UNREST

*C*HE PATTERN of political behavior evolving in the American colonies during the eighteenth century was determined, in large part, by the long duration of international conflict from 1739 to 1763. What this pattern might have been had the century been a peaceful one can only be guessed. During this protracted conflict, significant campaigns were fought in America, and the burdens and responsibilities imposed upon the colonies by these actions prevented a normal political evolution. The disturbances and trauma caused by the necessities and hazards of intense warfare changed the probable course of their political behavior. During this war-torn era, the colonists were forced to assume much political responsibility and to learn new political functions. These operations caused them to construct more comprehensive patterns of self-government and to become adept in the creation and use of political mechanisms necessary to carry on these functions. This period of warfare also provided the colonies with certain opportunities for united action and gave them a sense of common interest which undoubtedly stimulated the growth of a capacity, still in an embryo stage, for confederated self-government based upon a sense of self-identification apart from Britain. It was the germ of nationalism.

The colonies, by their situation, must perforce fight. Expeditions organized in large part or in whole by them were significant features in all these wars. In the first and second conflicts at the end of the previous century, Port Royal in Nova Scotia had been captured by colonial arms. In the ill-fated War of Jenkin's Ear colonial militia participated in Admiral Edward Vernon's unsuccessful attack on Cartagena in South America. Glory crowned their flags when they reduced Fort Louisbourg at the mouth of the St. Lawrence in King George's War, only to see it returned to the French in 1748. At length their role had developed to the point that their efforts started warlike chains of reaction in Europe. The next war, the French and Indian, or Seven Years' War, was in large part fought because of actions of the colonials.

Virginia and Pennsylvania were especial rivals for control of the interior of the British area, particularly in the Ohio Valley, and when the French undertook to create a link between their Canadian and Louisiana possessions by claiming that area, the British government and the colonies were at one in seeking to stop French advance. A group largely from Virginia organized a stock company, the Ohio Company, and secured a great grant of land. The governor of Virginia sought to aid them by sending a messenger to the French commander who was building up settlements in what was to become western Pennsylvania, ordering the French to leave. When this mission proved ineffectual, the Virginia governor sent some men to build a counterpost at what is now Pittsburgh. The French soon seized this work and completed it as Fort Duquesne. The Virginia governor thereupon sent a larger force which, after an initial success, was besieged and captured. Thus, in 1753 and 1754, Virginia and France had started a war.

At this point the home government stepped in and sent over troops. This effort, like most of the English operations to date, was badly managed, the advice of experienced colonial militia officers was ignored, and for three years there was only disaster. The fighting and the diplomatic fencing became more complicated as Austria, Prussia, and Spain joined in, and the colonies found themselves at war on their southern borders and in the West Indies.

This enlarged warmaking placed great responsibilities upon the colonies and tested their political capacities. They must plan their own defense and organize an offense. They mobilized troops, built forts, and conducted campaigns beyond their own borders. They were compelled to secure arms and equipment, and to supply food, quarters, and transportation. Officers had to be found capable of training and leading the militia. Better communication with the other colonies and the home government had to be contrived. They not only must learn to administer but they must reconcile themselves to increasing financial responsibility, to tax themselves. In other words, they must enlarge their proficiency in self-government and in the art of politics.

Not the least of their lessons in political action came in the field of public finance, in appropriations, taxation, and revenue collection. In this realm they discovered that a basic question in any frontier com-

munity attempting large-scale operations far from the centers of capital mobilization was the scarcity of coin characteristic of these distant
societies. The proper provision for money supply had become, and
was to remain for some two centuries, a problem, and therefore an
issue, in American politics. The introduction of this issue in the first
large operation was a significant step in the evolution of American
democratic practice.

As early as 1690 Massachusetts began to use the solution so often
advocated: the Bay Colony issued paper money. In the second of the
conflicts other colonies followed. South Carolina, harassed by the
Spaniards during Queen Anne's War, 1701–13, not only issued paper
money, but made it legal tender. Furthermore, she organized a land
bank to issue more paper money on the security of the colony's unoccupied lands. Rhode Island likewise indulged, and Massachusetts resumed the practice. Within the next twenty years Pennsylvania and
Maryland joined in the emission, and Virginia, in 1755.

This inflation, this resort to paper money on a large scale was to
have decided political repercussions. So generous were these issues
that they undermined property values by enabling debtors to pay
their obligations with money of small value. Men of substance, creditors particularly, protested to the home government, and Parliament
proceeded to respond. Acts of 1741 and 1751 were designed to control emission of paper money, to forbid land banks, and to prevent
the issue of legal tenders, particularly in New England. These measures aroused great and lasting resentment in the money-issuing colonies. One in particular was to have far-reaching results. In Massachusetts one of the promoters of the land bank which was dissolved
had been a certain Deacon Samuel Adams, a man with great capacity
for political organization. When the Massachusetts bank was liquidated, he had to surrender most of his property for the purpose and
was thereby impoverished. His son, Samuel, never forgot the ruin nor
the ruthlessness of the process administered by British officialdom. A
financial grievance against Great Britain had been established, and the
people's parties fighting the king's governors could make vigorous use
of it. Furthermore, the colonies must face debts at the end of the war
period of something under £1,000,000, and their concern was obvious.

Not only had the colonies acquired greater capacity for self-government and certain grievances, but they had gained a sense of self-
definition. Warmaking had encouraged them to acquire a spirit of
independence and to display a callous disregard for the military suc-

cess of the mother country. Some of the most obvious manifestations of this attitude were various efforts at promoting colonial self-interest regardless of the British military requirements. Colonial trade with the French West Indies had always been lucrative and the war made it even more so. The British navy hampered French communication and trade with their American colonies, and the British colonies could profit by this interruption. They therefore entered this business despite the fact that they thereby aided the enemies of Britain. This trade probably prolonged the war by supplying the enemy and definitely hampered the efforts of the British forces to reduce the French West Indies.

Local profits also interfered with effective conduct of the war on the mainland, with some interesting corollaries. New York interests, which were close to the dominant De Lancey party, did not want the war to injure their fur-trading and land-speculating prospects. If New York mobilized the Iroquois and attacked the French, this action would mean an interruption of the fur trade and an obligation to stop their efforts to get the Iroquois lands for their real estate operations; furthermore, with warfare on the border, such real estate development was impossible. The New York machine, therefore, advocated a policy of neutrality. They spent little or nothing on defense, played down antagonism to Britain's French foes, and continued to aggravate the Iroquois by seeking their lands. In the meantime French activity in western Pennsylvania and the Ohio Valley, almost completely unopposed by the British, so impressed the Indians that it seemed that the Iroquois might defect to the French.

The British government was disturbed by this danger and endeavored, through their Indian agent in New York, Sir William Johnson, and certain colonists who were Indian traders dealing with the Iroquois, to get New York out of its "neutrality" and back into cooperating to defeat the French. As one of the moves in this direction the Board of Trade called an intercolonial conference to meet in Albany in July 1754.[1] Delegates from New York, Pennsylvania, Maryland, and the New England colonies attended, but Virginia, one of the chief parties at interest, was not represented.

As far as the main objective was concerned, the conference accomplished little. De Lancey, who attended, was not convinced by Johnson, and the delegates, having no power, had to be content with

1. Intercolonial cooperation had been experimented with in the New England Confederation and during the first of the Anglo-French Wars, 1689–1703, an intercolonial congress had met in 1690 at New York.

recommendations. They urged more defense measures, they recognized the grievances of the Iroquois, and they recorded themselves as against local real estate operations in Indian country. Finally, they proposed that colonial western boundaries be set at the Appalachian mountains and that new machinery be created to care for affairs west of those ranges.

It was this latter proposal that gave the conference significance in the advance of American politics. Benjamin Franklin, representing Pennsylvania, attempted to grapple with the problem of creating a mechanism to insure cooperative action. He proposed that the crown appoint a governor general for the American continental colonies and that the colonies send representatives to a grand council or continental congress. The governor and congress would have charge of the British responsibilities west of the mountains, Indian relations, trade, defense, and settlement. The colonies would supply money for this operation by taxing themselves, and the representation of each in the congress would depend on the size of the colony's financial contribution.

Nothing came of this plan immediately. The colonies were opposed to such a "super government." Certain of them, like Virginia, had large claims in the West and wanted to develop these independently. This proposal would have liquidated their Ohio Company and its ambitious operations. The British government on its part did not want to turn over its western responsibilities to colonials; British interests were planning land companies too. So the whole idea collapsed. But the plan of union was not forgotten and was awaiting resurrection when a convenient time came some twenty years later.

The failure of the Albany Congress of 1754, which was followed by General Edward Braddock's defeat and the Earl of Loudoun's frustrations, was but one of a number of misfortunes in these war years. The colonies found themselves invaded. Fort Oswego and Fort William Henry were captured in the colony of New York, and the attack on Louisbourg, during this fourth war in which American effort was greatly involved, was a failure. In 1758, however, the tide turned. William Pitt and the colonial governments had learned at length how to make more successful plans. Lord Jeffrey Amherst and General James Wolfe at long last could and did command success. Mobilizing British and colonial forces, they finally brought the war to a triumphant conclusion in 1759, and the diplomats secured the addition of French Canada and Florida to the Empire.

From their participation in this great effort the colonials had gained much political experience and had learned to do things for themselves in a big way. They had gained faith in their own political capacity, and among them had been awakened an emotion, a sense of self-identification, the beginnings of a nationalism which was at length to demand republican independence, an existence apart from the Empire. The eighteenth century experience of the colonies had provided them with an equilibrium in their institutional patterns and a political maturity. They were now prepared to meet a crisis and promote a basic change.

In the first years of relaxation which followed the cessation of hostilities in 1759, no one perhaps realized that the seeming political equilibrium within the Empire, so painstakingly achieved in the first half of the eighteenth century, was in process of disintegration. Few, if any, grasped the fact that the hard lessons in self-government learned by the colonists had made their position as dependents upon the far-distant imperial metropolis, London, so unrealistic as to be no longer tenable. They had in effect become too independent in thought and action to remain colonies in the old sense. They must become autonomous or independent. The problems of adjusting to peace were making a basic change inevitable.

Peace meant demobilization and relaxation. Many now had to make adjustments in their lives, and they had to do it during the hard times of postwar deflation. Colonial governments had been running in high gear and now had to slow down and make the painful discovery of how much they owed. They also had to learn that the Empire had changed. It was much enlarged; new and alien populations in Canada and Florida were now their neighbors within, not without, the Empire. French, Spanish, and Indians had to be assimilated. All these new duties had to be undertaken in an atmosphere made gloomy by debt, increased expense, new taxes, and postwar emotional letdown. But during the war years the colonies had learned to respect their own capacity and to be contemptuous of Britain's incapacity. They entered this period of adjustment with confidence.

Colonial politics were complicated by the difficulties in which the British ministers found themselves as they attempted to fit Canada and Florida into the imperial pattern. For this was to be no easy task; the new population was alien and had been brought up in a tradition of hostility to the British. Their religion likewise was different; they were Catholic. Furthermore, within the French and Spanish empires the people had had little practice in the self-government so prominent in the pattern of the thirteen British colonies. The presence of hostile tribes of Indians who began fighting under Pontiac in 1759 and the clashing interests of rival land speculators meant that the frontiers must still be guarded. There was also good reason to believe that the French and Spaniards would try to regain their lost possessions. For these reasons expensive garrisons were needed in America. At the same time government was required for the new acquisitions and such government could not be constructed from the patterns of self-government in use in the thirteen. All this would not only take much money, money to be raised at a time when the British government was financially exhausted and heavily in debt, but more important, it would take a high degree of statesmanship. Unfortunately, the British government was exhausted, its statesmanship seemingly bankrupt. An old generation of politicos was dead or dying, there was a young new king, and a dangerous chaos in political organization.

During the period of demobilization and relaxation, the colonial governments must busy themselves with meeting new conditions, and it was something of a letdown. No longer must they strain every nerve to mobilize and dispatch expeditions. Rather they must wrestle with debts and deal with inflated currency. To some extent they were concerned about defense against Indians, such as Pontiac. The frontier, moreover, had a positive attraction. Some of those at loose ends were thinking of finding homes in the lands to the west of Virginia and North Carolina and in the Ohio Valley. Land companies were organized to sell these lands and some of the colonies believed that by these sales they could pay their debts and take care of certain of their restless population. The colonials were also resuming trade with the West Indies and Canada, in the hope that the cloud of postwar depression might soon be lifted. In all this, for the nonce, the politicos had little to do and some undoubtedly missed the hustle and bustle of warmaking and the quarreling with British officers, supercilious and bullheaded as they were. The British ministers on their part were likewise struggling with debt and administration, and it was not long before they gave the colonists something which stirred their newly acquired political skills.

The colonial use of paper money had produced inflation and made the collection of debts at anywhere near their original value extremely difficult. The British government had to have money. The colonies were careless in paying customs dues and their indifference to trade regulations was notorious. Their irregular trade propensities had been particularly illustrated by their lucrative trade with the enemy in the West Indies duing the late war, so the first step was to attempt to clamp down on colonial irregularities and to really collect the revenue due. A series of measures was formulated by the ministry.

An act of the Virginia assembly to make it possible to pay stated obligations in depreciated currency was vetoed. An order was issued to colonial governors forbidding them to grant further permits to colonial merchants to trade with the French and Dutch West Indies. A new governor sent to Massachusetts was instructed to tighten up on smugglers and was given authority to use blank writs of assistance, i.e., search warrants, in the process. A proclamation was issued shutting off settlement beyond the Appalachians, designed to keep the colonists away from Indian dangers and from lands desired by British operators but which Americans believed to be their own. New customs regulations were issued giving the admiralty courts, which had no juries, more authority to enforce rules and making officers of the British navy customs collectors. New customs duties and restrictions were prescribed in the Sugar Act of 1764 and further new taxes were ordered by the Stamp Act of 1765. Finally, the home government was determined that the colonies should make a substantial contribution to the expense of maintaining a garrison army in America for protection against Indians and possible disaffection of the French Canadian population, even to the extent of quartering it on the people.

In each of the colonies there were conditions which made it inevitable that speedy political use would be made of these measures designed for revenue and defense. Most of the colonies had a history of disputes with crown or proprietors, except the self-governing colonies, and in them there had been apprehension lest their charters might be recalled following the unhappy Massachusetts precedent. Inevitably, these new policies meant the reopening of old wounds, the revival of old quarrels. The short-lived emotional vacuum formed by the coming of peace would soon be filled under the guidance of practiced politicos.

The new course of political action began in the most mature and politically sophisticated colony, Massachusetts. This colony, once self-governing, had developed the most advanced techniques of partisan mechanism of any of the thirteen and because of its former independence was probably most sensitive to grievance.

The Bay Colony had 168 towns holding town meetings and sending representatives to the Great and General Court. These town meetings not only elected representatives but they frequently provided them with written instructions. Boston, despite its size (over 15,000 people), was governed by a town meeting which the qualified voters were presumed to attend. However, so large a body was unwieldy and an inner mechanism had been devised, a group without legal standing, which managed the town meeting. This steering committee was headed by Sam Adams, who had inherited the interest from his father, Deacon Samuel Adams. This latter politician had worked through political clubs of his own organizing, creating an Alpha group of great skill. One of these in North Boston drew many of its members from dock workers along the waterfront. As a number of them caulked ships for a living and were known as caulkers, this club became known as the Caucus Club. Members of these and other like organizations could be counted on to attend town meetings and to follow the lead of the Adamses, father and son. These groups met in various "garrets" over the taverns or in the "long rooms" of inns. Tom Dawes was proprietor of the garret where the Caucus met. Adjutant Trowell had a long garret where the Masons congregated. The newspapermen, Edes and Gill who published the Boston *Gazette*, had a similar place of meeting; so did the Salutation and the Green Dragon taverns. Here, in these smoke-filled rooms, much politics was talked and many political tactics planned in the atmosphere warmed by steaming bowls of rum punch. Here Alpha functioned vigorously.

Political activity in these clubs was stimulated by a growing restiveness among artisans and other wage earners. They felt underprivileged, particularly in terms such as those of unemployment, depression, and postwar relaxation. They could be made easy prey to a sense of grievance skillfully suggested by their leaders. Their political effectiveness was enhanced by a prevailing tendency to turbulence which was characteristic of Boston. These clubs, formed by the underprivileged, for a number of years had been celebrating Guy Fawkes Day, known locally as Pope's Day, in the most boisterous fashion. The North End and the South End clubs were accustomed to bring out two large wagons and put on each a giant image of a "pope," together with a devil and some other figures. These would be illuminated and, manipulated by cords, like marionettes, made to perform antics. These wagons, surrounded by mobs, would start out from their headquarters raising all sorts of racket and seek each other out for a sanguinary street fight. Night would be made hideous and on each November 5 property would be destroyed if liquid refreshment was not forthcoming; many would get drunk; a number would be hurt; and occasionally someone would be killed. While this was going on, law and order disappeared, and Boston was in the hands of the mob. However, there was some leadership, and the rabble was not always as much out of control as it seemed. Here was a force which could be mobilized for protest.

These town meeting leaders in Boston with their clubs and their followers controlled the deliberations of the city government. They were not above calling town meetings unexpectedly at obscure places, occasionally on a notice posted inconspicuously where but few would see it. Likewise, they were in touch with leaders in many of the towns where small groups often exercised control as effective, if less turbulent or devious. Then in the legislature they were part of the loose organization, the country party, opposed to the governor's court party and worked closely with their fellow legislators from the interior. Few governors could prevail against this combination.

Not only did Massachusetts have this somewhat complex and effective political organization, but it had merchants who were alert and interested in politics. No sooner did word come of impending new taxes and administrative changes than they began activity. In April 1763 the Boston merchants organized a "Society for encouraging Trade and Commerce within the Province of Massachusetts Bay," something of a chamber of commerce. This group created a committee structure designed to organize opinion against unjust taxes and hardship regulation, to mobilize merchants in other colonies, to secure newspaper support for their position, and to stir up sympathy in England through correspondence with colonial agents and members of Parliament. From their efforts and example arose other mercantile organizations, articles were published in newspapers, legislative resolutions of protest were adopted, and petitions sent to the British government. The colonials were on the road to making intercolonial agreements for coercive measures which would, it was hoped, rouse British merchants, moved by self-interest, to espouse their cause.

Thus in the 1760's Massachusetts was well prepared to take political action. Her merchants started it off, but her politicians were not too far behind. Word of the Molasses Act and the new mercantile enforcement and quartering regulation arrived in the spring of 1764 as the towns were preparing for the annual meeting of the legislature. Sam Adams and his Boston associates prepared instructions for Boston's representatives which were adopted by the town meeting. Other towns did likewise, and when the legislature met in June, that body

not only adopted protests and petitions but they appointed a committee of correspondence to get in touch with the other colonial legislatures urging that they claim the full rights of Britons and demand that
there be no taxation without representation. James Otis, chairman of
the committee of correspondence, appealed to the various colonies for
"united assistance." Thus the Boston merchants were working with
their fellows in other cities, and the Massachusetts legislative leaders
were co-opting their opposite numbers up and down the coast.

The idea of official correspondence among the colonials had been
developed during the recent wars and the custom was not difficult to
revive. Some of the colonies already had committees who corresponded with London agents of the legislatures, and petitions and
protests could be handled by them. Also, the press was increasing in
size and influence, and it became an increasingly efficient engine of
propaganda. In 1750 there had been but thirteen newspapers, but by
1764 the number had increased to twenty-three. Only New Jersey
and Delaware were without local journals. These four-page sheets
could not offer quantities of news, but what they printed was read
greedily and the sheets were passed on from hand to hand. Much in
them was mere notice of events, for the idea of dealing with principles or providing propaganda was very, very new. Certain of the
printers thought of their function as a literary one and published
poems, prose homilies, and bits of fiction, sometimes in installments.
As printers were occasionally postmasters, they had access to the
mails for their sheets, and on occasion could by the same power discourage competitors. As dissatisfaction and apprehension began to
increase, these newspapers, carried by the postriders, spread the word
of protest and independent thinking up and down the seaboard and
into the back country.

In the southern colonies there were variations of the New England
behavior of political protest. In Virginia the Williamsburg coterie
who ruled were aware, not only of these new grievances, but of an
undercurrent of political uneasiness. The war era had left the Old
Dominion with heavy political responsibilities. The colony had spent
much in defense and in aggressive campaigning. Some of the operations had taken place on Virginia soil, and at least one of the colony's
citizens, the burgess from Fairfax, George Washington, had learned
firsthand of the inefficiency and wrongheadedness of British functionaries. The economic condition of the colony was likewise bad.
Not only had the government spent much money and gone heavily

into debt but the tobacco crop was so unprofitable that many of the leading planters were in debt to London factors. The colonial leaders had hoped to extricate themselves from their debts by using paper money and by speculating in the vast real estate areas beyond the mountains. To lead in these new moves a younger generation was coming into the picture, including men like George Washington and Patrick Henry.

When word came that the British government had disallowed a law which Virginia had passed to ease her obligations by permitting them to be satisfied with paper money, had issued a proclamation forbidding her citizens to use "her" western lands, and had imposed new trade restrictions and taxes, indignation began to mount in Williamsburg. Not only did the burdened planters wax indignant, but the small farmers and frontiersmen in the back country, often in danger from the Indians and lacking in adequate representation in the legislature, were ripe for protest. Some of the younger men were eager to come forward and supply more vigorous leadership. When the word of Massachusetts' actions in protest against the new Customs Act was received, Virginia responded with a similar protest to the crown and sent instructions to the colony agent in London to promote it. But news of the Stamp Act struck more fire, probably because of a new local issue introduced into the House of Burgesses.

That spring of 1765 the ruling group was moved to an unusual course. They sought to secure from the legislature authority to borrow money in London and loan it to the local landholders on the security of their plantation acres. But a young man had just been elected from one of the western counties to fill an opportune vacancy. Patrick Henry had already made something of a name for himself as a lawyer who had pleaded the colony's constitutional rights against English interference. Now he rose and attacked this proposal as an effort to favor the extravagant, debt-ridden planters at the expense of the taxpayers. This attack may have had behind it some knowledge not yet public of the use by planters of public money for their own ends. Patrick Henry and others, generally representing newer and westerly counties, secured the defeat of this proposal.

Almost immediately after Henry's 1765 success, word came of the probable passage of the Stamp Act. The session was nearly at an end and many of the House had already departed for home, thinking the session's work over, but in the last hour a motion was made to consider steps necessary because of this impending tax. Patrick Henry seconded this motion and then proceeded to introduce a series of resolutions which in no uncertain terms denied the right of Parliament to lay this tax, declaring that the Virginia legislature had "the only and exclusive Right and Power" to tax Virginians. In defending these resolutions, Henry uttered his famous warning to the king that as other monarchs had had their Brutus and Cromwell, George the Third might well "profit by their example! . . . If that be treason, make the most of it." Henry and his more radical friends triumphed for the moment by a narrow margin, but the next day the most radical of the resolutions was stricken out. However, the original set of resolves had been sent out in manuscript and was published in other colonies as though they all had been passed and had become the official act of Virginia.

On the same day that the Henry resolves came under debate, the Massachusetts General Court met and within a fortnight had invited a conference of representatives of the colonies to meet at New York in October to consider the menace of the Stamp Act. Each colonial assembly was to appoint delegates. It was apparent to the two most effectively political of the colonies that vigorous protest must be made against this invasion of colonial rights. Furthermore, Massachusetts realized that united action was necessary to make their protests effective. During the war years there had been some glimmer of the need for such cooperation but it had never really developed. Now for the first time an effort at such coordination was to be made with general spontaneity.

The response was neither unanimous nor in all cases enthusiastic. Only six colonies sent delegates chosen by their assemblies: Massachusetts, South Carolina, Rhode Island, Pennsylvania, Connecticut, and Maryland. The governors of Virginia, North Carolina, and Georgia would not call the assemblies, and nobody did anything about representation. New York, New Jersey, and Delaware were in the same situation, but irregular representatives appeared. The New Hampshire assembly, though in session and seemingly sympathetic, sent nobody. In October, therefore, twenty-seven delegates appeared from nine colonies. These delegates prepared a theoretical platform stating their rights and grievances and addressed petitions for repeal to the king, lords, and commons.

These efforts were of no avail. The Sugar Act was not repealed, and the threatened Stamp Tax was enacted in 1765, since no colonial legislatures provided any of the necessary money by their own action or suggestion as the ministry had requested. Word came that certain colonials had been appointed stamp agents in each colony, that the stamps were on their way, and that on November 1 little colonial mercantile business or law practice could be carried on legally without the use of stamps. The Bostonian politicos now girded themselves for a new pattern of political behavior, for they found the situation in their colony particularly aggravating. Governor Thomas Hutchinson, Massachusetts-born and bred, had many of the instincts of a late nineteenth-century ward boss. He believed in the patronage system and he never missed an opportunity to seize an office for himself or for a relative. He had vigorously opposed the land bank, which was liquidated by the British government to the ruin of the senior Samuel Adams, and he had deprived James Otis of a judicial appointment which Otis claimed had been promised to him. The governor was consequently hated by Adams and Otis on personal grounds. Now it appeared that he had secured the stamp agency for his brother-in-law, Andrew Oliver, who was already well cared for at public expense. Some sort of an explosion was due, and on August 14, 1765, it shattered such of Boston's calm as remained.

On that day, a large elm, thereafter known as the Liberty Tree, was put to strange use. An effigy was hung there, the likeness of Mr. Oliver, and with it some Pope's Day symbols. That night, as the Governor and council were in session in one of the upper rooms of the Colony House, a crowd took down the effigy and bore it through the ground floor of the little capitol to Oliver's wharf, where an office had recently been built, it was assumed, to house his stamp tax functioning. This was quickly demolished. Then the shouting throng, carrying the effigy aloft, proceeded to Oliver's house which they gutted, without regard to the protests of the terrified family. After completely destroying the garden, they pressed on up to Fort Hill where they buried the effigy. Some local leaders had co-opted the leaders of the Pope's Day riots in staging this violence. Next day the *Gazette* in describing the riot quoted from a speech in Parliament by a Major Barré; these men were truly "Sons of Liberty." Oliver resigned.

But this was not all. Another night and another crowd gathered in front of Governor Hutchinson's mansion. They demanded that he appear on the balcony and purge himself, that he declare to them that he had never advised the British government to levy the stamp duties. This he would not do, but sat silently behind barred shutters. Some windows were broken, speeches were made to the milling crowd, but at length when a neighbor assured them that the governor was at his country place in Milton, the crowd dispersed. For a day or so they would take it out in merely spitting at the governor's carriage.

The climax, however, was not long delayed. August 26 had been a brutally hot day and even at nightfall no cooling breeze came in from the sea. As darkness fell someone strangely enough added to the intolerable heat by lighting a fire in front of the Colony House; not long afterward men by the hundreds began to gather at the wharves. First they converged upon the house of the surveyor of the port. Fortunately for him, he was not at home, and a keg of punch was available at a neighboring tavern. Then the crowd went on to the houses of the register in admiralty and the comptroller of customs; these they gutted, paying particular attention to the wine cellar of the latter. Their next objective was Hutchinson's. The governor had just time to flee with his family by the back entrance. By morning the governor's mansion was a wreck. Though some of the rioters were arrested, another crowd rushed the jailer and freed them.

After all this there was to be a final act and a postlude. On November 1 when the Stamp Act was to go into effect, bells tolled, an effigy of Lord Grenville was hanged on Liberty Tree and later in the day on the public gallows. Yet on this day there was no violence. The North and South End clubs marched in solemn procession to the accompaniment of a band. Finally, on December 17, rumor was flying that Oliver was reconsidering his resignation, so he was forced to stand under the Liberty Tree and, in the presence of some two thousand, to read, sign, and swear to his resignation. Needless to add, the Stamp Act was a dead letter in Massachusetts.

Tactics of this sort were not generally employed throughout the colonies but their influence was felt everywhere. By November 1, 1765, the date on which the act was to go into effect, all tax collectors had given up any idea of functioning. On that date the Sons of Liberty and others posted warnings in many places, and in New York City there was a riot. The act never really went into effect anywhere. In 1766 the Parliament, upon motion of a new ministry, repealed the Stamp Tax, contenting itself with a Declaratory Act affirming the authority of Parliament to tax, if it saw fit.

Thus the Stamp Tax in various ways had mobilized community opinion for political action. Committees of correspondence, sundry enforcement associations of merchants pledged to nonimportation, the Sons of Liberty, and the intercolonial congress had all taken their parts in the drama. As a consequence, numerous people had been inducted into politics as amateurs. They tangled with the duly constituted representatives of the king's authority, they "persuaded" stamp distributors to resign, they set up rules of nonimportation and non-exportation, they watched their neighbors, and they dealt with infractions. They developed a sense of group conflict with the court circle and became a political action group, or faction.

Some form of organized political opposition appeared in every one of the thirteen colonies. It took different shape in each one, and in each it followed some pattern of partisanship already formed. Almost everywhere in these self-governing colonies, except in Connecticut and Rhode Island, there had been a struggle going on intermittently between a local elite and a court party representing king or proprietor. In each colony there was some fairly well-established faction which could and did find it to its advantage to take up these grievances.

The satisfaction at the repeal of the Stamp Act which the politically-minded colonists could take from their effective protests and acts was to be short-lived. The British government had not solved its financial problems, and the insubordination of the colonies continued to rankle. So in 1767 a third ministry, guided by "Champagne Charley" Townshend, proposed a new program. Different taxes, this time external only, on paint, paper, glass, lead, and tea were to be imposed, administration of the customs regulation was tightened, and the quartering of troops was insisted on. New York City had been chosen headquarters of the British army in America, but the colony of New York would not contribute to the expense, the Quartering Act to the contrary notwithstanding. So together with the Townshend program of taxation Parliament passed an act suspending the functioning of the New York assembly unless the money was forthcoming. This was inviting a new wave of political action in the colonies.

VII

NEGOTIATED POLITICAL
COOPERATION

*T*HE EXPERIENCED Massachusetts political activists, now as previously, rose first in protest. When the passage of the Townshend Acts was announced, Boston's town meeting managers and the colonial legislative leaders formulated protests, and the latter caused the legislature to send out a circular letter calling upon the other colonies to join in resistance. The legislature of Virginia approved Massachusetts' proposal and sent out a circular letter of its own voicing agreement. Feeling among the colonies reached a new high when the ministry retaliated by ordering Massachusetts to disavow her letter and, when the colony refused in June 1768, ordered the governor to prorogue the legislature. Now two legislatures, those of New York and Massachusetts, had been coerced. Such interference with the right of self-government invited a new and more radical step. The merchants of Massachusetts entered into an agreement to stop imports, and similar steps were taken promptly in Virginia but more slowly in New York and Pennsylvania, in fact not until a year had passed.

The slow action of New York and Pennsylvania demonstrated the fact that resentment at the British policies was far from unamimous or even uniform. The forces in New York, particularly in New York City, were composed of elements which were diverse and, on the face of it, somewhat contradictory. At the time, the Livingston faction was in power, led by Hudson River aristocrats, who marshaled their tenants, and by city lawyers, who were enlisting the proletariat from the city. Here were artisans, laborers, sailors, and stevedores who had no political privileges and whose only mode of expression was in mass demonstrations and riots. From these often unstable elements, New York units of the Sons of Liberty had been recruited by John Morin Scott, who worked through men like Isaac Sears, John Lamb, and Alexander McDougall, popular with those in humble walks of life.

Actionists of this character had been vigorous in enforcing agreements not to deal in British goods while the Stamp Act was on the statute books, and they had also attempted to prevent the sale of stamps.

New York, however, was too aristocratic and conservative a society to appreciate violence or to tolerate it as complacently as did Massachusetts; the De Lancey faction was of this temper. The result was that doubts as to the mechanism of their protests began to arise early among those opposed to British policies. There were many second thoughts. The assembly indirectly modified its refusal to provide money for the British garrison and made some appropriation. There were likewise defections from the Livingston party, and in 1769 the De Lanceys regained the legislature. New York would probably not have joined in the mercantile nonimportation agreements at all had not the home government unwisely demanded the payment of customs duties in coin at the same time that it disallowed an act providing more paper money. Matters were further complicated when the royal governor, emboldened by the victory of the De Lancey party, undertook to throw one of the leaders of the Sons of Liberty, Alexander McDougall, into jail. This started street fighting with the British garrison, climaxing in the so-called battle of Golden Hill, January 17, 1770. Notwithstanding this outbreak, the zeal for protest was clearly less strong in the middle colonies than in either the South or New England.

II

In the various northern colonies the Townshend policies had aroused opposition to a new fever heat. That portion of the program which was designed to stamp out smuggling brought out more violence. Newly appointed customs officials in Boston seized a ship, *The Liberty*, belonging to John Hancock. This action caused such a rough handling of customs officials by townsmen sympathizing with Hancock that even the Royal Navy could not handle the situation, and the customs men had to retreat to the fortifications in the harbor. In consequence of such defiance, a large garrison was stationed at Boston in the fall of 1768. As the colonial legislature refused to contribute, the troops were quartered in public buildings. Their duties included patrolling the streets, and some of them in their spare time sought to eke out their low pay by working in competition with local laborers and artisans. Although it was not long before most of the troops were removed, enough remained to keep alive the grievance. However, their numbers were not sufficient to handle any emergency which might arise, and when local activists contrived to taunt and badger the redcoats sufficiently, the tension snapped, and on March 5, 1770, there was bloodshed, the Boston Massacre.

By curious irony, the nonimportation agreements had in the meantime done their work, and under British mercantile pressure the home government had repealed all the Townshend duties save those on tea on almost the same day in March 1770 on which the Boston Massacre had taken place. The removal of the troops from the streets of Boston and the news of the repeal were sufficient to quiet colonial opposition, despite the continuance of the tea tax. The flame of revolt died down and nowhere faster than in New York and Pennsylvania where once again these colonies demonstrated their temperamental contrast with their neighbors north and south.

The quiet which succeeded the repeal of the Townshend Acts and the Boston Massacre was not long-lived. The British government was in the process of completing a new political equilibrium of its own in which at last George III and certain politicians working in the name of the royal prerogative had achieved a consolidation of interests. After a decade of effort the "king's friends" secured a working majority rather than an unsteady coalition in Parliament. The success of this new coalition provided its ministry a greater opportunity for tighter administration and more consistent policy. This faction undertook in 1772 to make some of the colonial judiciary more independent by causing the ministry, rather than the colonial legislatures, to pay their salaries. Also, after a revenue cutter fought an action disastrous to itself with smugglers who went unpunished, the government sought to have those accused of revenue violations thereafter brought to England for trial.

The climax came unexpectedly when in order to help the East India Company, which was overstocked with tea, the government devised a plan to permit it to sell its crop in the colonies cheaper than the local merchants could market the leaf. This policy favoring the great corporation at the expense of colonial storekeepers roused emotion again, and the Massachusetts and Virginia leaders began planning for new committees of correspondence. Another Virginia circular letter of March 1773 stirred the four New England colonies and South Carolina to renew their former cooperation, and instruments which had been laid aside were now grasped again. The committees of correspondence were reorganized and the Sons of Liberty reactivated. Direct action flared up once more, most spectacularly in its place of origin, Boston. Here the famous Boston Tea Party was organized, and the East India Company's tea consignments sent over under the new plan were dumped into the harbor by men disguised as Indians. This act of violence, this destruction of property, this defiance of the crown, these were the last straws. The ministry cracked down and Parliament passed the Intolerable Acts. Boston port was to be closed and Massachusetts' charter further abrogated. With starvation seemingly staring them in the face, the citizens of Boston on May 12, 1774, appealed to the other colonies for help.

Virginia's reaction to the news from Massachusetts was in line with her previous emotions. Immediately, May 24, 1774, the House of Burgesses called upon Virginians to join in a day of fasting and humiliation. For this the governor, Lord Dunmore, at once dismissed them, and as in previous crises of this sort, the Burgesses went into session at the Raleigh Tavern. There on May 27 they called upon the colonies to join them in a Continental Congress to plan remonstrance and cooperation. The response was general up and down the coast, and the extent to which feeling had been aroused was shown by the fact that it was strong in New York and Pennsylvania, hitherto reluctant.

The two middle colonies had been slow to act in large part because of their size, the variety of their interests, often conflicting, and their polyglot populations embracing so many groups. Consequently, their political mechanisms were more complicated and more difficult to manage. However, the machinery of political procedure had been slowly evolving, especially in New York, and now in this crisis it was ready for operation.

New York's politically minded leadership for some time had been experimenting with the device of political committees, particularly during the ten years following the French and Indian War. These committees had been designed to mobilize effective opposition, either to the governor or to the De Lancey machine. Now this mechanism could be put to work in opposition to British policy. Such committees were set up in the far-flung counties, manors, villages, towns, districts, and cities, in fact wherever there were governmental units. The members of these groups were particularly concerned with communicating with others of like interest and with providing news of local conditions and actions. In a day when there were few newspaper facilities, these agencies were important in mobilizing public opinion. Now that the Intolerable Acts showed the British government pat-

ently disregarding the cherished rights of the colonies, these committees swung into action.

The issue had been sharply drawn even before this when the East
India Company's tea consignment arrived in New York harbor. Here
a second tea party was staged, April 22, 1774, by the Sons of Liberty.
When the news of the Intolerable Acts arrived within the month,
even the more conservative forces were aroused, and open and concerted action now began. A meeting of merchants and all others interested in protest and resistance was called at Fraunces' Tavern.
Would the conservatives or the radicals direct procedure? The Sons
of Liberty hoped to dominate and planned to propose a slate for a
directing committee of twenty-five representing all factions, particularly those who had been active in resisting the tea tax. So many
conservatives attended, however, that a larger place had to be found
for the meeting, and when the count was taken, the conservatives
were in the majority. They then proposed a committee, not of
twenty-five, but of fifty, and finally, on May 19, 1774, a Committee
of Fifty-one was agreed to. Of these, twenty-two were conservative,
eleven radical, and eighteen in between.

The expanded committee was to have the responsibility for fixing
policy and administering the colony's action in the crisis. The new
organization would not accede to the desire of Massachusetts for cutting off trade with England completely. Instead it merely expressed
sympathy and suggested an intercolonial conference to plan united
action. In the meantime the Committee of Fifty-one sent out a letter
to the county treasurers, who were in turn to send a copy to each of
the local communities. The letter was an invitation for each county
and lesser political unit to use the committee mechanism and to appoint a local group to keep in touch with the central body. In the
meantime the radicals showed their dissatisfaction with this type of
moderation. Their members withdrew from the Fifty-one and associated with a Committee of Mechanics. Thus there were still two parties and two central committees.

Though the counties were not as yet generally ready to act, a
number of the towns began a boycott of British trade and appointed
committees of enforcement, sometimes called Associations, or Committees of Safety. Observing this local support, the radicals through
the Committee of Mechanics sought to secure a convention from all
parts of the colony to choose representatives to the intercolonial congress. Not to be outdone, the conservative Committee of Fifty-one
wrote to the counties urging them either to appoint delegates to this

congress or to authorize the New York delegates, appointed by the Committee of Fifty-one, to do it. Five counties designated representatives and four others authorized the New York City men to represent them. In this manner the New York delegation to the First Continental Congress, which was to be held in Philadelphia, was chosen and the conservatives and moderates were predominant.

Pennsylvania's reaction to the British policies of 1760–74 had been even more tardy, influenced by its own complex politics. Like New York, it was large and embraced a variegated population with many interests. The Quaker party was predominant, despite its "peace testimony," and yet it was constantly embarrassed by the military necessity of the colony's exposed position. The official conclusion of the French and Indian War had not brought peace to the Pennsylvania frontier, and there were constant demands made upon the assembly for men and money to defend the western settlements from the Indians. Outraged frontiersmen marched on Philadelphia to enforce their demands at gunpoint in 1763 and had to be turned back by skillful diplomacy. The situation was complicated by the proprietors' change of religion, from Quaker to Anglican, and their insistence that their vast estates should remain untaxed. Franklin and the Quaker party, therefore, contended that Pennsylvania would be better off if the proprietors were superseded by the crown. Franklin, the Quakers, and a number of the German pietistic sects began organizing to promote this basic change. The proprietors on their part, in cooperation with the Presbyterians and others, were trying to protect their interests.

So engrossed were Pennsylvanians in these dangers and controversies that little attention was paid to the new imperial taxes and administrative changes. The year 1764 had been one of a bitter political contest on local issues. The proprietary party mobilized every source of strength to protect themselves against Franklin's campaign to make the colony the property of the crown. Success repaid their efforts in October 1764, when in the Philadelphia city election, Franklin and his associates were defeated, although his party still controlled the assembly. This body, despite the Philadelphia defeat, sent Franklin to England to work for the transfer of Pennsylvania to the crown.

Pennsylvania thus literally had little political energy available for remonstrance at taxation. But with news of the Stamp Act some tardy resentment had flared up. Franklin and the Quakers at first seemed inclined to go along with the tax, they may even have thought that support of it would aid their efforts to have the crown take over the colony. But the proprietary party, perhaps for equally "political" reasons, would have none of it. They determined to fight it and led the move in the Pennsylvania assembly which sent a delegation hostile to the crown to the Stamp Act Congress in September 1765, though by only one vote. Despite the general hostility to the Stamp Act and the charges that Franklin and the people's party were accepting it, the latter party recovered from their defeat of 1764 and won the election of 1765 in Philadelphia.

These conditions illustrated the fact that in Pennsylvania, as in New York, there was sharp division between conservatives and radicals. Likewise, the sides were very evenly matched. The Quaker-German party was generally victorious in the annual elections and, despite the fact of heavy mercantile interest, very hesitant to join in boycotts and fearful of violence. Belatedly, the Philadelphia merchants agreed not to trade with England after the enactment of the Townshend duties but withdrew from the boycott with extreme celerity after their repeal in 1770. As in New York, however, the tea tax roused emotions. The Philadelphia radicals forced the tea ship to leave without unloading, and when Paul Revere arrived in Philadelphia with news of the closing of the port of Boston, it was apparent that some action would be demanded, although opinion was divided as to what. No one defended the Intolerable Acts, but there was sharp difference as to the wording of the expression of resentment or the degree of resistance. The leaders of the General Assembly, chief of whom was the speaker, Joseph Galloway, wanted to work for a better imperial organization with a recognition of greater autonomy and power for the colonies.

The more radical group had been working up a committee system like New York's in the various towns to take the lead in resistance to tyrannical acts and unwanted taxes out of the hands of the Philadelphia merchants who were to them too cautious. At Philadelphia the force of the radicals was augmented by the formation of a Mechanics Association similar to that in New York City.

A new activity toward protest began the day after Paul Revere's arrival with the news of the passage of the Intolerable Acts. On May 20, 1774, a skillfully planned mass meeting was held in Philadelphia. A committee of correspondence composed of ten radicals and ten conservatives was set up to reply to Boston's plea for aid. But the letter which they sent to Boston was displeasing to the radicals, and they were further disturbed when the Quakers would not participate in a day of mourning on June 1 when the port of Boston was closed. So they were prepared to take the next step in response to Virginia's call for an intercolonial conference. Here again the radicals were busy. They circulated a petition to the governor to call the assembly. But he refused. Then some merchants of Philadelphia summoned a mass meeting at which a committee of correspondence was appointed to respond to a communication from a similar meeting in New York. The more radical leaders, however, met in the American Philosophical Society and called a city-wide meeting for June 18. In this move the Mechanics Association was particularly active. Some eight thousand attended this rally. Resolutions were passed supporting the intercolonial conference, and a central committee of forty-three was authorized to work with a committee in every county. Thomas Mifflin, John Dickinson, and Charles Thomson then made a tour of the colony and finding sentiment favorable, so reported, and a convention of the representatives of the county conventions was called for July 18.

The obvious fact that such a provincial congress would meet finally moved the governor to call the assembly for the same day. The delegates to the provincial congress were chosen on July 15, and three days later they met at the same time that the assembly was gathering. The convention endorsed the Continental Congress, suggested that the assembly appoint delegates, listed those whom they thought should be in the delegation, and advised what their instructions should contain. These points were duly presented to the assembly. They appointed delegates but only from their own membership, thus omitting John Dickinson and including Joseph Galloway, the leading conservative. The assembly issued instructions to the delegates which were less specific and radical than those submitted by the convention. Despite these modifications, the convention accepted this program and adjourned. In Pennsylvania, as in New York, the radicals had been forced to accept a moderation of their program.

As the response of New York and Pennsylvania would indicate, the sentiment for an intercolonial conference was general. The interference with the process of self-government in Massachusetts was held to be too ominous a sign. The other colonies, including the self-governing colonies, who had always feared the loss of their charters, were now alert. They would send food to starving Boston and arm themselves. The royal governors sought to check their actions by proroguing or failing to summon the legislatures. But the colonists would not be stopped. Mass meetings, conventions, and committees appeared at various times, and in all save the self-governing colonies, a new organ of government appeared in the form of such spontaneous provincial bodies as had been initiated in New York and Pennsylvania in May and June 1774. In July these were followed by similar moves in New Hampshire, New Jersey, and South Carolina and by Virginia and North Carolina in August. These bodies were chosen in the same way used to select the lower house of the legislature and they immediately began to take over the direction of public opinion in the colonies. The result was that all the colonies save Georgia responded to Virginia's May invitation and undertook to send delegates to the Continental Congress scheduled to meet in Philadelphia in September 1774.

Most of these delegates were appointed by the new provincial congresses, councils, or conventions. In New York there was a species of popular election in scattered wards and towns. In South Carolina a mass meeting of the Whigs of the province met in Charleston and prepared a slate of delegates, later approved by the legislature. In Connecticut the delegates were designated by the committee of correspondence upon authorization of the legislature. Only in Pennsylvania, Rhode Island, and Massachusetts were the delegations chosen by the legislatures themselves, and in the latter colony by the lower house acting on its own responsibility.

This first Congress much resembled a party convention attended by representatives of the various colonial Whig parties to the number of fifty-five. The process of calling and convening the Congress illustrated the extent to which factions representing different political attitudes had developed since 1764. During this decade it had been apparent that the resentment at the British policies was not universal. There continued to be many who were bound to the crown and to the royal governors by ties of patriotism, conservatism, social connection, political service, personal advantage, or just habit. They frequently represented the more wealthy with well-established social recognition, but the active part played by the colonial merchants in opposition to the crown policies shows the weakness of any such generalization. Likewise, there were then as now as many conservatives, who preferred to acquiesce in things as they were, among the less favored by fortune or enterprise as among those in the higher income brackets. So as early as 1764 a political cleavage began to appear. Later on, when more radical groups appeared in protest against the Stamp Act, those who were opposed to force and violence let this dislike upon occasion overcome their distaste for taxes and supported loyalty to law and order. Representatives of this group had appeared among those attending the Stamp Act Congress, and one of their number from Massachusetts had been chosen as its president. He carried his disapproval of their proceedings to the point of refusing to sign the resolutions and petitions which were their main product.

In the days of the nonimportation agreements in protest against the Townshend Acts, this division had been less apparent, although a new religious cleavage turned up. Many viewed with alarm a move which was gaining momentum among Episcopalians to secure an American bishop to protect and expand the Church of England in the colonies. The well-established non-Anglican churches, particularly in New England, resented and feared this. So the Whigs in America began an attack upon Anglicans which the latter, in turn, resented. The bitterness caused many of the Church of England to grow more out of sympathy with opposition to the crown.

By the time that the Continental Congress began to be planned for, it was apparent, furthermore, that the Whigs themselves were not too thoroughly united upon the question of how far opposition should go. These divisions of opinion can be more clearly understood by reference once again to the situation in Pennsylvania, where the convention was to meet.

Despite the surge of resentment aroused in Pennsylvania by the plight of Boston, the Quaker colony did not lose its wonted attitude of caution. The Society of Friends and many German pietists were dedicated to pacifism and thus reluctant to countenance any action that implied the possibility of violence. Their influence was still to be reckoned with, and its strength was underlined by the fact that the speaker of the Pennsylvania assembly was Joseph Galloway, a conservative who felt that the problems could be solved by some accommodation of differences within the Empire, a view perhaps suggested by Franklin's proposal submitted to the Albany Congress twenty years before. This tendency to compromise and adjust would be in the air at Philadelphia.

This fact was soon discovered as the delegates began to assemble. A vigorous group, of whom the Adamses, Samuel and John, were the chief, had come to Philadelphia to urge united action, not only to aid Boston, but to insure the rights and liberties of all. To them this meant not only sending supplies to Boston and the drafting of ringing documents of protest and defiance, but also the organizing of a continental army and a possible shedding of blood in defense of freedom.

When these men arrived in Philadelphia, they began to sense a contrary spirit pervading political and social circles prominent in the city. Sam Adams' organizing genius took command. He knew that the conservative influence expected the Congress to meet at the Province House where Galloway and his conciliatory associates had their headquarters. The Adames realized that such an arrangement was not to the advantage of those desiring radical measures.

The Massachusetts leaders scouted about and got in touch with a more radical group in Pennsylvania, mostly resident in Philadelphia, who represented a more liberal, liberty-loving element and who included representatives of the submerged nonproperty-owning artisans and other population groups, such as the frontiersmen and a vigorous Scotch-Irish Presbyterian element. Some of these people had warned the Adamses against the Province House and perhaps arranged an invitation from the Carpenters' guild to use their hall. The radical group thought that acceptance of this invitation would give evidence of broader sympathy and more genuine love of liberty. So Adams and his group secured agreement that they would stop in at Carpenters Hall on their way to the Province House and try it.

To the dismay of Speaker Galloway of the Pennsylvania assembly, legalistic conservative, the members liked the new hall so much that they voted to stay there without further ado and then elected a local radical, Charles Thomson, who was not even a member of the Congress as the secretary. No one then dreamed that he would remain at this post for fifteen years and wield immeasurable influence over its actions; he was one of the most effective of Betas. Thus from the first day it was apparent that there were two factions and that the more radical was in control.

The conservatives were not to be overborne without contest, however, and sought to arrest the radical program with a compromise. Speaker Galloway proposed a plan reorganizing the Empire and giving the colonists a greater degree of autonomy and self-rule while admitting the supremacy of Parliament. After vigorous debate this was tabled by a vote of six states to five and the way cleared for the positive action which was eventually to lead to independence. The radical group now perfected what the conservatives wished to avoid and to avert which they had urged the meeting of the Congress, namely economic coercion. Congress formed a Continental Association, a political mechanism to enforce a boycott. There would be nonimportation, nonexportation, and nonconsumption.

VIII

BEGINNING INDEPENDENT ACTION

*T*HE ASSOCIATION was the fruit of experience. The political leaders ascribed the failure of the nonintercourse policy of 1769–70 to the fact that its enforcement had been in the hands of the merchants and that they had allowed their desire for profit to get the better of their zeal for liberty.

Now each county, city, and town was to have a political committee of enforcement chosen by those qualified to vote for representation in the legislature. In each colony the committee of correspondence was likewise charged with general oversight of the plan. Furthermore, the colonial citizens were asked to pledge themselves not to buy imports, thus, it was hoped, effectually cutting off temptation to colonial merchants to continue to import. The committees were to keep watch and ward, inspect customhouse entries, keep tab on what was on the merchants' shelves or in their warehouses, and draw further attention to violations. The possible consequence of noncompliance might be tar and feathers.

This new mechanism of political action was not consummated without resort to a political device which was to be essential in operating the politics of the American republic. As soon as details of the Association began to be discussed, it was apparent that there was not only a temperamental and ideological factionalism in the Congress but a sectional division as well. These were based on the different folkways and cultural patterns resulting from the physiographical differences conditioned by the wide range of latitude and longitude. When the question of nonexportation arose, certain of the more southerly colonies who depended upon the sale abroad of staple crops, notably South Carolina and Virginia, saw disadvantage to themselves. Not until the date of operation was postponed and it was agreed to permit the export of rice, though not indigo, was unanimous sanction of the Association secured. This first intercolonial organization to enforce a plan of positive action, accepted October 20, 1774, was the first of the political instruments of what was to be a new republic. It was put in operation after factionalism and sectionalism had forced compromise, establishing a pattern which was to be basic to the operation of what was to become a federal system.

The Association designed by the Continental Congress would not be implemented by the colonial legislatures still associated with royal and proprietary executives. The impetus to create provincial congresses, therefore, was stimulated by the advice of the Congress to the colonies to organize agencies to enforce the Association's policies.

Massachusetts forged ahead in this direction. The lower house of her legislature had already met independently of their normal relationship with the governor and council when they elected the delegates to Philadelphia. Now they came into direct conflict with the governor, General Thomas Gage. In the spring he had issued the usual writs for the fall elections, but as a result of the legislature's insubordination in meeting independently, he recalled these writs, expecting to prevent any election and for the time being eliminating the legislature. The people of Massachusetts paid no heed to the governor's recall of the writs and as usual chose representatives. These men avoided Boston but assembled at Concord in October 1774 where they proceeded to organize and to style themselves the provincial congress. They assumed the authority to govern the colony without reference to Governor Gage and his council. They then undertook to organize enforcement through the Association.

In New York the Committee of Fifty-one continued to function. When the Congress advised the colonies to enforce the Association and when the legislature would take no action, this Committee undertook to set up county, city, and town committees to do the job. When the colonial legislature finally refused in January 1775 to join the Association or even to appoint delegates to the Second Continental Congress, planned for May, the Committee of Fifty-one suggested a provincial convention to elect them. Delegates from nine counties responded, and on April 20, in convention, they chose men to represent New York at this second intercolonial gathering.

In Virginia soon after the delegates returned from the first meeting in Philadelphia, committees were organized as suggested by the Congress, and the militia looked to their officers and their arms. Some of these had lately been in service on the frontier where in the so-called Lord Dunmore's War they had vanquished some Indians. Special military associations were created to arm companies of riflemen to be clad in hunting shirts. Furthermore, as the Philadelphia Congress had recommended that each colony choose representatives to a second assembly, the head of the Virginia delegation in the first body, authorized to do so by Virginia's provincial congress of the preceding August, now called each county to choose delegates to a second provincial congress to meet in Richmond, March 20, 1775. Here the delegates approved the work of the First Continental Congress and chose representatives to the Second. Likewise, they proceeded to consider further readying of the militia and heard Patrick Henry's famous call to arms: "We must fight." To him liberty was so dear that he was willing to give his life for it. "Give me liberty or give me death!" The militia was cooperative. When Lord Dunmore attempted to prevent them from collecting munitions, the Rangers, or "shirt men," descended on him at Williamsburg and made him restore some powder he had taken from the magazine.

In Pennsylvania another pattern was followed. In the summer of 1774 a convention and the assembly had been in session at the same time and the assembly had seen fit to do the convention's bidding with one obvious exception. The next regular annual elections were held in October 1774; the assembly then chosen approved the work of the First Continental Congress and elected delegates to the Second, including John Dickinson, recently returned to the assembly. The local committees recommended by the Continental Congress were reactivated and were eagerly joined by many who were not voters. The Quakers, however, were instucted not to serve. In the meantime, the general Committee of Forty-three issued a call for another provincial convention, and the county committee chose delegates. This convention met January 23, 1775, and undertook to supervise the assembly. Thus a dual authority continued to exist in uneasy partial agreement. After Lexington and Concord, military associations were formed which the assembly perforce had to approve and support by issues of paper money. This dual authority operated during 1775.

The development of such various types of provincial congresses in these and other colonies was evidence that in all save the self-governing provinces a new political power had been created, independent of the duly constituted colonial governments, even though, as in Pennsylvania, it was in the form of a curious dual operation. This independence came to the attention of the home government just as the new party of the king's friends had emerged victorious from parliamentary elections. With unusual confidence they turned to the colonial problem. They would meet colonial defiance. When the petition of the Continental Congress was presented to Parliament, January 19, 1775, that body speedily rejected it almost 3 to 1. The efforts of Pitt and Burke to promote reconciliation failed, and on March 13 the king signed the New England Restraining Act forbidding the Americans to trade with other nations.

In the meantime, the second provincial congress of Massachusetts assembled at Cambridge, February 1, 1775. This body encouraged the provincial committee of safety, led by John Hancock and Joseph Warren, to perfect the defenses of the colony. When word came of the action of Parliament, the Massachusetts congress appointed a day of prayer and fasting and decided to raise an army. General Gage realized he could hardly tolerate this, so he again sought to discover accumulated supplies of arms and munitions and take them from the colonials as he had the previous September. This time his actions brought spectacular results.

One of his expeditions, consisting of some eight hundred men who were ordered to destroy a supply dump at Concord, set out on an April night. Word of this leaked out; hence the night dash of William Dawes and Paul Revere to alert the countryside. When the troops arrived at Lexington, they found a detachment of militia assembled to oppose them. This was brushed aside with a few casualties, and another skirmish took place at Concord. The British destroyed what supplies they could find and then set out to march back to Boston. By this time the countryside was alive with militia, and the troops had to pass through a scattered barrage of shots from behind stone walls along the road. The British were saved by a thousand reinforcements and got back to Boston but only after severe loss. The colonists lost nearly one hundred men and the British somewhat less than three hundred. A shot had been fired "heard round the world," and blood had been shed.

The joining of battle and the shedding of blood hastened on the trend of events. The news finally swung New York into decisive action. The assembly had not been willing to assume any real responsibility for resistance. As it was about to adjourn on May 3, the Committee of Fifty-one came forward with a plea for the election of a provincial congress to take over the assembly's functions. This time every county responded to the appeal. Their delegates met May 22, 1775, as the first New York provincial congress and assumed the power to govern the colony. In the meantime the Committee of Fifty-one had been deemed too conservative and the more radical had formed a Committee of One Hundred which took over the governing of New York City, May 1. Despite radical dominance, "Loyalists" had been included in this new group.

The provincial congress completed the committee organization of New York. A standing committee of correspondence was appointed to arrange for a committee in every county and subcommittees in towns and districts. These committees were to enforce the Association by requiring the citizens to sign an agreement not to trade with England. These committees were also to organize and equip militia, to tax, to fix prices, to sequester Loyalist property, to try recalcitrants who, if convicted, would be sent to jail. In an emergency they could call the militia to action. When the provincial congress was not in session, the colony was to be in charge of a committee of safety. Succeeding provincial congresses met in the winter of 1775 and the spring of 1776.

The action at Lexington and Concord, furthermore, had transformed what had been a party contest into a civil war. In a sense, some of the atmosphere of the Puritan Revolution of the preceding century was re-created. Those who were earnest to protect their rights and liberties now had to take on the responsibility of organizing armies and waging war. Those who opposed them must, by so doing, side with the crown and join with its agents in defeating the American armed forces.

The new conditions made the names Whig and Tory over into Patriot and Loyalist, although they still were used more or less interchangeably. Each one of the thirteen colonies had these two factions, and in each one the Whig or Patriot group had created or gained control of the government. These new governments sought to protect themselves and their constituents from those who would restore the authority of England. Consequently, they officially confiscated the property of Tories and in some cases banished them. On the other hand, the Tories fought back, either by joining the king's forces or by organizing guerrilla bands to harass Patriots by destroying their property or making away with it and on occasion killing them in the desultory civil war which developed in some colonies. The strife was made more bitter because defeat of either side could be considered as making probable condign punishment. The Patriots would then be defeated rebels, liable to the penalties prescribed for traitors. The Tories, on their part, if defeated, could apprehend more general banishment and confiscation. In the meantime, however, many of the

Tories either were disqualified or disqualified themselves from the regular participation in factional politics as it manifested itself in elections and lawmaking.

The disappearance of the Tories from the election contests and from the congresses, conventions, and legislatures did not mean an era of unanimity. It only ushered in a new type of factionalism, or partisanship. War had begun but what was to be its end? When the Second Continental Congress assembled at Philadelphia, the colonies were still in the midst of the excitement caused by the fighting at Lexington and Concord. In each of the colonies except Connecticut and Rhode Island, there was some form of emergency political mechanism in operation, and in all of them armed forces were being mobilized and equipped. In all of the colonies there was bound to be questioning and division about the objectives of these extralegal governments and the use of these troops. Was this activity merely for defense of rights and liberties, or was this effort leading toward freedom from the British yoke, toward independence?

Naturally, this questioning and these differences were reflected in local contests and in congressional discussions. In the course of these debates it soon became apparent that there were factions among the Patriots. Of the sixty-three who made up the roster of the Second Continental Congress, nine were in a mood which makes it appropriate to speak of them as conciliationists. At the other pole were the eighteen radicals who were on the road to independence. A third group, as in most legislative bodies, stood somewhere in the middle. As in the First Continental Congress the more aggressive group came from the two most politically mature colonies, Massachusetts and Virginia, while the leaders of the conciliatory group, as before, were from Pennsylvania and New York.

The radicals were able to secure the support of most of the middle group for the creation of an army and for the appointment of their choice, George Washington of the Virginia delegation, as its commander. On the other hand, the conciliationists achieved the approval of the idea of sending another appeal to the ministry, in the form of the Olive Branch petition indited by John Dickinson.

There were similar factions among the Patriots in various of the colonies. In all save the self-governing colonies there was the same question. Should there not be a new and independent political mechanism set up? How long should they attempt to operate the present makeshifts? As usual, there were the divisions between the daring and the cautious and the radical and the more conservative. The radicals in Massachusetts, through the provincial congress, sought to get a directive from the Continental Congress. But they were too early. The conciliationists and the moderates in Congress were still determined to wait until the response to the Olive Branch was known. So Congress merely advised Massachusetts to hold an election for the lower house of their assembly, then to choose an upper house as they had before the Intolerable Acts, and so carry on until a governor was appointed who would rule according to the terms of their 1690 charter.

A new political problem arose out of the necessities of further warmaking. General Washington must do everything possible to strengthen his military position and to weaken that of General Gage, but General Gage was a legally constituted law enforcement officer, engaged on assignment from the crown within the Empire. As such, he considered Washington and his associates as traitors. On the other hand, Washington maintained that he was the commander of a duly constituted military force; that his power arose from the fact that he was "the uncorrupted choice of a brave and free people" and that this choice was the "purest source and original fountain of all power." He knew that he must maintain this stand. At the same time he must also protect his army and hinder the chances of Gage's success by aiding in the creation of new and strong colonial governments which would cooperate with him in seeing to it that Gage received the minimum of aid from the residents of the colonies, particularly in the vicinity of any British encampment. It was essential to have some political mechanism whereby a new loyalty could be created and a new type of treason defined and punished. In other words, there must be some way of dealing with the Tories. Washington, therefore, was concerned with two political objectives: one was new and independent colonial governments, and the other was the creation of a new national state which would have as its instruments of government the Continental Congress and the Continental Army. Washington, in cooperation with his generals and with the radical wing in Congress, undertook a formidable task of political organization.

Washington was very careful in working with Congress, because he realized that one of his principal jobs was winning over the moderates in that body. Congress at the same time sought to keep in touch with him and sent a committee which spent some time with him in camp during October 1775. This committee consisted of three well-disposed friends: Benjamin Franklin of Pennsylvania, Benjamin Harrison of Virginia, and Thomas Lynch of North Carolina. With

Washington and his congressional associates was working the logic of events. In a sense it may be said that once Congress organized the Continental Army, independence was inevitable, but it took thirteen months of uncertainty before the issue could be finally resolved. Important links in the chain of events which drew the colonies closer to independence were the decision by Congress to authorize the importation of war material and the granting of permissions to export colonial products in order to pay for the same, which were decreed in July 1775 and implemented in September by the creation of a "secret committee" set up by Congress to secure supplies. Shortly after the Congress opened up avenues of trade, Washington undertook to organize a naval arm of his forces in Massachusetts so that he could harass the British by stopping their supply ships from reaching Boston. These actions meant that warfare was now open on the high seas and privateering was indicated. All of these operations implied in reality the assumption of attributes of sovereignty; they were steps on the road to independence.

These steps also necessitated legislation, and Washington was working with his backers in Congress to get adequate rules and regulations, particularly a definition of punitive treatment for such Tories and others who hampered Washington's operations by giving aid and comfort to the king's forces. Washington realized that it was vital that there be created a power to punish Tories and the "new treason." This was difficult to define as long as the colonies maintained that they were loyal subjects of the king, for so were the Tories. So it would be necessary to legislate a new loyalty and a new allegiance, and this was, of course, another assumption of sovereignty and a very long step on the road to independence.

Washington took the lead in the political activity necessary to persuade Congress to take these steps and, in effect, headed a political as well as a military force. He worked not only through the committee which came up to visit him in Cambridge, but by correspondence and by the use of agents. His efforts and the logic of events—with great help from the British measures for putting down the rebellion, which included burning coast towns, seeking to rouse the slaves, and hiring Hessians—secured most of what he desired. But the Congress could not feel itself justified in taking the final step—declaring independence—without instructions from the states. So Washington and the Independence party had been looking to the states, seeking to stimulate political action there.

Washington, as general, was particularly concerned to have

stalwart governments in the colonies upon which he could depend. This was particularly true in New England where his first operations were conducted. When he took command, Massachusetts and New Hampshire had each the king's government and a provincial Patriot government. Connecticut and Rhode Island were, as usual, ruling themselves, but they had taken no stand on the question of the status of Tories and the protection of the Continental Army against any aid or comfort which the Tories might give to the king's forces. So in the course of the organization of the army and the besieging of Boston, Washington gave some attention to the political situations in these neighboring colonies. In this activity he depended a good deal upon the generals whom Congress had appointed to be associated with him. Several of these were from the New England colonies, and they were his political as well as his military aides.

General Washington's interest in the politics of the New England states was quickened by activities of the British in the vicinity. New Hampshire was directly concerned, especially after the burning of the Maine seaport of Falmouth. What happened at Falmouth might happen at Portsmouth, so as early as October 18, New Hampshire had asked Congress' advice as to what procedure was to be followed in creating a government to take the place of the colonial establishment which had been operating under the royal governor, John Wentworth. In the meantime, early in November, Congress had received word of the burning of Falmouth and of the king's final answer to their petitions, namely, the Proclamation of Rebellion. At the same time the committee which had been working with Washington at Cambridge had returned. These matters made it easier for Congress to follow the plans which Washington had worked out with the congressional committee and to give more definite advice to New Hampshire and to South Carolina, who was also asking the same question, than they had to Massachusetts.

Between November 4 and December 6, Congress took an extremely significant series of actions. They defined spies and traitors and authorized courts-martial to inflict the death penalty upon any convicted. They authorized retaliation upon those who should "favor, aid or abet the system of ministerial oppression," doing so "in the name of the people of these united colonies" and by virtue of authority derived from them "according to the purest maxims of representation." They adopted rules for the new navy, they authorized the capture of prizes, and they created a committee of secret correspondence which was to seek foreign aid diplomatically and financially and to that end to organize a diplomatic service. They authorized New Hampshire and South Carolina to call together representatives of the people within those colonies for the purpose of establishing such a form of government as would best serve their needs "during the continuance of the present dispute" between Great Britain and the colonies.

These actions gave Washington and the patriots in New Hampshire what was needed. The General sent military protection to them and instructions for dealing with Tories, which included using crown officials as hostages. In December New Hampshire's voters chose delegates who met in Exeter and drew up a constitution. Washington likewise acted in Connecticut, sending instructions regarding Tories which the Connecticut legislature at its meeting in December followed, enacting a strong measure. Rhode Island in the meantime had acted independently with a similar law. In December the Massachusetts provincial congress elected a new delegation to Congress, omitting the conciliationists who had previously somewhat counterbalanced the enthusiasm of the Adamses and issued to the new delegation instructions authorizing them to do whatever they thought necessary "to establish the right and liberty of the American colonies on a basis permanent and secure." Thus Washington and his generals, working in close cooperation with the New England Patriots, had strengthened their political power and had taken measures to isolate and punish the Tories if they aided the king's troops while Washington was organizing an effective siege of Boston.

Washington and the Patriot leaders were of course aware that their task was broader than merely showing concern for New England, and the commander's political interests led him to try his hand in the middle colonies, which were notoriously reluctant to take much positive action. In November he sent his military secretary, Joseph Reed, to Pennsylvania to use his political genius in advancing the Patriot cause, and a few weeks later he authorized General Charles Lee to go to New York for the same purpose. Neither of these efforts bore immediate fruit, and Lee's attempt to isolate and punish Tories was such a failure that he had to be removed from New York operations.

In the meantime, things moved faster in the South. There again British policy was very helpful. In Virginia Lord Dunmore had succeeded in raising a force and establishing a headquarters at Norfolk, where in November he had issued a proclamation and had offered the

slaves their freedom if they would revolt. This action was very disturbing to the Virginian General Washington and stirred Congress to
advise the Old Dominion to follow the same line which had been
suggested to New Hampshire and South Carolina. When in late February news came that the British parliament had passed an act ratifying the king's Proclamation of Rebellion, destroying colonial trade
and requiring unconditional surrender, the South began to act. Upon
the motion of one of the South Carolina congressmen, General
Charles Lee was sent to the southern colonies with four brigadier
generals to assist him in rallying the southern Patriots. He established
himself in Virginia and immediately got in touch with the Patriot
leaders in both the Carolinas. The activity of General Lee and his
brigadiers, plus the logic of events, spurred action. On March 26
South Carolina adopted a constitution. On April 12 North Carolina
authorized its delegation in Congress to join with others in voting for
independence, and when South Carolina heard of that, she declared
herself independent. A few days before, the provincial congress of
Georgia had likewise empowered its delegates to vote for independence. The climax came when Virginia on May 15 authorized her
delegates in Congress to take the same course.

In the meantime, the final bastion to be scaled was that erected by
the middle colonies. Pennsylvania, New York, New Jersey, Delaware, and Maryland were evidently less inclined to positive action
than other colonies. But Washington had been endeavoring to stimulate them to move, as we have already seen, by sending Joseph Reed
to Pennsylvania and General Lee to New York. Reed plunged immediately into Pennsylvania politics and was elected to the assembly
which met in January 1776. The Pennsylvania situation tended to
conservatism in large part because the privilege of voting was so narrowly restricted and because the powerful river counties had consist-
ently refused to enlarge the legislature by making counties of proper
size out of the growing western communities. However, there were
signs that this trend was to be reversed. The January 1776 session
authorized the enlargement of the assembly by introducing more
counties, and this larger assembly was chosen in May. This new and
larger body, however, proved still to be under the domination of
conservative influence, and John Dickinson was its leader. In the
meantime, news from abroad was even less reassuring than before, for
tidings were arriving that the British government was hiring more
German mercenary troops and planning a new expedition. The
troops which Washington had driven out of Boston and which had

gone to Halifax for refreshing could now be expected almost any time to descend upon some colonial seaport, probably New York, accompanied by the Hessian mercenaries.

Philadelphia was as apprehensive as, or more so than, New York, and the radical leaders, acting through the Pennsylvania military associators, petitioned for a survey of the defenses of Philadelphia. Congress almost immediately summoned Washington to come to Philadelphia, and this visit from the Commander in Chief enabled him not only to size up the military situation, but also to have important political conferences with men like Richard Henry Lee, his associate from Virginia. As a result of the news and the conferences, Congress drew up a new military plan, and on the fourth of June John Hancock sent a message to the colonies. Nearly a month before, on May 10, Congress had recommended that any colony without an adequate government should take steps to form one and had passed a very significant resolution declaring that "the exercise of every kind of authority under the said Crown should be totally suppressed," for as the resolution proclaimed, "all the powers of government" were hereafter to be "exerted under the authority of the people of the colonies." Now, on June 4, came Hancock's circular informing each colony of its military obligation under this plan.

The stage was thus set for the final act in the drama. On June 7 Richard Henry Lee rose in his place, fresh from conference with George Washington, and moved the famous resolution "that these united colonies are and of right ought to be free and independent states." His resolution was referred to the famous committee to prepare, in eighteenth-century fashion, a declaration to be addressed to a "candid world." While this committee was deliberating, events began to move. The day after Lee's motion, the Pennsylvania assembly, meeting in the same building, withdrew its cautious instructions and authorized Pennsylvania's delegates in the Congress to concur. Joseph Reed then rejoined Washington. That same day the New York delegation in Congress wrote to their parent body in New York for new instructions.

Washington, in the meantime, was planning the defense of New York City and was negotiating through the intrepid George Clinton with the conservative New York committee of safety. At the same time a Tory plot was uncovered in New York City which indicated that funds disbursed by the British through the mayor of New York had been used to tamper with members of Washington's bodyguard. While these unpleasant details were being uncovered, Delaware finally ordered its officers to act in the name of the colony instead of the king. New Jersey appointed five new delegates to Congress—men authorized to vote for independence—and Maryland, having received Hancock's letter, decided to comply with its military requirements and voted to concur in independence.

Despite the imminence of invasion and the discovery of the Tory plot, New York still hesitated, and not until a special election had been held in which the people voted in favor of independence did New York act. On May 27 the provincial congress of that colony virtually declared New York independent. However, it did not instruct its delegates, so July 4 approached with the New York members the only ones not authorized to favor the Virginia resolution. When Lee's motion came up on July 2, three delegations were in doubt. The New Yorkers had no instructions, a majority of the Pennsylvania group were opposed, and of the Delaware delegation of three, only two were present—one for, one against. By the time of the roll call, however, Caesar Rodney had ridden up from Delaware to make his delegation 2 to 1 for the resolution. Those opposed in the Pennsylvania delegation refrained from voting so that Pennsylvania's voice might be given for independence, and New York abstained. Not until July 9 did the provincial congress of the new Empire State authorize its delegates to concur.

Thus, the campaign for independence had been won, as far as legislative action could win it. Shrewd political organization, in which Washington and his generals had an important part, plus the logic of events had brought the victory.

·❧[IX]❧·

THE POLITICS OF CREATING
A RATIONAL SYSTEM OF
SELF-GOVERNMENT

*T*HE STEP had been taken. The thirteen colonies, through their representatives in Congress assembled, had declared themselves an independent republic. They would join the Swiss Confederation as another such government in a world of monarchies. Thus was a new "empire," as it was sometimes called, dedicated to self-government, though as yet it was almost wholly undefined. As it had been established in the eighteenth century, a century of well-formulated rationalization, the necessity which was to compel these erstwhile British subjects to experiment with a new politics would be conditioned by the canons of the Age of Reason.

Each one of the colonies, now that it had become an independent political body, must redefine itself. This redefinition involved much politics which would mold political behavior in new forms. The differences of opinion as to the self-governing devices to be used by the new body politic were diverse. These variations were to produce factions in politics which would make necessary the writing of a new chapter in the history of American political behavior. The basic question was what kind of a political power was to be created. This had to be worked out on two levels, state and central.

At first, government had been carried on by the provincial congresses which had induced the Revolution but this of necessity was a temporary phase. As early as 1775 those seeking independence, the Patriots, began planning new orders of government spelled out in new constitutions. Massachusetts moved first. On the advice of the Continental Congress its provincial lawmakers invited the towns to send representatives to an assembly which should rule until a royal governor undertook to act according to the terms of the charter abrogated by the Intolerable Acts of 1774. New Hampshire, following later congressional advice, drew up in January 1776 a new constitution to serve "during the present unhappy and unnatural contest with Great Britain." In the spring of 1776 South Carolina adopted an instrument to be used until "an accommodation of the unhappy differences between Great Britain and America" could be achieved.

After Congress in May 1776 recommended that the states "adopt such government as shall best conduce to the happiness and safety" of their citizens, a new series of constitutions was developed. Virginia and New Jersey completed theirs before July 4. Virginia repudiated the crown, while in plainer terms New Jersey decreed that "all civil authority [under the king] is necessarily at an end." The other states followed straightway, Connecticut and Rhode Island merely continuing to use their colonial charters, while disowning their allegiance to the crown. As the initial work had been hastily done in Massachusetts, New Hampshire, and South Carolina, their permanent constitutions were completed in 1780, 1784, and 1778, respectively. Most of this political structure was erected by congresses, legislatures, or more irregular revolutionary bodies. No state sought popular approval of the work.

The Pennsylvania constitution of 1776 was produced in face of the same opposition which marked all steps in that commonwealth leading to independence. As the events of 1776 began to drive in the direction of separation, the assembly continued its resistance to the move. But Congress then helped the Patriots by its call upon the colonies of May 15. The Pennsylvania revolutionaries responded immediately.

The Patriots prescribed their own procedure. They called a convention which arranged for an election to be held July 8 for the purpose of choosing the membership of a constitutional convention. They opened the franchise to many hitherto not privileged. Any male over twenty-one who would abjure allegiance to the crown might vote if he had dwelt in Pennsylvania for a year and at any time paid some taxes.

A campaign was organized under the direction of the Revolutionary committees and the military associates, who manned the polls. In due course the members of the convention were chosen. The constitutional convention assembled and remained in session from July 15 to September 28. It prepared a democratic plan which, dispensing with a governor, placed all authority in the hands of a unicameral legislature. Such executive function as was provided was assigned to a supreme executive council which could not veto acts of the assembly. Every seven years a council of censors was to survey the acts of the government during the preceding years. If they thought changes warranted, the censors might summon another constitutional convention to consider amendments to the fundamental law. The convention put its creation into operation without submitting it to the voters and set November 5 as the day on which the new legislature was to be elected.

The process of establishing state government moved most slowly in New York State. Provincial congresses continued to exercise governmental functions. A third, elected in April, assembled May 14, 1776. This body proclaimed New York a virtually independent state. However, it would not authorize the state's delegates at Philadelphia to vote for united independence until the voters had chosen a fourth provincial congress. The election for members of the new body would serve as a referendum. This congress, duly chosen, met at Whites Plains to avoid the impending hostilities around New York City. There on July 9 approval of the Declaration of Independence was voted, and in due course New York's delegates signed the historic document, for which the state's delay had prevented them from voting on July 2 and 4. Their next concern was the drafting of a state constitution.

A committee of thirteen was appointed to perform this task and John Jay proved to be the creative member. Their work was much interrupted by the fighting in which New York City was captured and which reached even up to White Plains. Their work was finally approved by the convention on April 20, 1777, and then a council of safety was designated to carry on until the first state election could be held. A sharp contest for governor ensued. The more conservative of the voters were divided between General Philip Schuyler and John Jay. Urban voters were appealed to by John Morin Scott of New York City, while the man most attractive to the yeomen farmers was General George Clinton, then under arms. The voters preferred Clinton, who left the army and was sworn in on July 30. The new legislature, however, was hindered by the fighting and did not succeed in assembling a quorum until September 10, when they attempted to work at Kingston. Here they found themselves again in difficulties when the British burned the town in October. It was not until February 1778 that they could finish their work in the comparative quiet of Poughkeepsie. In the meantime, the fourth congress still functioned on occasion, while the council of safety and then the new governor carried on as best they might in the troubled months of 1777 following the capture and occupation of New York City. That metropolis remained in British hands for the duration of the war.

The constitutions thus carefully created or improvised in the thirteen states made the legislatures all powerful. The representatives of the people were to bear the full responsibility. Almost unanimously the new states decided to place the power to rule in the hands of all-powerful legislatures generally chosen annually. In some of these states, notably Pennsylvania, Georgia, North Carolina, and New Hampshire, the suffrage was greatly widened by the omission of property qualification for voting. Only in five states—Maryland, Massachusetts, New York, South Carolina, and Virginia—did a conservative trend manifest itself. In general the rural communities were to have the dominating influence in the new states, leaving the smaller urban areas, where businessmen and speculators congregated, largely without great influence. Weak executives reflected the Patriots' fear of the crown and its royal governors. They, like the judges, were generally to be chosen by the legislatures, and a tendency quickly developed to keep these ceremonial figures in office for long periods. The judiciary too were thought of as a stabilizing force to be kept independent by appointment for indeterminate periods described as "during good behavior."

While the new states were creating their political structures, a new mechanism had to be provided on the second level. The British imperial government had been expelled, and no central government, no central power, had been devised to take its place. Such central government as there was existed by common consent without any constitutional form or sanction save such as was supplied by the so-called Continental Congress. Many of those who had been leaders in the cause of independence felt little or no need for any substitute for the British Empire. In fact they feared tyranny, such as might be developed by any new power.

Despite this distrust of central authority, there was general recognition that there must be some form of general government. A committee was in consequence appointed to construct a plan for one at the same time that the committee to prepare a Declaration of Independence was constituted. Its chairman was John Dickinson of Pennsylvania, an able but conservative lawyer who had been most wary of independence. He and others of his fellow conciliationists really believed in a central power with some strength. His plan would have given the new government authority to veto state legislation, to provide uniform laws, and to maintain a force capable of putting down any violence in the states. This government would likewise control the public lands, vast in quantity, claimed also by Virginia, Massachusetts, New York, Connecticut, North Carolina, South Carolina, and Georgia. These lands could be sold to ensure revenue, and there were companies already formed, some of whom had grants, who were busy with plans for wealth.

Dickinson and his more conservative associates ran afoul of a radical group who could see little need for any but local government. This revolutionary junto, led by the Virginia and Massachusetts Patriots, like Richard Henry Lee and the Adamses, were, if they could, going to take the teeth out of the articles drawn up by Dickinson. When they got through with his plan little was left but a league of independent states with practically no central power. One thing they did leave to the new government was control of the great western lands. Theirs, however, was a different concept of the use of the estate. To Dickinson and the more conservative the public lands were to be for colonial, speculative uses. They would be sold and the settlers governed by Congress. But to their more radical opponents these lands when inhabited would be made into states and added as equal partners to the Confederation. The radical view prevailed: the articles sent to the states for ratification on November 17, 1777, took little power from them and could only go into effect if accepted by all of them.

By July 1778 all states had consented but three: New Jersey, Delaware, and Maryland. The first two soon joined, but Maryland dashed hopes of ratification by announcing she would not agree until the "landed" states gave up their claims beyond the mountains. This demand was aimed primarily at Virginia, whose giant claims to the northwest gave many an envious complex. In the background too were land companies who were hoping that a compliant Congress, rather than Virginia, would have control of the disposal of these lands. The promoters of such companies came generally from the "landless" states, Maryland, New Jersey, Delaware, Pennsylvania, and Rhode Island. Under their pressure some of the landed states began at length to give in. Between February 19, 1780, and January 2, 1781, New York, Connecticut, and finally Virginia made cessions of their claims to Congress. Thereupon, Maryland, who was put under pressure by the French minister who indicated that otherwise the Chesapeake might not be protected by the French fleet, signed March 1, 1781, and the articles straightway went into effect.

Despite their victory in imposing the Articles of Confederation, the power of the radicals was about to go into an eclipse. The ratifica-

tion of the new central system came at a time when the war fortunes
of the Confederation were reaching a peak. French aid was arriving in
force, and General Washington had decided to attempt to capture
another British army, that of Cornwallis which had been campaigning in the southern states. At this particular point, believing the objective won, the radical party leaders dropped out of the Congress leaving conservatives with an opportunity to put some of their ideas of
government into effect. They felt that the method of operating government by committees, so much used during the fighting, was inefficient and dangerous, even though it had so far seemed to work.
Committees had managed to organize an army, secure supplies, conduct diplomacy, secure an alliance, and raise money, but the propo-
nents of better organization now in 1781 planned and put in operation a series of improved administrative measures. Departments of
foreign affairs, war, and marine were constituted. A superintendent
of finance was given charge of the Treasury, and the Bank of North
America was chartered. Unfortunately the measure to provide regular revenue through customs duties was defeated by the refusal of
Rhode Island to consent. A post office department of sorts was continued, using the old system which Franklin had operated under the
crown. As long as he was in command, General Washington was to
have almost dictatorial powers. The coming of peace, however,
seemed to spell the end of any concern about central power. Political
activity tended to concentrate in the states.

The radical leaders were back in the localities, where the problems of
demobilization, unemployment, debt, foreclosure, and loss of property were taxing their powers. In the newly defined society, communities were widely scattered in an age when communication was slow
—no faster than could be supplied by horse, wheels, or sailboat—so
local personalities and interests predominated. Associations were limited, and the minds and emotions that acted and reacted one upon the
other, or in the mass, were those of societies often with some geographical determination, like a river region, a seacoast, a piedmont, or
a transmontane area.

During the period of English control of the colonies, each had
some such determinants of population location, and as they grew,
each developed patterns of partition and division into social subunits.
In each one of these were the leaders and the led, the elite and the
average, the expressive and the incoherent, the active and the pas-
sive.

Now in the period of postwar readjustment, the Patriots continued their leadership in these various localities. During the war itself the responsibilities incident to warmaking had brought out the talent of the officers in the ranks of the Continental Army and the militia, the members of the congresses and their myriad committees, as well as of those civilians who had been occupied in keeping the armed forces equipped, who had issued propaganda, and of others who had begun to regulate the lives of their fellow men. Among all these were many who had grown used to command and to taking part in public service. The Patriots, in fact, had become a new elite, an accepted leadership in the new American establishment.

Within the several states political partisanship continued. These new elites were opposed by the old, whose leaders had not infrequently been Tories. Memories were long. The guerrilla warfare with its depredations was not forgotten. Nor had those who had more directly given aid and comfort to the British armies been forgiven. There were some attempts at reprisal now by confiscation, by banishment, and sometimes by applying tar and feathers. Even on unrelated issues, old Patriot and Tory lines formed on opposite sides, sometimes with different names.

Such divisions were complicated by factions which had already appeared within the ranks of the Patriots: radical and conservative. The former had generally favored a quicker strike for independence and a more decisive line of action. Even after the adoption of the Declaration of Independence, these differences had not died, and in the various new state governments they reappeared. Sometimes they figured in the contests for the new governorships, for example in New York, where Jay and Schuyler of the Livingston faction had to give way to the country lawyer and popular general from Ulster, George Clinton, who was serving with his troops in the field.

Certain long-standing causes of political division had not been changed markedly by the Revolution. Though more liberal, the new constitutions did not entirely let down the bars to the franchise. Property holding and taxpaying were still usually the necessary qualifications. Also, despite the continental experience, the outlook of many continued to be provincial, and significant numbers of these Patriot elites were content with the narrow view. Men like Patrick Henry, Richard Henry Lee, George Clinton, and the Pennsylvania radicals were immersed in the affairs of their Iberian villages and were not dreaming of Rome.

But there were others who were not content, and some who were alarmed. The new republic was neither strong nor respected. There were significant signs of instability and weakness: property was not safe, the boundaries of the republic were undefended, and there were hints of disintegration. Responsible men began to work for strength and stability. That which the Patriots had begun needed to be finished by a group of stabilizers. Some of them had been active in the war; others had been too young.

To them something was missing. The colonies had always had a superior power, the crown, but now independence had created a gap. There was no superior power, no establishment to turn to for aid. Yet there were so many difficulties which a central power might help solve. There were unpaid soldiers, artisans out of work, and a postwar depression. There were heavy debts owed by the states and the Confederation; the hard-money supply was being drained out of the country. A disordered commerce, restricted by foreign powers, prevented earning money to pay the debts. The British, the Spanish, and, worst, the erstwhile French allies were prohibiting business with the West Indies. In the newly proclaimed states there were foreclosures of mortgages and distress. Local politicians, often Patriots or radicals, heeded popular demands, passed stay laws preventing foreclosures, and authorized paper money. In seven of the states, paper money was printed copiously, enabling many debtors to free themselves at bargain rates, thus in effect depriving their creditors of a portion of their capital.

Efforts to strengthen and stabilize the polity uncovered embarrassing and even frightening impotence. When diplomatic efforts were made to improve commercial relations abroad, the powers rebuffed the diplomats of the new republic. When some progress seemed possible with Spain, it was found that concessions in trade had to be purchased at the price of internal strife. When the diplomats agreed to open Spanish commerce at the price of according Spain control of the Mississippi, the eastern diplomats, who thus negotiated, stirred up a western opposition that revealed a sectional cleavage that threatened disruption of the new republic even before it was well established.

The Congress was further hampered by the fact that it could collect no certain revenue. The first effort to secure the right to levy customs duties had been blocked by Rhode Island, and when a second, more limited grant was sought, that was vetoed by New York. Congress had still to depend on a requisition system which the states in their own economic distress were unable or unwilling fully to honor. The Continental debt continued to mount up, and even the interest on the foreign debt went unpaid. The credit of the new nation was approaching zero.

The most threatening of these circumstances was the appearance of domestic violence. In 1786 in western Massachusetts efforts to collect debts by foreclosure roused some unpaid veterans. Under the leadership of Daniel Shays they undertook violent measures to protect their homes. These yeomen resisted officers, forcibly prevented courts from meeting, and destroyed records. The governor of Massachusetts had to send an armed force to restore the courts.

These were the conditions which stirred the stabilizers to efforts to overcome them. They could take advantage of a spirit of enterprise that was abroad, despite these handicaps. The new nation had great potential wealth. There were industrial, commercial, transportation, and real estate opportunities for investment and enterprise which promised much, and certain new ventures had been begun under the benign influence of peace, urged on by both opportunity and need. These same opportunities and needs, together with the perils and emergencies, were bound to have political consequences.

The great resources that appealed to the enterprising as a way out of some of the difficulties were the development of the great real estate resources of the new nation, particularly beyond the mountains, and the development of trade, both domestic and foreign. Real estate operation had always been in the forefront of the American imagination, and not only individuals but a series of land companies were at that time active. Their ambitions had been a strong element in the process of organizing the initial central government, the Confederation, and after the final ratification of the articles, their interest continued. When, in 1780, Congress had asked the states to surrender their western lands, the decision had been made to organize these areas into new states and thereby enlarge the Confederation. But there was delay in implementing this plan, because Virginia in her cession of January 2, 1781, had stipulated that Congress must annul land company claims in that region and guarantee Kentucky to be hers. The land companies, which included prominent Pennsylvania and Maryland politicians, fought the acceptance of Virginia's conditions, and it was not until March 1, 1784, that the necessary negotiations and maneuvers finally resulted in the actual defeat of the speculators and the virtual acceptance of Virginia's conditions. On that date Virginia executed a deed, and Congress could go ahead to carry out the decision to sell the land to the citizens of future states.

Jefferson prepared a report outlining the process to be followed. This, Congress adopted that same year and implemented by passing an ordinance in 1785. Under these two enactments settlers were authorized to go into the region north of present Tennessee and east of the Mississippi. This vast area was laid out in ten potential states: Sylvania, Cherronesus, Michigania, Assenisipia, Metropotamia, Illinoia, Washington, Saratoga, Polypotamia, and Pelisipi. These units would be surveyed and divided up into ranges consisting of square townships made up of square sections. Each township should be six miles square and consist of 36 sections, each containing 640 acres, or one square mile. These sections should be the minimum amount purchasable and would be sold at not less than one dollar an acre.

Self-government and civil rights were guaranteed to the settlers, and a section was set aside in each township to be used to support public education. Under the stimulus of this plan Massachusetts and Connecticut completed the surrender of their claims, except that the latter state held out a section called the Western Reserve which she did not part with until 1800. Virginia continued to hold Kentucky; and North Carolina, after surrendering Tennessee in 1784, quickly reclaimed it in 1785. South Carolina yielded her small strip in 1787, although Georgia hung on with disastrous consequences to her Yazoo region until much later. It would seem as though western development could be a great resource which would serve as a political laboratory for democratic experiment.

Much of this planning depended, however, upon transportation development. These regions were far away and beyond the Appalachian Mountains. Proper travel and trade routes must be achieved, projects both difficult and expensive. These enterprises were to call for a series of political and economic moves with results of enormous consequence to the development of American democracy. They were engaging the attention of some of the new republic's responsible citizens.

Some of those most active in the Revolution, even George Washington himself, were looking for new opportunities. The general was much concerned about making the Potomac navigable, and shortly after his return from the conflict, he began to seek a charter for a Potomac River company. As the river was the boundary between Virginia and Maryland, its navigation must be the concern of both. Washington was the leader in securing incorporation for this company from both states, although these negotiations were undertaken in an atmosphere of some hostility. Maryland maintained that her boundary was the south bank of the Potomac and therefore the control of the river hers. In view of this claim, it was believed that Maryland was seeking to harass Virginia's trade. Virginia, on the other hand, was expected to retaliate by excluding Maryland from the Chesapeake. However, before any real difficulty arose Virginia ceded her western lands, and this encouraged Maryland to respond with a gesture of good will. So Jefferson arranged with a Maryland delegate to sponsor the appointment of commissioners from both states to make an agreement about the navigation of the Potomac. James Madison made a similar move in the Virginia legislature and soon four commissioners were authorized. In the resolution the Virginia commissioners were instructed to invite Pennsylvania to consultation because she was vitally interested in navigation in the Chesapeake, into which the Potomac fed.

Maryland accepted Virginia's invitation, and after some delay and misunderstanding, the Maryland and Virginia commissioners met at Alexandria, Virginia, in March 1785. While the Maryland delegation and two Virginia commissioners were waiting the arrival of the two other Virginians, Washington invited them to stay at Mount Vernon. These commissioners, among their recommendations, suggested an annual conference on commerce.

Under this stimulus Virginia invited Congress to call such a conference, to meet in Annapolis in September 1786 and to which all states would be invited, to discuss the general commerce of the new nation and to draft a trade act which might be adopted by Congress to improve all phases of the trade of the young republic. Congress issued such an invitation, but although ten states concurred in one way or another, delegations appeared only from Maryland, Virginia, and New Jersey, with two representatives from New York and one from Delaware, twelve in all; none came from regions south of Virginia or east of the Hudson. This small gathering, with Alexander Hamilton the most striking figure, did not take long to discover that there was little that so few could do. Yet commerce was suffering, so this small group recommended a full-scale convention to study revision of the Articles of Confederation. At first the Congress refused to issue this call, but after Virginia accepted the idea and appointed commissioners, Congress issued an invitation on February 21, 1787, which Massachusetts at once accepted. Virginia and Massachusetts were again associates, and the convention was to meet in Philadelphia in May.

This call met an instinctive need. The experience of the years since the close of the war had emphasized the fact that something was lacking—some symbol of the achievement of nationality. The Confederation was too much like a band of discontented and revolting colonies. Many, particularly the stabilizers, instinctively felt there was a need for something more. There was no head. All other nations had kings, some symbolic personification of the nation. The new republic had nothing save a weak ceremonial figure, the President of the Congress, to receive foreign ministers. In diplomacy, in commerce, in public finance, in armed might, there was no one to assume responsibility in danger or in difficulty except a committee which might not be in session or a Congress which might have only a few members bothering to attend. In effect the new republic missed the Empire, the crown.

As the uncertainties of these years had increased, a growing feeling developed that something must be done in the way of creating a responsible political authority, a new surrogate. Thus, when the Congress at length summoned the states to conference, this need insured a sufficiently favorable response. This interest was not general, but it was large enough to initiate action which eventually led to results. There were potent political elements among those responding. In the first place were those who disliked weakness and wished to promote strength in government. These were the people who were dissatisfied with the defenseless position of the republic, who smarted at the humiliating place which the new nation had to take in international affairs, who feared the mob, the destruction of property values, the heavy mountain of debt, and most of all, the lack of any individual or agency to do anything about it. Prominent in this response were the stabilizers. Likewise, there were a number of younger men with political ambitions who were not satisfied with the negative attitudes of elder leaders like Patrick Henry in Virginia, George Clinton in New York, Sam Adams and John Hancock in Massachusetts. In so many states local governors and ruling groups who were made up of the Patriot elite, the new state establishments, seemed permanently set up, with no interest outside of the state. But the nation still needed leadership; the republic required a surrogate.

·∘[X]∘·

THE NEW SURROGATE

*I*N EACH of the states save one, men were now ready to assume the political responsibility for attempting a new equilibrium. Generally they were younger men, men with imagination and new ideas about politics. Only in one state did they seem lacking, in Rhode Island, still the home of the otherwise-minded. They were coming, fifty-five of them, representing a well-distributed cross section of the population of twelve states; another nineteen chosen, however, did not come, including some prominent in the radical junto, and their absence was an omen of controversy.

Those who came to this convention were in most cases men who shared a desire for stability. In the words of James Madison, the government which they wished to devise would be designed "to protect the people against their rulers." Beyond that, however, Madison and some of his associates felt that the people must be protected against themselves. He felt that they were subject to "transient impressions" and "temporary errors." Therefore, they were "liable to err from Fickleness and passion." Madison believed that "a necessary fence against this danger [would] be to select a portion of enlightened citizens [to legislate], whose limited number and firmness [might] seasonably interpose against impetuous councils." The task of these delegates was to create such a power in a newly designed central government.

The delegations from Virginia, Pennsylvania, and Massachusetts assumed leadership and undertook to support an agenda to be known thereafter as the Virginia plan. This was a project conceived by nationalists, who believed in efficient centralized government. They proposed a new Congress of two houses, not a unicameral meeting of representatives of a series of sovereign states chosen by their legislatures. The lower house should be chosen by the people of the United States directly, in proportion to their numbers. Large states should have more representatives than small states. This popular House should then choose a Senate and an Executive: the size of the Senate was to be proportionate to the nation's population and wealth. No congressman could be re-elected and they might be recalled during their terms. There should also be a Supreme Court. The Congress could veto the laws of the states. The Executive and Supreme Court could veto national laws, but they might be passed over this veto by a vote larger than a majority.

This plan from Virginia was brought to Philadelphia, and the Pennsylvania and Massachusetts delegations agreed to advance it. They also proposed a slate of officers for the convention. Benjamin Franklin was to nominate George Washington for the presidency of the convention, just as the Adamses had proposed him for the command of the army twelve years before. However, the weather was bad and Franklin confined to his home, so Robert Morris made the motion, which was unanimously carried. William Jackson, English by birth, a Revolutionary officer who had dwelt in South Carolina, a member of Washington's military staff during the war, but then residing in Philadelphia, was chosen secretary. The real record, however, was to be kept unofficially and fully by young James Madison of Virginia who spent most of his time taking voluminous notes, which he wrote up every night. And well he did, for the sessions were private and through his tireless industry we have the record which otherwise never would have been made.

The formalities of organization over, the delegates' vote practically unanimously decided the real question. Congress had instructed them to report some revisions of the Articles of Confederation. The convention decided to start fresh and to build a new system without reference to the old. They would abolish a confederation vaguely governed by a council of plenipotentiaries. They would make a government of three equal and coordinate branches and give it power, something the old Congress never had enjoyed. National power therefore was endorsed during the first week by the convention, voting then as thereafter by states, each state one vote. Thereupon the debate proceeded for nearly four months on the mechanisms for exercising and limiting power and for choosing those who were to wield it.

Despite this seeming unanimity, there was a deep-seated division. Certain of the smaller states were not reconciled to the concentration of power in the hands of the large states. They had to find some way of checking this preponderance, and Connecticut, Delaware, New Jersey, and New York got together to support a New Jersey plan which would have retained the structure of the Articles of Confederation, retaining for each state one vote, but yielding to a Congress so organized the taxing power denied to the old Congress and providing for an executive and judiciary of sorts. Lines were now formed between large and small states with a real possibility of a tie when New Hampshire should arrive and if Maryland persisted in voting with the small states.

As the discussions continued, a second division became apparent. There was a second cultural clash based, not on size, but on physiography. This was the difference between North and South. On this basis a tie was possible because of the absence of Rhode Island. This North-South division was notably apparent in the consideration of two basic power questions. The Virginia plan called for representation by population, the large states having the largest votes. And in discussing the question of taxation, this division was also a determinant. In levying direct taxes, it was generally agreed that this should be done by population, with the largest states paying the most taxes. But what was population? And here the sectional cleavage appeared. What of the slaves? Since they had no civil status were they population in the political sense? The southern states wished them counted as people when figuring the basis of representation, but they were not so interested in having them so counted as a base for taxation.

This sectional division was also operative in the discussion of the third great power question, that of control of commerce. Here, as in the question of representation and taxation, the basic cultural differences, notably emphasized by the existence of a slave-operated, plantation agricultural society in the South, came to the fore. It was featured in the discussion of the question of whether the national power over commerce, if achieved, would be used to prohibit the importation of a continuous supply of Negro slaves.

With these basic differences between large and small states and slave and free, each with a potential tie vote probable, could any agreement be reached which would do more than continue the impotence of the Confederation? After four months of strenuous work, it was found that the answer was Yes. Washington, Franklin, Morris, and their associates, many of whom were younger men, by the formation of a series of deftly devised compromises and the construction of a most ingeniously complex political mechanism, made the Constitution.

The basic compromise was that which constituted the House as representatives of the people, giving each state the number warranted by its fraction of the total national population, while the Senate was to represent the states, each state to have two senators. The question of the definition of population was compromised by counting three-fifths of the slaves, as they had been counted by the Confederation in making requisitions, and there was further compromise by counting this proportion, not only as a basis for representation, but also as a basis for direct taxation. Enough southern votes were secured for the clause granting the new government power over interstate and foreign commerce by an agreement that there should be no interference with the slave trade for twenty years. The purchases of Negroes made in the interim and the natural increase thereafter would presumably suffice.

The document itself, when finally drafted, represented the greatest of the compromises. The Articles of Confederation, and in reality the New Jersey plan as well, represented decentralization and the paramount power of the states. The Virginia plan, on the other hand, was a centralized, nationalistic plan which would have placed the power in the hands of a central government, in turn dominated by the large states. The final agreement was neither. A federal, not a confederated or a nationalistic, system was achieved, based upon an intricate division of power.

There were to be three equal and coordinate branches. The legislative was to be made up of a Senate, two from each state, chosen by the legislatures thereof for six-year terms, staggered so that only one-third of the Senate must stand for election every two years, and the terms of no two senators from any state should expire at the same time. The members of the House of Representatives were to be chosen for two-year terms and must all be elected every two years. The Executive should be a President elected for a four-year term by an Electoral College. This Electoral College was to be chosen as the states might direct, each state being entitled to a number of votes equal to the total of its national senators and representatives. The judiciary were to be appointed by the President, by and with the advice of the Senate, to serve during good behavior. The judges and the President were subject to impeachment. Each group listed above was chosen by different agencies for terms of different lengths. It would never be possible by peaceful means to completely change the personnel of the government at any one time. There would always be continuity by holdovers.

The power which these agencies and parallel agencies in the states would organize was nicely divided. There were to be two kinds of law, federal and state. The new Congress was given a number of specific powers. Both the Congress and the state legislatures were prohibited from exercising certain powers, and to whom the remaining powers were to be assigned was left an open question. There were to be a federal executive and the state executives; therefore there were to be federal and state employees, each operating thereafter within a specifically or indefinitely defined sphere. There were to be two court systems, federal and state. This meant that there would be two systems of police, two jury systems. Although the Constitution and the laws of the United States were to be the supreme law of the land, the relation of the federal courts to state law and judicature, as well as to federal law, was to take years to work out. One of the strengths of the Constituion, it developed, was the fact that it left so many questions to be answered when convenient and appropriate—there was so much room to move around. Most significant, there were to be two systems of politics.

This ingenious and supremely wise document on September 17, 1787, received the assent of the majority of the delegates then present from each state. Sixteen of the fifty-five refused to sign it; a majority from New York and Virginia and half the delegations from Massachusetts and Georgia were absent, thus permitting those who remained to cast the votes of these states. It had received the assent of a majority from but eight of the thirteen states. New Hampshire, Pennsylvania, Delaware, and South Carolina were the only delegations to give it unanimous approval. If account is taken of the nineteen elected delegates who refused to come to Philadelphia at all, it appears that only Pennsylvania, Delaware, and South Carolina had a majority of those originally appointed signing the document; New Hampshire, Connecticut, and New Jersey were tied. Massachusetts, Maryland, North Carolina, and Georgia, as well as New York and Virginia, were negative, and Rhode Island was not there. The presence at the final session and the affirmative votes of thirty-nine of seventy-four delegates made it possible for the rubric of subscription to assert that it was "Done in Convention by the Unanimous consent of the States present," and the further words, "In Witness whereof We have hereunto subscribed our names," made it possible for a few of the reluctants to gain immortality by their autographs, merely signing the document as witnesses without agreeing to its contents.

The document thus achieved had then to be submitted to three stages of political scrutiny. The proposed Constitution must first be reported to the Congress sitting in New York. This feeble body would undoubtedly send it on to the states. In each, the legislature must receive it and then provide for the election of a special convention to decide whether the state would ratify. After these election campaigns, thirteen state conventions would deliberate and act. Twenty-seven bodies, therefore, would have to take cognizance of the document, of which thirteen would be chosen in special elections. If and when nine of these thirteen acted favorably, the new system would be put into operation.

Public reaction to the new document was confused. Few could really know much about it, in the early stages at least, and to many the project became a symbol of either good or evil and was supported as such rather than on critical judgment of its contents. There were some four classes of reaction. Many now could feel relieved of anxiety and were prepared to accept the new scheme at once. A second group was opposed to the new plan and was determined to reject or at least to modify it. A third saw in it an opportunity to improve a local situation and by supporting or opposing it to secure political advantage over their opponents. A fourth and probably painfully large segment of the population was either ignorant or indifferent or both.

The opponents, those of the second group, seem to have been the first to think in terms of political action, and this because they were already politically so well organized. The opposition was to be led by three of the most experienced of American political operators: the governor of New York, George Clinton, and his machine; former Governor Patrick Henry of Virginia with his oratorical reputation and his following in the Old Dominion; and the Pennsylvania Revolutionary party, the radicals of 1776 who had spearheaded the move for independence in their reluctant commonwealth and who had been in power much of the time since. These interests were well established, wanted no superior power, and were prepared through their organizations to head the opposition.

This intransigence appeared early in New York. Two of the state's three delegates withdrew July 7 and never returned. As early as August Governor Clinton began preparing to keep New York out of this new system. Newspaper attacks appeared in September and Clinton himself had ready a series of articles which appeared in the New York press as soon as the text of the Constitution was ready.

The old Revolutionary machinery was oiled. Opposition campaigning clubs were organized. Rallies were planned and held. The trusty committees of correspondence sharpened their pens. State office-holders directed from the New York City customhouse were marshaled. Documents were printed and distributed not only in the Empire State, but anti-Constitutional leaders were contacted in all the states, and newspaper and pamphlet material supplied them.

This hostility had to be countered. Important Virginians, notably George Washington and James Madison, had a great stake in the new plan, and besides, they knew what they were up against at home with Patrick Henry in opposition and because of the refusal of Governor Edmund Randolph and George Mason to sign the new proposal. Further north, George Clinton had powerful enemies in New York opposed to him, such as that part of the New York City legal and Hudson Valley landlord interest represented by the Livingstons; John Jay; General Schuyler and his son-in-law, Alexander Hamilton; and the landholder Van Cortlandt. They would join with Washington and Madison in the war of influence. No sooner had the "Cato" letters of Clinton begun to appear in the New York press, than Hamilton, Madison, and Jay began a series of newspaper letters signed "Publius," which have ever since been known as the *Federalist Papers*. These writings demonstrated the value to the new republic of the strength and stability designed to prevent disintegration and destruction.

Closely associated with these supporters was a determined and resourceful group in Pennsylvania. In that commonwealth a stiff battle for power was mounting. The radicals who had been in control since 1776 were opposed by certain conservative leaders in social, business, and political circles who wanted to revise the state constitution and to provide more safeguards against equalitarian disregard for conservative influence. These men, under the leadership of Robert Morris and those associated with the Bank of North America and other budding interests, had been making headway; they had recently been winning annual elections, and they had sent one of the strongest delegations to the Constitutional Convention. The radical party were on the defensive and worried lest their loss of power might become permanent. Their organs began to develop hostility to the work of the convention in August. Pamphlets from the Bryans and John Nicholson were prepared and printed. In this desperate struggle for ratification in Pennsylvania, the Federalists were powerful, ingenious, and wealthy enough to obtain press material from the pens of Noah

Webster and Tench Coxe and to use influence which could be made available throughout the Confederation. New York City and Philadelphia were to be the centers of propaganda, and the postriders and private messengers were constantly transporting printed matter and manuscript. Friends of the proposed Constitution, through control of the Post Office, were accused of delaying, if not suppressing, mail opposing it. These influences were designed to inspire the convinced to greater effort and to awaken the interest of some of the mass of the indifferent.

Those supporting the plan, it developed, had the greater advantage. In various states acceptance was general, even eager. Some states were so lacking in resources for successful independence, so burdened by obligations, so exposed to danger from invasion, or so imposed upon by their neighbors that they welcomed the relief which would come as part of a powerful republic which could aid and protect them while giving them a place of dignity within it. This attitude appeared dominant in Delaware, New Jersey, Georgia, Connecticut, and Maryland and of some importance in South Carolina and New Hampshire. Also among the population were many who feared instability, the possibility of other Shays' Rebellions which attacked the law or urged measures disturbing to vested interests and property values. Disgruntled veterans and too-generous resort to paper money could be frightening. Such an apprehension would make a strong party in favor in Massachusetts, the home of Shays. The odds seemed to be in favor of ratification in eight states.

The process of ratification had been cleverly devised. It was provided that if nine of the thirteen states approved, these nine could thereupon establish the new government, leaving as many as four states to shift for themselves. Thus, with approval probable in eight states and with little to be expected in Rhode Island, New York, or North Carolina, the contest would probably be decided in either Pennsylvania or Virginia.

From September 1787 through July 1788 there was a concentrated period of discussion, electioneering, debate, and decision. There was an elaborate, highly rationalized, theoretical·debate over political principles. Those who feared tyranny and loss of liberty saw the Constitution even as an approach to monarchy. Where in this document was any bill of rights, any guarantee of liberty? Would not the power to tax deprive the states of their revenues and impoverish them? On the other hand, the supporters declared: let the states protect civil rights; it would be the responsibility of the new government to keep order and to make the nation strong and powerful in the eyes of the world.

Besides this debate, there was the force of certain intangibles. There was the personal influence of Washington and Franklin whose names were signed to the Constitution and whose reputations were revered. Many who had fought under Washington in the war and had become his associates in the Society of the Cincinnati could be expected to follow his lead. Many younger men whose ambitions had not been satisfied under the rule of the Patriot elite saw futures in the new regime and supported it. An even less tangible factor arose out of a fundamental human division. Those who disliked change and were inclined to accept, even defend, things as they found them, opposed this daring change, while those who liked novelty and saw greener pastures elsewhere were for the new. Alpha carried both messages. After taking into consideration all elements of those for or against, it is plain that the secret to the successful fight for approval was the same political capacity which devised the general plan of ratification now projected into the states. This was particularly in evidence in five: Pennsylvania, Connecticut, New Hampshire, Massachusetts, and Virginia. In these bodies politic a variety of techniques proved effective.

Had people been able to recognize it, the battle was over early in December 1787, and it was won in Pennsylvania, the second state to ratify. The Constitutional Convention and the legislature of Pennsylvania met in the same building, Independence Hall. The legislative chamber was the place of meeting of the convention. As its deliberations took longer than anticipated, it had not adjourned when the annual meeting of the legislature scheduled for September took place. The legislature therefore met upstairs. When the Constitutional Convention finished its work on September 17, there were but twelve days left of the Pennsylvania legislative session.

The friends of the Constitution had a majority in this legislature; they did not know how they would fare in the next one, to be chosen in October. Therefore they were anxious for the body upstairs to call a convention to consider the new document. But there was a legal obstacle in the way. The Constitution had to be sent to New York to the Congress who then must decide how it was to be submitted to the states. Until that was done, the Pennsylvania legislature officially had nothing before it. The document was sent to New York, but the Congress dallied. The friends of the Constitution in Philadelphia became more and more concerned, but finally the Congress did submit the document, and it was dashed across New Jersey in the care of a swift dispatch rider.

When it arrived, the Pennsylvania legislature had but a few hours left of its session. Under its rules it took two-thirds of the membership to make a quorum. The foes of the Constitution, though a minority, had sufficient membership which if absent could break a quorum and prevent business. At this juncture they left the hall and the sergeant at arms could not prevail upon them to return. But their strategy was to no avail. A group of determined men seized two of them and brought them to the session. These two, held in their chairs, made the necessary quorum, and the legislation calling a convention was passed. Had this action not been taken, Pennsylvania could not have held its ratification convention in November 1787, and the time of its meeting was of great significance.

In Connecticut appeared similar political skill. Here there was a careful calculation designed to head off possible opposition. A series of articles began to appear in Connecticut newspapers as early as August. These built up a confidence in the convention by dilating on the strength of the members, particularly Washington and Franklin. Moreover, these articles fanned the flame of fear of monarchy and stressed the idea that the work of this convention was probably the only defense against the creation of a king. Less direct but equally effective were criticisms of certain public figures whom the writers seemed to think might oppose the new document. Whether due to this newspaper campaign or not, the Connecticut convention voted 4 to 1 for ratification, and those political opponents against whom this admonitory barrage was fired gave their support to this new system.

In New Hampshire shrewd politics took another turn. Here the great enemy was indifference. New Hampshire's population outside of Portsmouth was widely scattered and difficult to reach. Many people lived in isolated communities with practically no contact with the outside world and cared nothing about any government save their own control of their own affairs. So indifferent were they that so many of the legislators stayed away from a special session to provide for a ratifying convention that no quorum could be had. The legislature, nothing daunted, called the convention and to insure at least a minimum attendance designated that it meet simultaneously with the legislature. The same men might attend both and thus spare expense. Likewise, the supporters provided propaganda in the Portsmouth press. Unfortunately this did not circulate very widely, and when the convention assembled, the Constitutionalists were in a minority. Ingeniously they developed strategy. After a few days, instead of permitting a vote and accepting defeat, the leaders again resorted to shrewd operation. They adjourned the convention for some weeks and then sent postriders into the more inaccessible parts of the state with their view. The result was obvious when June came. The convention reconvened, and lo! the antagonistic majority had melted and the erstwhile minority, risking a vote, found themselves in command, and New Hampshire became the ninth state to act. Its ratification insured the success of the new system.

In Massachusetts there occurred another variation of tactics. Her convention was by far the largest of those held in the states, numbering 355. Two of the most influential of the Revolutionary leaders, Sam Adams and John Hancock, seemed unfavorably disposed, and another, Elbridge Gerry, had refused to sign the document. Gerry was defeated in his bid for a place at the ratifying convention so was not very effective in opposition, but it might be different with Adams and Hancock. Here no chances could be taken. A rally was gotten up among Adams' favorite constituents, the Boston populace, and when they gathered at the Green Dragon Inn to support the Constitution vociferously, two days before the convention met, his tendency to oppose evaporated. Regarding Hancock, their tactics were different. Vanity and love of place were his well-known characteristics. So it was subtly intimated to him that if the new system came into being, he would be a most fitting Vice President to serve with the great Washington, or even perhaps if Washington would not leave his retirement, Hancock himself might be the first Chief Magistrate. Hancock, like Adams, became sympathetic. Then clever newspaper work and an elaborately staged debate of the Constitution by the convention, clause by clause, capped the effort, and the Constitution was ratified by a close vote of 187 to 168.

The contest in Virginia was expected to be crucial, and its leaders were among the most effective of the political figures in the nation. It was disconcerting to have Patrick Henry in opposition and to have the governor, Edmund Randolph, and George Mason decline to sign the document. The refusal of Thomas Jefferson, Richard Henry Lee, and Arthur Lee of Revolutionary fame to give support was also discouraging. But this weight of objection did not hinder the orderly procedure of submission. In the months between the submission in September until the ratifying convention, which spent almost all of June in deliberation, the friends of the new system were busy.

Their great strength was the commanding figure of George Washington. His great name carried much weight, and the friends of the document saw to it that many veterans of the Revolution ran for membership in Virginia's June convention. Then James Madison, always fertile in expedient and thorough master of the contents of the document, not only was writing "Federalist" papers for the press, but he was quietly working to get Governor Randolph to reconsider his rejection. Furthermore, Madison was going to be the floor leader at the convention.

When that body assembled June 2, the Constitutionalists were fortunate from the start. Henry and Mason did not dare oppose the beloved chancellor of the commonwealth, Edmund Pendleton, as chairman of the convention, and Pendleton was in favor of ratification. And when they decided to demand that the Constitution be discussed at length, clause by clause, they played into the hands of the friends of federalism. The lines were close. The supporters had a slight majority, but a careful and deliberate analysis such as Madison could give was bound to be convincing, so this deliberate approach led by Madison could and did strengthen and increase the supporters. The thing to be avoided was any opportunity for Patrick Henry to sweep the convention by one of his fabulous bursts of oratory. This was precluded by discussing the document in committee of the whole. Here no final decisions could be reached, no binding votes taken, and Pendleton, freed from the burden of the chair, could participate in the discussion at will. Added to these advantages, Henry handled himself badly, even approaching prevarication, and Edmund Randolph came back to the federalists.

The able debate was dignified and convincing, and in the end the plans of the opponents to demand a new general convention or to tack on amendments in the form of a bill of rights conditional to ratification failed, although the amendments were submitted by Congress and later proved useful.

In most of the other states ratification had been relatively simple; Delaware, New Jersey, Georgia, South Carolina, Maryland came in smoothly. But in three there was a determination to be negative. In New York, Governor Clinton's machine triumphed in the election for the constitutional convention. These opponents won forty-six out of the sixty-five seats. The nineteen favorable to the document came from New York City and three neighboring counties. However, the back of this resistance was broken by the ratification of ten states, the knowledge that the new plan was going into effect, and threats that

New York City and its environs might join the new government. All these circumstances combined to bring a reluctant ratification, July 26, 1788. Thus eleven states had consented, though North Carolina and Rhode Island would have none of it. So Congress went ahead to provide for the organization of the government prescribed by the Constitution.

The plain truth of the matter was that the Constitution was ratified because of its ingenious character and because its supporters were gifted in the arts of politics. Whether the Constitution was the positive act of the people of the United States expressing the desire of a majority can never be known. But that it was duly ratified by regular procedures after vigorous and widespread political activity is obvious. Enough people feared that "anarchy would soon [ensue] . . . the seeds being readily sown in every soil." There must be strength in government. They believed that this strength was to be provided, and adequately so, by the support of Washington and Franklin. One newspaper writer wished to call the supporters of the Constitution Washingtonians and the opponents Shayites, and there was growing sentiment for ratification of the document so that Washington could speedily become President. The gap left by discarding the British king might be filled by General Washington administering the Constitution. The nation wanted a surrogate to be some substitute for the Empire. The Articles were obviously not that, so they were quickly disposed of. Perhaps because of the accident of Washington's character and availability, they did not seek a king, the normal ruler of the time.

Much of the work of projecting the pattern of independent American political behavior had been completed. The thirteen colonies had transformed themselves into states, each with a constitution of its own. The Articles of Confederation had been tried briefly and quickly discarded for the Constitution. But these fifteen constitutions did not provide all the mechanisms necessary to establish the American democracy. Another instrument had to be invented to meet the needs which the process of growth would entail.

It was already evident that the pattern of population movement and expansion which had been followed since the first migration was not going to stop with the Revolution nor at the Appalachians. As at other times, adventurous migrants were going out on the frontier and were adapting political institutions which they knew to conditions which they found. Already Congress had recognized this tendency, had decided that there should be new political units recognized, and had made some effort to plan for them. However, to date their efforts had availed little. The real accomplishments were being achieved out on the frontiers where scattered groups had taken matters into their own hands and were once again improvising. Here too they were devising politics.

This process had recommenced as far back as the end of the French and Indian War. The Peace of Paris in 1763 had theoretically removed the French and Indian barrier to the expansion of population and land speculation. In New Hampshire and in New York two speculative colonial executives, Governor Benning Wentworth and Lieutenant Governor Cadwallader Colden, had been alive to the possibilities of profit in the region between the Connecticut River and Lake Champlain, to be known as Vermont. Virginia likewise sought to exploit her great estate. Land companies with prominent stockholders in Pennsylvania, Maryland, and New Jersey had their eyes on the Ohio Valley region, which Virginia believed to be hers, and planned rival developments. Active speculators in North Carolina were trying to operate in Kentucky, which Virginia included in her domain, and likewise were beginning the penetration of the Holston and Cumberland valleys in present-day Tennessee. In these distant enclaves the process of creating self-government was beginning anew.

In these river valleys of the West, adventurous pathfinders from Pennsylvania, Virginia, and North Carolina had been busy since the early 1770's. Virginians settled in the valley of the Holston at the Watauga settlements beginning in 1769, thinking they were within the bounds of their own colony, and they were shortly joined by refugees from North Carolina who, having sought to resist corruption as Regulators, had been defeated at the battle of the Alamance in 1771. When these settlers on the Holston found they were really in North Carolina, not Virginia, they decided that independence was what they really wanted. Forthwith a convention was assembled, and in 1772 in true American fashion they began again the creation of government. The process of constitution-making by American-born citizens here began, and the Watauga Association adopted a written frame of government. A legislative body of thirteen was constituted, of whom five were to be a commission to perform executive and judicial functions. The laws of Virginia were adapted to their purposes. A sheriff, a clerk, and a public attorney were provided for, and an office of probate and a land title registry set up. After four years of such independent existence the War of the Revolution broke out, and new dangers led them to petition for membership in the North Carolina legislature. The embryo of Tennessee, however, was in gestation.

During this same period the western ranges of Virginia, known as Kentucky, the dark and bloody ground, began to be the scene of new politics. An adventurous group under the leadership of the Pennsylvanian James Harrod founded Harrodsburg in 1774. Next year another Pennsylvanian led a second and more significant settlement. Daniel Boone some years before had gone into North Carolina and from thence had explored Kentucky. Judge Richard Henderson of the Old North State gathered together some associates in a real estate speculation to be promoted by their Transylvania Company. In their employ Boone founded Boonesborough in Kentucky. Like the early proprietors, these operators planned a self-governing colony, and on May 23, 1775, they sponsored a convention to which delegates from Boonesborough, Harrodsburg, and two other Kentucky settlements were invited and elected "by free choice of Individuals." They adopted a constitution of sorts providing a legislature and vesting executive authority in the proprietors. However, the colony of Transylvania did not last long. Virginia claimed it to be within her jurisdiction, and in 1776 the Transylvanians agreed to accept status as a county of Virginia. Henderson, thus thwarted, soon developed other plans and before the decade was out planted a settlement near French Lick in the Cumberland Valley at what is now Nashville, Tennessee.

A third evidence that there must be recognition of the fact that new politics were in the process of evolving was in an area far from the region west of the mountains. On the northern frontier there was a green and mountainous region between New Hampshire and New York which was too far away for early settlement, particularly with the French almost within gunshot. But the end of the French and Indian War made even this distant cranny attractive to the speculator. Almost immediately rivalry set in: New Hampshire and New York both claimed the region. The New Hampshire governor acted first and numerous New Hampshire grants were made; by 1763 some 131 townships had been created. Then the New York authorities made grants and in 1765 created Cumberland County in that region. The battle raged in the colonial courts and in London, and sometimes there was rough handling of surveyors and agents on the ground. New York gained some legal advantages, but the New Hampshire grantees were in possession. Under the leadership of the intrepid

Allen brothers, Ethan, Ira, Levi, Heman, and Heber, these Green
Mountain Boys organized to defend the homes they had in all good
faith established in Vermont.

The answer to this problem in the minds of those Vermont leaders
who frequented the Catamount Tavern in Bennington was recognition by the crown as a separate colony, and in typical fashion they
undertook to organize and to petition. A convention met in April
1775 and voted to "wholly renounce and resist" the Yorkers' pretensions. Then came the Revolution and Ethan Allen and his Green
Mountain Boys performed their great exploit at Fort Ticonderoga.
For a time there seemed to be an inclination to participate in the
committee and convention system springing up in both New Hampshire and New York. However, the idea of separate organization
grew stronger, and the zealous Vermonters sent a delegate, Heman
Allen, to the Second Continental Congress. When this body suggested that they join New York, this was not the news they wanted
to hear and they remained aloof. The climax came in January 1777
when another convention assembled and declared Vermont independent. In still another conclave in July delegates remodeled Pennsylvania's constitution, called itself Vermont, and undertook to organize a state government. In due time this was accomplished, after
Burgoyne had been defeated, and in March 1778 the first legislature
met, chose a governor, organized militia, and made laws. Some of the
inhabitants and the new state of New York protested, but all they
could do was to keep Vermont out of the Continental Congress and
the Confederation. But in the meantime Vermont maintained and
perfected its independence, and in 1780 New Hampshire relinquished
her claims.

During the 1780's real estate ambitions continued to flourish
whenever there was thought of the vast area north of the Ohio which
Virginia was in the process of relinquishing. Some few settlers had
started homes there on the site of present Cincinnati as early as 1780,
but no efforts had been made at formal political activity. Virginia,
too, had marked off a region between the Scioto and the Little Miami
as lands for military bounties to her veterans, and Fort Harmar had
been built at the mouth of the Muskingum. But the plan of Jefferson
and the Congress to make extensive sales there under the Land Ordinance of 1785 had not materialized: few people had $640 to buy a
section as proposed. Congressional action in refusing to recognize the
claims of the Illinois-Wabash Company, headed by James Wilson of
Pennsylvania, and of the Indiana Company to parts of Virginia's

western estate dimmed the hopes of those speculators, and for a while there was little activity north of the Ohio. But the growing demands of veterans for land bonuses and the independent political activities in Vermont, Kentucky, and Tennessee emphasized to Congress that the problem of regular western political expansion had not been solved.

The Kentuckians had never been too happy as a Virginia county and once again they began to dream of independence. In 1784 they gathered in convention at Danville to start once more on the road to independence. Virginia, who had just ceded her great northwest claims, was not too reluctant and within two years, after more convening and petitioning, was ready to agree. But the region was huge, distances were great, population scattered, and communication almost nonexistent, so Kentucky's independence was delayed. In the same year, 1784, North Carolina surrendered her claims to the Watauga and Nashville, Tennessee, region to the United States and in a sense abandoned these distant outposts. Here the frontiersmen immediately took up the opportunity and, despite the fact that North Carolina soon changed her mind, organized the State of Frankland, or Franklin, under the leadership of John Sevier, December 14, 1784. Internal difficulties soon developed, and after a species of civil war, in which the citizens of the new state engaged with the officials appointed by North Carolina, ended in a battle and Sevier was defeated, North Carolina resumed jurisdiction. But it was not too difficult to predict that a new state was in the making.

Influences were beginning to converge on Congress urging the restudy of the previous implementing of the pledge to make new states in the West. Evidently that made in 1784–85 was not functioning. Individuals were not going to buy $640 plots, even if they were a mile square. The veterans and speculators entered the picture. Various plans were circulated among Revolutionary soldiers proposing to provide grants of land for them as partial compensation for their military service. One of these called for the creation of a military colony in the region north of the Ohio. However, the need which Congress had for funds never permitted this plan any real hope of success. Congress proceeded to arrange for surveys according to the design of the Land Ordinance of 1785 in preparation for sales. The United States geographer directing these surveys and his associate were both Revolutionary officers resident in Massachusetts, and when in the course of their exploration they saw the great empire, they undertook to revive interest among their fellow veterans. They were instrumental in promoting a meeting at the Bunch of Grapes Tavern in Boston, where on March 1, 1786, a company was formed known as the Ohio Company of Associates. They proposed to collect territory. They put their project in the hands of the Reverend Manasseh Cutler, who came to New York to lobby the purchase through Congress. At first he seemed to be getting nowhere, and then ingenuity had to serve. Another land project, known as the Scioto scheme, was being actively pushed by William Duer, secretary of the Board of the Treasury, on behalf of himself and certain members of Congress. He and Cutler united forces. Then they let it be known that the President of the Congress, General Arthur St. Clair, would be an admirable leader to go out into this great region as its governor. With these interests united, a bill was at length possible.

The new Northwest Ordinance was not as democratic as the plan of Jefferson, but it was nevertheless a great document and very vital to the nation's growth. Jefferson had planned to invite settlers to go into his ten potential states whereupon either "on their own petition, or on the order of Congress" they would "receive authority . . . for their free males . . . to meet together for the establishing of a temporary government, to adopt the constitution and laws of any one of the original states," and then plan for a legislature of their own choosing, thereafter to make the laws. The plan of 1787 was more conservative. Congress would appoint a governor, a secretary, and three judges. These men should repair to the new region, set up a government, and, as a committee of five, make the laws for it and then enforce and interpret them. Not until five thousand inhabitants had migrated could the settlers have any part in the government. At that point they might choose a legislature and subsequently make their own laws. However only those could vote who had been citizens three years, had resided there three years, and had become owners of two hundred acres of land.

This plan meant that the early land laws and legal definitions of property and its safeguards would be in the hands of appointees of Congress and that the early voters and lawmakers would be likewise men of property. No easygoing frontier concepts were to rule. It was the document of a businessman, not of a political theorist of liberal outlook. Upon this rather conservative base a liberal structure should be erected. Civil rights and religious liberty were guaranteed. There should be neither slavery nor involuntary servitude. And when the number of people reached 60,000, they might be admitted as a state. Education, too, was insured, because the land ordinance had set aside one lot in every township, 640 acres, for the support of public schools.

After the passage of this ordinance, the Ohio Company purchased 5,000,000 acres, nominally at two-thirds of a dollar per acre. One and a half million acres were for the company, while the remainder were for the shadowy Scioto Company in which Alexander Hamilton, William Duer, Arthur St. Clair, and Richard Henry Lee were interested. The price was to be paid in certificates of indebtedness, and as they were selling at a heavy discount, the great tract was secured for something less than a half-million dollars. In due course the next year, in 1788, the first settlement was founded at Marietta. General Arthur St. Clair and Winthrop Sargent of the Congress were appointed governor and secretary as agreed, and they proceeded to the West to establish the first territory of the United States, to be known as Ohio.

Thus in the great year 1787 representatives of the American people had created another great instrument complementing the Constitution. One provided a great plan of self-government, the other the mechanism permitting political growth. If the United States had determined to remain static, thirteen members with colonies or frontier marches controlled by them, the nation would have been something different, with two classes of citizens, those with self-government and those who were colonials. But this decision to admit new states not only insured an adjustment to take care of growth, but it meant that the United States would be a laboratory for constant experiment in new units of self-government, in new systems of politics. New constitutions would be constantly in the making and new governments in process of formation.

It had been a great period of planning and formulating. In true eighteenth-century fashion, these rational men of virtue and frugality sat down with their quill pens and prepared twenty frames of government, only four of which had to be discarded. In these thirteen state constitutions, the two Northwest Ordinances, and the Constitution, the founding fathers had contrived a pattern of political behavior which was not only new to the world but was to prove unbelievably practical. It was not to be a temporary enthusiasm or a temporary expedient but a successful machine still operating most effectively 180 years later.

These elaborate plans thus fulfilled the desire to create government within a framework of a society greater than the individual states and to go forth and organize new units according to self-defined specifications. The original urge had been for local autonomy within the Empire, not independence. When autonomy was denied, the colonists undertook to create, not complete unitary independence, but a new superstructure, a federalism of their own design, within which their creative instinct could still perform—but within a system. These states would not go each his own way—if they would not work within the familiar Empire, they would erect a new shelter, provide a new mother country. By a stroke of genius they were able to create what they needed, a new system, and then under the comforting illusion of its shelter proceed to make their dreams come true, not within the Kingdom of Great Britain and Ireland, but within the United States of America, where they could construct a new establishment. They must operate under the inspiration and protection of a superior order. But what had they created—later on there had to be one war of definition—do we yet know?

·❧[XI]❧·

PUTTING A MACHINE IN OPERATION

ON JULY 2, 1788, Cyrus Griffin of Virginia, President of the Congress of the United States, announced to his colleagues that the Constitution had been duly ratified. This announcement meant that a new era in American political evolution was about to begin. Federal power and a power structure must now be created. At the end of the Revolutionary War power lapsed, and until 1789 there had been a power vacuum. A political mechanism new in the world must now be designed. Congress, together with the states, must now arrange to put this new political machine into operation. The new states by the act of ratification had resolved to take a further step in self-government and face more realistically the problem of creating political power. Gone were king and parliament, abandoned was the weak Confederation. Power there was to be, but power based upon the elective principle. The executive and the legislative arms were to be chosen by the people or by agents of their choice. Then they must be organized and begin their functioning. Though the responsibility for the next moves was largely in the hands of the states, the legislators of the Confederation must set the stage and arrange the time schedule.

The old Congress moved cumbrously to perform its small part. Most of two months, July 14 to September 13, was spent in considering where the seat of the new government should be. The main stumbling block was a contest between New York and Philadelphia for the honor. At one time a compromise city, Baltimore, was agreed upon but not for long. In the end it was decided to remain in New York City where the Congress and the few Confederation officers had been at work since 1785. This question decided, it did not take much more time to set up a calendar.

Presidential electors were to be appointed, as each state should prescribe, on the first Wednesday in January 1789. These electors should meet in their respective state capitols on the first Wednesday in February, each to write two names on a ballot. The tallies of these ballots would be sent to New York in due time. On the first Wednesday in March the newly elected senators and congressmen would assemble and organize. The electoral votes would be counted by them; the man receiving a majority of the electoral votes was to be announced as President and the second highest man as Vice President. If no one received a majority, the House would choose a President from the five highest, each state having one vote. As soon after the announcement of the result as practicable, the President and Vice President would be sworn in.

The real responsibility for implementation, however, rested with the states. They were to define the qualifications for the voters for electors and representatives and prescribe the conditions determining the election of senators. New horizons were to be revealed to the American voters. Never before had the individual in any of the American communities had to look much beyond his own home locality in making choices of members of the legislature of his state. Now for the first time voters were to be called upon to choose men who were from other communities who were to be electors or to go to the new government as their congressmen. The mechanics of choice would not be uniform but would depend upon the political sophistication and habits of the various states. Methods would range from the complicated devices needed in large states to the simple forms in use in the small commonwealths.

Between October 4, 1788, and January 27, 1789, the eleven states perfected their new laws for the choices necessary. Pennsylvania, in fact, chose her senators September 30. Elections to the House took place on various dates from November 24 to March 3. Only two were held on the same day, when Delaware and Maryland voted for theirs on the day prescribed for the choice of electors. All those voting for representatives and electors must be property holders, save in Pennsylvania, where taxpaying was sufficient qualification. The various states otherwise showed their individuality, for no two behaved exactly alike. The chief difference involved in the choice of congressmen was whether the states' delegations should be chosen by districts or on a general ticket with each voter balloting for a complete state-wide delegation. Massachusetts and Virginia devised a plain and simple district system; New York, South Carolina, and Georgia made slight modifications. Delaware, having only one representative, did not have to choose. Pennsylvania, Connecticut, New

Hampshire, and New Jersey had general tickets, and Maryland had a system of its own whereby each voter voted for six candidates, one from each of the six districts, and the highest coming from each of their respective districts was elected to represent it.

There were likewise various methods of nominating candidates for Congress. The most elaborate was devised in Pennsylvania. On September 3, even before the election law was enacted, the Antifederalists held a convention to plan a campaign to secure amendments to the federal Constitution and to discuss candidates to go to the new Congress to promote that purpose. During the next few weeks the Antifederalists corresponded about such candidates and on November 12 published a slate. This was sometimes referred to as a Whig ticket. In the meantime a Federalist convention met November 3 to nominate both representatives and electors. Prior to this meeting various methods were used to choose the delegates who would compose it; some were chosen by city conventions, some by county meetings, and the like. This convention made up a slate which got into the press November 8. The powerful German element disliked both these tickets, but as the election was to be November 26, there was no time for much action. German leaders therefore published German Federalist and Antifederalist tickets, substituting two German names on the Federalist and one German name on the Antifederalist ticket. There was a busy campaign for two weeks and then the German Federalist ticket won. Their high man received 8,736 votes out of some 14,600 cast.

In Connecticut, New Hampshire, and New Jersey the individual voter had a hand in nomination. In Connecticut each voter wrote twelve names on a ticket. These were tabulated by the legislature and the twelve receiving the highest votes became a slate from whom the voters must then select five. In New Hamsphire each voter wrote three names. If any one received a majority he was elected, but if not, the legislature would send back the six highest and from these the voters would select three. In New Jersey each voter could hand four names to the clerk of each county court. The governor would then tabulate these nominations and publish them as a list. Then each voter was to vote for four from that list and the four highest were elected. Interestingly enough, a legislative caucus meeting in the Princeton College library suggested a list of four who were ultimately elected. In Maryland, likewise, a legislative caucus of Federalists nominated a ticket which was eventually chosen.

There were sharp congressional contests between Federalists and

Antifederalists in Pennsylvania, Maryland, South Carolina, New York, Massachusetts, and Virginia. The contests in the other states seem to have been fought on local or personal issues. Of the fifty-nine representatives chosen, eleven were Antifederals. South Carolina was the only state with an Antifederal majority, four out of five; New York had two Antifederals out of six; Massachusetts, two out of eight; and Virginia, three out of ten. Somewhere in the neighborhood of 100,000 voted, or approximately 6 percent of the white males.

Senators were chosen by the legislatures without much event of moment. There was some disagreement over whether they should be chosen by joint or concurrent meetings of the houses. Three chose concurrent meetings: New Hampshire, Massachusetts, and eventually New York. Pennsylvania and Georgia each had only one house, and the rest used the joint session. In only two states was there anything of particular partisan significance. In Virginia, Patrick Henry and his Antifederalists were in control, and they defeated James Madison; two Antifederal senators were chosen. In New York Clinton's control of the lower house and the Federalist superiority in the upper meant that no agreement as to method could be reached, and New York proved unable to select senators for several months. The first Senate was even more predominantly Federalist than the House as there were only two out of twenty avowedly Antifederal.

The legislatures at the same time arranged for the choice of electors on January 7, 1789, the date set by Congress. These electors were voted for by the people in five states, though in New Hampshire if candidates did not secure the support of a majority of the voters, the legislature would make the choice. In Massachusetts the people in the several districts nominated double the number and the legislature chose. In New Jersey the governor and council appointed the electors, while in Georgia, South Carolina, and Connecticut it was done by the legislature. In New York it had been decreed that the electors should be chosen by the legislature but there developed a deadlock. The senate was anti-Clinton, and thus Federalist, while the house was dominated by the governor. The house insisted that the two houses sit together, thus a majority would have been Antifederal. The senate would not accept this, holding out for separate sessions which would probably have meant that each group would secure a senator and half the electors. As the houses did not agree during that session, New York chose no electors.

The new Constitution by requiring the election of a federal Executive, even by so indirect a process as the operation of the Electoral

College, started the new nation on the great task of national presidential elections, the great hallmark of American democracy. The election of the Executive was an ancient incident in British experience, though latterly only in so far as Parliament upon rare occasions had assumed the task. Connecticut, Massachusetts, and Rhode Island had essayed it in the colonial era, but it had not been advanced much in the new state constitutions: only New York and, in a sense, New Hampshire had adopted it. But now the choice of the President and Vice President was to start the direction of the political thought and action of the American voters to the quadrennial choice of a leader. This responsibility was eventually to become the basis for national partisan politics in the republic, in a highly original and largely unforeseen development.

However, in 1788–89 there was nothing even faintly resembling a national presidential campaign. The consensus was general that Washington should be the first Chief Magistrate, despite the fact that Franklin was approached and some in New England thought of John Adams. There was no such unanimity, however, about the second choice. Here the name most frequently mentioned was John Adams, but he was opposed with something like organized effort made by some who were out of sympathy with the Constitution and wanted a new convention to amend it.

This centered in New York where the organization which Clinton had mobilized to prevent the ratification of the Constitution was continued to work for his election as Vice President and for constitutional amendment. His coadjutors sent out a circular in his behalf to correspondents in other states and, as before, were in touch with Patrick Henry's group in Virginia, hoping that the Old Dominion's electors might write Clinton's name on their ballots with Washington's.

Adams was in fact not too popular. There was a good deal of hesitancy about supporting him in the South and in spite of Washington's final acceptance of him as the best available number two man, there was coolness among the General's friends. Washington's most active supporter who essayed the role of something resembling a campaign manager was his former military aide Alexander Hamilton. The latter had no love for Adams, but he naturally had to move circumspectly as Washington was willing and New England was eager to support him. Whether he believed he could defeat Adams is debatable, but he did write to various correspondents that he feared New England might not give full support to Washington and suggested that the second votes in the South be not all given to Adams. Later he sent word to New England that the South was not unanimous for Washington and if the Connecticut electors did not scatter some of their second votes, Washington might be defeated by Adams and the will of the people thwarted. Probably what he wanted to avoid was a tie vote, with Washington and Adams each receiving the same number.

The result of these maneuverings avoided that outcome, if there had ever been any danger of it. Washington indeed received every vote of the sixty-nine electors chosen and voting; four did not bother to act. Of the second votes Patrick Henry was able to deliver three of Virginia's ten to Clinton, the only votes he received. The only southern votes which went to Adams were five from Virginia, half the state's quota. He secured the ten votes of Massachusetts and the five of New Hampshire, though Connecticut scattered two votes out of seven as Hamilton had suggested. Adams' total of thirty-four was completed by eight of Pennsylvania's ten and one of New Jersey's six. Jay, whom Hamilton probably preferred to Adams, got only nine votes: Delaware's three, five of New Jersey's six, and one from Virginia.

The new system had been inaugurated with a minimum of deviation from accepted patterns. Congressmen had been elected in the same manner as members of the state legislatures and senators had been chosen as had delegates to the Continental Congress. All that was new was the choice of presidential electors. These new tasks accomplished, politics continued to be of the state variety to which all were accustomed, and nothing was to occur to alter these patterns for some years. In the southern states the old courthouse and statehouse politics of the colonial custom continued with the landholding "squires" much in evidence and with Alphas and Betas actively carrying on. In New England the town meeting coteries were the powers, and due deference was paid to the town elders, who often were leaders in the Congregational establishment. The politics of New York and Pennsylvania continued to exhibit the greatest degrees of sophistication, and it was in these states that political innovation was to have its greatest place of experiment.

Local issues and personalities continued to be the principal interest of the communities. But gradually a new political design was to be indicated to meet the needs of the federal system. Upon the base of local patterns a new federal structure was to be superimposed. This was not accomplished easily or quickly. It proceeded by fits and starts, and there were long periods in which there seemed to be little federal activity and no progress. Not until thirty years had passed did the outlines of the new design begin to appear with any clarity. Attention has been focused on the emergence of this pattern as though it were a steady and inevitable process, conceived in its final design from the start. This is not true. At first it was an interest of but a few, and they had no real comprehension of what kind of politics the federal system would require. It really did not start as early as is usually assumed. Much of the time it was not a matter of interest to many, and there were long gaps in its operation. For nearly fifty years popular attention in politics was absorbed in operating the local system, already 150 years old. Interest in the new federal politics developed with extreme deliberation.

As the first Wednesday in March of 1789 happened to be the fourth, that was then and thereafter to be the beginning of the successive four-year presidential administrations. On that day in this first year of federal operation nothing was ready. Local New York City merchants had subscribed money to fix up the Old City Hall in Wall Street for a federal Capitol, but it was still in the hands of workmen when the guns and church bells saluted the birth of the new government. On that day only eight senators and thirteen representatives were in the city, not nearly a quorum of either house, the memberships of which numbered twenty and fifty-nine. Not until March 30 was there the number required in the House, and the Senate failed to muster enough before April 6. On that date the two houses met together and counted the electoral votes. George Washington and John Adams were sent for; on April 21 Adams was sworn in and on April 30 General Washington was duly inaugurated. The new government was in operation.

But would it run efficiently? This question was to be answered initially by these small groups of men meeting in two rooms, faced with difficult problems; almost everything depended on their behavior. Some of them were old acquaintances, others were meeting each other for the first time. Some were experienced in lawmaking, others were tyros. For the time being they were assembled in New York, in an isolation dictated by the lack of communication characteristic of that era. Mail service and travel were slow and hazardous, newspapers few and small. These men were to operate almost in a vacuum of public opinion. Conflicting views, antagonistic personalities, clashing ambitions, and attitudes shaped to various social environments were inevitable.

Even before Washington had been inaugurated, preparations were made to start legislation. James Madison, expecting to cooperate with Washington, undertook to set up an agenda. The first item was revenue legislation. After years of vainly making requisitions, Congress now had the power to tax, and the empty treasury made imperative the writing of a tariff. James Madison, with the blessing of Washington, undertook the duties of floor leader of the House where the financial legislation must originate. In the process of planning these imposts, the variety of communities and their interests appeared, and there was a series of divisions over what should be taxed and how much. The conflicting views of southern agricultural interests, commercial New England, and the varied ventures of the middle states clashed, as they had in the First Continental Congress and ever since, and various trades and deals helped the process of agreeing to a bill.

In the meantime the civil service, if it may be so called, of the Confederation had been carrying on. The offices of the Department of Foreign Affairs, the War Department, the Board of Treasury, and the Post Office had been functioning in their limited fashion. Congress undertook to reorganize these bureaus and to establish a federal customs service. Consequently bills were passed providing for the continuation of the departments of Foreign Affairs and War and the Post Office, but the Treasury was reorganized. There should now be a department with a Secretary who should report directly to Congress. Also a federal court system—Supreme Court, Circuit Court of Appeals, and district courts—was provided, with an Attorney General and a series of clerks, marshals, and district attorneys. This legislation was passed during the summer, and Washington busied himself with appointments. He began with customhouse officers and then proceeded to choose his department heads and the judges and officers connected with the new courts.

He asked his former aide to be his fiscal officer, and Alexander Hamilton assumed the Treasury. The Secretary of War, General Henry Knox, he continued, and likewise he reappointed Samuel Osgood as Postmaster General. He wished Thomas Jefferson to conduct foreign affairs and shortly other domestic concerns in what was going to be called the Department of State. However, Jefferson was still in France, so Washington persuaded John Jay to hold over in the foreign office. In the meantime the President sought to create a federal judiciary, an Attorney General and lesser court functionaries. When Washington was through, it was apparent that Jefferson, Hamilton, Knox, Osgood, and a strong panel of lawyers, including Jay and Randolph, were going to make up the new government.

Washington naturally and quite uniformly appointed those friendly to the Constitution to take office.

He was probably consciously undertaking to create an American establishment, which might be compared with that existing in England where crown, Church, titled families, country squires, and city professional men and mercantile leaders, together with a few emerging industrial magnates, were the group to whom deference was accorded. That which the new republic was creating would include the Patriots and certain elites which had developed in the thirteen states. To them Washington was now adding a group of department heads, judicial officers, and federal civil servants. Washington himself was its great personification, the aegis of the republic.

When Washington had concluded his appointments, the man whom he designated as Secretary of State, Thomas Jefferson, was still in France, and as Knox and Osgood were already in office, there were but two immediate newcomers: Hamilton, who was a resident of New York City and therefore right at home; and Edmund Randolph of Virginia. It is of interest to note that the Virginia President invited two from his own state, kept on two from Masssachusetts, and added to them a New Yorker. And it was upon this New Yorker that public attention was going to focus.

That the new Congress would divide into groups and factions, that these groups and factions would be influenced by the nature of the personalities involved, and that they would be shaped in part by the units of society from which their members came was inevitable. It was also probable that much of this divisive factionalism would be dependent upon accident and opportunism. It was accident and the logic of events which did much to shape the early stages of the new federal politics of the United States.

The first factors were the financial chaos of the new government, to which were added some accidental features, such as the nature of James Madison, the fact that Washington brought Alexander Hamilton into the picture, and finally that Thomas Jefferson was six months late in joining Washington's official family. It was this group of more or less accidental factors combined with the pressing needs of the American society which shaped the new politics of 1789–91.

The question which was to be the most obvious factor in this politics of the new republic was the extent to which the central government would seek and succeed in exercising power. If it did little, it would stir up as little politics as had the Confederation, but if it acted contrariwise, there could be no predicting the nature of the resulting

divisions of opinion and of factionalism. Had Washington chosen a
routine administrator for the Treasury and left Madison to develop
an Administration program in Congress, there is no telling what
might then have transpired politically, except that government would
have been pretty much in the hands of Virginians. But Washington
chose Hamilton, and a new chapter of politics began to be written.

Hamilton had the mind of a statesman, he wanted the new government to be effective, and to that end he felt that it must have
credit in the world of finance and the support of the substantial men
who could advance its enterprise. He also liked power. So as soon as
he became Secretary of the Treasury, he began to work on devising
the measures which Congress should pass to give the new federal
society stability and strength. When the second session returned to
New York City in January 1790, he was ready with a program. He
recommended that the Congress agree to pay the depreciated debt,
foreign and domestic, federal and state, at face value. He would
obligate the new government to raise securities fallen way below par
to 100 percent of their face value. Furthermore, as the federal government had deprived the states of much of their revenue, he urged
Congress to assume the debts of the states as well and to be responsible for their payment. This ambitious plan Hamilton submitted to
Congress, expecting that body to enact it forthwith. In planning this
undertaking he more or less ignored the fact that Madison was the
established House floor leader, and instead of attempting to work out
with him a practical cooperative sponsorship, he deemed his word to
be sufficient with the lawmakers.

Though Hamilton had the intellect of a statesman when it came
to creating measures, he did not always have the ability of the politician to eliminate opposition. His measures and his method of handling
them initiated opposition that for the time being split the Congress.
The great objection to his program was that it rewarded speculators
who had bought the debt cheap after it had deteriorated in value and
who would now reap rewards at the expense of the public. The poor
debtors, often veterans, who had lent the money or supplied the services and who had sold their certificates for as little as twenty-five
cents on the dollar, now could calculate the enormity of their losses
and the great increase of speculators' fortunes.

Also, this measure was not liked in the South, where it was looked
upon as a device to make the rich northern businessmen all the richer.
It would despoil the poor farmer and enrich the city capitalists. It was
a device of the rich to gain wealth at the expense of the poor. It was

iniquitous. So those who thought it was evil, unfair, and unjust—a device of speculators, conceived to advantage the North at the expense of southern interests—now began to voice vigorous opposition. They were joined by many in certain states, notably Virginia, who, though they had paid much of their debt, would have to share in paying taxes to satisfy the obligations of the less provident. It was a very close issue and Hamilton feared that his measure might be lost. But he had learned something. Perhaps he was not so powerful as he thought; he must now become the politician, and he therefore undertook to take steps.

When he found that he lacked Virginia votes essential to carry assumption, he sought the aid of Jefferson almost as soon as the latter arrived in New York to take over the State Department in March 1790. One day he ran into Jefferson as they were both going to the President's, and he broached a proposition to him as they walked up and down in front of Washington's dwelling. As the fortunes of some of the more hard-pressed states were in the balance, the national credit was in danger. As a fellow administrator, he urged that Jefferson join him in an appeal to the President to call a mass meeting to regulate the American dollar. To increase his persuasion Hamilton brought in another question. Where was the permanent capital to be located in which the new golden age was to flourish? Some wanted the seat of government to remain in New York City. Others were speaking for Philadelphia, for another spot on the shores of the Delaware or the Susquehanna, or for Baltimore. Where would Congress establish the capital in a federal district ten miles square? Might it not be on the Potomac?

Jefferson was quick to understand. He had just returned from the French court where he had had to handle the difficulties of negotiating with European bankers while American credit rating was so poor, and he could understand the Treasury's weakness. He could also see Hamilton's point when he brought up the question of the capital and suggested that it might be situated on the banks of the Potomac, in Virginia and Maryland. Jefferson was not averse to bringing the question of assumption and the Potomac site before his fellow Virginians from the Potomac districts who were hostile to Hamilton's program. He arranged a dinner party to which the Virginians were invited, and he and Hamilton had a full discussion with them. The result was an accommodation. Assumption was passed and the capital would be located on the Potomac after a ten-year sojourn at Philadelphia, insisted upon by some of the Pennsylvanians and their Delaware Valley allies.

The inevitable tendency to divide on issues involved in the creation and exercise of power which had manifested themselves in the writing of the tariff had thus come forward again in more intense fashion over Hamilton's proposals to manage national finance and service the debt in a manner which would add to the power of a "financial interest." This plan, designed to secure for the Treasury and the new government the support and the financial backing of an enterprising and speculative group with a large supply of new money had decided political implications.

On almost the same day in March 1790 that assumption came under discussion, revealing statements were committed to paper indicating certain traces of the politics which was emerging in these first years of the government's operation. Senator Samuel Johnston of North Carolina recorded that "the sentiments of the Northern or Eastern, and Southern members constantly clash, even when local interests are out of the question . . . even the lawyers from these different quarters cannot agree on the principles and construction of law." At the same time a friend from Virginia reported to Washington: "A spirit of jealousy which may become dangerous to the Union towards the Eastern States seems to be growing fast among us. It is represented that the Northern phalanx is so firmly united as to bear down all opposition, while Virginia [is] unsupported even by those whose interests were similar to hers."

Yet from New England was expressed a different view. "The southern gentry have been guided by their hot tempers and stubborn prejudices and pride in regard to southern importance and negro slavery . . . and they have shown an uncommon want of prudence as well as moderation; they have teased and bullied the House out of their good temper, and driven them to vote in earnest on a subject which at first they did not care much about." One of Hamilton's associates in the Treasury summed it up after Congress had gone home. "All the disputes of this session may, in my opinion, be traced to the rival claims for pre-eminence between Massachusetts and Virginia, New York and Pennsylvania. These states have very important interests at stake which cannot be easily reconciled, and the consciousness which they have of their weight in the government, prevents them from exercising all the moderation which our present circumstances require."

Hamilton's statesmanship, despite this opposition, did secure support for the new government, but it also emphasized sectionalism and a basic lack of unity, conditioned by physiography and also by an ideological difference. The new government could be thought of as aristocratic, favoring the rich at the expense of the poor, the city at the expense of the country, the North at the expense of the South, the speculator at the expense of the farmer. Was Hamilton aiming at a monarchy and using Washington to that end?

Congress finished its second session with the friends of Hamilton in control and with Jefferson an ally. The Washington Administration was acting as a unit. During the autumn, the establishment had left New York City, and when the lawmakers came together again in December 1790, it was in Philadelphia, where they settled down under the benign shadow of Independence Hall. Hamilton was ready with the capstone of his financial edifice. He needed more taxes and he proposed the chartering of a national bank to serve as fiscal agent of the Treasury. The taxes were to be excise levies on alcoholic beverages, notably whiskey, imposts that would affect the incomes and the money supply of the poor and the farmer, particularly in the more remote regions where whiskey served as a vital medium of exchange. The bank, of course, was obviously a financiers' device to be located and to operate in cities, of slight benefit to rural society, and probably a drain upon their resources. Besides, it raised a grave issue: Where in the Constitution was there any power to charter any corporation, let alone a central bank?

Once more hackles were raised. The same interests disturbed by Hamilton's funding plans were now again in arms, but by this time Jefferson and Hamilton had proved incompatible, and the Secretary of State was with them and cooperating with Madison. However, as in the previous session, they did not have the votes. Excise and bank bills passed. Jefferson advised Washington to veto the latter as unconstitutional, but the President accepted the contrary advice of his Secretary of the Treasury and signed the act. The Administration was no longer a unit.

Thus by the end of the first Congress a pattern of political attitudes about the new government and of behavior determined by them had begun to take shape. Hamilton's personality and his brilliantly conceived financial plans had been the controls. His proposals had been accepted, but they were proving unpopular in certain quarters. His schemes were attractive to those desiring strong government and to speculators, but they had profited from them at the expense of many humbler folk. Veterans and other certificate holders who had been induced to part with their paper at a great discount by schemers with foreknowledge learned with dismay of their loss and others' profit at their expense. Southern planters saw financial power and wealth concentrated in distant northern cities, they believed, to their disadvantage.

In more specific terms Jefferson had not only had to endure the fact that Washington often preferred Hamilton's advice to his, but he was constantly aggravated by his colleague's bearing. Hamilton was more glib, quicker in speech, more scintillating and brilliant in company than he. Also, he would interfere in all phases of government, particularly in foreign affairs. Hamilton was constantly in touch with the British embassy, encouraging its personnel to work with him rather than with the State Department. In short, Hamilton had gotten on the nerves of Jefferson and Madison because of his manner, his personality, and his arrogant assumption of superiority.

It was furthermore obvious that the exercise of power by the new government had begotten a natural opposition. This opposition was creating division. Some people therefore had to be in the minority, a minority including those either disappointed, frustrated, or determined to win next time and who were motivated by any or all of these urges to make vigorous political effort to this end. Attitudes conditioned by these factors were beginning to spread. Word of the measures of government and the behavior of their authors was circulated by letter, by the newspapers which were brought by the post-riders or which were printed locally, and by word of mouth from travelers and the local Alphas. Suspicion became current that a corrupt squadron was connected with the new government and that there were perhaps even some who were plotting monarchy.

Jefferson and Madison undertook to learn what popular reactions were in order that they might put to politcal use what they learned. "There is a vast mass of discontent gathered in the South and how and when it will break God knows," Jefferson advised the chancellor of New York State, who was likewise disturbed by Hamilton's pervasive activity. The Secretary of State was convinced that "the only corrective of what is corrupt in our present form of government [can be made by] the augmentation of the numbers in the lower house, so as to get more agricultural representation, which may put that interest above that of the stock jobbers." He concluded, "Zeal and talents added to the republican scale will do no harm in Congress." This writing of his on March 13, 1791, is an early indication of the use of a new political label. Those in command of organizing the new government and directing its first congressional program were obviously federalists, friends of the Constitution and closer association. But their actions and their policies led to the questioning of their objectives: Were they not also aristocrats seeking to create a monarchy? This was becoming a very real question in the minds of Jefferson and those who for one reason or another opposed them. It was a simple rallying point, easy to understand: the republic was in danger; it was the responsibility of a "republican interest" to seek to protect that which was in peril against evil.

Even before the first Congress adjourned and while these political patterns were forming, the election of the Second Congress had begun. As in the choice of the First, there was no uniformity of procedure, no schedule of time, no appearance of innovation. Each state chose its representatives according to its own sense of convenience and propriety following accustomed schedules, and few states used a common election day. During this period no political organization of national significance was apparent nor any but local campaigns conducted. At the conclusion of the voting it would be noted that, although a number of changes had taken place, the general situation was the same. Five of the original senators, now become twenty-six because New York had finally elected two and North Carolina and Rhode Island had ratified the Constitution, did not return. The only significant change, however, was that Burr succeeded Hamilton's father-in-law, Senator Schuyler, who had been elected from New York in July 1789. In the House twenty-eight of the original sixty-five were succeeded by newcomers, but there was no political significance in this turnover. The Washington Administration could count on general support, although the bloc of consistent Federalists numbered only about fifteen. The speaker to be chosen would be Jonathan Trumbull of Connecticut, a more reliable Federalist than Frederick A. Muhlenberg of Pennsylvania, the first incumbent, had been. On the other hand, Madison could only depend on seventeen. The majority of the congressmen held themselves independent of any consistent classification.

Despite the general Federalist success in the First Congress and the failure of any change to be indicated by the elections to the Second, there were signs of some efforts at the mobilization of an opposition, largely directed by local rather than federal situations. It was already becoming apparent that political behavior in the new republic was to develop on two levels and that while the contest in Congress between those favoring the Federalist-Hamiltonian program and its opponents was significant, the interest in state contests based on local situations and the public esteem of local characters was just as compelling, if not more so. The new state-federal relationship was to be a two-way communication. Events in state politics were to affect federal patterns as well as vice versa.

When the first Congress finally adjourned in March 1791, there was a general exodus from Philadelphia. Even President Washington felt the need of a respite and made an extensive tour of the South. Perhaps the most significant change of scene was that which first Madison and then Jefferson and Madison experienced. Shortly after the adjournment Madison went up to New York City for an extensive sojourn. Here he observed a deep political schism and sought to make use of it.

The force of state politics was impressed upon Madison during his sojourn in New York. Throughout the history of American democracy, no state was to be more sophisticated or powerful in setting the patterns of political behavior. Its first governor, the Revolutionary general, George Clinton, had been in office since 1777. Like Patrick Henry he had been unfavorable to establishing a new and more powerful federal government. Hamilton, therefore, when he had at length defeated the governor and his co-workers in opposition at the state ratifying convention, had commenced almost at once to get Clinton out of the governorship. He and certain of his associates who had fought for the Constitution had begun to work on a plan as early as 1789 to put the Federalists in power. They felt that Clinton was too strong to be defeated by an obvious Federalist, so they sought to split Clinton's forces by nominating one of his supporters. At a meeting held February 11, 1789, in Bardin's Tavern in New York City, a group of Federalists proposed to support an Antifederalist state judge, Robert Yates, for governor. Committees of correspondence were organized in New York City and Albany. This move almost succeeded, for in April Clinton won by a majority of only 429 votes.

Hamilton's party, on the other hand, gained the legislature and the belated choice of United States senators could be made. Hamilton's father-in-law, General Philip Schuyler, had been elected to what proved the short term expiring in 1791, while a newcomer in the state, Rufus King, recently a migrant from Massachusetts, secured the second place with the longer term; these two senators belatedly took their seats in July 1789. The Federalists, in this matter and in the allotting of the federal patronage, followed Hamilton's judgment and ignored the powerful Livingston family. The chancellor, Robert R. Livingston, who had sworn in President Washington, received nothing nor did any of his numerous and politically powerful family. The Livingstons did not forget this slight.

It was this situation that Madison observed in New York that spring of 1791, and it was of no little significance that Madison then stayed so long in Gotham. It was perhaps even more significant that Jefferson joined him there in May and that together they went on a "botanizing" expedition up into New York state and New England. While Madison was in New York City he fellowshiped with certain of the disaffected Federalists, notably Livingston, and while he and Jefferson were examining the flora of New York and Connecticut, they had meetings which caused one of Hamilton's associates to write him that "there was every appearance of a passionate courtship between the Chancellor [Robert Livingston], Burr, Jefferson and Madison when the two latter were in town." Madison was also planning further investigations of political opinion on a trip into New England with John Beckley of Virginia, clerk of the United States House of Representatives, who had a sharp nose for political information. Madison eventually decided he could not take this second trip but Beckley did and sent back numerous reports which Madison shared with Jefferson.

Out of this local situation which Madison particularly, and Jefferson incidentally, explored in the spring and early summer of 1791 was arising the possibility of a political alliance between Virginia and New York which might break down Hamilton, cast aside New England, and create a new power which might take over whenever Washington should step down. If the disgrunted Livingstons with their counsel, the astute Burr, could associate with the Jefferson-Madison "republican interest," such a new power might be created.

Further evidence of the organizing of opposition and of the planning of maneuvering was provided by the emergence of a political press. The Washington Administration had early recognized the need of an official gazette, such as had been developed by the English government, to contain government communications, to publish orders and promotions, to print the laws, and otherwise act as government organ. John Fenno, a Massachusetts newspaperman and printer who had migrated to New York City, had set up a paper, *The Gazette of the United States*, in April 1789, to be supported in part by government advertising and printing. He had brought it to Philadelphia when the government moved. This paper hewed to the Washington-Hamilton official line and was obviously trying to help their friends to be elected to the Second Congress.

Just when Jefferson and Madison began to think of a press in the republican interest, it is not possible to say. Newspapers opened attack on Hamilton's proposals in 1790. Thomas Greenleaf in the New York *Journal* and the editors of the *Independent Chronicle* of Boston and the *Pennsylvania Gazette* and the *General Advertiser*, both of Philadelphia, the latter edited by Benjamin F. Bache, Franklin's son-in-law, were opposed. Washington was included in the attack when he signed the bill moving the capital away from New York. This was more than Greenleaf would stand, and despite reverence for the General, he let him have it with his rather small barrel. In thinking about an opposition press, Madison and Jefferson found none of these suitable for their purposes: their circulations were too local and Bache's *Advertiser* was a daily. A weekly paper to be distributed by mail was needed. Late in the winter of 1790–91, Madison heard that a Princeton classmate, the poet Philip Freneau, was unhappy in New York and was hoping to set up a newspaper elsewhere. Madison suggested that he might be induced to come to Philadelphia and urged that Jefferson appoint him as a translator in the State Department. Jefferson agreed and made the poet an offer which, however, he declined. When he went up to New York in the spring, Madison saw a good deal of his classmate and broached to him the idea of setting up a newspaper in Philadelphia. Nothing happened, however, until after the "botanizing" expedition. Then in August Freneau accepted the translator's post at $250 a year, not a princely sum. Francis Childs and John Swaine, New York publishers of the *Daily Advertiser*, a Federalist sheet, agreed to assume the financial risk of a republican weekly to be published in Philadelphia under Freneau's editorial control. On October 31, 1791, the first number of the *National Gazette* appeared. The "Republican interest" now had an organ. Soon the new postal law of 1792 would provide cheap mail rates for newspapers and thus for political propaganda.

This organ promptly began its work. A broader platform was being constructed which would carry more than opposition to Hamiltonian financial legislation. The antagonists of Washington and Hamilton were moved to spread a more vital apprehension, for they professed to feel that republicanism was in danger. Washington, with his six-horse coach, his formal receptions, his state dinners, was accused of affecting the ceremonial of a monarch. Jefferson came to believe that Hamilton was at heart a monarchist planning to make Washington a king, and some of Vice President Adams' writing indicated that he was hoping for the development of an aristocratic state. A letter of Jefferson's was published without his knowledge which was interpreted as an attack on Adams as an aristocratic foe of liberty. His son, John Quincy Adams, defended his father in the Boston *Columbian Centinel*, and then a "host of republican volunteers" replied. As Attorney General Randolph wrote, "Since the standard of republicanism has been erected, it has been resorted to by a numerous corps." One Federalist reported that in Congress "faction glows within like a coalpit."

This political tension was increased and the propaganda strengthened by a financial crisis. During the winter of 1791–92 there was disaster. William Duer, official assistant to Hamilton, had been speculating in the national debt, and in March 1792 he failed. This disaster enabled Jefferson to charge with greater plausibility that the U.S. Bank was stimulating speculations reaching to the proportions of mania and once again to attack "stock jobbers." Hamilton now was aroused, believing that "Madison, cooperating with Mr. Jefferson, is at the head of a faction hostile to me and my administration . . . actuated by views . . . subversive of the principles of good government and dangerous to the Union, peace and happiness of the country." Jefferson on his part was concerned because "a sect has shewn itself among us, who declared they espoused the new constitution, not as a good and sufficient thing itself, but only as a step to an English constitution. . . . Too many of these stock jobbers and king-jobbers have come into [Congress], or rather too many [congressmen] have become stock jobbers and king-jobbers."

Hamilton, stung by charges of jobbery and corruption, some of which Jefferson later implied to Washington against him, seized upon the fact that Freneau, the "Republican" editor was on the payroll of the State Department and in print charged Madison and Jefferson with conniving to subsidize Freneau from the public funds to attack the Administration. A pamphlet likewise appeared in midsummer entitled *The Politics and Views of a Certain Party*. This accused Jefferson and Madison of organizing a party to make Jefferson Washington's successor, a faction becoming known informally as Democratic Republican.

Jefferson and his cohorts replied and war was on. In the resulting vivid pamphlet and press controversy of 1792 Jefferson was the more subtle and less obvious. He left the real work to others—Freneau, Madison, Randolph, all disguised by classical pseudonyms. Hamilton's assumption of any opportunity to interfere was probably the real basis for Republican bitterness. It can be wondered whether if he had stayed out of foreign affairs there would have been so much said about the corrupt squadron fattening on Treasury plunder. Hamilton seemingly had taken the support of Jefferson and Madison for granted and could never understand why he did not have it and why they resented him. When he at length went after them, there was nothing subtle about his attack. Hamilton in fact had secret ambitions to succeed Washington and so must forestall any Virginian pretension.

Those who were politically conscious knew that 1792 was a presidential year and that President Washington was not well. The heavy duties of his office weighed upon him. Most galling of all were the attacks upon him personally which went to the lengths of impugning his integrity. He had gone so far, in fact, as to ask Madison's aid in preparing a farewell address. Clearly at one time early in 1792 he was making up his mind to retire. However no one wanted him to withdraw. Madison and Jefferson were just as insistent that he remain as Hamilton was. As a matter of fact, the pamphlet and press war was designed really to get rid of Jefferson and Hamilton. Washington, as the great aegis, was felt to be indispensable in these uncertain days of novelty.

Under such circumstances no one had the temerity to think of running against Washington, and as he kept silence about his plans, any direct political maneuvering for the first office was unthinkable. The technique of any opposition would be to deprive John Adams of the second post, to attempt to move someone else into the line of succession. The man first thought of was Governor George Clinton of New York. The understandings, friendships, or whatever they may be called, which had developed during Madison's and Jefferson's visits to New York began to bear fruit, watered as they were by a Pennsylvania interest.

John Beckley, clerk of the House, born in Virginia but then living in Philadelphia and an intimate of the Virginians, undertook another mission as one of the republic's first political trouble shooters. He was sent over to New York City by Dr. Benjamin Rush to make sure that Aaron Burr was aware of a Pennsylvania interest in supporting Clinton against Adams. However, this objective did not suit all. Certain Philadelphians, including Alexander J. Dallas, thought Burr would be a stronger candidate—they perhaps were stimulated by Burr himself. Letters were sent to Madison and Monroe and to others in the South from both Philadelphia and New York urging a shift from Clinton to Burr. This proposal found no favor in Virginia, which was always to be Burr's Waterloo, and the Old Dominion leaders sought to interpose a veto.

This difference of opinion called for a conference, and on October 16, 1792, there occurred in Philadelphia what appears to have been the first national nominating conference, and it was to promote the Republican interest. Melancton Smith, New York supporter of Burr, came over and met with Jefferson, Beckley, Pierce Butler of South Carolina, several Pennsylvanians, and perhaps others. There the opposition of Virginia to Burr prevailed, and it was agreed that Clinton should be the man. He was in the process of running for reelection as governor of New York, but this fact did not seem to deter anybody. After this conference New York closed ranks behind Clinton. Melancton Smith undertook to visit Rhode Island, Connecticut, and Massachusetts in his behalf. Patrick Henry was urged to write to his friends in North Carolina, and others corresponded with key men in South Carolina and Georgia.

Whatever political management the Federalists undertook for Adams was directed by Hamilton despite his long-standing dislike for the Vice President. Hamilton noted the activity in behalf of Clinton and Burr and sought to head it off by letter writing, working with federal officeholders in the states. He was suspicious that this Clinton support was part of a plot to divide the votes of the middle and New England states and then have southern votes elect Jefferson over Adams. He took charge and even issued directions to Adams chiding him for staying away from his post in Philadelphia. "I fear," he wrote the Vice President, "that this will give some handle to your enemies to misrepresent. Permit me to say it best suits the firmness and elevation of your character to meet all events, whether auspicious or otherwise, on the ground where station and duty call you."

But though there was little or no political organization or campaigning on a national level, the arts were developing in the states, notably in New York and Pennsylvania. The spring of 1792 was to witness another of New York's triennial gubernatorial contests. George Clinton was of course going to run again, and Hamilton and the Federalists were scheduling another effort to beat him. Hamilton was still smarting from the Clinton-Livingston combination which

drove his father-in-law, General Schuyler, from the Senate and replaced him with Burr. But who could Hamilton and Schuyler persuade to run against Clinton? Judge Yates would not, Stephen Van
Rensselaer would not, and then to their horror a move developed
among the lesser known Federalists to have, of all persons, Burr as the
party's candidate. Under this urging Hamilton persuaded Chief Justice Jay to run at the invitation of a Federalist mass meeting organized
by Hamilton and endorsed by Judge Yates. Even then the danger was
not over, for some Republicans tried to replace Clinton with Burr.
This move was quashed by the latter. So it was Jay against the peren-
nial Clinton.

The supporters of Jay and Clinton contrived the use of committees of correspondence as the chief electioneering mechanism, a use
initiated during the Revolution. These committees had been active in
the state election of 1789 and were now at work for both Clinton and
Jay. The direction of Jay's campaign was undertaken by a committee
located in Albany. These men planned a series of local nominating
meetings like that at Rye where a "general meeting of Freeholders
and inhabitants" gathered presumably at an inn, voted to support Jay,
and set up a committee to promote his cause. The Clintonians held
similar meetings, likewise presumably inspired by a central committee. These Albany committees, also by correspondence, sought to
enlist the support of influential individuals. In this contest no ideological political designations were used. The aggregations, such as they
were, were called Jayites or Clintonians, and there was no organized
fight for the legislature. In New York City, for instance, there were
three tickets: Jayite, Clintonian, and a third sponsored by "a considerable number of the Merchants of New York." Some of the candidates were on more than one of these lists and they all fared about
equally.

The contest was bitter and close, and Jay seemed at length to have
been elected in April by a majority of four hundred. The legislative
canvassers then by sharp practice, due to the partisan advantage of
the Republicans and the clever participation of Burr, caused the legislature to revise the returns on the grounds of some irregularities in
three western counties and to count Clinton in. This seeming fraud
deepened the animosities between Hamilton, Jay, Schuyler, and King
on the one hand and Clinton, the Livingstons, and Burr on the other.
These animosities were to lead to ever greater hatred, tragedy, death,
disgrace, and a blasted career, sparked by unscrupulous power lust
and ambition.

Pennsylvania, like New York, continued its early political sophistication. The Commonwealth during the post-Revolutionary period had produced two rather equally matched groups, those who had come into power with the Revolution and those who thought that their radical constitution of 1776 should be altered—a radical and a conservative group. The conservatives won enough strength to secure the ratification of the United States Constitution and a new Pennsylvania constitution, but their margin of control was so narrow that their new charter was a compromise with a liberal slant. The senators and representatives chosen to the federal Congress were those favorable to the Constitution, but they split over Hamilton's plans, and William Maclay, one of the senators from the western part of the state, became bitterly opposed to the other senator, Robert Morris, and to most of the congressmen. Morris, Thomas Fitzsimons, and others of the congressional delegation, when the new constitution was finished in September 1790, sought to secure the election of General Arthur St. Clair as governor, but the popular president of Pennsylvania, General Thomas Mifflin, with the support of the old radicals and many others snowed St. Clair under. The legislature showed itself nearly equally divided between eastern and western influences, conservative and radical. In the last decade of the eighteenth century, Federalists were generally slightly ahead, but the margin was always narrow.

Pennsylvania continued to display the political sophistication which she had acquired, because her large and complex area and population dictated it. Also, Philadelphia was the national capital from 1790 to 1800 and thus was the seat of both the state and the national government. Those administering the state and the nation and making both federal and state law were in the closest proximity. Furthermore it was Franklin's state and the city where his grandson, Benjamin Franklin Bache, published first the *General Advertiser*, and later the *Aurora*, which became one of the chief Jeffersonian newspapers. Here, too, John Beckley had made his home and was strategically located.

During this decade the Pennsylvania political operators continued to be the center of innovation, experimenting with the formalized nominating procedures which they had inaugurated in selecting their representatives to the First Congress. By the time the Third Congress was to be elected in 1792, a new set of circumstances dominated. Congress was required to reapportion the seats among the states on the basis of the census of 1790 just completed. However, they delayed until after the Pennsylvania legislature was due to adjourn. So

the Pennsylvania lawmakers must provide for the election of con-
gressmen-at-large in whatever number Congress was later to prescribe.

When this number was known, the Federalist junto proposed a
plan for creating the machinery of nomination. They proposed a
public meeting at the State House in Philadelphia which would invite
a state convention of county committees to choose a congressional
slate. The opponents of this junto, however, attended the Philadelphia meeting and sought to take over. They were immediately on
their feet, and the huge Dr. James Hutchinson charged that the proceedings were all cut and dried and that the assembled throng were
merely there to ratify a conclusion already determined. Hutchinson,
Alexander James Dallas, and others demanded that a committee of
correspondence be designated to write around and get suggestions
which the committee might later work into a slate. The Federalists,
however, persisted with their plan and held their projected gathering
at Lancaster on September 20, where they nominated a ticket of
eleven Federalists and two Republicans. This ticket was called the
slate of the Conferees. The Republicans in the meantime had solicited
nominations by correspondence, sending 520 letters into 21 counties.
On September 27 their committee announced the results of their letter writing in the form of a ticket of eight Republicans and five
Federalists selected from a suggested list of forty-four. This was
called the slate of the Correspondents. The names of seven of the
nominees were on both tickets—two Republicans and five Federalists,
though of the latter group two or three were rather uncertain in their
Federalism. So the contest was to be between the six Federalists and
the six Republicans who were named by only one of the tickets.

There was no real constituted organization behind these contestants. Some people were indignant at convention nominations, charg-
ing that they were a device to take the choice out of the hands of the
people, "an invasion of the right of the citizens at large to think,
judge, and act for themselves." As a result there was a good deal of
independent ticket-making. A variety were sent around by mail and
advertised in the newspapers under the signatures of "Momus,"
"Mirabeau," "A Republican," or other designations. It would appear
that the so-called Correspondents ticket was actually made up by
Hutchinson and Dallas in cooperation with Albert Gallatin in the
western part of the state. It was all very informal and both major
tickets were the work of self-appointed political operators. There was
little organization and no discipline. When the votes were counted,
the seven on both tickets were overwhelmingly elected, and for the

other six, three Federalists and three Republicans were chosen. Those selected therefore consisted of five firm Federalists, five good Republicans and three waverers who had once been Federalists; Jefferson reported nine of the thirteen as of his persuasion. The Republicans claimed a victory which was hardly theirs, particularly as few paid any attention in the November balloting for electors to their ticket which Dr. Hutchinson had circulated. Pennsylvania was continuing to be sharply divided, rallying to the two standards in nearly equal strength.

The results of the balloting showed Washington again the unanimous choice of the 132 voting electors, but the opposition to Hamiltonian pretensions was indicated by some 50 votes from New York, Virginia, North Carolina, and Georgia, with one from Pennsylvania against Adams and in favor of Clinton. Jefferson received the second votes of the new state of Kentucky and Burr received one from South Carolina. Three electors did not bother to vote. Adams' total of 77 insured him a second term as Vice President and kept him in the line of succession.

The political behavior patterns so far developed were all very rudimentary. It was obvious that in Pennsylvania and in New York there was a tendency toward nominating meetings, local and statewide. But the bulk of the nominating was done by caucusing and public invitation through signed statements in the press. It was still very informal, and nothing like organized parties had emerged. Jefferson resented the fact that Hamilton, in Fenno's *Gazette*, dared "to call the republican party a faction." But that was all it was. Parties as we know them, depending as they do on organization, did not exist. It had been more or less the responsibility of a few, and there is little evidence of any general interest in the mechanics of choice. Washington was the acknowledged leader of all, and public attention had no reason to be focused on anybody else. The details of administration and lawmaking were not available to many nor was there particular interest in who was chosen in the few elections prescribed. The years from 1789 to 1793 were something of a trial heat stirring up little attention; the accustomed local politics was dominant. On the national scene there was little more than the personal relations developing in the chambers of Congress and in the drawing rooms and boarding places in the capital city of Philadelphia. There was little organized connection between Independence Hall and the scattered statehouses. The force operating political behavior was largely such dynamics as are produced in small groups.

··⊰[XII]⊱··

INSTALLING A NEW ENGINE

*T*HE RUDIMENTARY federal politics of the new republic had so far been largely personal, dominated by local conditions and officialdom. Men had come to New York and to Philadelphia, had deliberated in the halls of Congress, and had mingled in the inns, rooming houses and drawing rooms of these cities. They had walked together in the streets. They had corresponded with their connections at home and, at the ends of the sessions, had generally returned thither. Presumably they kept in touch with the elites which were operating most of the state governments. There is little indication that men like Jefferson, Madison, and Hamilton were much in the public eye or that there was a great deal of popular emotion aroused either by Hamilton's finance or at first by the possibility of monarchy. Washington was in command and public confidence in him quieted apprehension: he was such an appropriate instrument to create an American establishment.

The evolution of the various patterns of American political behavior over the years, however, was to demonstrate a basic fact: Unpredictable events that occur anywhere in the world may be politically serviceable despite the fact that they appear to have little relevance to American domestic concerns. Foreign developments on many occasions can quite opportunistically be put to political use.

One of the first and most potent forces which was to be significant in crystallizing the initial phase of the national political machine came, not from home, but from across the seas. This was in fact but another manifestation of a political determinant of long standing. The colonies had always been jealous of their autonomy, of their freedom to manage their own affairs. They had been very conscious—and fearful—of possible interference from Europe, whether from the mother country or from the Continent. They were accustomed to be wary of Europe. And now came new reminders of this old apprehension. The fear of Europe was revived with new force by events across the sea. This force was surrounded by a romantic aura which was particularly influential because so few ever felt it directly. There was little common, matter-of-fact, or everyday about it. In an age which was on the verge of the romantic and in a mood to respond emotionally, such a force was to be potent—it was the French Revolution.

This tumult proved a handy instrument for use in American politics. It began almost simultaneously with Washington's Administration and was to have American repercussions for much more than a decade. At first, news of the revolt was received with rejoicing. Here was tangible evidence that the American political example was an effective agent in bringing liberty to the nation's great friend and ally. The destruction of the Bastille, the Declaration of the Rights of Man, the Constitution of 1791, these all were reminiscent of the recent struggle for liberty on American soil, and these successive steps induced the pleasant feeling that American influence was having an increasing weight in Europe, that it was reforming an ancient and powerful monarchy.

Many in America watched with increasing sympathy and apprehension the attempted encirclement of the new power by the reactionary monarchs of Europe, and at about the time that news of the outbreak of the War of the First Coalition came, this interest and enthusiasm took the form of organization. In June 1792 some ardent friends of France formed a Jacobin Club in Philadelphia. The fortunes of the French armies were followed by these friends of France, first with apprehension but after Valmy with rejoicing.

American interest, however, was not all pro-French by any means. Washington himself had not been too happy about the Constitution of 1791, and he had been disappointed when Louis XVI failed to escape from France in June 1792. These attitudes served to confirm Jefferson in his belief that there were monarchists in America and that Washington or someone else might be a potential king. But a vigorous anti-French opinion did not really take shape until word came in 1793 that Louis XVI had been beheaded and later when the antireligious phases of the Revolution became even more clear. These attacks upon authority and religion aroused disgust and antagonism among many who were wedded to regular and stable life. Then too the outbreak of the general European war was complicating American interests, particularly after Great Britain became involved in February 1793.

The eventual emergence of the Republic of France and the victories of the Republican armies over the forces of the Monarchies awakened anew the French enthusiasm in America. Here were two sister republics, France and the United States. In the American Revolution France had helped the revolting states; now as the new French Republic was threatened it was time to return the aid. The idea of clubs to celebrate the onward march of republicanism began to spread, particularly as war hazards were causing anti-French sentiment to appear.

Those who were naturally friendly to Britain, either emotionally or commercially, were now stimulated to expression by the incidents of the war. In a misguided moment the French Republic sent over as its first minister an enthusiast, Citizen Genêt, who ostentatiously violated American neutrality by using Atlantic coast seaports as bases for French privateer operation and by other forms of behavior diplomatically objectionable. Even Jefferson, ardent friend of France that he was, had to join in dismissing him and to draft the papers involved. On the other hand, a contrary situation was intensified when British war vessels began to drive American ships out of a lucrative trade supplying France and to impress "British deserters" in the American merchant marine.

The sum total of all this was to arouse once more the emotions of the American Revolution. Love of France for her aid, hatred of the British who now were charged with a desire to destroy the French Republic and American commerce, suspicions of French anarchists and atheists who were believed to be seeking to destroy constituted authority and religion, these contrary emotions stirred public opinion. Those who wanted to keep on good terms commercially with Great Britain, despite her aggravating incursions on certain branches of American commerce, vied with those who denounced impressment and seizure as invasions of American rights. So changes were rung again on love of liberty and hatred of tyranny, on the one hand, and on defiance of dangerous radicalism and the need to maintain profitable business relations with the great commercial power, on the other. And little of this affected many people directly, for most of it was far away—but it was so emotionally satisfying. These materials could be useful in any political contest. Hamilton and Jefferson and his associates could use them in their maneuvering.

Washington, in conducting the establishment, was much troubled by these contrary emotional expressions. He took an eminently practical attitude. His government could not afford war in its infancy, particularly with a great naval power when he had no navy with which to fight. So he proclaimed neutrality and endeavored to work for a diplomatic settlement with Great Britain. To this end he sent Chief Justice John Jay on a special mission to London in May 1794. There the British were not of much help, and eventually Jay came home with a treaty which had some features that proved politically very vulnerable.

While Jay was negotiating, more oil was poured on the political fires. Most of Hamilton's finance had not created a very perceptible popular ripple. But there was one element in it which had begun to exhibit politically usable features. In searching for sources of revenue, Hamilton had proposed to tax luxuries, notably liquor, as perhaps as painless a form of exaction as could be devised. However, it developed that certain of these excise levies would be due from frontier whiskey distillers who were short of cash, as they lived largely by barter. Besides, they dwelt in communities where whiskey was a medium of exchange as well as a standard article of diet and where citizens were naturally resentful of any governmental restraint or exaction. It was only a matter of time before some political incident would occur in which lawbreaking and insubordination would threaten and perhaps precipitate violence.

The most disaffected area was western Pennsylvania. Incidents had been occurring for two years. When these had taken the form of a defiant convention, Washington had issued a proclamation in 1792, admonishing citizens to refrain from obstructing the collection of the excise tax, but the climax did not occur until 1794 when open resistance to federal authority could be described picturesquely as the Whiskey Insurrection. The local federal collector was defied by force of arms in a move which culminated in an attack upon the home of John Neville, the excise inspector of Allegheny County; in the melee the house was burned down and one attacker killed.

This violence and resistance to law was not confined to Pennsylvania. There were examples in the Carolinas in relation to the excise, and in Virginia there were outbreaks against the Nonintercourse Acts which Congress had passed to coerce Great Britain in retaliation for her attacks on American commerce with France. These explosions were connected in the eyes of the Federalist leaders with the factional politics stirred up by the organization and spread of the so-called "Democratic" societies.

These political clubs were modeled in part on American prototypes which had emerged in the Revolution, such as the Sons of Liberty and, later, Franklin's Society for Political Enquiries of 1787 and the Sons of Tammany formed in Philadelphia and New York in 1789. More immediate in their influence were the political clubs formed in Paris during the early phase of the French Revolution, and from which the American clubs drew their inspiration.

In America these clubs were most active in 1793 and 1794 and numbered all told about forty-two scattered throughout the states, with nine in Pennsylvania. They were frequented by those who were friendly to France, and they served to promote a current fad of adopting French republican customs. They used the new forms of address, "Citizen" and "Citizeness," they sang *Ça ira* and the *Marseillaise*, and their convivial atmosphere was a vivid thread in the social pattern. Their talk was mainly of politics, and the word "Republican" began to have local use. They were sometimes referred to as promoting the "republican interest," as it was called, implying of course that there was a "monarchist" interest to be combated and that prominent in that interest were Hamilton and his associates working to strengthen central government, Washington's establishment.

The events of the summer of 1794 in western Pennsylvania helped to define and sharpen political division. When President Washington learned that the United States marshal had been resisted violently and the inspector of revenue attacked and burned out, he concluded that unless some stern measures were taken, federal authority would be reduced to zero. So he decided upon a great show of force, mobilized 15,000 militia from Pennsylvania, New Jersey, Delaware, and Maryland, and marched them into western Pennsylvania. Conciliators had been sent on ahead and they and the large number of troops prevented any clash. When Washington reported the matter to Congress in November, he connected the "Democratic" societies with the insurrection, referring to the agency performed by "certain self-created societies" which, he declared, had been active to defeat the law. The implication of Washington's words to the undiscriminating public was that he believed the "Democratic" societies were dangerous, subversive, and anarchistic, encouraging citizens to wanton disregard of law and order.

The so-called insurrection in the West had brought before Washington a problem basic in democracy, the problem of the tolerance of opposition by those in authority. So far there had not yet been any national political contest: Washington had been elected by acclamation. Now there was armed defiance to federal authority in western Pennsylvania. Was the American system going to concede "the consent to loose" and suffer an opposition to be left free to grow without

interference from authority? President Washington found this a difficult assignment. He and certain of the well-established elites in New
England appeared to think of the growing opposition groups as con-
spirators plotting the overthrow of established government, despite
the fact that these "Democratic" societies were quite open in their
operations. The truth was that the New England elites were the ones
who operated in secrecy. They shunned publicity and liked to keep
their meetings and their decision-making profound secrets.

These novelties in political behavior made the year 1794 indeed a
memorable one. This was the time to choose the Fourth Congress,
and a new thread was added to the pattern of political contest. This
had become almost inevitable after 1792 as the furor over the more
violent phase of the French Revolution and the repercussions of the
war between France and England were increasingly felt.

When Great Britain began to bear down on American trade with
France, the "Democratic" societies took a generally truculent attitude
toward England and demanded that friends of Britain and foes of
liberty and freedom of trade be defeated for Congress. The membership of the "Democratic" societies was prominent in this. They
sought to mobilize sentiment against the congressmen or candidates
who were in this category. They promoted the support of candidates
who were pro-French in sympathy and undertook to get out the
vote. However, by the time Washington's allusions to these self-
constituted societies which had been stimulated by the Whiskey Insurrection became current, most of the elections were over. Those
keeping count were now aware that this Fourth Congress was definitely different in its composition from its predecessors. It was cur-
rently believed that this result was due in some part to the activities of
these clubs. This, however, was probably farfetched, for they were
rather pressure groups than political machines, and Jefferson, Madison, or other national figures were not connected with them. But the
phenomenon of contest for control of the House had to a certain
degree entered into American political life. Also, despite fear of subversive activity and the growth of the idea of controlling free association, the consent to loose was being established. The establishment
had lost control of the lower house, not on any domestic issue, but
because of events in Europe which revived patterns of thinking current in 1776.

The first real contest for power was projected on a national scene
by some who were interested in contesting the presidential election of
1796. Never again would the spirit of acclamation return that had

dominated 1788 and 1792. Yet no one was thinking of a campaign to persuade voters to support any ticket, party, or person, because the electors were still largely appointed by the legislatures of the states and few questioned the assumed fact that electors were men of independent judgment. As the legislatures did most of the choosing, the election to that extent was in the hands of statehouse operators, the Betas. But there were new developments in political behavior that were suggesting new patterns.

Some of these were occurring in Philadelphia where the new nation's representatives continued their association on Independence Square and its neighboring streets. On this stage the cast was changing. Jefferson left the State Department and went back to Monticello as 1793 came to an end. Hamilton was subjected to increasing scrutiny by his opponents, who were always suspecting corruption in Treasury operations but finding only somewhat arbitrary but honest administration on the part of the Secretary. Early in 1795 he tired of this and went back to New York City. This left Madison, William B. Giles, and other Virginians to marshal the Republican interest, as in fact they always had, for Jefferson had not done much real organizing work. Fisher Ames, Theodore Sedgwick, and their associates could be thought of as Administration leaders.

Madison had always been the floor leader of the opposition in the House, but for the first two Congresses his leadership had been almost wholly negative. He and his associates opposed the Treasury policies of Hamilton, particularly its later phases, notably the creation of a bank. Their appeal was to section and class. The advent of the European general war in 1793 presented a new opportunity to Madison and his associates, an opportunity for a republican program, one designed to rally all groups and sections. This policy demanded an aggressive attitude toward Great Britain, who was destroying American commercial freedom in her efforts to defeat France. By resolutions and other maneuvers Madison and his associates attempted to rouse the normal antagonism to Britain which had existed since the Revolution and to create a reliably consistent Republican bloc in Congress by the organization of the first elementary party caucus. This they would do, not by innovation, but by following well-known emotional grooves.

Their efforts during the Third Congress, 1793–95, had not borne much fruit. But the Fourth Congress presented a greater opportunity. When this body assembled in December 1795, significant changes had taken place. French sympathy, the Democratic societies, a natural desire for change, interest in new faces, and unfortunate antagonisms had done their work. For the first time, the Republican bloc was larger than the Federalist corps and now commanded a majority of the membership, the first time any identifiable group had done so. There were fifty-seven Republicans, forty Federalists and only seven independent members. However, despite this majority, a Federalist, Jonathan Dayton of New Jersey, was chosen speaker, because his association with some Republicans gave him their votes as well as those of the Federalists. Political groupings and loyalties were still in the fluid stage. Yet a closer concert was developing among the Philadelphia contenders, the Federal establishment and the Republican interest, and people of like mind in the states. The opposition congressmen were seeking to arouse sentiment and gain support in their constituencies. They were writing back home to the local elites or courthouse associates and stimulating them to persuade others to hold meetings, to pass resolutions. Likewise, they communicated with the legislative leaders at home, attempting to influence them to provide official state pronouncements to be sent to senators and congressmen to demonstrate either the strength of the opposition to the establishment or popular support of its measures.

For there was a second new circumstance, namely there was the bill to appropriate the money to implement the Jay treaty with England recently ratified by the Senate and which was now before the House. The opportunity was therefore at hand for a political maneuver which the Virginians were planning. The appropriation of this money, under the Constitution, must be initiated in the House. John Beckley, the Virginia clerk of the National House, is credited with proposing a scheme to rally the opponents to the Establishment to defeat the appropriation, thereby solidifying a phalanx strong enough to carry the election of 1796. Patterns used in the Revolution and fitted to the limited communication facilities of the day were utilized. As in colonial times, one of the legislatures would make a proposal and invite response from similar bodies in the other capitols. These resolves and responses would be circulated, collected, and presented to Congress as evidence that popular opinion was opposed to the treaty.

In one of the first attempts at operating a coordination of federal politics on the two-level basis, the beginning of a new type of political machinery was made manifest in 1796 on the eve of the third presidential election as an instrument designed to direct it. Virginia proceeded to pass resolutions congratulating the two Virginia sena-

tors for voting against the ratification of Jay's instrument and calling
for a constitutional amendment to give the House a part in treaty-
making. Supporting resolutions were invited from other states. This
move proved a failure. Not only did other states prove indifferent or
hostile to Virginia's plea but the Federalists were aroused to action.
They organized the signing of a flood of petitions favorable to the
Jay treaty. Hamilton got his ward leaders in New York City to work
to obtain signatures approaching in number the totals in the most
vigorously contested elections. Under this stream of influence the
House majority against the treaty, which was well over a score, despite Madison's effort to organize a caucus to hold the Republicans
together, dwindled to nothing and the appropriation was made. The
Republicans were thus badly defeated in a move designed to mobilize
their forces for victory in the presidential election. The Federalists
were now alerted and organized, and the spring elections in New
York, Massachusetts, and elsewhere showed the tide again turning in
their favor. The voters were more interested in peace than in the
politics of the Jeffersonian faction. The plans of Madison and Beckley
to organize a favorable agency to resist British pretensions had failed.
Hamilton was still the superior tactician.

Accompanying this effort at organization was some slight effort at
creating a nominating mechanism. Any such developments were
hindered greatly because few knew what Washington planned to do.
If he would stand again, there was little point in making any effort,
and he made no public announcement. He had confided in Adams as
early as March that he would not serve again and that he expected
Adams to succeed him. On the other hand, as early as 1794 the
French minister had reported that he had expected Jefferson to succeed. Until Washington spoke, however, nobody could be sure.
Jefferson himself was back in Monticello seemingly with no political
effort in contemplation. And there were no announcements.

Despite this silence and lack of activity, there was some movement
in political waters, particularly in Virginia. The political activists of
the Old Dominion already had developed a sense of responsibility for
supplying leadership. Theirs was the native state of President Washington; of two of his Secretaries of State, Thomas Jefferson and
Edmund Randolph; and of James Madison who was probably the
man of greatest influence in Congress and the one who had become
the legislative leader of the maneuvers to contain Hamilton and protect the Republican interest. Madison's concern was to prevent
Hamilton from determining who should succeed Washington and to

promote Jefferson's chances to defeat the Vice President, John Adams, who in those simple days of the first establishment seemed the obvious choice to succeed the President. Jefferson himself did not "run" in any sense of the word. He and Adams were old associates in the Revolutionary effort, and he preferred Madison to stand against Adams if anyone did. Madison, however, was promoting Jefferson's candidacy and was thinking in terms of Jefferson and Burr. Clinton had just retired from the governorship of New York on account of "ill health," somewhat discredited by the sharp means used in 1792 to count him in, and had been succeeded by Jay. Burr had many friends among the Federalists, and some of their electors might give him one of their votes.

Among the Federalists, Hamilton, now back home in New York, was undertaking to play the decisive role. He was keeping in touch with Philadelphia through Senator Rufus King. He never liked Adams—some thought he tried to block him in 1789—and it seems that secretly he hoped that he, Hamilton, might succeed Washington. At any rate he seemed determined to be the kingmaker. His choice was Jay, but when the Jay treaty proved too unpopular, he began to look elsewhere. He, together with Jay, now governor of New York, and Senator Rufus King, began to search for someone from the South who could run with Adams, the idea seeming to be that this southern vice presidential candidate might get more votes than Adams, who was unpopular in the South, and thus slip in ahead. Through John Marshall, Hamilton first tried to get Patrick Henry to accept this role. John Marshall sounded out the ancient Patriot through Lee but had to report failure. Then Hamilton, at King's suggestion, fixed on General Thomas Pinckney of South Carolina, negotiator of the popular Pinckney treaty with Spain and still in Europe. He then in effect wrote his intimates that Adams and Pinckney would be the two best names, with the clear intimation that enough southerners were expected to vote for Pinckney but not Adams and thus ensure Pinckney's election. Therefore in May 1796, before Congress adjourned June 1, it was determined at a "quasi caucus" in Philadelphia that Adams and Pinckney were the names to be used.

The Republican interest believed that more formal action was essential. During the congressional session in the spring of 1796 at Philadelphia, Madison and that convenient Republican legman, John Beckley, were at work attempting to get some formal agreement on a ticket uniting the Virginia and New York interest, which Madison had been engineering since 1791. The building of this combination was slow work because Burr was not trusted by some people of importance. A caucus of United States senators of the Republican interest had been tried, the first of its kind. It had approved Burr by a majority of one vote over Pierce Butler of South Carolina who was favored to prevent the South Carolina electors from voting for Thomas Pinckney. Then Senator John Langdon of New Hampshire came in and made it a tie, and the meeting broke up as the Butler supporters walked out. When Madison went home early in June, there had been no binding decision reached. Beckley carried on further negotiation with Gallatin and David Rittenhouse in Pennsylvania and with the Livingston clan in New York. The principal argument for endorsing Burr was to keep him from joining the Federalists. By July there appeared to be some agreement to pair Jefferson and Burr.

There was still much uncertainty as to who, if anybody, was running for anything and, if so, for what, yet a certain amount of pamphleteering and newspaper writing was stimulated. Adams' friends had something in the nature of a slogan that sounded like "Peace and Prosperity," while Jefferson was proclaimed the friend of the Rights of Man and foe of advocates of any "hereditary power and distinction"; his friends attempted to invoke a Spirit of Ninety-six, again looking backward to the Revolutionary experience. Adams was attacked as an aristocrat, a dangerous monarchist who acquiesced in the unequal distribution of wealth and who opposed the Constitution, a Tory friend of Great Britain. He would turn the republic over to speculators and stockjobbers, he was the enemy of the sturdy farmer and the poor man, bound body and soul to the interests of commerce. As an agent of the northern merchants, he was a foe to the South. He was pictured as "frigid in council, phlegmatic in determination, and slow in the execution of his resolves."

Jefferson was denounced as a red Republican, an atheist, a leveler, a radical who flouted sound government and condoned violence, a revolutionary and friend of France who had opposed the Constitution and was careless of property rights. He was a destroying agent who would let the nation go bankrupt and its business languish. He lacked firmness of character, he had failed as governor of Virginia during the Revolution and had quit the State Department at a critical time. His friends denied these charges and defended his administrative capacity. Washington was reported as desiring Jefferson for his successor. Some professed to believe that he was the only man who could reconcile contending factions. Southern Federalists devoted some energy to advancing Pinckney. They labored to show that he was neither a British Tory nor a Francophile, neither a tool of Hamilton nor a Jeffersonian physiocrat who would sacrifice all to the agricultural interest.

But this campaign of scurrilous abuse and ardent defense did not get under way until late. Popular interest during the summer was slight. Washington was still a potential candidate who made no public statement as to his plans. Jefferson himself seemed to prefer to be Vice President with Adams, to carry on the idea of an establishment. Not until early fall, less than six weeks before the scheduled choice of electors, did public interest seem to waken, and this was in part due to Washington's belated announcement of his own withdrawal.

Many who read the General's farewell address which he published late in September did not fail to note his trenchant observations on the baneful influence of foreign interest upon American political behavior or his stern judgment against parties and party spirit. These influences had troubled Washington much during his Presidency. He had never been sympathetic to the French Revolution's more violent course, and its reflection in the factional developments in the United States had been a veritable plague. He had demanded the recall of the French diplomat Genêt and had dismissed his own Secretary of State, Randolph, when he came to believe he was encouraging this interference. Now he was too well aware that another French representative, Pierre Auguste Adet, was at it again. In the spring of 1796 it had transpired that the diplomat had sent two agents into the western states specially instructed to promote the fortunes of the Republican interest, as friends of France, and late in the summer he received authorization to do what he could to insure the election of Jefferson by publication of a British program of reprisal upon American shipping if Jefferson won. Adet made a trip into New England to encourage Adams' enemies there, and on the eve of the election in Pennsylvania he began a campaign designed to show that the election of Adams meant war. He published a series of proclamations and letters from France to this effect in the hope that these would cause the peaceful to join the Republicans in voting for Jefferson.

A sense of contest became more manifest when at length it was apparent that Adams and Jefferson were being supported for the office and that a personal rivalry, which probably didn't exist, was being advertised. Candidates for elector were beginning to announce their preferences as they bid for votes. In New York party tickets appeared, one called a Federal Republican ticket and another a Republican ticket. In Boston there was a Republican Federal list. But the most clear-cut partisan battle was to be fought in Pennsylvania. The Federalist faction had been reasonably successful there to date, and the Federalist legislature hoped to make sure of the selection of a full ticket of Federalist electors by returning to the general ticket system. The Federalist members had then chosen a routine electoral ticket including several men designed to attract German support. They expected to depend upon the fact that a variety of county seat elites had control of the election machinery, that voters had little interest in these four-year contests for electors and did not come out to the polls in any large number. The county town people would get out enough of the neighbors and that would suffice.

But there was an enterprising operator at work with other ideas. John Beckley was now a Pennsylvania citizen and a resident of Philadelphia. He and some associates planned a secret campaign to appeal to country voters and get them out in sufficient quantity to overwhelm the county seat elites. A secret state convention was called to meet during a gathering at Carlisle ostensibly to dispose of lands which the commonwealth held for taxes. There a big-name electoral ticket was chosen which had on it some of Pennsylvania's best-known sons. This was to be kept secret. It was to be communicated first to key men in each county to be passed around by word of mouth among the country folk. Then pamphlets were printed and distributed pointing out advantages of having a southern rather than a New England President. Beckley also sent around bulletins from time to time giving out false information showing Jefferson way out ahead, even to the point of announcing Hamilton as advising Jefferson's election to keep the nation out of a war with France. He sought vigorously to defeat members of Congress who had supported the Jay treaty. Handbills were distributed, and then finally, late in October, a corps of party workers bearing printed lists were sent to each county, and as all votes had to be handwritten, the county workers were urged to see that the voters had tickets properly copied out to take to the polls. Adet also sought to add his weight and worked hard to get friends of France to wear red, white, and blue cockades and march to the polls so decorated.

This well-planned organization threw what was thought by the confident Federalists to be a sure thing into the doubtful column in Pennsylvania. Early returns showed everything in doubt, and the returns were slow. Finally the official date for announcing the result, November 18, arrived, but returns from three counties—Greene, Fayette, and Westmoreland—were not in. If the governor proclaimed the result without those three counties, the Federalists had the ticket. He temporized, referred the matter to the state supreme court, and finally a week later, even without Greene County, he proclaimed the result. Thirteen Jeffersonians, one Federalist, and one committed to both were elected. Would this put Jefferson into Washington's seat?

The swing in Pennsylvania indicated a very close election, and in October and November certain interesting maneuvers by correspondence developed. Hamilton again sought to guide the Federalist electors; this time he probably feared that their tactics might elect Jefferson despite the fact that it appeared that Adams would have a slim majority, razor thin. He realized that some southern electors might vote for Pinckney and not Adams in the hope of electing the former and that, anticipating this, some New England electors might drop Pinckney. So narrow was the margin between Adams and Jefferson probably going to be that, if this game were played, Adams and Pinckney might both come below Jefferson. Therefore Hamilton tried his best to get the New England electors to give equal support to Adams and Pinckney. Hamilton proved he would stop at little in his effort to get these New England electors to give such support. Just as the Massachusetts electors were meeting, he supplied an item which appeared in the Boston *Centinel* to the effect that the vote of the Vermont electors was invalid because their authority to act was based on a resolution of the legislature rather than on a statute. There was no truth in this at all, but the fear of the loss to Adams of that state's four votes and the consequent greater possibility of the election of Jefferson led all but three of Massachusetts' sixteen electors to vote for Pinckney as well as Adams rather than scatter their second votes. This maneuver did not change the result, as Vermont's votes were regular and counted, but had they been invalid, Jefferson would have been elected, for so many of New England's second votes had been thrown away that Pinckney could not have beaten him. To Hamilton, had this maneuver elected Pinckney, it would have been so much the better. The defeat of Jefferson was, however, probably his great objective.

There also was a Burr intrigue, particularly in New England. His friend Speaker Jonathan Dayton of New Jersey advised certain of his friends there that Adams and Pinckney were doomed and unless some New Englanders voted for Burr, they were sure to have Jefferson. A final confusing element in New England was provided by Adet's interference. One of the reasons why Connecticut electors would not vote for Pinckney was Adet's intrigue. The people of the Nut-meg State dreaded the "corrupting French influence" which they foresaw if Adams were defeated. One writer in the *Connecticut Courier* pointed out the possible need for the secession of New England in the near future and the destruction of the Union if this dangerous Franco-Republican influence prevailed—and this some twenty years before the Hartford Convention.

The sum total of these maneuvers and intrigues demonstrated that the electors showed a good deal of independence in their second choices. Many were suspicious of the backers of Pinckney and Burr, believing them to be instruments to defeat either Adams or Jefferson. The result was that the electors from Federalist New Hampshire, Rhode Island, and Connecticut, together with three each from Massachusetts and Maryland, would not support Pinckney. Burr lost badly, for Virginia, North and South Carolina, and Georgia turned against him. He got less than half as many votes as Jefferson; only thirty of Jefferson's electors voted for him. Virginia voted for Sam Adams instead of Burr, and it appears that some of the latter's supporters hoped that John Adams might be re-elected Vice President to serve with Jefferson in the first place. The loss of Pennsylvania by Adams by a slim margin of some two hundred votes would have cost him the election had not a lone Federalist elector carried his district in Virginia, another won in Pennsylvania on the general ticket, and a third announced North Carolina Federalist had been chosen by the North Carolina legislature with eleven Jeffersonian companions. South Carolina voted for Jefferson and Pinckney, and had not eighteen of New England's electors voted for other people, Pinckney would have been elected. Did they do this because of Hamilton's urging, and if so, where does the result leave the score in regard to Hamilton's judgment motivation? Certainly the day of the straight party ticket was not yet.

Even today there is no surety as to motivation. There is no way of calculating who the people wanted, so various were the agencies of choice. In the eight states which chose their electors by popular vote Adams lost the large commonwealths of Virginia and Pennsylvania, in the latter by the closest of margins. Every indication is that the nation was nearly evenly divided. The result showed no trend, no national leadership. There is little evidence that anybody but Washington had captured the popular imagination. The outcome was in a sense, save perhaps in Pennsylvania, in the hands of the political elites in the sixteen states. Their condition, characteristics, interests, personalities, prejudices, and whims were to determine the result.

Summing up these sixteen variables, the nearest factor discernible is that the electoral votes followed geography and location more than anything else in the absence of any national leadership of commanding emotional appeal. There were eight northern and eight southern states, with seventy-three and sixty-five votes each. Adams could have expected seventy-three plus the ten votes of border states Delaware and Maryland. Actually, clever and unexpected organization took from him fourteen Pennsylvania votes, and he failed to get three in Maryland, but he added one each from Virginia and North Carolina. The final result, 71 to 68, was a remarkably accurate correspondence to the sectional distribution of votes. Adams won because the northern states had a slightly larger number of electoral votes than the southern. The predominant factor was proximity, local and sectional interest. The Federalist Adams had the advantage of being in office, his supporters represented accepted and recognized power, the new American establishment. The Republican interest had not attracted enough attention or support, despite their use of the 1776 tactics. Nor had they achieved sufficient organization to provide them with strength enough to turn out a seated power.

The final indication of the uniqueness of this contest is found in the evidence provided by the so-called contestants themselves. Jefferson perhaps preferred to serve as Vice President with Adams than to work for the chief place, and Adams preferred to have Jefferson as Vice President rather than his ostensible running mate, Thomas Pinckney. There was never to be anything like this again. But as yet there was no effective central party organization or discipline. Results were decided in state capitols, and attempts at national direction counted for little. For the moment the new establishment seemed in the way of perpetuating itself.

·⊰[XIII]⊱·

THE CRYSTALLIZATION OF FACTION

*T*HOSE IN the full political floodlight in this first decade did not think much in terms of national political strategy. Organized politics on that level can hardly be said to have existed, despite the federal two-level pattern of government. The ambitious played by ear or by sitting down and writing something. Also, there were the Philadelphia and statehouse elite causeries. The power in politics still remained in the state governments and they had provided little in the way of innovation. When the policies of the new federal government had been formulated, it was done in the small groups of men operating in New York and Philadelphia. There the principal forces had been those characteristic of such small groups from scattered localities without much facility for communication with their constituencies. Much depended on the personal relations and capabilities of a few men. Those in the first dominant group were innovators, with Hamilton as the creative mind, if not the political intelligence. His innovations, which Washington supported, and the way in which they were enacted had stirred up the opposition of Madison and Jefferson. But they themselves were not presently innovators, rather they looked backward and tried to revive the Patriot emotion against monarchical tyranny which their aggravated imaginations could accuse Hamilton of plotting behind Washington's great reputation.

This Patriot revival failed, despite the novelty and appeal of the Democratic societies idea imported from France, and the new republic passed through the presidential elections of 1792 and 1796 without any effective organized opposition on the federal level. The result appeared to be a union of Adams and Jefferson in office with a pattern which would have made Jefferson's succession to Adams and the continuance of the establishment inevitable. Adams, after two terms as Vice President, was succeeding Washington, and Jefferson, now Vice President, might be thought of as similarly succeeding Adams.

Jefferson was not yet an innovator, and he might well have been content with this possibility: he was only fifty-six, eleven years younger than Washington, eight years younger than Adams. So when Adams and Jefferson took the oaths on March 4, 1797, they probably thought little of 1800, but rather of what to do about Anglo-French relations. Whether Adams and Jefferson would have given much attention to 1800 if left to themselves we may not hazard, but their hands and minds were to be forced by Hamilton and Burr and the complexities which their ambitions and behavior advanced. The French and the British were also to have much to do with it—as Washington had feared.

From the standpoint of Philadelphia operation, the Federalists had improved their position; for the time being Jefferson and his associates were on the sidelines. Jefferson was probably again thinking more negatively than positively. He wanted to head off Hamilton and probably would have been content to work with John Adams along lines of anti-Hamiltonian cooperation.

Foreign affairs continued to dominate the emerging American politics in a way which became spectacular. The continued warfare between France and England and the rising star of French military glory involved the United States very seriously. The refusal of the republic to take sides was met by French reprisals on American commerce and rejection of American representatives unless, as was intimated in the foreign office at Paris, they would pay what amounted to bribes. This humiliating situation, communicated to Congress by President Adams in the spring of 1798, set off a political chain reaction. President Adams and the Federalists responded to the anger against France with legislation for increased armament and preparations for the war which seemed imminent. Adams found himself popular and gave vent to fervent sentiments by voice to crowds who assembled at his doorstep and by pen to the many who would read his words in print.

The Republicans were loath to believe these dispatches. They were libelous, they hoped, a Federalist plant. Jefferson felt that they were being used by Adams and the majority in Congress as an excuse to pass laws which in effect would overthrow liberty and free government and establish monarchy or some form of police state. Feeling ran high. Federalists paraded the streets of Philadelphia mounting the black cockade, and President Adams put on a military uniform, a sword, and a similar cockade before coming to his front door to harangue the marchers. Republicans, identified by red, white, and blue cockades, likewise took to the streets, shouting praise of much maligned France. Some of these groups tangled. Adams feared the "reds" might attack his residence and smuggled arms and ammunition through the back entrance. His servants were armed and the house barricaded. On the night of May 9, the President slept little. Guards were at his door. There was some street fighting, and one man was arrested as the local light-horse cavalry patrolled the streets.

To William Cobbett, editor of *Porcupine's Gazette*, this Republican activity was treason. Irish immigrants and French fugitives were uniting in a plot to overthrow the government. Dangerous "red" aliens were poised to strike. The Federalist majority in Congress rushed to the breach. Not only did they vote men, ships, and taxes, but they enacted alien, sedition, and naturalization laws designed to rid the nation of undesirable foreigners and to stop the abuse of Adams and his party in the opposition press. These were direct assaults upon the Rights of Man, and the Jeffersonians once more could look back to the Revolution.

During most of this furor Jefferson had to face the bitter realization that France was destroying the political power of its Republican friends. He found himself politically and socially much on the outside and without influence, certainly in Philadelphia. The Federalists were firmly entrenched as they had regained control of the House in 1796 and seemed sure to increase their power in the mid-term congressional elections of 1798. The Vice President found himself in an intolerable situation. He was further activated by the fact that the Federalists were planning to raise an army and that Washington and Hamilton were to have command of it.[1] President Adams himself was being maneuvered into the background with the connivance of the Cabinet of Hamilton men which he had inherited from Washington. Furthermore, Adams continued to be absent from Philadelphia for much of the year and tried to administer the government by mail from Brain-

1. In July to September 1798 everyone was in favor of Washington for commander of the reactivated army. He would accept if he could have Hamilton for Inspector General and active field officer. So it was Hamilton, C. E. Pinckney, and Knox, major generals; and William North, adjutant general; with Jonathan Dayton and William S. Smith, brigadier generals. These were confirmed by the Senate except Smith, who was the President's son-in-law. This list put Knox, who was senior, at the bottom. Adams up in Quincy reversed the order and dated the commissions Knox, Pinckney, and Hamilton. The Cabinet resented this; Secretary Wolcott's skillful diplomacy was put in motion and by the time Washington's protest got to Adams, he had agreed to date commissions all on the same day and permit Washington to decide as to duties. Washington then set up the list Hamilton, Pinckney, and Knox. Both of the latter outranked Hamilton, and Knox then refused the commission.

tree, Massachusetts. As the Alien and Sedition Acts began to be enforced, Jefferson's fears of monarchy again were pronounced.

Under these pressures Jefferson now really sought to organize the Republican interest and to seek the Presidency. Heretofore he had not been of single purpose; often he had been negatively rather than positively oriented. He had wished to oppose and prevent rather than to promote and win. However, over the years he had been developing a political correspondence with people in the various states, and he had been careful of his relations with Burr, whom he probably neither liked nor trusted. He had on occasion given direction and advice to Madison. Now in the summer of 1798 he began to organize in a fashion typical of Patriot days.

The passage of the Federalist tax measures and the Alien and Sedition Acts were signals for the revival of Revolutionary political tactics. Here were another Stamp Act, new attacks on liberty, and fresh evidence that the Federalists wished to outlaw opposition, to make political partisanship and criticism illegal. The great Washington had condemned opposition, and the Federalist members of Congress now had gone further and taken steps toward making it unlawful. It was both natural and easy for the Jeffersonians again to look back to the halcyon days of 1776. They would raise "liberty poles" and issue manifestoes against tyranny, invoking a Spirit of '98.

Jefferson and those associates would prepare a platform—had ·he not been principal author of the Declaration of Independence?—and attempt to have it accepted in the various states. As in the Revolution the legislatures would be the means. The Virginians would start by securing the cooperation of some state legislature other than Virginia's and then supply resolutions to be adopted and sent to the other state lawmakers for endorsement. The first idea had been to start in North Carolina, but the Federalists won a victory there that made the state doubtful, so Kentucky was selected. Jefferson and his circle prepared a set of resolutions which were transmitted to Kentucky, through agents who were kept unaware of Jefferson's part in their preparation. In these resolutions each state was held to be the judge of whether a federal law was constitutional. The Kentucky legislature thereupon declared the Alien and Sedition Acts to be "altogether void and of no effect" and called upon other states to do likewise. Madison prepared resolutions less sweeping which were passed by the Virginia legislature. The states must protect the republic against a military dictatorship and protest against the Alien and Sedition Acts as subversive "of the general principles of free government" and "levelled against the right of freely examining public characters and measures, and of free communication among the people." These famous resolutions of 1798 declared the condemned acts unconstitutional and invited other states to cooperate "in maintaining unimpaired the authorities, rights and liberties reserved to the states . . . or to the people." The Virginia resolves, however, did not go as far as the Kentucky pronouncement, which declared for the principle of nullification.

Jefferson now for the first time was busily engaged in party leadership. He continued to develop a new line of propaganda. The Federalists had finally deprived Beckley of the clerkship of the U.S. House of Representatives which had supported him since 1789, but Jefferson persuaded Judge Thomas McKean, just elected governor of Pennsylvania, to appoint him clerk of the Philadelphia mayor's court and also clerk of the orphans court of Philadelphia County. Beckley likewise became chairman of the Republican Philadelphia committee of correspondence and began to write. He prepared an *Epitome and Vindication of the Public Life and Character of Thomas Jefferson,* and five thousand of these were printed. Jefferson collected money to pay the bills, and they were distributed, Burr being one of the chief agents. Albert Gallatin and Tench Coxe were likewise busy.

Jefferson himself drafted a program, which he communicated in a letter to Elbridge Gerry. He stood for economy and free trade. He was opposed to a standing army and would depend on militia and a small navy for coast defense. He wanted no new treaties, no entangling alliances. He was for freedom of religion and the press. Reason rather than force should be used to refute criticism.

The President on his part was for some time uncertain as to his future and his support. He wanted a second term, but he had opponents in his own party who were making efforts to supersede him, particularly after his peace efforts. Some influence was exerted to persuade Washington to run again. He would have none of it and died before any great pressure could be put upon him. Adams meanwhile had finally taken the bit in his own teeth. In the congressional elections of 1798–99, the Republicans had been decisively beaten, and he made a significant decision. The American people really wanted peace and he would do his best to secure it. He was done with uniforms, swords, and warlike speeches. He would negotiate with France and kill off General Hamilton's opportunities to gain fame in arms. So he dismissed his Secretary of State, Timothy Pickering, and secured the resignation of James McHenry, his Secretary of War, who had been serving Hamilton rather than Adams.

Then he turned to a situation which had emerged in Pennsylvania. In that commonwealth there had been a concerted effort to resist the levying of the federal tax to support the increase of arms. Certain men under the leadership of an auctioneer, John Fries, had been convicted of treason for this intransigence. Adams now pardoned them. At the same time he proceeded very slowly in enforcing the sedition law, and in appointing the officers called for to organize the enlarged army, he attempted to woo Republican support. By December 1799 he had made clear his purpose to encourage a third, or middle-ground, faction, which would repudiate the extreme Federalist position of intolerance and the leadership of Hamilton. In that same month at an informal caucus at Senator Bingham's, certain Federalists decided to support Adams for the Presidency on this moderate basis. The Chief Executive continued his battle for peace, and Congress followed his recommendation, passing an act to disband the volunteer army. But in the end it turned out that the result in 1800 did not hinge on what either Adams or Jefferson did. The battle, so far as there was one, and it must be borne in mind that there was little popular interest in presidential contests in those days, was decided more or less by what was done in the states.

In the states, unfortunately for Adams, the Federalists had advanced little in developing a capacity for organization although in New York and Pennsylvania they had made progress and in Virginia they put forth some effort, following the example of their opponents. In New England, where they were strongest, they had their own peculiar elites who drew their strengths from the custom of long-standing reverence of their establishments. They depended upon their press to develop a propaganda which was both venomous and scurrilous in its attacks upon Jefferson's morals and ethics, even accusing him of scientific animal vivisection.

Neither Federal nor Republican organization advanced in efficiency, or even existence, in any very perceptible fashion in the South. There the population was largely rural and scattered. The old English tradition of the influence of the landed magnate was prevalent. Elections were partly social events, enjoyed by many of the voters who came for a holiday made relaxing by the custom of treats offered by the candidates. But the problem of electing Jefferson so impressed certain of his Virginia associates that organization in the Old Dominion was essential. In 1796 Adams had been elected because single electors from Virginia and North Carolina had voted for Adams. There, too, four Federalists had been elected to Congress in the 1798–99 elections. Federal success was a threat.

The Virginia Republicans took two steps in 1800. They secured the passage of a law which required that the electors should be voted for on a general ticket, thus practically preventing any stray votes for their opponents. The second step was the creating of party machinery. A caucus of the Republicans in the legislature and "a number of other respectable persons" on January 21, 1800, nominated a slate of twenty-one for electors. They also provided a plan of thorough political organization patterned after Revolutionary models. They created a central corresponding committee of five to operate in Richmond and to work through committees of five established in each county. The Federalists shortly followed suit. Finally Governor James Monroe appointed committees of three in each county to superintend the voting for electors. Of these 279, 188 were already Republican committeemen. These Republican workers distributed Jefferson's literature and sent out a circular letter with the list of electoral candidates. As the law required tickets to be written out and signed on the reverse by the voters, this circular contained directions for preparing the written ballots.

But it was New York that was going to play the deciding role. Burr had been increasing his power in New York City and was winning his bitter contest with Hamilton for political command in the metropolis. He had built up an efficient committee system. He had a general city committee and committees in each of the seven wards. The New York legislature still chose the electors, so New York's vote for President depended on who controlled that body, and the political complexion of New York State was such that the control would probably depend upon who was elected from New York City. Recently the city had been Federalist, so it was Burr's responsibility to change it. He hit upon the device of a big-name ticket for the assembly. The Federalist were nominating men of no particular appeal, but Burr persuaded such prominent figures as General George Clinton, General Horatio Gates, and Brockholst Livingston to stand for the assembly. Then by indefatigable committee work he got the Republicans to the polls. The result was that New York City was carried by five hundred votes in April, and the legislature was safely Republican. This was a good omen for Republican success nationally.

This year more electors were to be chosen by the voters. Not only was this true in Virginia, but Rhode Island, Maryland, North Carolina, and Kentucky had joined the ranks. Party names were still not consistent. In Rhode Island the Republicans were called American Republican Federalists. In New Jersey, South Carolina, Massachusetts, and New York the Federalists were called Federal Republicans. In Virginia it was the American Republican ticket whom Jeffersonians were to support. Republicans too were often called Jacobins.

A nearer approach to formal nomination was made. About May 8, the Federalists in Congress met in their first formal caucus and designated Adams and Charles Cotesworth Pinckney of South Carolina to be candidates for President and Vice President. This member of the Pinckney family was substituted for Thomas, his younger brother, at Hamilton's insistence. In the squabble over the rank of Adams' newly appointed major generals, he had stepped aside to make way for Hamilton's precedence. As in 1796 it was thought essential to have a South Carolina Pinckney on the ticket in the hope that the South Carolina electors would vote for Jefferson and him as they had in 1796 and thus make him President, a plan again attributed to Hamilton's dislike of Adams. This caucus Bache's Philadelphia *Aurora* called a "Jacobinical conclave" and criticized it so severely that Bache was had up before the bar of the U.S. Senate for rebuke.

Shortly after the Republicans' victory in New York and about the time the Federalist caucus designated Adams and Pinckney, the Jeffersonians turned to making up a ticket. The choice of Jefferson was conceded, but who should be the Vice President? Here was Burr fresh from his New York City triumph—should they not try him again? Then there was another possibility, not from New York, in the person of Elbridge Gerry of Massachusetts, who had been the Republican member of the diplomatic team which Washington had sent to France and who was active in trying to build up Republican strength in Massachusetts. He had come home, and in the spring election he had nearly unseated the Federalist governor. Tench Coxe and others asked whether it would not be well to try to make inroads in New England. A caucus decided against this, however, and decreed that the honor should continue to go to New York. But whom did New York Republicans want? Many might prefer Clinton to Burr. Albert Gallatin was designated to find out through his father-in-law, Commodore James Nicholson.

Nicholson called upon Clinton. The former governor was properly coy; he was not really interested unless party success demanded his acceptance. The commodore's call on Burr found the latter rather sure he could be governor of New York and still resentful of southern failure to support him in 1796. The messenger gathered, however, that Burr would accept if he could have assurance of southern good faith. Nicholson therefore advised Gallatin that Clinton declined and that for this reason Burr was New York's preference. Consequently, on May 11, forty-three Republican members of Congress met at Marache's boardinghouse in Philadelphia and designated Burr.

The chief effort of the Republicans was the use of the printing press. Beckley, despite illness, misfortune, and sorrow, and others wrote and Jefferson distributed. Burr was on the road. He took the lead in endeavoring to make inroads in Federal New England. He worked particularly in Connecticut and Massachusetts and endeavored to get the governor of Rhode Island, who was expected to be chosen an elector, to agree to give one of his votes for Jefferson. This pledge came to nothing as the governor at length decided not to run. The Federalists sought vigorously to counteract this by attacking Jefferson's stand on religion in press and pamphlet. The Vice President was an infidel, an atheist, and if he were elected, meeting houses in New England would be burned. A divine, sometime acting president of Queens College in New Jersey, wrote a pamphlet entitled "Serious Considerations: God and a religious president or impiously declare for Jefferson—and no God."

On the Federalist side, however, there was some working at cross-purposes, because Adams, realizing that Hamilton and the ultra anti-French Federalists were not too loyal to him, was seeking to build up a great moderate support. The President even indulged in some rudimentary stump speaking, using an official journey to inspect the new capital city of Washington, to which he and the government were going to move in the fall. During this tour he stopped to speak at Lancaster, Pennsylvania, and at Frederick, Annapolis, and Baltimore, Maryland; and he gave quite an oration at Washington itself. On his summer trip to his Quincy home, he made more appearances.

On his part Hamilton played an equivocal role in which he demonstrated a high degree of ineptitude. He was again thinking in terms of the possibility of beating Jefferson with Pinckney if Adams could not make it. On a journey to New England in July he labored to persuade the New England electors, as he had done in 1796, to vote unanimously for Pinckney as well as Adams. His hope was that this full vote would keep Adams ahead of Jefferson, and then the South Carolina votes he expected for Pinckney would put the latter ahead of Adams and defeat him. He also prepared a pamphlet for very private circulation pointing out Adams' weaknesses and failures. This presumably was to aid Pinckney's chances. But here Burr stepped in. He procured a copy, had it printed in a large edition and distributed widely to show up the internal disharmony of the Federalists. Noah

Webster undertook to answer Hamilton in Adams' defense, but all this did was to advertise Federalist confusion.

Hamilton's final evidence of ineptitude was his attempt to persuade Governor Jay to call a special session of New York's expiring legislature, which was Federalist. He designed to get the legislature to pass a law requiring the election of New York's electors by popular vote in districts. This would salvage a few for the Federalists. Jay refused to make this move, and the schism in Federalist ranks was even wider.

In the end, all Hamilton's plans failed, even in South Carolina. There some hoped that the electors would repeat their procedure of 1796 when they voted for Jefferson and Pinckney. However, Charles Cotesworth Pinckney, not Thomas, was running this time, and he refused to accept any votes not paired with Adams. Also, another Pinckney, Charles, a second cousin of the brothers, was moving among the legislators with suggestions of preferment from Jefferson if Jeffersonian and Burr electors were chosen. They were, and Charles Pinckney's "suggestions" were later received with favor. He himself became minister to Spain. Had the South Carolinians voted for Jefferson and for Pinckney, instead of Burr, the South Carolinian would have had seventy-two votes to Jefferson's seventy-three and would have become Vice President.

The votes of the electors showed the fact that some rudimentary organization was now nearer to crystallizing. Every Republican elector voted for Jefferson and Burr, every Federalist but one voted for Adams and Pinckney; one Rhode Island elector threw his second vote for Jay rather than Pinckney to prevent a tie. The Federalists had carefully planned to avoid such a contingency, a formality the Republicans had also contrived but then had failed to carry out. A South Carolina elector had been expected to throw away a vote, and Burr had arranged that one in Rhode Island would do likewise. But the situation in South Carolina had become so tense that no elector was willing to carry out this plan and in Rhode Island the Federalists won. Jefferson had all the southern votes, save Delaware's and four of North Carolina's twelve, and Adams secured all in New England. In the middle states, Burr's spring stratagem had given New York to Jefferson and himself; New Jersey went for Adams, while Pennsylvania's peculiar politics produced a peculiar result.

The commonwealth had been a much trodden drill ground. The year previously the Republicans had won a resounding triumph. Thomas McKean had been elected governor with a friendly house although hampered by a Federalist senate. Copying New York, he immediately began a house cleaning of Federalist officeholders, a move that anticipated later spoils practices. He had given Beckley two jobs to make up for his removal by the Federalists as clerk of the United States House, and the latter was as usual highly effective. Pennsylvania was said by a not unbiased Federalist to be controlled by the Masons, the Irish, and the most "God provoking Democrats this side of Hell." Because the Federalists controlled the senate, they had prevented the choice of the electors by popular vote. And now at the last minute they created a situation which split the electors. As the two houses had not been able to agree on an election law in the spring of 1800, no popular election for electors had been held. After the October election failed to change the complexion of the two houses, the governor must call a special session if the state was to have any electors at all. Here again the houses could not agree and finally a compromise was engineered. Each house would nominate eight, then the two houses would meet in joint session and choose the state's fifteen electors from the sixteen nominated. The house nominated eight Republicans, the senate eight Federalists. The joint session chose eight Republicans and seven Federalists and these electors voted eight for Jefferson, seven for Adams.

The basic determinant in the electoral choice was the same that had been apparent in 1796. The electors voted in general for the candidate nearest their homes. The northern states voted for Adams and the southern for Jefferson. Had there been no unusual activity in New York, Adams would have been re-elected, but this spurt in New York City under Burr's direction caused his defeat. It would appear that Adams was stronger in 1800 and more popular than he had been in 1796, even though he lost. The truth was that there had been very little change in voting between 1796 and 1800. Adams in 1796 had seventy-one, Jefferson sixty-eight; now Adams had sixty-five and Jefferson seventy-three. Adams' gain of six in Pennsylvania could not offset his loss of twelve in New York, hence the result. As this year only five states chose electors by popular vote, there is no way of presenting any statistical evidence of any great change in popular sentiment, of any popular uprising by the common man against an aristocrat. Burr's clever footwork, outsmarting Hamilton in New York City, seems to have been the key. It was Burr's sophistication and skill in ward politics, rather than Jefferson's principles, that accomplished the result. Perhaps this was the revolution.

The final result when announced showed that Jefferson and Burr were tied, each with seventy-three, and the election must now go to the House of Representatives. Here each of the sixteen states had one vote, of which the victor must secure nine. While the result was still not officially known, Jefferson communicated with Burr in most friendly fashion, indicating he had been considering him for his official family were he not elected, and Burr replied saying he expected Jefferson to win and that his friends certainly would all vote for him. He further wrote, "I will cheerfully abandon the office of Vice President if it shall be thought that I can be more useful in any Active Station." Jefferson, however, never was to offer him any "active station."

The House, which met on February 11, 1801, was curiously divided. It was a Federalist-controlled body, having been elected in the furious days of 1798–99. It must now choose a Republican, must choose between Jefferson and Burr. Despite the fact that in numbers the Federalists predominated in the House, the counting by states— each state one vote—destroyed their control. The Republicans had a majority in the delegations of eight states but the Federalists only in six, for in two, Vermont and Maryland, there was an equal division. The southern and middle states, save South Carolina and Delaware, cast eight votes for Jefferson. The latter two and four from New England gave six for Burr; Vermont and Maryland could not agree, so abstained. Counting all the votes, Burr had fifty-five to Jefferson's fifty-one. Thus it was obvious that some Federalist or Federalists would have to vote for Jefferson or some Republicans for Burr. Federalists had been in communication with Burr, and while the New Yorker seems not to have responded, Jefferson had become convinced that he was bargaining with them and even with Republicans against him, and he therefore did not offer the Cabinet post; thereafter he had no use for his former ally. What Burr was doing has never become clear. The Federalists had no way of commanding nine votes, so he may really have been working for the Republican votes needed to put him in the White House. On their part the Federalist congressional leaders toyed with the idea of causing a deadlock and passing a law making the president pro tempore of the Senate the President until another election could be held at a date set by act of Congress. This president pro tempore could have been John E. Howard of Maryland, who had been chosen in November, or some other Federalist.

From one o'clock in the afternoon on February 11 until eight the following morning, twenty-seven votes were taken. The House had no heat, there was a bitter snowfall whitening the out-of-doors. One

man, Joseph Nicholson of Maryland, had come out despite a high
fever and lay suffering on a cot in a House committee room all that
night to save Maryland from going to Burr. At eight the House
finally recessed until noon. At that hour there were a few more
ballots. By Friday there had been thirty-three tries with no variation,
so an adjournment was voted until Monday.

Over the weekend there came a change. The Federalists tired of
Burr—whether because he refused to give them certain assurances
can not be definitely stated. At the same time, conference with Jefferson turned out more reassuringly. Also, Hamilton had been striving
hard to keep Federalists from voting for Burr. General Samuel Smith
of Maryland saw Jefferson on behalf of the Federalists who held the
balance: Bayard of Delaware, Baer and Craik of Maryland, and Morris of Vermont. They wanted the same assurance which Hamilton
wanted, namely that the financial system be undisturbed, the navy
enlarged, and many smaller Federalist officeholders left in office.
What if anything Jefferson promised is in dispute, but probably there
was a cryptic understanding rather than a promise. On February 17,
on the thirty-sixth ballot, the Federalist congressmen from Delaware,
Maryland, South Carolina, and Vermont did not vote for anybody.
Thus the votes of Maryland and Vermont were cast for Jefferson,
giving him ten votes, one more than needed. South Carolina and
Delaware voted blank, leaving Burr with but four states. No Federalist voted for Jefferson. Jefferson was to have as his Vice President
Aaron Burr, whom he now thoroughly distrusted. The new Congress
was to be Republican.

Thus, twelve years of experience had brought certain tangible
results. In the years preceding 1789 there had been an interstate
mobilization of the erstwhile colonies to preserve their autonomy.
After the adoption of the Constitution, the political task continued to
be the development of an establishment better to preserve this autonomy. On the state level this was a continuance of what they had
achieved during the Revolution. During that struggle whatever was
needed on a larger stage had been achieved by gatherings of state
delegates. The war had been won and the Constitution had been
achieved by this method.

But with the assembling of the new Congress in 1789 something
new had to be learned. The Congress was made up only in part of
representatives of the states; the lower, though more numerous,
branch represented a vague, ill-defined mass which could be described
as the people. The "people" now had to learn how to choose their

"representatives." Initially the method was simple though various. By a series of communication devices, names were presented to the public in much the same way that candidates for the state legislatures had been presented. From these names voters had made choices. Quite frequently the result was achieved because a given individual inspired more confidence and more liking than any others, or perhaps more people thought he could be more useful to the community, the nation, or to more narrowly constituted groups. It is realistic to say that they were in reality named by local elites of various sorts, some of them of relatively great age, going back even before the Revolution.

Was the determinant of choice to Congress going to remain in the locality, dominated by local influences and circumstances? The answer to this question turned out to be "predominantly, yes." But as people were forced to recognize that they lived not only in a state but also in a federal republic and that things were happening often at a greater distance in places like New York, Philadelphia, and later Washington where representatives whom they had helped to choose were dealing with federal and international problems and powers, they were forced to think more comprehensively, and what they thought and felt about these more distant affairs was shaping their motivations for expression and political action. This had created a federal politics as over against a state politics, though neither could ever be really independent and distinct.

It was inevitable that the patterns of the new federal politics of choice would begin to emerge when they did. A new practice of the art had appeared in the states during the Revolutionary War and had been in operation for some score of years—the life of a generation. In most of the states some form of elite establishment—courthouse, town meeting, urban ring (in a very rudimentary sense)—had been created. More important, the necessary discontents, frustrations, incompatibilities had accumulated. There was an increasing number who wanted to get somebody out, often because they might in the process get somebody in. It may be said to have been inevitable that about the middle 1790's there should be a definite wave of opposition to the accepted power structure in many of the states. But what ammunition would the opposition use? Some of those early in the fray tried to employ the financial measures of the new government, others found its foreign policy useful or tried to. The facts of war, taxation, and the Bank, with their expense and destruction, particularly commercial, were tried out. But the time was not yet ripe for crystallization.

Then came the hour and the issue. The issue was a chronic one, one appropriate for a republic; it was the issue of power. In a number of the states there were many who wanted to retire power aggregates, elites, establishments, or at least to change their personnel. So in the 1790's antipower associations began to form. Those participating in these political opposition moves cannot be described accurately by any such easy terms as class, occupation, region, religion, nationality, or even culture. These people wanted a change in the power structure for reasons which might or might not be related to any of their circumstances of existence, save their own ways of behaving.

It was convenient, useful, and desirable to enough people to oppose others, who were in power and were attempting to keep them out, in the name of well-known and reasonably well-defined antipower principles which had been common in the Anglo-American experience for centuries, certainly since the seventeenth-century revolutions.

In the southern states there had survived an almost feudal state of government by consent or by contests among local rural landholders where the "gentlemen freeholders" usually got along without issues or divisive organization. The complexities of culture patterns in the states north of the Mason-Dixon line dictated a more involved politics, particularly in the middle states. In New England in most instances the Patriots of the Revolution and the supporters of the Constitution had inherited the idea of a revered elite, partly ecclesiastical, in the towns. Here the revival of the Revolutionary opposition-to-power psychology was to prove particularly useful, for despite the firm situation of the establishment there was a good deal of insecurity and dissatisfaction, largely because of the ancient position of the establishment. But the leaven was working even there; those who were dissatisfied or working for change found certain situations and issues ready at hand. They began to be circulated by the Alphas and combated by the Betas.

During this era although the nation had learned to tolerate opposition and had demonstrated this by 1796 and although an established power had consented to loose and hand over authority, as had been done in 1800, there had been an obvious failure: the method of choosing a President by electors had broken down. The fathers presumably had planned the Electoral College as a nominating body which would present several candidates to the House for its choice. Instead of acting as independent men of judgment, the electors had first of all unanimously chosen Washington twice and then substituted the judgment of a congressional caucus and a factional contest for their own independence. Only in 1796 had there been independence of judgment. In 1800 every one of the majority voted for the same two men, leaving it to Congress, ironically a Federalist Congress, to choose between two Republicans. Only by what was almost an accident was the man designated for Vice President not preferred for President. Voters participated to any degree in President-making in but a few states. The Electoral College, Congress, and divided legislatures still had more to do with the assignment of power than did the people.

This complex experience suggests that the word party cannot be used in this period with much of today's significance. American parties are now really competing trade associations of professionals who operate highly organized groups which are federal, that is, they work on state and national levels. Their central organization of salaried staff deals with well-organized, independent, and often tough-minded locals. In the 1790's no such situation existed. Factional juntos in Congress were endeavoring to give direction, usually without much success, to a variety of independent state orders, some of them hardly possessed of any organization. These so-called partisans did not grasp the real meaning of the federal system of politics. They thought and were long to continue to think in terms either of centralization or dispersion, not in terms of shared power.

CREATING A REPUBLICAN
ESTABLISHMENT IN WASHINGTON

$\mathcal{T}$HE MOVING of the capital to the shores of the Potomac in October 1800 brought a new element into the dynamics of the evolution of American political behavior. This new element was the atmosphere of the District of Columbia as a dwelling place for those attempting to direct the political process. This city from the beginning was to be unlike any other, certainly in the United States. It was created in a pocket of a river valley which was to prove a meteorological horror, and there it was built almost literally from nothing. At one end there was a little Maryand corporation, Georgetown, while across the river from it was Alexandria, Virginia. On the eastward expanse of the Potomac flats, which was relieved by some hills, the gifted Pierre L'Enfant began his work, the work of laying out a city of magnificent distances and surveyor's stakes.

By 1800 there were sticking starkly up out of the plain two unfinished show buildings, the Capitol and the Executive Mansion, the latter modeled on the design of an Irish country estate. Some speculative builders had begun erecting residences for bureaucrats and diplomats together with certain business structures, while some adventurous entrepreneurs had opened boardinghouses around the base of Capitol Hill to accommodate the senators and congressmen who had been sentenced to exile in this barren waste of mud or dust. Here they would be plagued with influenza in winter and malaria in summer, biting cold and mortifying heat, the latter made almost maddening because of the drone and buzzing of biting mosquitoes and swarming flies.

In this infant metropolis the art of government and the game of politics were to be practiced under circumstances of the maximum disadvantage. The White House was an inhospitable barn, damp and unheatable. The boardinghouses were crowded and ill-kept by slatternly servants. There was no society, little service, few markets.

Before long there was also the sure promise of ill health, boredom, and dangerous and expensive relaxation. Probably no group creating a power structure and a system of politics ever worked under greater disadvantage. Cliques and messes lived together in the boarding-houses, which were either Jeffersonian or Federalist, and there the members consoled themselves by long political discussions because there was literally little else to do. Later, of course, gambling halls and fancy houses would be arranged for, but that was to take a little time. At the western end of Pennsylvania Avenue President Jefferson and the heads of departments were to do business and organize some social life, and there the diplomats, often sour exiles to this barbarous village, did their part to contribute a somewhat vinegary taste to the raw "society" of this "republican court." The exasperating phase of it is that no historian can properly evaluate the force of this combination of horrors in shaping the machinery necessary to run the political system then in the designing.

When the new President came to Washington to live in the White House, he was without too clear an idea of the political implications of his success. He had at least one preoccupation: he desired to play down as much as possible the divisive results of his rise to power, to woo his enemies, for he recognized the stigma attached to "parties," and so in his inaugural he proclaimed, "We are all Republicans, we are all Federalists"—now that the election was over and the change made. And in these words he expressed a sincere though vain hope that he, like Washington, might command a general and united support, devoid of the factionalism that Washington had so deplored and condemned. But he was sufficiently realistic to know that certain difficulties had to be dealt with.

In the first place, whether he admitted it to himself or not, he was no Washington, nor did he have either the General's prestige or his popular esteem. He must also reckon with two men whom he could not stomach: Alexander Hamilton and Aaron Burr. Furthermore, the sectional character of political division was a challenge. He was well aware of the hostility of northern opinion, particularly in New England.

Jefferson's election in no sense should be thought of in late nineteenth- or early twentieth-century terms. It did not bring a new organization to power. There was nothing like a united, ordered party ready to step in to create a new administration imbued with the purpose of solidifying its hold on power. Quite the contrary, the new

President and Vice President were at loggerheads. The House of Representatives was Republican by majorities variously calculated as from 24 to 33 in a body of 106. The hold of the Jeffersonians on the Senate was slighter, amounting to an uncertain majority of 3, which on occasion was destroyed by absences, resignations, or the hostility of Vice President Burr. In neither branch of Congress was Republican talent notable.

In effect, therefore, the election of Jefferson meant scarcely more than that he had come into the White House. Whatever political power those who called themselves Republicans might achieve was yet undecided. Presumably, each of the contesting groups had seven states, and in two, Maryland and Pennsylvania, there was a close division, with the Federalists at slight advantage in Maryland and the Republicans in Pennsylvania. That was the verdict in the Electoral College. In the House, the Republicans had advantage in nine states, the Federalists in four, and there were three ties: Vermont and North and South Carolina. Could the Federalists win back their strength in Vermont, Rhode Island, New Jersey, and Maryland, they would again control Congress, and had they carried Maryland's entire electoral vote instead of but half of it or had they retained New York City, Adams would still have been in the White House. The Federalists on paper were by no means dead, and Jefferson knew it.

The President, having been initiated into political leadership, now seemingly sensed that he must continue to act in that capacity and without much help. He therefore sought to encourage the press and insure some journalistic support. He would patronize a journal with a reliable editor, and one was at hand. Samuel Harrison Smith had set up a paper almost as soon as Washington began to be the capital city, and now the President found the columns of the *National Intelligencer* useful as a quasi-official gazette and as a propaganda sheet. Smith often got the inside story, although Jefferson at times objected to being held responsible for all his editorials. Benjamin Franklin Bache of Philadelphia also had ambitions to be considered the "organ." He set up a branch office in Washington and became a competitor with Smith for the official printing and for stationery contracts. Both "organists" hoped to support their journalism on the fruits of this patronage. In this Bache was the less fortunate. Jefferson was also mindful of the press elsewhere and most significantly, as later events were to prove, helped set up Thomas Ritchie in 1805 as editor and proprietor of the Richmond, Virginia, *Enquirer*.

Jefferson also paid close attention to his support in Congress, perhaps in part because there did not seem to be much Republican leadership talent there. The President and his associates looked carefully to its organization and aided in shaping patterns of continuing significance. There had been some use of occasional caucuses in previous Congresses and of committees to frame or to shape legislation. Now the speaker of the House, Nathaniel Macon, gave careful consideration to the role of these groups, and they assumed a new importance. Macon made his friend John Randolph of Roanoke the chairman of the House Ways and Means Committee, and he soon assumed a large measure of control over legislation. Jefferson watched matters in the House and had many of the congressmen to his frequent dinners. He could not function so effectively in the Senate because of the hostility between him and Vice President Burr.

Furthermore, in shaping his political course Jefferson for the first time in the history of the new republic must deal with the possibility of patronage in connection with a change of administration. There had been no such concept when Adams succeeded Washington, but now that Jefferson had defeated the head of the Federal establishment, there came the question of appointments. What would be Jefferson's policy toward the appointed officials of the federal government, all of whom had been commissioned by Washington, Adams, or their appointees? The new President was at the head of a civil service of something under three thousand, of which between four and five hundred could be appointments made directly by him. These people had been designated by either Washington or Adams and were for the most part of the Federalist establishment. In handling the problem of whether or not to make removals, he was not so much interested in rewarding his own supporters as he was in making certain that the key positions should be filled by those upon whom he could count.

Jefferson was troubled by the task, for he was sincerely committed to freedom of expression and did not believe in proscribing men for their opinions. He may also have given some assurances to a few Federalists during his election by the House. But if he were to consolidate his position and build up his strength for greater security, he must have loyal adherents devoted to this cause. And his determination to make some changes was intensified by the fact that Adams and the Federalists had reorganized and enlarged the federal judiciary, and even up until the last evening of his tenure Adams had been making "mid-night" appointments. These latter, numbering some forty, Jefferson determined to ignore. Of the rest of the officeholders whom he appointed, he made public announcement that he would remove about half and leave the balance to death and resignation. One computation suggests he removed 109 out of a possible 433. Whatever the actual figure, it is clear that he used much restraint and tried to make removals principally where incapacity or malfeasance seemed present. He was most concerned about the judiciary and was particularly interested in removing marshals who showed adverse political interest.

He rewarded certain of those who had helped him in the House in February. Faith was kept with the Federalist James Bayard and perhaps others by not removing their henchmen. And at the same time he turned on Burr. His most significant purpose was to eliminate the Vice President, both as a leading figure in Administration councils and as a potential successor. He could not forget what he believed to be the latter's subtle effort to defeat him in the recent contest in Congress.

Before Jefferson's intentions were recognized, Burr and the Livingstons in Washington, who were Senator Armstrong and Edward Livingston in the House, provided the President with a slate on which supporters of Burr were proposed for the principal offices. These names Jefferson passed on to Clinton, who challenged the Burrites; they were passed over. The Livingstons in the meantime had been detached from Burr by Jefferson's appointment of the chancellor to the French mission and of lesser members of the clan to other offices and by favors from the Clinton-controlled New York State council of appointment, who were to give generous recognition to the Livingstons at the same time that they largely ignored Burr.

The reverberations of the Jefferson-Burr split were matched and overmatched by mightier tremors in New York. The Federalist governor, John Jay, wished to retire and refused to run in April 1801. "Old" (he was only sixty-two) Governor George Clinton came forth again and defeated Stephen Van Rensselaer in the spring balloting. Clinton's nephew DeWitt now became the power in the council of appointment, which took a leaf out of the Federalists' book. As in 1793 a Federalist council had made a clean sweep, so DeWitt Clinton now maneuvered a house cleaning which threw out some six to seven thousand employees of Federalist tinge. But few Burr men were numbered among their replacements. The Clintons and the Livingstons took everything, for DeWitt Clinton hated Burr as much as did Hamilton. In the midst of this carnage Burr went back to Washington and began working with Federalists with the slogan "A Union of all *Honest* Men." The unity of the Republicans did not seem remarkable and would not the feud with Burr contribute to Federalist strength?

As Jefferson was dealing with appointments, he was also concerned with extending his support in the section where he had the least influence, namely New England. In this area there was a well-entrenched series of town establishments. In many of these the clergy and lay leaders of the Congregational Church, set up by law and supported by tax money, bore a controlling part. They were allied with certain professional men, businessmen, and others who appreciated the stability which continuing orders of this character could provide. Such people were conscious of a unique definition as New Englanders and were aware of the fact that fellow citizens from other sections had different characteristics and interests. One of their own number, John Adams, had been in the center of the new government from the beginning. Now, however, there was no New Englander either dwelling in the White House or presiding over the Senate. A Virginia–New York combination was in control, and of this the New England elite was very conscious.

The Jeffersonians were immediately to demonstrate that they had already grasped much better than their opponents the tactical significance of creating organizations. The new President proceeded to display his talent in planning to move in New England. In constructing his Administration, he chose two of his five Cabinet members—Henry Dearborn, Secretary of War, and Levi Lincoln, Attorney General, as well as Gideon Granger, the Postmaster General, then not of Cabinet rank—from that section. Though they were not politically aggressive, they had a symbolic usefulness. In the meantime, lesser men undertook by propaganda and personal mobilization to build up an opposition in many of these New England communities which would outvote the establishments in town meetings and send new people to the statehouses.

The politics now stirring in New England was forming new patterns useful to the Jeffersonians. The entrenched order, based on Patriot activity during the Revolution and the town-Congregational organization in town meeting and church, had reached a point in time when it was bound to be questioned. Any stated order which lasts long enough finds a new generation rising, new people coming in, a growing number whose demands or whose ambitions have been refused or frustrated, and a frontier where new communities just created are realizing that places and power are monopolized by the older settlements. When these determinants of opinion have generated enough force, the established order is faced by a cumulating threat of the loss of its status and power. At this point the growing opposition will seize upon any issue which proves promising.

This stage was now being reached in New England. In fact it had begun to appear about 1795. Those who wanted a change were fostering a series of discontents and apprehensions arising from the foreign and commercial problems accompanying the French Revolution. These included the Jay treaty, the Alien and Sedition Acts, and Jefferson's deism. These factors could be used by the ambitious, the frustrated, the dissenters, the frontiersmen, as well as by the worried and the apprehensive, as convenient instruments to effect the defeat of the old order which their complex discontents were demanding. The rising Republican political force could thrive in part because of the fact that there were enough "new people," politically speaking, enough who were insecure, enough looking for political status to take advantage of whatever opportunity was present. Those seeking advantage could play a politics colored by anything at hand to enable them to assume an image they might think convenient or useful. Much of this material would depend on the community pattern and how the community reacted to incidents, to conditions, and to situations which could be worked over into issues. In Massachusetts those who were on the frontier or in the back country might seize upon the idea that power was monopolized by those on the seacoast or at the ports. Poor farmers could protest against the town meeting ring. Businessmen could fight a government which did not protect commerce against foreign harassment. The unsuccessful could openly distrust a state bank which might not extend them credit. Patriots could attack Tories and praise the French. The conservatives could reverse the process.

In this general situation religion was likewise to play a significant part. As in the 1750's the Great Awakening had been a herald of the American Revolution, now at the entrance into the nineteenth century there was another revival, a "second Great Awakening." Here the forces of religious enthusiasm were surging up in protest against atheism, deism, and the calm and seemingly static indifference of the established Congregational elite to the deeper stirrings of the spirit moving people to regeneration and new birth. The more Calvinistic of the Congregationalists, together with Baptists, Methodists, and Quakers, could join in a concern that there was a state religion which had too little sympathy with "gospel religion." They called upon men to destroy this distinction and join together in a true Church of Christ. This Second Awakening in a sense was a herald of the destruction of this indifferent establishment and of a triumph which Jefferson and his followers, who believed that the supreme power lies in the people, would inaugurate.

Taking advantage of all these complicated circumstances favoring their objects, the Jeffersonians to accomplish their purpose devised a political organization consisting of a hierarchy of committees, stemming usually from a central legislative caucus of party leaders which formed a state central committee, and county and town committees as well. These workers were to contact as many individuals as possible, indoctrinate them with the principles of Jeffersonianism, and get them to vote against the "ins." The principles they were to preach were those of popular rule, equal political rights for all, the separation of Church and State, the glorious liberty of the citizen, and the leadership of Thomas Jefferson. In foreign affairs British offensiveness was to be stressed, smoldering hatred of the Tory fanned. Such organization was created and developed publicly and efficiently. Models already in use in Virginia and Pennsylvania, and to some extent in Maryland and New York, were copied. They harked back to the committee system of the Revolutionary epoch.

This effort produced an interesting reaction symptomatic of the incomplete development of the democratic concept of popular rule. The elite, certainly in Massachusetts and less generally elsewhere in New England, likewise had a caucus system and a spate of committees in which nominations and decisions were made. But these operations were secret and based on the concept that the wise and good would decide and then at the appropriate time make known their will to the lesser folk for obedient acceptance and ratification with due deference. The New England Federalist leadership now looked upon this open organization and propaganda as subversive and called it conspiracy and insurgency. To them it was a revolutionary attempt to overthrow the established order. Jacobins were trying to institute a terror. Atheists were plotting to overthrow the Church. Hostile southern interests wished to dominate and overthrow New England's commercial structure. Jefferson, the Antichrist, would reign and bring Tom Paine back to confound the clergy.

The time was indeed ripe for the Republican operation. Certain of the leadership of the Federalists, particularly the members of the Essex Junto in Massachusetts, men like Timothy Pickering, aristocrats like George Cabot and others, were not particularly attractive to a group of citizenry who were independent and enterprising. Voters in frontier communities like Vermont and the Maine district of Massachusetts were naturally not reconciled to centralized control nor were the otherwise-minded who dwelt in Rhode Island. Many voters responded to the Jeffersonian appeal. The Federalist governmental structure eventually collapsed like a house of cards. That which had been dominant since 1787 collapsed in 1807 when Massachusetts elected James Sullivan Republican governor. This was probably inevitable, as power aggregates seldom last most than twenty years.

While the Republican campaign to invade and contain New England was advancing with a considerable degree of success despite Federalist rallies, the New York situation was entering a new phase which was likewise to involve New England. Governor George Clinton and particularly his nephew, DeWitt Clinton, continued to pursue Burr relentlessly. The Vice President had been working through a group called the Martling men who met in Martling's Tavern and controlled New York City. In order to drive him from that stronghold, DeWitt Clinton through his English editor, James Cheetham, in his paper the *American Citizen* began a series of articles to show that Burr had tried to defeat Jefferson and elevate himself in 1801. Furthermore, Governor Clinton appointed DeWitt, Mayor of New York, to invade Burr's own bailiwick. Burr fought back through a series of "Aristides" letters in which he sought to expose "DeWitt Clinton as a cruel and corrupt intriguer who controlled the Council of Appointment, whose name had become synonymous with vice."

The approaching state election in New York and the national contest of 1804[1] were to offer new fields of bloody fighting. Jefferson

---

1. The election was to be carried on under a new mechanism. The tie vote of 1800 which, because of rudimentary party structure, seemed likely to be repeated now that each elector was voting for the two caucus designees. This situation indicated that a change was needed, so the Jeffersonians in Congress had drafted a Twelfth Amendment to the Constitution, which had been sent to the states on December 12, 1802. Thirteen of the seventeen states ratified it. Most of New England—Massachusetts, Connecticut, and New Hampshire—together with Delaware, all Federalist inclined, rejected it. The amendment was declared in effect on September 25, 1804. Under the original system, the electors had merely voted for two people, with no designation as to first choice. If no one gained a majority of the electors, the House would choose from the five highest, each state with one vote and a majority of states necessary for a choice. The next highest would be Vice President, but if there was a tie for second place, the Senate would choose. Now under the Twelfth Amendment, the electors were to label their two candidates, one for President, the other for Vice President. If no one designated for the Presidency had a majority, the House would elect a Chief Magistrate from the three highest, and the Senate in a similar event would choose the Vice President from the two highest.

and his close associates wanted James Madison to succeed him in 1808, so in choosing a Vice President in 1804 they must have someone with influence who would not be in a position to seek the succession four years later. There was some intimation that they were thinking of Governor George Clinton. He was attracted by the idea and therefore refused to run again for governor of New York. This was not to DeWitt Clinton's taste, for he found his uncle useful. He went so far as to try to get Jefferson to give up the idea but without success. So a successor to the governor had to be found in New York. The Clinton-Livingston leaders shortly selected Chancellor John Lansing, who reluctantly consented to run for governor.

Hardly had this choice been made when Burr appeared in the picture, seemingly determined to split the party. A group of his friends in the legislature nominated him for the governorship, presumably with some expectation that he might receive Federalist support. Hamilton, however, tried to prevent this union by coming out in favor of Lansing. This confusion, which the chancellor had not expected, plus the fact that he found that the Clinton-Livingston bosses wanted complete control of the patronage, decided the chancellor to stay on the bench. In this dilemma Clinton accepted Chief Justice Morgan Lewis, brother-in-law of Robert and Edward Livingston as his candidate. When, despite Hamilton's urging, Rufus King refused to stand, the Federalists made no nomination. Burr was expected to get much of their support and the sympathy of Lansing and his followers.

Strange help was coming from New England for Burr. The Federalist leaders in New England particularly the Essex Junto, feared that Jeffersonian radicalism was going to destroy the republic, and the more suspicious of them, such as Pickering, almost immediately detected in Jefferson's proposal to annex Louisiana what they professed to believe was the President's real objective: The addition of this great agricultural potential would diminish the relative strength of New England in the United States and definitely relegate this section to the humiliating position of an insignificant minority. Some, like Pickering, began to propose a New England secession before it was too late. The leaders of the Essex Junto went into action. Dismayed by the implications of the annexation of Louisiana, they would not have been averse perhaps to breaking the Jeffersonian control even at the cost of splitting the Union. They talked of engineering the secession of New England and New York and to this end they would aid Burr in his race for governor of New York, encouraging New York

Federalists to back him. They and Burr could even a number of scores with Jefferson, Hamilton, and the Clinton-Livingston alliance if the returns from New York in April were right. But from that point of view the returns were not right. Burr was defeated by Lewis, and the younger New England Federalists seeing how hopeless was this dream, turned to organization.

The Federalists of the first decade had indeed definite limitations as political leaders of the new republic. They could structure a self-governing nation and could create a body of administrative personnel who would bring intelligence and dedication to the task. But for this contribution they expected acceptance of their position as an elite without question. They assumed they would be recognized as a form of responsible aristocracy almost in European terms. They, on their part, were willing to contribute hard work and to labor in the interests of society, but they expected society to show them deference as their due. Then when at the end of the first decade an opposition formed which endeavored to dispute their authority and even to impugn their motives and their ability, they were often dismayed and resentful. But they disdained to summon any capacity which they may have had to appeal to the voters and often withdrew from politics. They showed little zeal or ability for the organization of a following or for campaigning.

The Jeffersonians, on the contrary, early developed a skill for organizing for combat, for contesting elections. Although in several instances in New York and Virginia, in the former as early as 1792 and in the latter in 1800 the Federalists had made some effort, it was not sustained and so did not persist. However, the triumph of Jefferson in 1800–1801 and the passage of time stirred a new spirit. A new generation of Federalists, younger men, were not willing to accept defeat. They could not help note the increasingly obvious Jeffersonian skills and their successful use in election contests. So there were various efforts to emulate them.

As the elite groups came under increasing fire and seemingly were quiet and unpublicized, these younger Federalists in many instances began to realize that they must meet these attacks with similar organization. So in the decade after 1800 there were numerous efforts to form counterorganizations and to make use of committees, caucuses, and conventions openly and within public view.

This younger generation began organization on several fronts. In January 1801 New York followed Delaware, which had been organized as early as 1795, and an "open caucus" was held in Albany where the Federalist legislators invited certain other Federalist leaders to constitute a "numerous and respectable meeting." This meeting provided a system of committees to be organized not only on a state-wide basis but also in various districts, counties, towns, cities, and wards. By 1808 other such efforts were made in the New England states, in New Jersey, Pennsylvania, Maryland, and Virginia, which can now be diagramed in organization charts. But these political activities were not national in their orientation; in fact the so-called party had disintegrated into a series of state operations. The Federalists who had been prominent prior to 1800 after Jefferson's victory likewise turned largely to state politics.

Shortly after 1800 there were slight efforts to reverse this trend, both Gouverneur Morris and Alexander Hamilton tried to set up a national group of corresponding committees, and the latter attempted a national meeting in connection with a meeting of the Society of the Cincinnati, but to no avail: the Federalists can hardly be said to have contested the re-election of Jefferson in 1804. However, their activity in state contests made elections there more significant and quite probably stimulated an increasing voter participation and at the same time curtailed the inherited tendency to deference. Electioneering devices were introduced. There were mass meetings and stump speaking. Occasionally there was a barbecue with plenty to eat and drink. Candidates traveled about speaking to groups and meeting individual voters. Holidays, such as the Fourth of July and Forefathers' Day, were used for parades and rallies, and even funerals were put to political use. Committees were organized for personal work, calling on voters, distributing tickets, providing carriages to get distant or infirm voters to the polls.

As the campaign of 1804 approached, Jefferson and his associates were determined to dispense with Burr. The device chosen for this purpose was to turn the responsibility over the the Jeffersonians in Congress, and 108 of them formed a caucus which met February 25, 1804. They called Senator Stephen R. Bradley of Vermont to the chair. Jefferson was nominated by acclamation, and then "to avoid unpleasant discussions" the caucus balloted without any presentation of candidates: each of those in the caucus wrote a name on a ballot. Not one voted for Burr. Sixty-seven preferred George Clinton. His nearest competitor had but twenty. So the ticket was to be Jefferson and Clinton. A committee of thirteen was set up "for the purpose of devising measures to promote the success of the republican nominations." None were included from Massachusetts, Connecticut, New Hampshire, or Ohio. This may be thought of as the first "national" campaign committee. On their part the Federalists held no official caucus, but somehow an understanding was reached that Charles Cotesworth Pinckney and Rufus King should be voted for.

Despite his successes, Jefferson was having his difficulties and cannot be said to have created a well-organized, smooth-running machine. To be sure, through his agency certain forces which were rising in New England in opposition to the ruling elite may have been stimulated to quicker evolution, but their advance was inevitable. The so-called party in New York and Pennsylvania was sadly torn by faction. A serious revolt was developing in Virginia and in the party in Congress, which seemed to threaten Jefferson's plans in so far as party leadership was concerned, particularly his desire to have Madison as his successor. The fact was that the Republicans had gained their power by their accumulated skill as an opposition. They had thriven on offense and now success threatened them. Rather than perfecting a party, they were disintegrating into factions.

The state of the Jeffersonians in New York had illustrated this weakness, and by about the time of the President's second inauguration it had become obvious that, though Burr had been defeated and Hamilton killed in a duel with the Vice President, the triumphant Livingston and Clinton alliance was about to break up. DeWitt Clinton had made enemies which included certain Burr, Livingston, and New York City Tammany elements who were determined to break his power come what might.

In Pennsylvania the most articulate factional leadership came from Philadelphia where the principal Republican editor, William Duane of the *Aurora,* and Congressman Michael Leib tried to speak for the Republicans. But Albert Gallatin, Secretary of the Treasury, their fellow Pennsylvanian, did not see fit to recognize their pretensions, nor did Jefferson or his Secretary give them much of the patronage. Then Duane quarreled violently with the Republican governor, McKean, and Jefferson gave evidence of working with the governor, which further disturbed the editor. During these last four years the schism had been growing wider and the waters had been muddied by some sympathy which developed on occasion between Governor McKean, Alexander James Dallas, who was the federal district attorney, and the Federalists. Jefferson had always hoped to woo the Federalists, so this had some countenance from him. Duane and Leib attacked this rapprochement, set themselves up as the real "Republicans," and dubbed the governor and his associates as apostates, "Tertium Quids," who were neither one thing nor the other, neither Republicans nor Federalists. Fortunately for Jefferson these splits in Pennsylvania and New York were not to be reflected in the presidential election of 1804, though such bitterness was an open powder keg which might explode at any time.

A situation more unpleasant for Jefferson to deal with was developing in Virginia and in Washington. The Virginians, as has already been indicated, played a politics all their own, a politics more concerned with personalities than issues. Virginians like Jefferson, Madison, Monroe, John Randolph of Roanoke, and John Taylor of Caroline had been long associated and over the years had worked together generally, though not always, in harmony. When Jefferson came to the Presidency, he chose Madison as his Secretary of State, and soon Monroe was sent abroad to collaborate with Chancellor Livingston in purchasing Louisiana. John Randolph was the Jeffersonian floor leader in the House and for four years carried the Administration program successfully through Congress. Then certain external factors entered into this association that produced rifts in the lute, although the basic conditions which made these rifts so ominous arose from the personality quirks which these associates possessed. These external factors included the series of disastrous consequences that followed the outbreak of another Napoleonic war in 1803, which frustrated Jefferson's plans to get Florida and Texas and brought humiliation and loss to the United States.

During these difficult years of war, while impressment and privateering were embarrassing American commerce, Monroe was kept in Europe endeavoring to improve American status. At this he was a dismal failure. Another factor was Jefferson's determination to purge the federal judiciary by impeachment of two district judges, Pickering and Chase, and probably the Chief Justice, John Marshall, another Virginian. As floor leader of the House, Randolph was entrusted with the impeachments. The removal of Pickering, who was insane, was not such a chore, but when the impeachment of Chase was taken up, it proved to be impossible. Despite Randolph's most violent efforts, the Senate refused to vote the judge guilty of a high crime or misdemeanor just because he was a violent partisan who sometimes harangued grand juries. This was a blow to Randolph's pride. He was highly strung and neurotic, almost to the point of being unbalanced, and prey to morbid fancies and violent prejudices. He seems to have wanted to retreat abroad as a diplomat in Monroe's place. He had grown violently jealous of Madison, whom Jefferson thought of as his successor. So he developed the idea that Monroe, not Madison, should succeed Jefferson and in the meantime that he go abroad. He and John Taylor of Caroline, together with some other Virginians, had also become convinced that Jefferson, in his efforts to woo the Federalists and in his attempts to expand the American possessions, had abandoned the pure Republican policies of 1798 and was in effect a Federalist or, at best, a "Quid." Therefore when he suffered the shame of his defeat in his efforts to impeach Chase and when Jefferson and Madison refused to send him abroad, he was ripe for violent revolt.

Randolph began a smear campaign which he was to continue *ad nauseam*, particularly against his preferred rival, Madison. A Georgia legislature in 1795 had made a large sale of land in the Yazoo River region to some New England land companies, for which all the legislators save one received a consideration. The next year the succeeding legislature had annulled the sale as corrupt. The new owners resisted being dispossessed and carried the case to the Supreme Court, which found in their favor. Under the decision, the United States undertook to pay damages to those whose investments were impaired by Georgia. This plan would largely favor New England citizens at a time when Jefferson was working to build support in that region. Madison, Gallatin, and General Benjamin Lincoln of Massachusetts were designated commissioners to determine the amounts to be paid. The Jefferson Administration then favored bills to pay the awards of the commissioners. Randolph when floor leader saw no evil in this, but now that he was out of favor he seized upon these awards as weapons to use in revenging himself on Jefferson and Madison. His snarling denunciation of these Yazoo frauds kept the smear constantly alive. His epithet "Yazoo" hurled against an opponent on the floor of the House was devastating, highly disconcerting to the allies of Jefferson and Madison in Congress.

This confusion among Republicans did not spread farther south than Virginia, largely, it may be surmised, because the politics in the three states of North and South Carolina and Georgia, as well as that in the frontier states of Kentucky and Tennessee, was still in a state of pristine disorganization. The population was very scattered over a rural society. In the southern states there were no state-wide campaigns as the legislature chose the state officers and electors. Courthouse and county court functionaries gave almost undetectable direction to state politics and no organization was called for. In the West things were somewhat ruder and rougher but just as embryonic. The factional quarreling and social complexity that was to demand organization was not found here. The Republicans did not find remedies.

As the Republicans were suffering from their factionalism, would the Federalists gain advantage from it? One of the significant characteristics of democracy is the freedom of any minority group to seek to convince the people that there should be a change of government. That this freedom was possible had been demonstrated in 1800, and a change had been consummated: a majority group in power for twelve years had been rejected and a new majority had taken over. Now a new problem in political behavior arose. How would a majority party which had been defeated comport itself? Could it adjust to defeat and make an effective bid to return to power? But no real interest developed in the Federalist ticket and even New England abandoned Federalism save in Connecticut. The latter state, Delaware, and Maryland gave the fourteen votes which were all the "Feds" could command. Despite his political disadvantages, Jefferson's re-election in 1804 can scarcely be said to have been contested. In fact the Federalists by 1804 seemed apparently unable to adjust to an effective minority status, but this the Young Federalists were determined to cure.

Power had been established and moved to Washington where it was to reside permanently. But Jefferson had seen fit to reduce this power to almost its lowest terms. As there was so little power, there was little to excite interest, either negative or positive, and therefore little to stimulate contest to secure it. As there was so little challenge to combat, there was little to condition partisanship, and partisanship seemed gradually fading out. Under these circumstances the seats of power were found elsewhere, in the state capitols of the young republic. The power-minded, therefore, had no reason to exile themselves in the unfinished, chaotic, and unpleasant seat of the federal government on the Potomac shore.

·❧[XV]❧·

A POLITICAL VACUUM

𝒯HE SO-CALLED partisanship of the first decade of the republic has been misnamed, for it had not produced any permanent system of election contests between organized competing factions. Organization, such as it was, existed only in the states. Such national political mobilization as had developed seemed created for single ends and operated as one-shot weapons. The Patriots mobilized to secure independence. The first group known as Federalists were dedicated to the adoption of the Constitution; the second of that name and sign, to the implementing of the document by organizing the federal system. The Jeffersonians had as their objective the elimination of the Adams-Hamilton Administration. This done, there seemed no further danger, particularly as Federalism appeared to be dispersed and impotent. As there was little of national import to challenge the Jeffersonians, they seemed to be fragmentizing, and whatever of a nascent party institution on a national scale there was appeared to be withering like Jonah's gourd. The election of 1804 could hardly be called a contest. Political battles now took the form of in-fighting.

But if this so-called partisanship had died down, factionalism had risen, and it was this factionalism that was to insure the return of political conflict and contest for power. The increase of disintegration and the consequent growth of disorganization were to inject into political battles a growing prejudice against the existence of the Jeffersonian regime, of the power called the Virginia Dynasty, sometimes smeared as the despotic "House of Austria." Some citizen of the Old Dominion had been Chief Magistrate since the beginning, save for the four unhappy years of John Adams' tenure, and there was a certain restiveness under this monopoly of Virginian leadership, which was particulary apparent in New England. Since the beginning there had been more or less latent rivalry, based upon cultural differences, between representatives of northern and southern communities. Might not this confusion profit the feeble opposition of the changing Federalists?

Previously, when each of the various groupings had attained its end, it had disintegrated. There was also a decided prejudice against "parties" as dangerous and disruptive, even subversive. Both Washington and Jefferson had to some extent shared this view. It seemed to survive only on the level of state operation. Signs of Jeffersonian disintegration continued. The "Quid" idea seemed to be spreading. Hardly had the first Congress of Jefferson's second term assembled than his erstwhile floor leader showed obvious signs of disaffection. Randolph sought to defeat significant phases of the President's foreign policy in the House. He charged that Jefferson was abandoning pure republican principles by seeking to enlarge central power. He demanded *laissez faire* and the maintenance of the seats of political power in the state capitals and not in Washington. Furthermore, knowing that Jefferson considered James Madison as heir-apparent, Randolph launched a boom for James Monroe as the party candidate in 1808. Jefferson stepped in and contained Randolph's antagonism by adroit moves, but despite this, the Republican purists were going to attempt to rally around Monroe.

In the meantime foreign affairs got worse. The American navy had been humiliated when the *Leopard* fired on the U.S.S. *Chesapeake*, and the insults arising from the French and British efforts to keep American commerce from helping either of these rival warring powers had become almost intolerable. To combat this, Jefferson and Madison had developed a policy of peaceful coercion similar to that which was in vogue during the years of the Revolution. They would refuse to trade with those who flouted the American flag. Pushed to its logical conclusion, this policy meant at length in 1807 that a complete embargo was laid. No American ships could leave American ports for Europe, transatlantic trade was dead.

This brought distress to the ports and hope to the surviving Federalists. Now at last they might rally. The Essex Junto began to capitalize this discontent, and New England began again to turn to thoughts of secession and a few even to alliance with Britain. In the spring election of 1808 the Federalists regained the legislature of Massachusetts and began a drive to prevent a war with England. Some of the leaders even entered into conversations with an Englishman from Canada, John Henry. These were communicated to the English ministry and indicated that Massachusetts might not only refuse to join in war on England but might even treat separately to obtain "a guarantee of its security."

Federalists prospects seemed further to brighten, particularly as local situations dangerous to the Jefferson Administration continued to develop in New York and Pennsylvania. The Federalists were indeed favored by one of Jefferson's peculiarities. By temperament he was not a nationwide political operator. He preferred to play palaceguard politics in Washington. He stayed out of local quarrels, particularly in Pennsylvania despite Gallatin's place in the intrigues of that commonwealth. When these situations began to loom on the 1808 horizon, the nature of the political behavior in these two states and the fact that each had an important metropolis added new patterns to American politics. In this creation Pennsylvania continued to take the lead. As early as 1801, after the early Republican successes in organization developed by Beckley et al. throughout the commonwealth, which had been such an effective instrument in winning the state, new devices were developed. Regular procedures were invented for organization and nomination. The convention system of nomination which had been used intermittently was refined. Jeffersonians in the city of Philadelphia met at the State House, where they chose delegates to join with those from Philadelphia and Delaware counties in naming candidates for state senator, and a similar device was charged with nominations for Congress. Assembly candidates were designated by delegates from the various election districts in Philadelphia County. The same meeting at the State House created a permanent organization. The voters in the several wards were urged to meet and choose permanent committees of five. These committees were to join together and select a general ward committee which was to make city nominations. Vigilance committees were designated to get citizens to vote, to supply ballots, and the like. Each year at a general city-wide gathering of the voters a general committee of superintendence was created to supervise the fortunes of the party. By 1803 this system of organization had become established.

Three years later New York perfected a similar system. Under the stimulus of the Tammany Society, which had reorganized in 1805, an obvious political organization was designed the next year. The Jeffersonians in each ward now met and chose a committee of three. These various ward committees held meetings and planned for elections. They became the Tammany Hall General Committee. At the same time the wards would send delegates to Martling's Tavern to nominate local candidates. In 1811 Tammany completed a Wigwam of its own and no longer met at Martling's. As the embargo brought its woes, the Federalists perked up in New York, as in New England. They must organize, too, in the form of a Washington Benevolent Society which set out to rival Tammany in New York City.

In the meantime the contest for control of the state was sharpening as the enemies of the masterful DeWitt Clinton continued their constant war upon him. He had broken with the Burrites and with the Martling men of the Tammany Society; he and the Livingstons had beaten Burr. Then he had quarreled with the Livingston governor. Now in 1807 he was determined to drive that executive and the Livingstons out of power. He made some effort to negotiate peace with Tammany, and despite failure, he succeeded in putting his own man into the governor's chair in the person of Daniel D. Tompkins. In the first year of his term, the embargo was passed and a storm broke in New York City. DeWitt Clinton, Vice President George Clinton, and their editor James Cheetham came out against the embargo, leaving Tompkins to follow the President.

This break seems in part due to the fact that old Vice President Clinton wanted to be President, and as Jefferson was intent on Madison, Clinton took a course which might win him Federalist support. He may have hoped for a combination of the latter and the Quids. Those in opposition to whatever group was in power had been thinking of George Clinton ever since 1792, and now in 1808 he sought another chance when in that year the New York legislature nominated him for President. Not only in New York was there interest in him, but support had been developing in Pennsylvania.

The rivalry in the Keystone State between the Philadelphia machine, led by Duane and Leib, and the Quids had grown more intense when a number of country leaders joined the Quids to carry the war into Philadelphia. An Irish editor, John Binns, had been set up there, and the fight with Duane was intensifying. Both sides seem to have resented Jefferson's indifference and in reprisal were looking with favor on George Clinton rather than Madison. Thus there had developed two candidates opposed to Madison—James Monroe and Vice President George Clinton.

Jefferson of course was not to be deflected by this opposition. He had announced shortly after his second inauguration that he would not run again, and it had been obvious all along that Madison was his choice. When the opposition candidacies developed, some pressure was put upon him to change his mind and run himself, but he would not.

The "pure" Republican foes of Madison in Virginia on their part endeavored to get an expression of support for Monroe from the Virginia legislative caucus on January 21, 1808, but they failed. Almost on the same day, January 20, the official congresssional caucus was called for January 23. A chain of continuity had now been established. Senator Bradley of Vermont, chairman of the 1804 caucus, assumed the responsibility of calling another in 1808 and sent out a printed call, not only to the 118 Republicans in the House and the 28 in the Senate, but to 2 or 3 Federalists as well. There was some objection to this and his authority to issue the call questioned, but in the end a number variously estimated at between 89 and 94 turned up. Madison received 83 votes, with 3 for Clinton and 3 for Monroe. For Vice President Clinton had 79. The ticket was to be Madison and Clinton. Again a national "committee of correspondence and arrangement" was appointed. This time Massachusetts, New Hampshire, and Ohio were given places but Connecticut and Delaware excluded. The caucus also adopted a resolution to meet opposition to their assumption of function: "The members of this meeting have acted only in their individual characters as citizens; that they have been induced to adopt this measure from the necessity of the case; from a deep conviction of the importance of union to the Republicans throughout all parts of the United States, in the present crisis of both our external and internal affairs; and as being the most practicable mode of consulting and respecting the interest and wishes of all."

Strangely enough, this nomination of Clinton for a second run for Vice President did not end his interest in the Presidency, and this continuing attitude encouraged the Federalists. If Clinton were given an endorsement for the first place by the Federalists, they, together with those Republicans opposed to Madison, might bring him in. Some Federalists favored that idea, so some sort of conference seemed indicated. As there were so few Federalists in Congress, a caucus merely of their representatives would not be effective, so a new device was needed. Some efforts had been made to develop nominating conventions. In Pennsylvania such state gatherings had been experimented with and also the augmented legislative caucus to which districts unrepresented in the legislature by the party in question were invited to send delegates. Certain of the Federalists who thought it might be possible to rally around George Clinton successfully thereupon sought to invoke the convention device and began planning for it. A certain amount of visiting and correspondence between Philadelphia and Massachusetts produced a letter from Philadelphia to Boston suggesting the Massachusetts caucus invite a meeting of Federalists at New York "from as many states as could be seasonably notified." Letters and messages were sent, not only from Boston, but from Philadelphia and New York as well. The Federalist legislative caucus in Massachusetts, which had been jolted by Republican victories in the state elections, appointed a "campaign" committee, which in turn resorted to the old Revolutionary technique of appointing a committee of correspondence. They wrote around to Federalists in other states and eventually arranged for the first national nominating convention to meet in New York City in the third week in August. Representatives to the number of twenty-five to thirty from eight states—Massachusetts, Connecticut, New Hampshire, Vermont, New York, Pennsylvania, Maryland, and South Carolina—were present. This meeting, conducted in clandestine fashion, interestingly enough, decided not to support George Clinton but rather C. C. Pinckney, who had been so badly beaten in 1804.

The campaign of the Federalists in the end was mostly intrigue. Senator Timothy Pickering of Massachusetts did his best to play up the idea that Jefferson and Madison were subservient to France. He wrote to Governor Sullivan of Massachusetts, making such a charge, and he sought to negotiate with the British envoy, George Rose, somewhat as Hamilton had done during Washington's regime. When the British agent, John Henry, came down from Canada to encourage the Federalists to keep this idea alive, they gave him their confidence, and he made reports which reached the British foreign office. None of this helped Jefferson and Madison who were seeking to get satisfaction from England in the matter of the searching of the U.S. war vessel *Chesapeake* for British "deserters." There were some who thought that Federalist intrigue with the British smacked of treason, and John Quincy Adams left them to join the foes of his father. The unpopularity of the embargo in the meantime helped the Federalists, who were encouraged by gains in the New York legislature.

Though thus organized and operating, the Federalists failed to win, but they increased their 14 electoral votes to 47. In New England, Massachusetts, New Hampshire, and Rhode Island were back in the Federalist fold with Connecticut. North Carolina cast 3 of her 14 votes for Pinckney in company with Delaware and the fraction from Maryland[1] which continued from 1804. New York cast 6 of her 19 for George Clinton. Madison polled 122 out of the 175 voting.

---

1. North Carolina and Maryland used the district system.

Jefferson's success as a party leader had in fact ended with his re-election to the Presidency in 1804. His second Administration had proved to be a period of general European war in which his major political efforts were devoted to another backward look, reviving the economic coercion of the Revolution in a futile attempt to control events by the embargo and to a successful project to pick his successor in the person of his Secretary of State, James Madison.

The controlling facts in the situation seem to have been that the federal government and the Jefferson Administration were failing to control events and losing public confidence. They could not arrest the European damage to American prestige.

The election of 1808 provided the first instance when a President in effect chose his own successor. Likewise, it was the first occasion when the Secretary of State, rather than the Vice President, succeeded to the Chief Magistracy. It was also the first election whose result sent a man not among the Revolutionary leaders to the White House. Finally, it was the first instance of a man of lesser status succeeding to the post hitherto held by men of first rank. Whatever may be said of his ability, Madison did not rate in public esteem on the same plane as Washington, Adams, and Jefferson.

This change of leadership and pattern of action was stimulated in part because the humiliating treatment which Great Britain and France inflicted upon the United States had not been stopped by Jefferson's policy of economic coercion embodied in the Embargo Act. To make matters worse, American commercial interests and public esteem for government in general had suffered from this restriction, particularly in New England, and the rising tide of dissatisfaction gave new opportunities to those who wished to strike at the Virginia Dynasty and the reputation and power of the federal government.

Though the opposition which had developed in Virginia, New York, and New England had been unable to concentrate on any candidate to oppose Madison, even at that, he had won largely because a certain proportion of the electors were chosen by state legislatures and these legislatures had been elected before the full effect of the embargo was realized. Had all the electors been chosen by the people in the latter half of 1808, Madison's defeat might well have been accomplished.

Public opinion was welling up to such a pitch that it seemed that it might be used politically, and the Federalist leadership again undertook to make the most of it in Jefferson's last session of Congress and in the New England legislatures in the spring of 1809. In Washington and in Boston that winter of 1808–9, the Essex Junto leaders undertook to advance the remedy to their situation which they had last considered in 1804, namely secession. They were tired of "Negro" Presidents and Congresses. The Virginia Dynasty, or the House of Austria, seemed to be in permanent ascendancy, and the only method to free themselves was to resort to the tactics of 1776, using the arguments of the Virginia and Kentucky resolutions of Jefferson and Madison. A concerted series of pronouncements under Federalist leadership was launched from the Massachusetts and Connecticut legislatures and various New England town meetings which were definitely pointing to a New England convention to consider secession, in a fashion to be achieved later at Hartford in 1815.

This eruption of resolutions against the embargo stirred up all the factionalism in Congress which had been restive against Jefferson and Madison and brought a revolt which was a bitter blow to Jefferson and an inauspicious prelude to Madison's inauguration. When Jefferson's partisans felt forced to repeal the embargo, the Federalist leaders ceased to talk of secession, but they continued to correspond with the British and with the British agent, John Henry, who had visited them in Boston in 1808 and was now back again, instructed perhaps to keep alive their separatist ideas.

The factionalism which had disturbed and finally sent Jefferson back to Monticello, disappointed and thwarted, continued even more vigorously under Madison. The senatorial group—Samuel Smith of Maryland, William Branch Giles of Virginia, Michael Leib of Pennsylvania, and Vice President Clinton—moved in on Madison while he was making up his Cabinet. He wanted Albert Gallatin to succeed him as Secretary of State but learned to his chagrin that these men and the Federalists could prevent his confirmation. Madison hoped he could persuade Samuel Smith to change his mind if the President would make his brother Robert, Jefferson's Secretary of the Navy, Secretary of the Treasury to administer that department with the help of Gallatin, the new Secretary of State. This, however, Gallatin would not agree to; he would not take on the new responsibilities and at the same time continue the old. So at length Madison continued Gallatin in the Treasury and appointed Robert Smith Secretary of State. This meant of course that Madison must do the work, for

Robert, though polite and cooperative, was not up to statesmanship.

Under such disadvantages, which were underlined by Federalist victories in 1809 in Massachusetts, New Hampshire, Rhode Island, and New York, Madison undertook a troubled residence in the White House. The prestige and power of the federal government had declined to such a point that during the War of 1812 it practically disintegrated. Politics was returning to the states where the courthouse and the town meeting orders took over again in the South and New England, while New York and Pennsylvania continued to experiment in their increasingly intricate sophistication. Anything lke federal two-level partisanship had died; the members of the Virginia establishment were merely perpetuating their kind.

For a while President Madison continued his interests more as foreign minister than as party leader or director of domestic policy. In fact he was not even able to prevent Gallatin's enemies in New York and in the South from defeating the recharter of the Bank of the United States. He was indeed a President in isolation, spending most of his time playing the intricate game of foreign policy with the unfortunate result that he got nowhere with the British and at the same time was smeared as pro-French. Some Federalists even went so far as to speak of his thirty-year career since the 1780's as one long effort to produce French advantage. His fortunes were not helped by victories for the Federalists in the fall elections of 1810 in Vermont, Connecticut, Rhode Island, and New Jersey, nor by the fact that he had to suffer a defeat at the hands of Smith, Giles, and Leib, sometimes described as the Invisibles because they tried to work in secret, who had caused him to lose a key foreign policy bill in Congress earlier in that year.

By the end of his second year in office, March 1811, the tide turned slightly in his direction; time was bringing forward a new generation. The congressional elections by and large were favorable. The voters of Massachusetts turned back to a Republican governor and elected a legislature that would defeat the arch Federalist Timothy Pickering for another term in the Senate. The next Congress was to have a large proportion of younger and abler men. At last Madison determined to act to free himself from the hindrances of association with the Invisibles, the Smith-Giles-Clinton-Leib-Duane faction which had humiliated him.

Gallatin may have brought Madison's resolution to a head. He had been a particular object of attack by Duane's *Aurora* and by those of like mind with the Invisibles. Gallatin was tired of being in the same Cabinet with Robert Smith and suffering defeat in Congress at the instance of Samuel Smith and his associates. So he resigned in March 1811. Now Madison moved. He dismissed Smith and made his former opponent James Monroe, Secretary of State and heir apparent to the Virginia Dynasty. He thereby reunited his Virginia cohorts behind him and strengthened the Republican establishment. Also, as Monroe was obviously an exponent of better relations with Great Britain, Madison sought to rid himself of the suspicion that he was a creature of Napoleon. He would thus re-form his party ranks and at the same time prepare for his own re-election in 1812.

Unfortunately he had reckoned without the Clintons and the British. One of the significant factors in early American political behavior was the place and influence of family. This was particularly strong in New York which since colonial days had been the home of the De Lanceys, the Livingstons, and the Clintons. One of the most vigorous of these clansmen was DeWitt Clinton. Working ostensibly and often sincerely in the interest of his uncle, George Clinton, he was most ambitious himself, and as his uncle grew older and failed in health, his own ambition grew. At first he had been eager to make his uncle President, but as 1812 approached he was undoubtedly thinking more of himself. Well established in New York, he had been U.S. senator, had been frequently in the legislature, and for much of the time mayor of New York City. He had bitter enemies, however; the Livingstons and the New York City Tammany machine were determined to stop him. Recently they had defeated him for the legislature: they did not want him to be in Albany when the legislative caucus nominated candidates and chose New York's members of the Electoral College. But in 1811 he took advantage of the death of the lieutenant governor and, despite his enemies, secured election in a state-wide contest to that office.

He was in fact making the first active campaign for a presidential nomination in American political history. He realized that if he could capitalize on the disaffection among Republicans in Pennsylvania and secure the support of New England these states together with New York, Delaware, and Maryland might make him President. The fact that in Pennsylvania Republicans held a convention in March and declared for Madison should have warned him that his plan was unlikely to succeed, but he counted on the support of Duane and Leib and the disaffection in Pennsylvania over the success of the federal government in making Pennsylvania pay some claims which the commonwealth had determined not to honor in defiance of the U.S. Supreme Court. He had great hope. And the Madisonians feared him even to the point of offering to take him as their vice presidential candidate instead of his uncle. This would have given him the inside track in 1816 for the succession of the Secretary of State was hardly firmly established. But no, he would not.

The Republican congressional caucus met in May and renominated Madison with John Langdon of New Hampshire, for George Clinton had died only a fortnight or so before. Langdon declined, so at a second meeting, seeing that DeWitt Clinton remained unapproachable, they nominated Elbridge Gerry, recently governor of Massachusetts, a man too old to be in line in 1816. A few days later, the Republicans in the New York legislature presented DeWitt Clinton. Efforts began at once to woo Pennsylvania, money was spent, and negotiations with the Federalists began. They were not unused to this as there had been exchanges before with Burr.

The reason for Clinton's confidence was the fact that the British would make no concessions, partly because of Federalist advice, and Madison and Monroe were fast becoming convinced that their situation was intolerable and that war was inevitable. They had been in communication before the recent Republican congressional caucus with some of the vigorous new congressmen, led by Henry Clay, John C. Calhoun, and others, already called war hawks, and it was only a matter of weeks before a declaration of war would be asked and voted. But there were many, particularly in the New England and the middle states where commercial interests were influential, who did not want war. They were desirous of finding a leader of a peace party, and Postmaster General Gideon Granger of Connecticut was already working on New York congressmen to enlist Clinton. Then when the war came in June, its early operations were neither impressive nor satisfying. Could the leading Federalists in New York be brought to join New England in supporting the Republican Clinton? The war was going to be increasingly unpopular, particularly in New England, and neither Madison nor his secretaries of War and of the Navy seemed to have much capacity to direct it. The nation was unprepared, money was scarce, and enlistments slow. Worse, there was much bitter and open opposition.

A tragedy stirred up politics in this presidential year. A Federalist newspaper in Baltimore which vigorously opposed the war was destroyed by a mob. This aroused certain of its supporters to start the paper again. A second mob attacked the new location, killed one Revolutionary veteran, a General Lingan, and badly crippled the famous "Light-Horse Harry" Lee who, out of friendship for one of the proprietors, was aiding him in defending his right of free utterance. This villainous example of mob tyranny roused a wave of protest and quickened the New England Federalists in their determination to support a peace candidate against Madison.

Just about this time negotiations were opened between Clinton and the leading New York Federalists, and for the first time there appeared an active candidate "making arrangements," using emmisaries, and even having a manager. On August 5 at Gouveneur Morris' mansion he met the great trio of Empire State Federalism: John Jay, Rufus King, and Morris. They spoke of peace and were evidently most desirous of learning whether he would head a peace ticket.

In the meantime the New Englanders had become more interested. A Connecticut committee had been corresponding with other states. They had enlisted a Pennsylvania committee to sound out the South. Clinton's emissaries had also been working in Pennsylvania and had spent a good deal of money in printing and circulating addresses urging Clinton's qualities. At length all these efforts, stimulated by the Baltimore tragedy and the lack of any success in warmaking, brought a group of Federalists from New England and as far south as South Carolina to meet in New York in secret for three days in September in a nominating consultation on a somewhat more elaborate scale than that tried in 1808. Delegates attended from eleven states. Although they kept their actions secret and made no announcement, their decision was to nominate no ticket of their own but to support Clinton, and this despite the contrary urging of Rufus King. Clinton was to have as his running mate Jared Ingersoll of Pennsylvania. Clinton never firmly committed himself to peace, but it was obvious that "peace" support would be welcome.

The battlegrounds proved to be in Pennsylvania and in New York, the one before the people and the other in the legislature. In the Keystone State, Federalists met in secret and made no public pronouncement, but it was apparent they would support Clinton. The Clinton electoral ticket was headed by the choleric old Quid former Governor McKean, and Leib more or less unobtrusively supported the slate. Duane and the *Aurora* on their part kept strangely aloof. In the end, custom and the desire to grant patriotic support to the government at war secured victory for the Madison ticket. So close seemed the race, however, that it was believed to be in doubt until the close.

The contest in New York was in the legislature. Here the Federalists had the assembly and the Republicans the senate, but on joint ballot the Republicans had a majority. Clinton was anxious to preserve the concept of party loyalty to the state caucus nomination of his party which had presented him in the spring. He did not want a split party or a victory by announced Federalist support. This needed some clever management, and it was at this point that there appeared one of the nation's astute managers, true successor of Aaron Burr without his weakness for women and treason. Martin Van Buren, then in his youth, a freshman senator, manipulated the joint session so that Madisonians either voted for Clinton or abstained, and the electoral vote went to Clinton seemingly as a Republican with no taint of open negotiation or coalition with Federalism. New York had taken another step forward in producing leaders of management.

When the votes were finally counted, Madison had been re-elected, 128 to 89. He had the South and West, save Delaware and five of Maryland's eleven votes. He had also won frontier Vermont. Clinton had the rest of New England, New York, and New Jersey, as well as Delaware, and Maryland's remaining votes. The battleground and the place of victory had really been Pennsylvania.[2] Had Clinton won her twenty-five votes he would have become President. But they went to Madison and he stayed in the White House. We hear little more of the Clintons in national politics, but they had left their mark on American democracy. Burr, the Clintons, and Van Buren were the creators of machinery which was to supply a large part of the operational technique of self-government.

This failure to nominate a candidate and the leaning toward De-Witt Clinton had probably been a mistake. The Young Federalists had been advancing organization through committees and conventions. A series of Washington Benevolent Societies was also springing up, somewhat in the manner of the earlier Democratic and Tammany societies. Federalist electioneering newspapers were overtaking, in numbers at least, their Republican competitors. The New England *Palladium*, the Connecticut *Courant*, the New York *Evening Post* and the revamped Philadelphia *Gazette of the United States* were preaching Federalist doctrine. The Young Federalists also cast aside

---

2. A number of the electors had been chosen early, before the warmaking incapacity of the Administration had become apparent. Had the electors been chosen in the fall of 1812 the result might have been different.

certain of the taboos of their senior and undertook to electioneer as the Jeffersonians were doing, organizing mass meetings, indulging in stump speaking, celebrating holidays to political advantage, organizing forces for house-to-house canvassing, distributing tickets, escorting voters to the polls, even resorting to coercion and corruption.

This practical effort was beginning to pay off under the favorable circumstances presented by resentment at the embargo and the less than satisfying results of Jefferson's and Madison's diplomacy. Therefore it was unfortunate to fail to nominate a presidential candidate in 1812. Though Clinton came within twenty-odd votes of success, he did not do as well as the Federalists might have done if their success in elections for state governors and legislators is taken into account or as their successes in 1813–14 might indicate.

War was a new experience for the federal republic and would undoubtedly bring unusual responsibilities and make experiments in political behavior necessary. The presidential election held in the first months of the fighting went off smoothly. In fact all during the war much of life was to go on as usual. To few people could the conflict seem very real, for a relatively small number participated in it. Save in one humiliating instance, it was fought on far distant borders or on the high seas. Communication was slow and poor, and news of what was transpiring could not be very good.

The political situation on the federal level was peculiarly unsatisfactory and weak. Neither President nor Congress had prepared adequately for the conflict despite the fact that it had been on the horizon as a distinct possibility for at least six years. In fact the federal government since 1800 had been trying to avoid any but routine functioning and had succeeded beautifully, save in the Louisiana Purchase. The army and navy had been permitted to decline, the Treasury had lost the services of the Bank, and Congress and Administration seemed immersed in small things and palace-guard politics. The game of diplomacy and factional maneuvering was played in isolation in Washington, far away from centers of activity and in a climate scarcely conducive to stimulating enterprise.

The war not only found the government inept but the country divided. Groups in the South and West may have been in favor of it and hopeful of acquiring Canada and Florida because of it, but New England in general and certain elements in the middle states were not. Commercial interests preferred the hazardous profits of troubled peace to the complete destruction of trade which they anticipated would arise from war. Enlistments were slow, and worse still, there was what amounted to a strike of the financiers and state banks: they would not lend the money necessary. Almost from the beginning New England state governments refused to heed the calls of the federal authorities. In fact the indirect communication which certain New England interests had maintained all along with England continued, and England exempted New England ports from blockade.

This situation stirred the younger Federalists to new life. But once again they demonstrated their incapacity to do anything but follow old patterns and to think only in terms of independent state action, the fashion of the Revolution. They capitalized on the unpopularity of the war and took advantage of Madison's lack of political "umph." By the second year of the war New Jersey and New Hampshire had joined the voters of Masschusetts, Connecticut, and Rhode Island in placing their governments in the hands of the Federalists. In New York, Delaware, and Maryland the Federalists had one house of the legislature. Only Pennsylvania, Vermont, and Ohio of the northern states remained Republican, and Vermont was soon to turn, although New Jersey shortly rejected Federalist guidance.

This political influence was reflected in the actions of some New England governors. In 1812 the governor of Massachusetts had refused to order militia to join the federal army. Governor Martin Chittenden of Vermont withdrew his state's troops in 1813, and when Sir George Prevost crossed the border of northern New York in the Champlain region the following year, Chittenden refused to call out his men, saying he had no authority to send them out of the state. Governor Caleb Strong of Massachusetts had never contributed any, and not until Maine was invaded, in September 1814, did he bestir himself. Then he organized the militia as a state army which he would not permit in any sense to be a part of the United States Army or under orders of its commanders. He did, however, expect the War Department to meet the expense; in this he was disappointed. At the same time—on the very day, in fact—that the British captured Washington, the governor of Connecticut withdrew his brigade of militia from the United States forces and set it up as an independent state army.

This pattern of Federalist minority behavior was but an indication of the general fact that the federal government had not yet reached maturity, nor its authority general acceptance. The War of 1812 was disillusioning in other respects. Communication with Washington was difficult all through the conflict due to the fact that most of it was fought on far distant frontiers to which there was no efficient transport: roads were not built and waterways did not flow in the right courses. The secretaries of War and Navy were not capable, and finally Monroe, the Secretary of State, took over the War Department. Also, Gallatin was no longer the Secretary of the Treasury, and an interim officer of no great talent or influence was assigned the job. The administrative difficulties were multiplied many times when enlistments could not be commanded, when state militia was withdrawn, when state armies were established, when so many defeats were sustained, at least on land, and when the money of the country went on strike. To cap the climax, the British captured Washington and burned important legislative and administrative centers. The government had to flee.

In truth the federal government collapsed, the Treasury defaulted, and the nation was ruled by state governments while the army and navy got along as best they could on their own. For a time the nation returned to situations similar to those in the Revolution and under the Confederation. Political behavior, partisan and administrative, can be said virtually to have ceased to exist on a federal level. Jeffersonian *laissez faire* had been carried almost to an anarchic conclusion. Fortunately it suited European situations to determine a peace, and then, after the war was officially over, Andrew Jackson won a decisive victory over the British at New Orleans.

The climax of political chaos had just been reached. On October 5, 1814, Governor Strong declared to a special session of the Massachusetts legislature that the federal government was prostrate, that Massachusetts was abandoned and must act for herself. The Boston *Centinel* proclaimed that the Union was practically dissolved. Under this stimulus the extreme Federalists at last carried their point. The legislature invited the New England states to send delegates to meet in Hartford on December 15 to take concerted action. It has often been thought that secession and a new confederation were in the minds of some. When the congressional elections were completed, it appeared that of New England's forty-one congressmen only two were Republicans. What might have happened had the war continued will never be known, but peace was at hand and the plans of the Hartford delegates came to naught: when they reached Hartford the war was over. The Federalists for the last time had lost their objective. As they had only issue—antiwar—their *raison d'être* was destroyed.

The overlooked truth of the matter was that for years few had really had any interest in the federal government save the Virginians, their Clintonian rivals, and a few die-hard Federalists like Timothy Pickering. The federal government exerted such limited functions—it had few favors to bestow or powers to exercise—that the republic had lost interest in it.

Madison, like Jefferson, had served out his two terms, narrowly escaping defeat in 1812, not because of any political skill showed by the Jeffersonians or their opponents, but because the Federalists had disintegrated and the schismatic Republican DeWitt Clinton, who opposed Madison, did not arouse enough interest to make enough people vote to change leaders during a war.

In the years between 1801 and 1824, federal politics had become routine, with organization almost wanting, leadership scarcely impressive. Public attention was not attracted to Washington, and interest was concentrated on state operations, where alone much political power was exercised. As far as the advance in machinery of government and in the conduct of the two-level politics which was required to operate the federal system successfully were concerned, the period approached a vacuum. Public attention was centered on the nation's peril in a world at war, and in that area of self-government the federal government was unimpressive in operation. The Federalists had really stirred but little since 1800, and in 1816 a congressional caucus had handed the White House over to another Virginian, James Monroe, largely it seemed because no one really wanted it enough to try and get it. Later in 1824 the Virginians would try to award it to another of themselves, William H. Crawford, whom Monroe had defeated in the caucus of 1816, but the rule of the House of Austria in reality was over. Politics was forced onward by a new dynamics which was building up new patterns of self-government. It was time for such a new politics, a politics in which Virginians were no longer to play an impressive role.

·◦[XVI]◦·

A NEW FRAME OF REFERENCE

*A*T THE conclusion of the War of 1812, the first political generation had to give place to a new group of younger men who would respond to the demands generated by the conditions which came in with the peace. These politicos began to appear as the republic was facing a new age, an age to be dominated, not by the uncertainties of a new venture nor by the quarrels of Europe, but by the opportunities which the United States, now doubled in size by the acquisition of Louisiana, could begin to grasp, undiverted by backward glances across the Atlantic. The tide of empire was moving westward.

The coming of peace had indeed changed the course of national development, and politics, which is a reflection of the moods of society, must of course change too. Prior to 1815 the new republic had been very conscious of its youth and of its insecurity. It seemed to be but a pawn in world politics with its destiny shaped in Europe. Now, however, Europe was to be engrossed in matters nearer at hand, and the United States could turn to developing its own patterns of behavior directed by its native force and opportunities.

American political behavior was to be shaped primarily by the republic's great estate, still so largely unoccupied, and by the swiftly growing population. Eighty percent of the nation had no white people in it, but natural increase and foreign immigration were rapidly to inflate the census figures. And the sparse settlement of the land invited people to move about seeking new opportunities, particularly in the new West, so recently increased in size by the great Purchase. This growing and moving population caused the constant creation of new communities, which in turn prescribed the establishment of new units of self-government and thereby increased political activity.

This constant settling of new self-governing communities was to produce a complex phase of American political evolution which was to tax American talent for self-government to the utmost, for it was to be marked by conflict and disaster. At one time it appeared that the task could not be performed and that the failure was to produce ruin. The idea of democracy had hitherto been tried only in small regions and with few people in rather static areas, but here were mobility, expansion, vast spaces, and great hordes. Ingenuity had produced the constitutions, federal and state, and the Northwest Ordinance. Would it suffice as the nation grew so large?

The process used to create communities, territories, and states was unique in human history. Nowhere had there been such a rational and regular extension of self-government. Four states—Vermont, Kentucky, Tennessee, and Ohio—had been admitted east of the Mississippi. Mississippi, Indiana, Michigan, Illinois, and Alabama had been set up as territories of the first and second class. The Louisiana Purchase, however, had introduced a new problem. The Purchase treaty bound the United States to give the inhabitants civil and political rights and to admit states from that nether region. But this produced complications. First there was the usual erection of territories.

East of the Mississippi this had created no problem. The provisions of the Northwest Ordinance and the Act for the Creation of a Territory South of the Ohio had been followed. But when it came to doing this in the region west of the Great River, in the Louisiana Purchase, the way was not so plain. In this enclave there were already inhabitants of another culture, used to another set of political institutions and these not particularly self-governing.

President Jefferson and his congressional associates, though pledged to ensuring the rights of man and to republicanism, did not believe that the French and Creole inhabitants of Louisiana were ready for Anglo-American self-government. Therefore the Act of 1804 which provided government bore slight resemblance to the Northwest Ordinance. A territory and a district were created. The Territory of Orleans, the present state of Louisiana, was given a governor and a council to be appointed by the President and to rule during his pleasure. This so disturbed the citizens that Jefferson found it hard to form a council, and shortly a delegation was in Washington demanding for the new citizens the right to elect their lawmakers. Congress was not long in yielding, and in 1805 a legislature elected by the people was provided. Meanwhile the so-called District of Louisiana, all the region north of the present state, with its capital at St. Louis, was at first merely put under the governor of the Territory of

Indiana at Vincennes, a most clumsy and unhandy arrangement. Not until 1812, when Orleans was admitted as the state of Louisiana, did this district receive its own officers and become the Territory of Missouri. Democratic self-government was assigned slowly and sparingly to the discontented Creoles.

When the War of 1812 came to an end, the stream of immigrating peoples swelled. Many of them left the eastern states, and a new element who were coming from across the seas to escape constant war and conscription joined them. They contributed to the making of new states out of some of these territories. There was a surge across the Great Water into Missouri; St. Louis was already on the road to becoming the metropolis of the Upper Valley. Then, too, the region to the south and southwest was attractive, and a proposal came before Congress to organize the Territory of Arkansas.

This process of state-making, of creating local units of settlement, of forming towns and counties, demonstrated a controlling factor in the extension of democracy; population was moving westward in parallel lines. The settlers west of New England and the middle states were transplanting the town and township local governments with some elements of the county and school district pattern, while the southern states were to transport the county unit with the county court as the primary ruling group. These county courts were drawn from the leading cotton planters in the lower South. Thus the sectional differences of the Atlantic seaboard would be projected beyond the mountains, and the rivalry for power would be intensified by expansion. Another source of conflict was also emphasized. Ever since the colonial years there had been cultural, and therefore political, conflict between tidewater and back country, seaboard and interior. Now there was to be the Old South and the New, the East and the West, the Seaboard and the Ohio Valley. The sectional character of the population was to have political repercussions as the cultural differences which they represented became crystallized.

While these new communities were in process of creation, the democratic patterns were being perfected in all parts of the nation. In the new states where land was easy to obtain and where there were few town dwellers or wage workers, there was little reason to set up a property qualification. Land was available to all, so in five of the eight new states suffrage was granted to white males over twenty-one. This provision followed a trend which had begun, not only with the state-makers, but in the East as well. The first state to be admitted, Vermont, gave suffrage to all males over twenty-one, and Kentucky, admitted the year following, added only the qualification "white." At the same time, and even before this, the older states had been surrendering some of the property-taxpaying qualifications. New Jersey, Maryland, South Carolina, and North Carolina in part gave up the idea before 1812.

The greatest advances toward universal manhood suffrage came when Connecticut, Massachusetts, and New York State yielded. The contest in the latter state was spectacular. The population of the Empire State had grown amazingly in the census period 1810 to 1820, notably in the western counties and in the municipalities—New York City and the Hudson Valley towns. Large numbers of people were coming from New England into the back country and into New York City as well. Political contests were sharp and the voters evenly divided between the followers of the Clinton dynasty and their Bucktail-Tammany opponents. The latter group believed that any increase in liberality of the franchise would benefit them and make the destruction of DeWitt Clinton the more certain. So they made the most of the fact that two agencies of the state government, the council of appointment and the council of revision, possessed arbitrary power to discharge public officials wholesale and to disallow popular enactments of the legislature. They therefore emphasized the abuses of these bodies as well as the fact that landlords and merchants were keeping many a hardy citizen from voting. Governor Clinton and his associates played into their hands by certain highhanded moves in attempting to block a popular vote on changing the fundamental law. These failed, and the result was the election of a constitutional convention of liberal hue which made a new body of fundamental law. It brought manhood suffrage nearer, though not until 1826 was the actual provision for it finally perfected. Only Virginia and Rhode Island held on to property qualification on the seaboard.

These advances along the road to purer democracy were accompanied by constitutional developments which increased the responsibility of the voters. The original constitutions had reflected suspicion of governors, engendered during colonial days of royal executives, and unbounded trust in legislatures chosen by representatives of property and people. However, experience had begun to indicate a need for checks and balances. So in the new constitutions governors were given more power, the vague and general grants of power to the legislatures were more carefully spelled out, the judiciary and more administrative officers were elected, and the judges, instead of being appointed for life or during good behavior, were elected for terms.

The presidential electors likewise were more often to be chosen by the voters than by the legislatures.

The result of these changes, prescribed in large part by the increase and the spread of the population, was threefold. There were more states, there were more voters, and the voters had larger responsibilities. Elections were more numerous, and the number of offices to be filled by the voters was greater. Those who had political ambitions found that they had more voters to persuade. Patterns of political behavior must perforce become more complicated.

The expansion of the population was not only creating new units of government and advancing democracy but it was also creating new governmental responsibilities. Population was not only moving westward but was also concentrating in eastern urban areas. Not only was commerce growing to supply the increasing population and thus increasing the size of ports and interior business centers, but a new industrialization was developing. The age of machine industry had begun twenty years before the War of 1812, and that conflict, by interrupting imports and limiting normal foreign commerce, had created a demand for manufactures which had induced owners of capital to invest in machines and factories. This process of industrialization was to increase urbanization and to invite population to come from the rural areas and from Europe to concentrate in cities and towns. This expansion and concentration of population in turn made necessary improved means of communication, more and better roads, artificial waterways, and eventually railroads. A great network of transportation facilities must be created to supplement the river system and coasting ocean traffic. Even here there were natural hindrances and obstructions to waterways and harbors which called for the application of human energy and ingenuity.

At the conclusion of the War of 1812, government could not help but be conscious of these developments, because they all induced demands for the exercise of the power of government. Both states and federal government were called upon. Means of communication were an essential need of society which must be supplied and maintained out of the general tax funds. The new industries, now that peace had come, were subject to bitter competition from abroad. Tariff protection must be secured or they would have to cease. More money must be mobilized and made available in larger amounts and more effectively than could be managed by small local banks. A second Bank of the United States was needed for this purpose. While roads and canals could be managed presumably by the localities, tariff protection and a national bank could not. River and harbor improvements, while theoretically state concerns, were tied up with interstate and foreign commerce which were under federal authority by constitutional definition. To what extent would state and, particularly, the federal government recognize these responsibilities and respond to these calls for taxing, expenditure, and financial policies? There were bound to be differences of opinion, opposition, rival plans, and constant controversy. Some indication of what this might be like had appeared in the days of Alexander Hamilton's activity in the new Treasury Department; now the political implications of these questions were again to show. They were to be important factors in a new politics.

In another area it was the day of bigger things. New enterprise could not be handled by individuals and there was need for more corporation activity. Turnpike companies, canal companies, manufacturing ventures, banks, railroads, all stimulated the increasing use of corporation organization. This meant turning to government, state and even federal, for charters, franchises, grants of land, and subsidies from the tax revenue. State legislatures, municipal boards, and, upon occasion, Congress were the source of such implementation, so to these bodies application had to be made. Here then were contests for grants, opposition to favors, and a sense in some instances that in return for such aids, the recipients ought to respond to the needs of the politicians who granted them. Thus there was laid the foundation for deals, graft, lobby activity, and "contributions."

The influence of these situations in shaping new patterns of political behavior appeared almost immediately after the War of 1812 and was most generally recognized on the federal level. The federal government, which had suffered such a loss of prestige during the troubled years of the war, assumed new importance with the coming of peace. The war had served to call attention to financial weakness, industrial immaturity, and inadequacy of communication, so Congress was called upon immediately to cast off the *laissez-faire* indifference of the prewar decade.

Three fields of significant legislation were cultivated. A new tariff policy with some protective features was enacted. A second Bank of the United States was chartered. A comprehensive system of internal communications was submitted to Congress. All of these policies were significant to the social and business life of the nation. They involved policies of great psychological and financial importance, and they were in many respects highly controversial. The assumption and the exercise of the power of government to deal with these weighty questions gave to the rather undeveloped and insignificant federal government a new importance which attracted the attention of the public and provided issues for the new politics which was in the making.

By a significant inversion these policies were taken over and promoted by the Republican party, the party of Jefferson, which originally had stressed *laissez faire*. Now the leaders were talking the language of Hamilton, leaving his few followers the uncongenial task of opposing measures of the type which the Federalist founders had created. Only on internal improvements did the Jeffersonians boggle, as on occasion Madison and Monroe vetoed these measures. So weak were the confused Federalists that for a time after 1815 protective tariff, national bank, and government spending did not supply fuel to rekindle partisan fires. More provocative seemed to be the question of creating new territories and admitting new states.

The Louisiana Purchase not only doubled the size of the young republic, but it introduced the necessity of assimilating a new, well-established culture. This necessity was found to imply a possible upset in the equilibrium achieved in the potential distribution of power in the federal system. From the beginning there was evidence of cultural change in the new republic. There were two well-defined groups of contrasting culture, North and South, free and slave labor groups. A harmonization of these two interests had to be achieved on all questions of major policy and in the distribution of the exercise of political power. In the evolution of the new states which had been admitted to the Union since its formation, there had been no disturbance of this balance. On the face of it, however, although the South had had a slight preference in that all of the Presidents save John Adams had come from that region, two free and two slave states had been admitted from the original area, and although there were nine free states to eight slave states, this did not seem to give any political combination any great advantage.

As soon as the proposal to annex the trans-Mississippi region began to be bruited about, however, the question of the balance was raised. Certain New England political spokesmen became more conscious than ever of the fact that New England's influence in an expanding federal system might be assumed to be shrinking, certainly their proportionate representation in Congress was. Now in this great estate across the Mississippi there were several potential states which were much more likely to be culturally in sympathy with the rural and slave labor areas than they would be with eastern mores. Representatives from the New England states sought to enlist opposition to the purchase of Louisiana and later to the admission of the settlements on the lower Mississippi as the state of Louisiana. Some few even threatened secession if the great area were purchased or if this state were admitted. To be submerged in a political system dominated by southern custom was dangerous and not to be tolerated. At the time these protests were not heeded, but they were ominous of the future.

By 1815 the push of population westward had attracted new settlers across the Mississippi, where they were to mingle with and soon outnumber the French and Spanish Creoles. For a time a balance was maintained. There were by 1819 twenty-two states, eleven free and eleven slave. But the postwar population movements seemed to be establishing a trend, or direction, of migration which justified the apprehensions of northern congressmen. This was a trend to the southwest which indicated a preference for potential communities where plantation operation and slave labor might prevail, and it proved to be a complicating factor in the new politics. When legislation for the admission of Missouri and the organization of Arkansas came into Congress, its introduction was the signal for a political outbreak. A number of circumstances combined to produce a bitter contest, which Jefferson in retirement declared to be as frightening as the sound of a fire bell in the night. Certain northern spokesmen, some of whom showed Federalist coloring, wanted to prevent the admission of a slave state which would make the South predominant in the Senate, at the moment equally balanced. As the free states had the greater number in the House because the population of the northern states was larger than that of the South, the question was, could this numerical superiority in the House be mobilized?

Here northern leadership could count on another advantage. Certain attitudes were pronounced in American society. One of these was displayed by militant religious groups who believed in the elimination of sin in order to approach social perfection and to demonstrate a means of grace indicating salvation. The sinfulness of human slavery could be proclaimed in striking terms and the South convicted of sin because of its support of the institution. Therefore the South and the nation must be saved from this sin, purged of the guilt. Also, there was the rational philosophy of the Revolution embracing equality and the Rights of Man. Certainly there was a contradiction, an irreconcilable difference between liberty and human slavery. It was utterly inconsistent with the basic principles of the American republic just to tolerate slavery, let alone permitting it to spread. These attitudes were quite generally cherished by American society, so it could be appealed to by those who wished to curb southern expansion and power. Their advance or even continuance in power must be fought in the name of human liberty to destroy the sin of slavery, an institution so inconsistent with republican ideals. So battle was joined which had disturbing implications.

In the parliamentary struggle that ensued the Senate was effectively managed by southern leadership, while the House was activated by its antisouthern majority. In the latter body efforts were made to destroy slavery in both Missouri and Arkansas, a proposition which had no chance of acceptance by the Senate. Hence there was the possibility of a deadlock which might arrest further expansion of government indefinitely, leaving to those seeking new opportunity only territorial status in Missouri and frontier anarchy in the balance of the Louisiana Purchase. Skillful management was necessary and it was at hand. The speaker of the House was Henry Clay of Kentucky. He was a brilliant and ambitious member of the younger generation who had been glittering on the Washington scene since he came to the Senate from Kentucky in 1806. He had made his mark later in the House as a war hawk and as its speaker. He now exerted his talents in promoting one of the strengths of the American democratic system of self-government, proficiency in the art of compromise. He was able to pilot through the House a Senate-created compromise. This measure took advantage of the fact that Massachusetts had consented to the admission of her expensive and inconvenient Maine district as a state and that most of the rest of the Louisiana Purchase was deemed uninhabitable because of its treeless prairies. Missouri and Maine would be admitted together as a slave and a free state, thus preserving the balance in the Senate, and the rest of the Louisiana Purchase would be divided by a line 36° 30′; north of this line slavery would be prohibited. Thus to offset Arkansas, a potential slave state, another free state would be guaranteed north of 36° 30′. Seemingly, the congressional imagination of that day did not foresee more than four more states: two slave, Arkansas and an undefined Oklahoma; and two free, Michigan east of the Mississippi, and an upper Missouri to the west of the Father of Waters. Clay gained a reputation for statesmanship from this episode which was supposed to remove slavery and southern domination as political issues.

Thus the tides of moving, expanding, and concentrating population had stimulated new struggles for the complex allocation of power which the intricate federal system indicated. They made likewise inevitable a greater assumption of power on the part of the federal government and a consequent resistance by the local units, the states. Furthermore, this struggle was complicated by the cultural conflict arising out of the immense geographical extent of the republic, spreading as it did over such a variety of physiographic and climatic conditions which had introduced cultural parallelism and cultural difference north and south. Finally, the passage of time introduced a new and controlling element, a most significant determinant of new political behavior patterns. The older generation of the founders was passing. Their political organization, such as it was, had all but disappeared. Now there were signs that a new generation was pressing to take the White House from this Virginia dynasty who had dwelt therein so long. In the process they were taking the lead in a new politics. The field was ripe for the harvest.

This politics now appearing in the republic was indeed new. What had hitherto appeared as partisan politics, in the twentieth-century use of the term, has often been described in terms that are now misleading. So far, such groupings as had been called parties had been discontinuous. Political activists had been pragmatic. They formed groups which were fluid and, in any modern sense, unstructured, formed for some immediate purpose, and when that purpose was achieved, they disintegrated. There had been the Revolutionary experience when the Patriots had acted for a purpose. Then when ratification of the Constitution was in question, its supporters were known as Federalists. The necessities of establishing the federal system, creating financial and foreign policies, defining power, and accommodating personal differences produced differences of opinion, factions, and parties but with only a minimum of organization. The first of these, again confusingly known as Federalists, accomplished its purposes during Washington's Presidency, and then the opposition, the Republicans, in Revolutionary fashion organized to get those controlling the new establishment out of power.

When this was achieved in 1800–1801, the new power established itself on a *laissez-faire* base of minimum action. This negative program had little potential to cause apprehension or to stir positive emotion. There was no political objective, so political interest died away as far as federal politics was concerned. The Jeffersonians in the Congress, under the guidance of their leader, had set up rudimentary machinery to give some national direction to their presidential choices in 1800, 1804, and 1808. Although this caucus among the Republicans

had persisted for two more of the quadrennial contests, it was dying
on its feet. The Federalists had never been able to do anything in
Washington. They were too few there, and their convention efforts
in 1808 and 1812 had done little.

By 1816, for all intents and purposes, the Federalists as a national
identity were through. Even the difficulties of the Napoleonic conflict and the War of 1812 failed to stir any effective party contest
save in the election of 1812. The Virginia Dynasty soon lost their
dynamic quality and more or less operated government by default.
Through these years a variety of political patterns had developed in
the states. Little concerted action on a national scale developed except
such as could be contrived during the sessions of Congress in Washington. The White House was more the seat of conference and connivance than of power.

During this decade or so in which there was a minimum of partisan contest in a national sense, political machinery had been used in
larger measure, not so much as an instrument of partisan contest, as a
convenient mechanism. In one state, New Jersey, where there were
no state-wide contests for officials, the convention system in county,
city, and township, with their organizing committees, operated almost
as a part of the state government, although without any legal establishment. Those who were making and executing the laws found it
convenient to have this type of organization to conduct elections.
With the return of national partisanship, one of its phenomena was
the falling apart of this extralegal campaigning structure; oftentimes
two conventions and committees took the place of one.

The real power and organized politics survived better in the
states. People in general had lost interest in "national politics" and
were indifferent to most of what went on in Washington. During the
War of 1812 the power and the glory had certainly departed. Politics
had disintegrated into state units and each had its own system. Parties,
if such they could be called, were fragmentized into factions with
little or no organization. Even in New York, Pennsylvania, and Virginia, machinery was reduced to a minimum. The embryonic concept
of national parties which had appeared in the first decade had not
caught on.

The pattern was still Revolutionary: a force was mobilized to
meet a crisis, minutemen were assembled through committees of correspondence. When the crisis disappeared, the force dissolved. In certain of the states there was evidence of more stable organization, but
it was not general. South of Virginia it could hardly be said to exist,

nor was it apparent in the new western communities. New England had an elite system all its own, partly ecclesiastical. There seemed to be a correlation between larger population and mixed heterogeneous societies, such as were characteristic of the middle states. When there was variety, there was greater need for organization.

Though nearly every one believed as 1816 approached that the next President would be a Republican, there were still Federalists in the land. They were not organized on the national level—in fact they never had been. They represented a state of mind rather than an association of bodies. They suffered from the stigma of opposing a war which the United States, officially at least, had won and from their futile gesture at the Hartford Convention. They were upon occasion smeared as traitors, and just as after the Glorious Revolution in 1688, supporters of the House of Stuart, the Jacobites, were under the ban, so were the Federalists. But they represented an attitude that was not uncommon: they liked order and were not attracted to innovation. They favored conservative policy and they had come to distrust such symbols of "irresponsibility" as Jefferson and Republicanism. They had never learned organization, nor did they understand its uses, yet they had some strongholds still in the states. In them they undertook to rule by small elite groups with little regard to popular interest or support. They could not appeal; they thought they should command.

For a time they had regained some strength because of the unpopularity of the embargo and the war, but when that episode ended for them with the disaster of the Hartford Convention, they were in difficulties. Then to make their condition worse, the Republicans, who were usually alert, saw the need for new measures to rebuild the national strength. They essayed the role of Hamilton and backed a program much like his. The Federalists now had no leaders, no reputation, and no program; all they could do was view with alarm and protest. As there are always those who so behave, their numbers were not negligible.

But what role would they play in the struggle for power? In 1816 they made no effort, not even such feeble moves as they had in 1808 and 1812. A few in the Philadelphia area had tried to suggest correspondence about candidates, but nothing came of it. On their part, the Jeffersonians were having what was to be a final congressional caucus. The custom had been growing to hand on the Presidency to the Secretary of State at a meeting of the Jeffersonian congressmen. So Madison and his associates planned to pass it on to James Monroe.

However, the remnant of the Old Republicans, including John Randolph and the Quids, picked out William H. Crawford, a Georgian of Virginia birth, for the role. They failed, and Monroe received the prize, but a general understanding was reached that the prize could come to Crawford in 1824. There could not be said to have been any campaign, and Monroe had no real opposition. The ruling groups in Connecticut, Massachusetts, and Delaware succeeded in appointing thirty-four electors who all voted for Rufus King without any formal understanding.

The activity involved in choosing a President in 1820 was even less noticeable. Senator Samuel Smith called the usual Republican congressional caucus, but so few attended, ostensibly because of a bad storm, that nothing was done and another was not called. The fact of the matter was that there was a revolt against the system, and certain state delegations had decided not to attend. The matter was left to the electors who, with one exception, voted for Monroe. One otherwise-minded New Hampshire man cast his ballot for John Quincy Adams. There was less unanimity about re-electing Vice President Danield D. Tompkins. Thirteen electors voted for others. Eight of these, Federalists, came from Massachusetts, and a majority of its delegation voted for Richard Stockton of New Jersey, the New Hampshire holdout voted for Richard Rush of Pennsylvania, Delaware's delegation voted for a native, Daniel Rodney, and one from Maryland cast his ballot for Robert G. Harper from that state.

The Federalist activities in the states after 1815 varied. In some, like Connecticut and Massuchusetts, they ran candidates, but in the main they sought to encourage, or at least take advantage of, Republican rifts and to support dissendent factions as they had helped Burr and DeWitt Clinton in New York. Their main use at times seemed to be as a smear instrument. Various Republicans attempted to weaken their rivals by fastening the stigma of "Federalist" upon them.

Were partisanship and factionalism dead? For a time there had seemed to be some hope. Washington and Jefferson had an aversion to parties, and Monroe, when he became President, undertook to do what he could to promote "the gradual elimination of all political factions." The practical second death of this faction in the election of 1816 seemed as evidence that this might be a possibility. Monroe made a journey into New England with this in mind. He talked fair and made various allusions to the destruction of faction and the encouragement of amalgamation. But Monroe had not done anything save appoint a few men from their ranks, most notably General Solomon

Van Rensselaer, who was made postmaster of Albany. The President seemed to discount the compulsion of change.

The truth was that with the coming of peace in 1815 all sense of crisis had evaporated, and the generation that had been guided by Revolutionary patterns had departed from places of responsibility. Therefore when new occasions were to teach new duties, they would teach new men. Without the control either of crisis or accustomed leadership after the coming of peace, there was no immediate force to shape popular behavior into any very definite political pattern. But the new dynamics in the making was creating a new politics.

·❧[XVII]❧·

ON THE BRINK OF CHAOS

*C*HE NEW politics, determined by forces appearing after the war, could be observed most strikingly in the presidential elections. The authors of the Constitution had found few precedents to guide them in prescribing for the election of the President, and none of them proved adequate. They had therefore been forced to create, and the result was a strange and, it proved, ineffective mechanism for the choice of the Chief Magistrate by an Electoral College. Within a decade the Presidents and the congressional leaders had added a gadget, an extralegal congressional caucus system for nominating candidates for the Presidency.

The caucus had been handing on the Presidency from President to Secretary of State, from Virginian to Virginian after the troubled term of John Adams. As 1824 loomed in the offing President Monroe had three presidential hopefuls in his Cabinet. Crawford sought to be the heir apparent in view of his withdrawal from the contest in 1816. John Quincy Adams and John C. Calhoun each nursed ambition in his own peculiar way. Then there was the speaker of the House, Henry Clay, spokesman of the new West. The indefatigable DeWitt Clinton of New York and his friend General Andrew Jackson of New Orleans fame and Tennessee residence had some backers, although the latter essayed to be a Warwick for Clinton rather than to seek the crown himself.

As Crawford had the best organization, with the support of at least eighty congressmen, it was feared that if a caucus were held he would be nominated. So his opponents determined to boycott any such gathering, and more than half the members signed a pledge not to attend. Therefore from the beginning the contest was to be a free-for-all, with a minimum of influence recognized as coming from the national capital. The country was indeed back to 1788–89 but with no Washington to whom all could turn nor any Jefferson with his political finesse and skill with the pen and the idea. Probably without realizing it, the politicos, such as they were in 1821, were going to be forced to use the ineffective scheme set up by the authors of the Constitution. Interestingly enough, it was to be the only time it was really to be employed. In other words, the Electoral College would nominate, not elect. It would present to the House of Representatives a slate of three candidates from whom that body would choose.

The members of this so-called new generation who were eager for power were really in fact not very new. Adams, Calhoun, Clay, Clinton, Crawford, and Jackson had long been before the public, even as presidential aspirants. Their average age was fifty-one and Adams and Jackson were fifty-seven. They had all been in public life since before the War of 1812 and Adams and Clinton much longer. Clinton had almost been elected in 1812. Crawford had yielded to Monroe in 1816. Jackson had been spoken of occasionally since his victory at New Orleans in 1815. As the old method of designation for the Presidency, the congressional caucus, had fallen into disrepute, there was a certain amount of experimenting with other devices to put these candidates before the voters. On December 18, 1821, the legislature of South Carolina presented the name of William Lowndes to the people of the United States as a favorite son. In 1822 John Quincy Adams gave his consent to have a legislative caucus in Massachusetts present him, provided only Republicans participated. Lest his Federalist background be too much remembered, he published a letter the next year in the Richmond *Enquirer* wooing the Old Republicans by proclaiming his loyalty to the Principles of '98. On July 20, 1822, the Tennessee legislature nominated Andrew Jackson. In November the Missouri and Kentucky lawmakers introduced the name of Henry Clay, followed by Ohio in January 1823. William H. Crawford was nominated by the legislature of North Carolina, November 24, 1823, despite a stroke of paralysis, and by Virginia on February 21, 1824. In the meantime Lowndes had died and South Carolina had made a second nomination when her legislature in November 1823 had presented John C. Calhoun. After preliminary consideration by a legislative caucus, a mass meeting organized at Faneuil Hall in Boston presented John Quincy Adams on February 15, 1824, as the favorite son of Massachusetts with Andrew Jackson as his running mate. This ticket was seconded in March by meetings in Virginia, Maryland, and Louisiana.

Confusion such as these moves proclaimed was bound to awaken some political actors possessed of a sense of order. One such appeared in New York, the graduate school of American politics. Martin Van Buren, chief opponent of DeWitt Clinton and leader of the Bucktails, had just been elected to the United States Senate and was planning to go to Washington, leaving New York State in charge of a regency at Albany which was to become famous. He was opposed to President Monroe whom he believed was trying to destroy faction by "amalgamation" with the Federalists. He particularly resented the appointment of the Federalist General Solomon Van Rensselaer, kinsman to the patroon, as postmaster at Albany. Furthermore he was a great believer in organization and he wanted to re-form the ranks of the Jeffersonian Republicans on a national scale in a fashion similar to that which he had employed in New York. In order to do this he proposed to re-establish the congressional caucus as the way to unite all Republicans on one candidate, thus settling the claims of the numerous contenders, all of whom assumed Republicanism. But the caucus was in disfavor.

In order to re-establish this institution he sought to revive the old New York-Virginia alliance which had been first, in a way, negotiated by Madison and Burr. When Van Buren took his Senate seat in December 1821, he began his maneuvers. His first move was to participate in a successful scheme to defeat a New York Federalist Clintonian for speaker of the House and to secure the election of a Virginian. He sought unsuccessfully to block Van Rensselaer's appointment as postmaster. At this time there also began to be some discussion of another instrument of nomination. One of the influential newspaper editors, Thomas Ritchie of the Richmond *Enquirer* and a Crawford supporter, realizing that his candidate had backers in all the states, proposed that a national convention be held so that the state operators in conference could arrive at a consensus which would focus public interest on one candidate—he probably hoped Crawford —and prevent the contest from being thrown into the House of Representatives. His editorials of July and August 1822 were given slight heed and the convention was not held. Rather, another effort was made to use the congressional caucus.

Van Buren was determined to try one. In March 1822 he had begun a series of trips to Virginia and, later, to points farther south. In the course of these journeyings he came to the conclusion that Crawford, rather than Calhoun, should be his choice. Crawford, born in Virginia and living in Georgia, had strong support in those states and in North Carolina. He was a good Republican, while Calhoun seemed to Van Buren to have Federalist ideas about federal power and spending, at least so Van Buren said. Perhaps the truth of the matter was that Van Buren shared Crawford's dislike of the rather austere and unyielding South Carolina intellectual.

Also, in preparing for the caucus, Van Buren tried to enlist the aid of Henry Clay, speaker of the House. He suggested that Clay run for Vice President. In view of the fact that Crawford had just had a stroke of paralysis, it would appear that Clay was not quite as shrewd as he might have been. But Clay would not agree, so Van Buren accepted Albert Gallatin as running mate because of his presumed influence in Pennsylvania. On February 14, 1824, the caucus assembled. Those who had signed the pledge to stay away kept it: only 66 of a congressional membership of 261 appeared. This rump included no Pennsylvanians; in fact eight states were not represented at all and a majority came from four states. Crawford was duly nominated and his choice for Vice President, Albert Gallatin, accepted. But Van Buren could not take much inspiration from his effort to re-form his party.

New interests, new sections, new communities, new masses of people, a new generation were all working together to promote new divisions among political activists that were bound to function when thought was given to Monroe's successor as 1824 approached.

Had the old routine persisted, the man would have been William H. Crawford. He expected it, and there was a certain amount of acquiescence among the operators within the establishment despite his illness. Crawford had a machine of sorts at work to secure it, and he had an effective spokesman in the person of Martin Van Buren. But there were too many ambitious men, sections, and interests to permit the inertia of the Crawford move to carry him along. Calhoun, the Secretary of War, opposed him from the South; John Quincy Adams, Secretary of State, opposed him from New England; Henry Clay and Andrew Jackson were hopeful in the West, and the former as the speaker and the latter as the hero of New Orleans had much appeal.

Partisanship was not viewed with unconcern nor was it taken for granted. Because of its character it was looked upon by even the great as undesirable, even as dangerous. As partisanship had started on a large scale as a Revolutionary instrument, it could suggest war and violence, internecine bitterness, venomous hostility. It was a divisive influence, which could be defined as subversive. Federalists and Republicans accused each other of being unpatriotic and of conniving with the nation's enemies. Madison was charged with being pro-French; Federalists, pro-British. In fact certain of the Essex Junto Federalists were exposed as plotting with a British agent. The Revolutionary term Tory was applied to the Federalists. During the War of 1812 Federalists had opposed the struggle and at its end had been preparing for some sort of vigorous repudiation, perhaps even secession. Despite the factionalism and the hostility to the conflict, the war had been won. But it is significant to note that some of its supporters still believed the triumph over the aristocrats and monarchs was equally as glorious as that over the British. There was fear of the Federalist faction, because there was still doubt as to whether the government was adequate, a projection of Revolutionary bitterness. What would be the part of these prejudices and antipathies in 1824? The various candidates were aware of their existence, and the voting power of those who cherished them might, in not a few instances, be significant, particularly with the field so divided.

Open support of Federalists might be embarrassing, even dangerous. Their endeavors to insinuate themselves into Monroe's good graces had not in the end brought much result. Yet when the campaign of 1824 began to be planned for, the several candidates, each in his own way, went after Federalist support. A series of almost comic maneuvers was undertaken designed to secure it. Crawford's efforts brought forth evidence that he had favored Federalists, and his Republican opponents published letters supporting him from such as Timothy Pickering, the most die-hard of Federalists. Calhoun was preaching that the old parties were dead and new ones forming; in such the Federalists would be welcome if they would cooperate. The idea was to work with Calhoun men in support of him. Webster seemed agreeable. Calhoun also had the support of the Pennsylvania Federalist James Buchanan, and there was hope in North Carolina. Henry Clay believed his American System of banks, protective tariff, and internal improvements would attract Federalists, and he had hopes that New York mercantile interests would appreciate his efforts to promote Latin American independence and trade. Jackson had been a favorite with many Federalists, and he believed he would have some of their support. He had always been favorable to them and had tried to persuade Monroe to include two of them in his first Cabinet, urging amalgamation.

Though the survival of the Federalists contributed nothing of significance to any political organizing, it did add to the confusion. Friends of the various Republican candidates tried to smear their opponents with the taint of Federalist support. Jackson's letters to Monroe urging Federalist appointments were dredged out, seemingly by larceny, and confusion became worse confounded. Adams had the most difficult time because he had once been a Federalist and knew that any overture he might make or any conversation he might have with Federalists would open him to suspicion of returning to his old fellowship with these traitors. The popular mind might be in the process of being conditioned to charges of corrupt bargaining.

The issues, if there were any, and the fates of these various candidates were to be decided in but a few of the states. The most significant developments were to take place in three: Pennsylvania, Tennessee, and New York. In the Keystone State there were three political interests. The Federalists had survived there longer than anywhere else save in New England. The Republicans for their part were badly split. The old school Leib-Duane group of Independent Republicans was at cross-purposes with the Snyder new school regime, which in its time harbored a faction known as the Family party wherein various kinsmen of Dallas and Wilkins were playing astute politics. Early in the 1820's the Family party was dominant and it favored Calhoun. Therefore this agency attempted to get the Pennsylvania Republican convention to endorse Calhoun in 1823. When they failed both in that year and in 1824 and when the latter gathering nominated Jackson for the first place, suggesting Calhoun for the second spot, Calhoun came to an unhappy conclusion; he must accept second place. He was facing a revolution in South Carolina where his old enemy, Judge William Smith, was working to put Calhoun at a disadvantage. South Carolina was feeling the expense of the postwar tariffs, designed to protect American industries, and the cost of internal improvements. These measures Calhoun had supported in 1816 to remedy war damage. But he found this was folly. So he now turned to *laissez faire* before William Smith could maneuver a coup. He became a states rights', Puritan fighting man; the nationalist in him was almost dead. He would withdraw from the main race and accept the nomination for the Vice Presidency. Jackson was an elder statesman, and his Vice President might be called on soon to succeed him.

In Tennessee some devious politics was to have unexpected results. In that distant region there was little political organization and nothing like partisan regularity. One of the numerous factions in that confused transmountain state saw a use for itself in Andrew Jackson's name and sought to appropriate it. This was a crowd who were anxious to defeat one of their senators, John Williams. They therefore undertook to present Jackson, perhaps without any serious expectation of helping him to the White House. They were merely using Jackson in their local situation; on the national scene they preferred Clay or Adams. On July 20, 1822, they proposed his name in the Tennessee legislature hoping to defeat Williams and his supporting faction who favored Crawford. This maneuver was not too fortunate as far as its immediate end was concerned, for they were only partly successful in gaining legislative strength to defeat Williams. They had found that the only way to finish the senator's career was to elect Jackson to his seat, a move they had not anticipated. Jackson himself had not taken his presidential candidacy very seriously. His original choice had been Clinton, and when the New Yorker's chances disappeared, Jackson had inclined to either Adams or Calhoun, whom he believed had supported him in his military campaign in Florida. Now he must perforce enter the United States Senate again, where he would find himself in the political center with his ambitions still unkindled.

The situation in New York was conditioned by the fast growth of the Empire State, particularly in New York City and the western counties and in the development of a new communication interest, the Erie Canal. These signs of enterprise vitally affected the fortunes of the officeholders and political factions of the Empire State, especially those of Clinton and Van Buren. These two presented a sharp contrast, the one the dominating statesman type of the old school of the founders, the other the suave, unobtrusive machine operator typifying a new brand of leader who would manipulate and arrange rather than lead and command.

Clinton had entered a new phase of his political life after his defeat for the Presidency in 1812. This new opportunity came at the close of the war when he grasped the possibility of a great waterway uniting the Hudson with the Great Lakes which would make New York City a major outlet for western trade. After five years and more of effort, he and his associates were instrumental in persuading the legislature to undertake this immense project. In 1816 it was taken up by a commission of which Clinton was a member. The work proceeded impressively, and when Governor Tompkins resigned the following year to become Monroe's Vice President, a state convention was organized to nominate Clinton for the vacant governorship, another indication of the growth of the convention as a nominating device to supersede the legislative caucus. Van Buren and his Tammany allies,

the Bucktail faction, could do little but suggest war hawk congressman Peter B. Porter to oppose Clinton. But of Porter, the voters
would have none, and Clinton was elected overwhelmingly. During
this new executive experience he pushed the canal ahead and was his
usual domineering self. Again he attracted Federalists and disturbed
the Jeffersonian advocates of *laissez faire* and little government. Van
Buren was able to capitalize this and again to mobilize Clinton's many
enemies. Tompkins was prevailed upon to run against his erstwhile
patron in 1820 at the same time he was standing for re-election as
Vice President. Again Clinton triumphed but by the narrowest of
margins.

Then Clinton undertook to block the successful move for a new
state constitution and destroyed his popularity to such a degree that
in 1822 he saw fit not to run again and turned his entire attention to
his work on the canal commission, which was bringing the construction of the Erie and Champlain canals to successful conclusion.

Clinton's unfortunate opposition to the popular demand for a new
constitution, which forced his retirement, seemed to spell the end of
his chances for the Presidency. But the regency was not relieved of
opposition. The Federalists secured a new stimulus to energy from
Calhoun and set up a paper, *The Patriot*, in May 1823, designed to
attack the power of Martin Van Buren and the Bucktails. Also, the
Clintonian faction hit upon a new issue. The presidential electors in
the Empire State were still appointed by the legislature. The growing
demand for broadened suffrage included a proposal that the electors
be chosen by the people. The opponents of the Bucktails advocated
this proposal, hoping that if the people chose electors they might
forget Clinton's opposition to the constitution and allow their local
pride to cause them to choose electors favorable to him as the great
canal builder.

At this point the regency showed poor judgment. When the New
York house approved the popular choice of electors, the regency-
controlled senate killed it in the hope of finishing Clinton's chances
once and for all. But then they took one further step to that end, even
more foolish. Clinton was still a member of the Erie Canal commission. The job was unsalaried and the work was about complete. But
now they would remove him, the great promoter of the work, and
thus complete his banishment to oblivion. But it turned out they were
not killing a foe, they were making a martyr.

The enemies of the regency immediately seized upon this foolish
vindictiveness. They raised up the martyr as a rallying figure to lead a

new People's party which would attract all opposed to the regency and on an issue of popular rights get back into power by running DeWitt Clinton yet again for governor. This maneuver was initiated in September 1824 at a state-wide convention. One of its chief architects was a young Rochester newspaper editor, Thurlow Weed, who that summer had become acquainted with a young lawyer from Auburn, William H. Seward. The convention formed the People's party and nominated Clinton for governor. Weed's newspaper announced its support for John Quincy Adams and Andrew Jackson for President and Vice President. Clinton and the People's party won a decisive victory in November 1824. As Van Buren, who had seemingly had no part in Clinton's removal from the canal board, ruefully remarked, "There is such a thing as killing a man too dead." What sort of an electoral ticket would the New York holdover legislature appoint? The regency controlled only the senate. The house was badly split.

This confused situation in New York and the fizzle of the congressional caucus from which Van Buren had hoped so much probably stirred him to new maneuvers in a fashion anticipating later high-level negotiations. Again he attempted to arrange for Clay to join Crawford and seek the Vice Presidency on his ticket. Such a junction of forces would be very profitable for Clay. Crawford's poor health might soon give Clay the Presidency. Was Clay nearer the Presidency at that moment than he was ever to be again? Who knows? Clay was coy but Van Buren pushed on. He persuaded Gallatin to withdraw from the caucus assignment. Despite this move, he got no satisfaction from Clay; perhaps he didn't expect any: men must be wary. But Van Buren did have the extra session of the New York legislature coming up to choose electors, and he hoped that the Crawford-Clay combination might win New York's thirty-six. Incidentally, a boomlet emerged designed to make Van Buren the vice presidential nominee instead of Gallatin. But there were few takers.

Van Buren was not the only exponent that year of organization and planned strategy. It was not yet the era of active public campaigning. Crawford's paralysis kept him out of any maneuvering. Calhoun had resigned himself to the Vice Presidency. Adams was unable to practice any obvious political arts. Jackson did not really think of himself as a candidate. Clinton was soon occupied by a local campaign in New York. But with Clay it was different. He was vigorous and ambitious. His western residence left him out of any of the little limelight there might be. He was going to be an innovator.

He organized a committee of correspondence to prepare campaign material for eastern circulation, and he appointed an informal campaign manager in the person of Josiah S. Johnston of Louisiana. These efforts were designed to augment his own active correspondence with men in New York, Pennsylvania, and Virginia, his birthplace. And it was in Virginia that another seed had been planted. Thomas Ritchie, editor of the Richmond *Enquirer* with whom Van Buren was to have long association, had unsuccessfully advocated a national nominating convention as a substitute for the caucus which Van Buren was pushing. These signs were all pointing to a new day—but it was a day which had not quite yet dawned.

The advancing months of 1824 meanwhile added to the bewildering variety of caucuses, conventions, meetings, resolutions, committees of correspondence, and negotiations. Money was raised, old newspapers took new stands, and new ones were established. Pamphlets and broadsides were printed and distributed. Voters were solicited more vigorously and variously than in any previous campaign. Electors were nominated and campaigned before the voters; tickets were printed which voters took to the ballot boxes. Never before or since has there been such a formless, unorganized, chaotic and confusing presidential election.

During these final months, the original promoters of Jackson in Tennessee and some rather obscure supporters in Pennsylvania, whom he had not been encouraging particularly, discovered they had built better than they knew. The voters were in a mood for a hero. After so many years of drab personalities in the White House, here was a colorful and dynamic man of power. The nation was approaching the fiftieth anniversary of the Revolution. It was a time of reviving memory, memories of Washington and the Patriot leaders. In various states an uncountable number of individuals were sensing a new leader. In some, such as Tennessee and Pennsylvania, skilled operators of the unorganized politics of the day could see in Jackson some useful purpose. These leaders in a sense became followers for reasons best known to themselves.

One by one the several states chose electors either at the polls or in their legislatures. After tedious waiting and scorekeeping during the months of 1824, it became reasonably certain that the election would have to take place in the House. But who would be the three candidates with the highest electoral score? By autumn there was no longer much doubt but that Jackson would be one, and Adams probably another. But who would be third, Crawford or Clay? It is hard to realize that Crawford's serious paralysis seemed of so little concern. But communication was minimal, the secret was well kept, and the candidate's condition was not a subject of remark.

Those who were keeping tab, for in that epoch the electors were chosen over a succession of months at a different time in each state, found Jackson in the lead but with not enough for a decision. He had won North and South Carolina, Alabama, Mississippi, and Tennessee together with a majority of Maryland's slate in the South; Indiana and part of Illinois in the West; and Pennsylvania and New Jersey in the East. Adams gained New England's fifty-one votes, and although he had carried Maryland by a plurality, the district system meant that he got but three of her eleven votes. Virginia and Georgia went for Crawford; Clay had Kentucky, Ohio, and Missouri. New York and Louisiana were about the last to vote, and the result depended on what their decisions might be. New York's thirty-six electors were the great prize.

In the meantime the cauldron of New York politics had boiled up once more. In November the People's party triumphantly put Clinton back into the governor's chair. Yet it was the expiring legislature that was coming back to choose the electors. And in this body no group was in control. The Bucktails had the senate 17–14, but the house was a bear garden. The regency could hold the senate for Crawford, but in the house Crawford had but 43, with Adams supported by 50 and Clay, 32. If the two houses had to meet in joint session, 157 strong, no one would be in control. Sixty would support Crawford, 57 Adams; each far away from the 79 needed. The outcome would evidently be in the hands of the 39 Clay supporters and the one uncommitted. Van Buren still hoped that Clay would settle for the Vice Presidency with Crawford.

On November 5 on the eve of meeting of the legislature a caucus was assembled at which the Bucktails met some Clay men. The conference was stormy because much was at stake. It had become reasonably apparent by this date that the election would have to be settled in the U.S. House of Representatives. Since Jackson and Adams at this point seemed likely to be two of the three in the balloting, the question was, would Clay or Crawford be the other? If Clay were included, his long-time influence in the House as speaker might make him the favorite. So it was to the interest of both the Adams and Crawford men to keep him out of the contest in the House, but they must have some of his votes or New York would cast no electoral ticket. The Clay men were demanding and the Crawford men in the New York legislature hesitant, but their need was equally great. So after protracted bargaining the regency-Van Buren-Crawford forces yielded the minimum and proposed a ticket of twenty-nine for Crawford, seven for Clay. Such a ticket might conceivably keep Adams out of the running and place the contest among Jackson, Crawford, and Clay. It was too early to tell. Clay men on their part were doubtful whether this combination would do their man any good, as well they might be.

Balloting began November 10, delayed by slow arrivals. On that day the Bucktail senate voted the ticket—twenty-nine Crawford, seven Clay—which they had offered. But in the house there was chaos. As predicted, Adams had fifty, Crawford forty-three, Clay thirty-two. The balloting produced no majority and there was a deadlock. If this persisted, no votes would be cast by New York, and Crawford would be definitely fourth man and out. Consequently, the Bucktails must pay any price to get the house to elect a slate so that the two houses could go into joint ballot, where Van Buren's agents would have a chance to "negotiate."

The regency came to a startling conclusion. During the session of November 12, Van Buren's lieutenant, Azariah Flagg, announced that next day the regency men would join the Adams men in the house and vote for thirty-six Adams electors. Thus, as the two houses would be in disagreement, they must go into joint session and there would then be a chance to do business. In this trading the Crawford and Adams men would be drawn together, possibly to the ruin of Clay. However, the Crawford men still had hopes of support from the latter, if they paid for it. So they now offered to vote for fifteen Clay men in return for support for twenty-one for Crawford. The Clay men would not agree, for even with this larger quota it was not certain that Clay would come in third. They might do better if Crawford got no votes from New York, provided they could secure enough from Adams to make Clay third.

On November 13 the regency men carried out their threat. They joined with the Adams men in supporting in the house a slate of thirty-six Adams electors. Thus they insured a joint session. The Clay men were furious at the regency and were in a mood to "confer" with Weed and the Adams men. A caucus was arranged for the weekend and the "negotiating" began.

The Adams men were in an unhappy position. They really did not want Clay in the running at all, because his influence as speaker might make him the winner, but they must have a sizable portion of the New York electors, or so they thought. The Adams People's party men were bitter foes of the regency, and they would not trade with Van Buren, so they must swallow a bitter dose and offer the Clay men a better deal than the regency. After several hours their leaders, Thurlow Weed, Henry Wheaton, and James Tallmadge, offered Adams electors to the Clay men if they would vote for a large proportion of the Adams men, even if this might bring Clay into the running. The Clay men understood that the Adams men would give them enough votes to make Clay third. To this they agreed, and Weed then proposed to print some tickets listing a combination of Adams and Clay men. He then retired to a newspaper office and did the printing himself. Then he and his associates canvassed the anti-Crawford men, distributing these tickets. In the instance of certain waverers, they required them to accept and cast tickets with the initials of Weed, endorsed on them, under pain of exposure if these tickets were not found in the box.

On Monday, November 15, the joint session gathered. Officially there were still 60 Crawford men, 57 Adams men, 39 Clay men, and one unpredictable, making 157, so each of the 36 electors had to receive 79 votes. The ballots were gathered and were put on the Bucktail presiding officer's desk. He unfolded one and found to his consternation a printed ballot with only Adams and Clay names on it, not the written Crawford and Clay combination which he had expected.

"A printed split ticket!" he exclaimed.

"Treason, by God!" cried an associate.

The vote was counted: ninety-five men had voted for seven Clay men, seventy-eight had voted for twenty-five Adams men, seventy-six voted for twenty-nine Crawford men, and three voted blanks. If seventy-nine votes were needed, only the seven Clay men had been elected. After a stormy scene and a walkout of some Bucktails, the fact that three had voted blank was accepted to mean that seventy-eight was a majority and that twenty-five Adams men had likewise been chosen.

The joint session adjourned for the night with four electors still to be appointed and everything still uncertain as to whether Clay or Crawford was in the House running. The Adams men still wanted to keep Clay out of the House where he might defeat Adams. So instead of redeeming their "assurance," enough of them joined with the regency next day to elect four Crawford men. This result left everything up in the air: if Clay carried Louisiana, he might be in; if he did not, the Adams men must then redeem their "pledge" if he were to be saved. So the choice of twenty-five Adams, seven Clay, and four Crawford men left the election possibly dependent upon either Louisiana or good faith.

On December 1 these electors were scheduled to meet in Albany, but there had been more work, dirty or otherwise, at the crossroads, and two of the "Clay" men did not appear. As was customary, the remaining electors filled the vacancies, and interestingly enough, the two newcomers voted for Adams; on the other hand, one Adams man defected to Crawford, and a Clay man voted for Jackson. So the New York vote finally stood: Adams twenty-six, Crawford five, Clay four, Jackson one. Thus, as things stood in the Electoral College, Crawford had forty-one, Clay only thirty-seven. Crawford had a chance because of New York's five votes. Clay was in only if he carried Louisiana's five. Had the Adams men honored their "assurance," they could have put Clay in regardless of Louisiana, but they just didn't want him there, so it was left to Louisiana.

Van Buren and the regency had got Crawford in the running but that was cold comfort. The only chance Crawford had had was if Van Buren's plan to unite Crawford and Clay had been accepted. Had the Clay men deadlocked the legislature and prevented New York from casting any electoral votes, Jackson would have had ninety-eight, Adams fifty-eight, Crawford only thirty-six, and Clay thirty-seven. Thus Clay might have been before the House and eventually elected.

In the meantime the slow-traveling news brought the tidings from Louisiana. Clay had lost. The Pelican legislature had chosen three Jackson and two Adams electors. This defeat came because two of his supporters driving to the legislature in a gig along muddy roads had been upset and mired so that they arrived too late to take part in the balloting, and two others of his supporters failed to appear at all.

Clay's supporters charged bitterly that the Adams men had double-crossed them. The Adams New Yorkers retorted that they had promised Clay's supporters only enough votes to get him in provided he carried Louisiana. This they had done and carried out their bargain; the only trouble was in Louisiana. Clay's supporters continued to charge bad faith and a deal with Van Buren's Crawford crowd.

By this complicated operation Adams had secured twenty-six electoral votes from New York. Had there been a popular referendum and the People's party which elected DeWitt Clinton governor had supported him, he might have secured thirty-six, which would not have affected the result. However, there was a ground swell for Jackson, and Clinton favored him. If Jackson had carried New York's thirty-six, he would have had a majority in the Electoral College and the election.

The contest was now thrown into the House, where the balloting would take place in February. What would Clay do? The accident in Louisiana and the intricacies of New York politics had kept him from a chance himself. Would he essay the role of Warwick? The successful candidate must secure the votes of the House delegations from thirteen states, for there were twenty-four states and each had one vote. Adams was sure of only the six from New England plus Louisiana and Illinois. In the latter state the lone congressman would vote for him despite the fact that a plurality of the state's voters had preferred Jackson. Early in January Clay let it be known that he would support Adams, and the three states he had carried in the electoral contest—Kentucky, Missouri, and Ohio—it appeared would follow his advice. Thus Adams was in the way of securing eleven of the thirteen needed votes in the House. The result hinged on Maryland and New York or Delaware. The voters of Maryland had chosen a split group of electors, but the majority of the electors had been Jackson men although a plurality of the voters supported Adams. The tortuous New York result just analyzed had produced a group of electors who were in large part for Adams.

What would the congressmen from Maryland, New York, and Delaware decide? The Maryland delegation of nine had only four Adams men, but there were among the majority a Federalist, a friend of Clay, and one whose district had voted for Adams. This seemed to open a field of negotiation. The New York congressional delegation of thirty-four had on it only seventeen Adams supporters. Could another, perhaps the Federalist, the patroon Stephen Van Rensselaer, be secured? Also, there was the Federalist state of Delaware. Its lone congressman was for Crawford. Which way would he turn?

This tight situation might now give the Federalists a power they had not enjoyed for a quarter of a century. Would they make use of it? One of their "giants," the godlike Daniel Webster, saw a possibility. He had been a Calhoun supporter, but when Pennsylvania buried the Carolinian, for the time being at least, in the Vice Presidency he was without a candidate. But he was a New Englander. He undertook to maneuver an advance of the political power of his section and of his party. He would secure, adroitly and discreetly, an adroit and discreet assurance from Adams that he would lift the ban on the appointment of Federalists to federal office which had been irking them so since the embargo and Hartford Convention days. With great finesse he he obtained from Adams this assurance, which he caused Lee of Maryland to see, and at the same time he worked on the patroon, Van Rensselaer. He was prepared likewise to press Louis McLane of Delaware if necessary.

His tactics with Van Rensselaer were going to provide the pay-off. The patroon was a very wealthy patrician with no emotional stability, a rich man, lonely in a democracy and with a psychotic craving to be liked. He was literally all things to all men. He was presumed to favor Jackson—they had been fellow military officers in the War of 1812. He was living in Washington in a mess where Van Buren kept close watch over him. To these tablemates he favored Crawford. Also, he was a Federalist. He had taken refuge, when asked, in saying he didn't think anybody would be chosen on the first ballot. Such pliable material Webster and Clay believed they could mold. Webster played on his Federalism. He said the Maryland congressman Lee was anxious to discover Adams' intentions about appointing Federalists. Would the patroon go to Adams and find out? The patroon was nothing if not obliging, so he dutifully called on Adams to learn his disposition. Adams, almost frantic, or as frantic as an Adams could get, told him as he had already told others, including Webster, that he was not in a proscriptive mood where Federalists were concerned. The patroon expressed gratification and went off to tell Lee what he already knew.

The day of the balloting came. The patroon left his boarding-house with assurances to Van Buren that he would not vote for Adams; anyway it wouldn't make any difference just then as nobody was to be chosen on the first ballot. However, George E. Mitchell of Maryland whose district had gone for Adams decided he had better follow the returns, so he was to make the fifth needed in that delegation, and Lee's hesitancy no longer mattered. Webster and Clay now saw a chance. They waited at a convenient spot to catch Van Rensselaer as he approached the House chamber. These were great and impressive men who could be persuasive and commanding, and the patroon was suggestible. They literally seized him as he was entering the House and bore down heavily on his moral sense. He had by his act of enquiry at Adams' lodging pledged himself to support Adams if he gave assurance that he would not proscribe Federalists. He had received that assurance and he was therefore in honor bound to redeem his pledge at least for one ballot. Besides, Jackson was a dangerous radical who would threaten the security of property. With the weight and might of Webster and Clay bearing down on him,

Van Rensselaer didn't have a chance. Besides, what did it matter? No one could be elected on the first ballot anyway.

When the box was passed the patroon put in an Adams ballot. But there was no second ballot. Maryland and New York had supported Adams on the first, and Adams was elected. Explanations were demanded of the confused patroon by Van Buren and others, so the statesman found one. He told friends that as the box was being passed he prayed for divine guidance. As he opened his eyes at the conclusion of his petition, he saw a ballot on the floor marked Adams. The box was before him, he picked up the paper and deposited it. To another he wrote more simply, "Mr. Clay's combination could not be resisted and to allay the excitement we agreed to vote for Adams." The apprehensions of a great conservative land owner had had their natural influence. Out of months of such confusion emerged a President for the United States in the person of John Quincy Adams. Such voters as could vote for electors, and in six states, including populous New York, none could, had registered an indecisive will. Jackson had 155,872; Adams, 105,321; Crawford, 44,282; Clay, 46,587. Who was the nation's choice? This was a secret undiscoverable.

This complex, long-drawn-out series of bewildering and usually unrelated incidents which finally ended in the election of John Quincy Adams by the narrowest of margins demonstrated the chaotic procedure which the constitutional provisions for the election of a President could permit. The growth of population, the expansion of the economy, the increase in the number of voters, the rise of a new generation all united to invite chaos, and under the Constitution and the laws there was no force to arrest it. A system so lacking in order and so unpredictable invited attention, and there were influences and events, persons and accidents which were to combine to create some innovations. In the meantime there was no mechanism and few recognizable groups or policies. Individuals and small groups in countless numbers were affiliating with those following this, that, or the other leader. No interest, section, philosophy, or individual leader was dominant or even possessed of much of a following. No longer was there a Hamilton-Jefferson contest over principles, over the definition of a power structure. The contending factions were followers of men rather than contestants over principles or definitions. As Nathaniel Macon wrote, "love of a snug office" was becoming a greater motivation for political activity and an adhesive, binding activists together in factions.

XVIII

DRAWING A NEW PATTERN

*T*HE COMPLEXITY of the confusion which marked the presidential choice of 1824–25 was sufficiently unsettling to stimulate significant changes of political behavior. After half a century of operation, the republic seemed to have made little progress; in fact, it had deteriorated in efficiency as far as electing the Chief Magistrate was concerned. The electorate had reached a state of appalling lack of confidence, probably undeserved, in the integrity of certain leading participants. Their image was not a wholesome one.

No one seemed capable of any conscious planning for constitutional or legal remedies for the procedural defects which had appeared; nevertheless, some changes of operation were undertaken. A new and better political mechanism of choice for the Presidency was needed beyond that provided by the Constitution, the Twelfth Amendment, or any federal or state statutes. The need for this instrumentation was not comprehended definitively, nor did any individual or group come to grips with the problem of producing it. The task was taken up instinctively rather than intellectually and the solution was not worked out in any programed or logical fashion, no document was drafted nor statute enacted. The resultant pattern was to be extraconstitutional, extralegal, and unwritten. It was to develop as a series of devices produced more or less spontaneously to meet a felt need.

In shaping the new methods indicated, there were various instruments which could be utilized. There were caucuses, conventions, committees of correspondence, political newspapers and pamphlets, and funds. There were managing political operators who directed, visited, and corresponded. There were leaders and followers, those who loved and hated, cheered and attacked, men who were loyal or double-crossing, who were honorable or cheating and devious, who were ambitious and self-seeking, or who liked the excitement and fun of the thing. There were likewise those who craved power and improved status, those who loved to play roles and to compensate themselves for failure in other stations by hoped-for success in politics, and there were those who wanted to try something new or to get another chance in a different environment. All these elements were present, but they had not been brought together in a full-fledged federal two-level operation or mechanism. Except in scattered units the American political machine was not yet on the drawing boards. The word "party" was sometimes used but in a different sense than people use it today; it did not imply organization or discipline.

From the complex situation which had been produced by the growth of population and the organization of so many new communities, there had arisen an interest in, and need for, novelty, adventure, and the excitement of devising new governments. In politics this was to produce the creation of the organized party machinery on the federal level, needed for directing the choice of Presidents. In presenting an analysis of the process of evolution which produced this invention, there is need of caution, for there is a tendency in history to permit spectacular events and unique personalities to overshadow the factors that made them possible. This era is commonly denominated the Age of Jackson, and it is easy to think of him as the one who commenced and commanded the evolution of the party mechanism, particularly the "Democratic" phase. But it is well to attempt keener perception.

The process involved was not so simple nor can it be ascribed to any uncomplicated situation. The growth of the population in numbers and the multiplication of communities in the western regions made more complex political organization of some sort inevitable. As long as the United States was committed to self-government, particularly to the frequent popular choice of a single Executive, the increasing number of voters to be reached called for some system of communication and mobilization. Leadership in such organization must be skilled to be effective. As it developed, there appeared several factors in its creation.

There were several significant innovators. After 1825 Jackson and his friends were highly motivated and assumed an activity which they had not displayed before the spectacular election of 1824. Jackson, the hero, had been robbed, and this wrong must be avenged. A second figure was the classically minded Vice President, John C. Calhoun, second man in the Adams Administration but opposed to it and determined if possible to overthrow it and enter the White House himself, if not in 1829, at least by 1833. But his methods of politics were conventional: he would formulate political papers, disseminate his ideas through the press, and conduct dignified personal negotiations, following a Jeffersonian pattern. A third element was called the Old Republicans, which included a group of Virginians known as the Richmond Junto. They thought of themselves as Jeffersonians, even purer than Jefferson, who were doctrinaire in their opposition to all centralization and subsidy and to most government assumption of power. Their spokesman was Thomas Ritchie, veteran editor of the Richmond *Enquirer,* which he had founded in 1804. He was thinking again in terms of a national convention such as he had suggested in the early 1820's to organize a party to overthrow Adams and Clay. But the most clever of this group of operators was Martin Van Buren, senator from New York, who had to his credit the management of the well-organized political machine which on occasion controlled the Empire State.

The catalytic forces marshaling the efforts of these agents at mobilization were not so much the activities of Jackson and his friends, nor the programs and plans of the others, as they were the American attitudes toward leadership and organization. Much work of this sort had been done on the state level. Here various efforts at machine construction had already progressed rather far, particularly in New York and Pennsylvania, the more complex of the local societies. During the previous four years some of the local units within these states had found it expedient to espouse the fortunes of Andrew Jackson. At home and in Congress a number of leaders had become associated with his name as Jackson men. In some instances this was purely a matter of expediency; some faction sought to use his popularity for its own benefit. In other instances there was personal loyalty to a hero; men were proud to support the great man and to be known as his confidants. So during the years and months prior to 1825 there were formed scattered elements of a Jackson following; indeed, there was something archaic and feudal about it; he was a chieftain or a *caudillo* with his retainers. It gave people a new sensation to be "Jackson Men." Whether anyone had thought of himself as a "Washington Man" or a "Jefferson Man" may have been possible but there was never that emotional, close personal attachment to them that there was to "Old Hickory." Something new had been added to American politics which could be expressed in informal, affectionate slang.

The train of political action which was to lead to the new behavior pattern was started by the fact that Clay's influence was thrown to Adams in the congressional balloting for President. When this was followed by Adam's choice of Clay as his Secretary of State, the election campaign of 1828 was on. Jackson remembered a bungling attempt of a Pennsylvania congressman, James Buchanan, to unite Clay and Jackson interests and jumped to the conclusion that Clay had sought to sell his influence to the highest bidder. Adams had won as the result of a "corrupt bargain."

This Adams-Clay association roused both Calhoun and Jackson. The first must take particular note because the implications were that Adams would be President for two terms and Clay eight years beyond that. No one else could have a chance until 1840 if the pattern established by Jefferson, Madison, and Monroe continued to be firm. Calhoun much preferred that set by Washington of having the Vice President rather than the Secretary of State succeed. One of the New York senators perceived that South Carolina was moving to form an opposition to the Adams Administration even before Adams was inaugurated and that Jackson and Calhoun were invited to a dinner for that purpose.

Jackson was soon to subscribe to the charge that he had been robbed by rogues. He voted against Clay's confirmation, resigned from the Senate and went home to Tennessee to assemble a posse of shock troops who would punish the perpetrators of this crime. In 1821 he had been an indifferent candidate; in 1825 he became a militant contender. A group of Jacksonians, the Nashville Committee, went to work that summer, and in October 1825 the legislature of Tennessee presented Jackson's name for a second time to the American people, calling upon them to vindicate the "hero" by defeating the criminals who had betrayed him. At a time when there were so many more people entitled to participate in the government if they could be attracted, it was significant that for the first time since the days of Washington there was a leader who could compel them. There was no longer much interest in the statesmanlike lack of popular appeal of the Adamses, Jefferson, Madison, and Monroe. The people wanted fire and ferver, a man of deeds and spectacular attraction. This was Old Hickory, a man who could command the simple uncomplicated human interest of a rather untutored mass. Such people were not to be marshaled into an ideological party. They were rallied as the Republican Friends of Jackson.

The work of organizing a host around Old Hickory's standard

was stepped up when Congress met in December 1825, and the senators and congressmen returned from their far-flung constituencies. Jackson was no longer there. Calhoun was presiding over the Senate. As the Adams men controlled the House, the opposition decided to work in the upper body. Van Buren must find a candidate as Crawford was no longer to be thought of. His first effort was to organize against Adams and to be noncommittal as to the man to be run in 1828. Jackson's cause was promoted primarily by the two Tennessee senators, then close friends of Jackson and members of the Nashville Committee. They were John H. Eaton, and Hugh L. White just elected to succeed Jackson. These men began consultation, correspondence, and negotiation by agents. Eaton made particular use of his brother-in-law, William B. Lewis, who was on the road a good deal seeking support and suggesting local organization. A number of such groups who had been at work in preparation for 1824 must be reactivated and more brought into being. These two Senators found sympathetic collaborators in Thomas Hart Benton of Missouri, Sam Houston of Tennessee and Texas, Edward Livingston of New York and Louisiana, John Randolph of Roanoke, and George McDuffie of South Carolina.

While these centrally located friends of Jackson were working in his behalf, committees of correspondence began to labor for him in several states where his support was growing. In these situations the size and nature of this backing depended much on local conditions and "characters." The definition of this opportunism was illustrated by the situation in New York. Here the struggle between Clinton and the Bucktails was as bitter as ever. Van Buren was attempting to run the Bucktails and the state government from Washington through a regency composed of such men as Silas Wright, William L. Marcy, Azariah Flagg, and Benjamin F. Butler. But his power was threatened anew by DeWitt Clinton, once more elected governor. Clinton had early jumped on the Jackson bandwagon and Old Hickory, always greatly swayed by personal loyalties, looked to him as his chief New York supporter. This was embarrassing to Van Buren. He had been the Crawford leader, but now Crawford could no longer be supported because of his health. Now, if because of his determination to defeat Adams, he supported Jackson, he must concede the New York leadership to Clinton, a situation most intolerable. Therefore the Bucktail leader undertook something of an oblique course, at least for the time being.

He would use his favorite skill, organization, and he would work, not from a pro-Jackson, but from an anti-Adams angle. He would attack the President's unconstitutional centralizing tendencies, his grasp for power. Without the consent of Congress President Adams had accepted an invitation to send representatives to a conference of the new Latin American republics, which was scheduled to be held at Panama. He submitted the names of his envoys to the Senate for confirmation and requested an appropriation from the House to pay them. Van Buren seized upon this act as an issue around which to mobilize the opposition party with which he hoped to unhorse Adams; to this end he undertook to work with Vice President Calhoun. Virginia and her allies joined in condemning this act as an arbitrary assumption of power, an engagement in an entangling alliance, a proof of a desire to expand central power at the expense of the states.

These allies sought to rally the real Republicans, those true to the principles of '98, against Adams and Clay who were promoting an expansive nationalism. In the end they did not prevent the passage of Adams' measures, but they delayed them so long that one of the envoys was dead and the conference over before the actions were taken. In the course of the debate the erratic Randolph had characterized Clay as "so brilliant and yet so corrupt that like a rotten mackerel by moonlight, [he] shines and stinks, and stinks and shines." The association of Adams and Clay he likened to an "association of a puritan and a blackleg." Randolph and Clay fought a duel which both survived; in the encounter Clay was more fortunate than Hamilton had been in his fight with Burr. Clay's shot tore Randolph's coat, so the Kentuckian gave him a new one. In this session of 1825–26 the nucleus of a new "combination" had formed but whom would it support? The contest had begun to narrow somewhat when Calhoun joined forces with Jackson in June 1826. Although Van Buren had worked with Calhoun against Adams in the Panama conference controversy, he had reserved judgment about supporting Jackson. He was still thinking in terms of organization and tactics rather than candidates.

The opponents of Adams had been building up a phalanx of journalists. Eaton undertook to set up a Jackson journal in Washington. Duff Green, a Kentuckian whose daughter had married Calhoun's son, at this time was editing a Jackson paper, the St. Louis *Enquirer*. He was persuaded to come to Washington. Here the Washington *City Gazette* was purchased with money raised in part by Eaton and renamed the *United States Telegraph.* The new venture was launched in February 1826. As a preliminary Eaton took Green to see Jackson. Green was "to keep . . . before the people" the story of the corrupt bargain between Adams and Clay and of how Jackson, the hero, had been defrauded. The perpetrators of the crime must be defeated in 1828. As Green and almost everybody else at that time thought of Jackson as serving only one term, the fact that Green was partial to Calhoun did not then create any tension. Green was to devote himself initially to continuing Calhoun as Vice President. Under these circumstances he came to Washington in October 1826.

Van Buren, as a Crawford man, was not too happy at having Green grind the new organ, so he began to work on the idea of bringing Ritchie to Washington to edit a paper favorable to the old Crawford interest in which they had both been prominent. Calhoun, on his part, was cold to this. When a close associate of Ritchie, P. N. Nicholas, wrote to Van Buren asking about plans for supporting some one against Adams, Van Buren merely reported that hostility to Jackson still persisted. But the New York senator was as always practical; he knew there must be concert on someone, so he was coming to believe that this might be Jackson. If Jackson would take Jeffersonian ground, Van Buren believed that the Crawford men would support him. Having made up his mind, he took his final step. He met Calhoun at a Christmas party over in Virginia at William H. Fitzhugh's, and there they agreed that Jackson was to be the man and that he was to be presented, not by a caucus as Van Buren proposed, but by a convention, at Calhoun's insistence.

The reason in part for this was that the situation in Virginia had changed. Ritchie and the Crawfordites had a real grievance. The Administration forces had come down into Virginia and had helped defeat Senator John Randolph of Roanoke for re-election. Randolph had been replaced by Clay's friend John Tyler. The Junto was now ready to support Jackson. This situation and the conferences with Calhoun led Van Buren to write a letter to Ritchie on January 13, 1827, which he showed Calhoun and Samuel D. Ingham of Pennsylvania's Family party. In this missive he invited an alliance between the "planters of the South and the plain Republicans of the North" to be consummated at such a national convention as Ritchie had advocated during the previous Administration. Directly or indirectly Jackson assured Ritchie and Van Buren that he was a Jeffersonian.

Within a month Senator Littleton W. Tazewell of Virginia, who had amibitions to make southern rule of the nation certain, wrote another letter to Ritchie with the concurrence of Van Buren who had originally had the idea. Ritchie was invited to move to Washington to establish a newspaper which would unite the Crawford, Jackson, and Clinton men in one great host. Duff Green for his part was too committed to Calhoun to do this. Van Buren was more than ever aware that he and the Vice President might not be compatible. Crawford hated Calhoun, and as Crawford's chief organizer, Van Buren had some of the virus. So he arranged a tie vote on a tariff bill before the Senate in 1827 and made Calhoun shoulder the opprobrium of defeating it. Then came disappointment: Ritchie would not leave Virginia to assume editorial sponsorship in Washington.

When Van Buren was re-elected to the Senate in February 1827, he was ready to go to work for Jackson, having received assurance that Jackson would stand on Jeffersonian principles. As soon as Congress adjourned in March 1827, Van Buren went on a southern journey. It was then pretty well realized that Adams had lost the next Congress, and Van Buren wanted to marshal a more compact support for Jackson. He visited in the southern states, going as far south as Georgia to confer with Crawford, who was now well enough to accept a local judgeship. He wanted to find out whether the Crawford men would join the followers of Calhoun in supporting Jackson. Knowing Crawford's antipathy for Calhoun, Van Buren realized that this was going to be difficult, but in the end he succeeded, largely because Crawford thought Jackson would kill off his mortal enemy Calhoun. A combination to push Jackson was another step nearer.

By September 1827 Van Buren was ready to undertake correspondence with Jackson only to be confronted with the fact that Old Hickory considered DeWitt Clinton his best friend in New York and to have it made plain that he had doubts about Van Buren's sincerity. Nor was he easy to change, though Van Buren sent Alexander Hamilton's son, James A., to take on the task of convincing him that Van Buren was a loyal advocate. In the meantime Calhoun's possible ambitions must be circumscribed. William B. Lewis and Sam Houston knew that it was supposed that Calhoun, as Monroe's Secretary of War, had recommended Jackson's censure for insubordination in the Florida war. They tried to get a statement of the facts from William H. Crawford, Calhoun's colleague in Monroe's Cabinet, but they failed. Therefore they put the idea aside; it had become less important as Calhoun was apparently willing to stand for Vice President on a Jackson-Calhoun ticket put up by the *United States Telegraph* in

January. Although the matter was shelved, it was to be heard from again. Calhoun, Ritchie, and Van Buren were working together for Jackson, and the South seemed in line.

When the new Congress assembled in December 1827 the Jacksonians took control. They elected a Virginian, Andrew Stevenson, speaker of the House, secured the committees, and gave Duff Green the subsidy of the Senate printing. In this winter of 1827–28 the majority group in Congress was for Jackson, and a caucus was formed to direct the advance of his fortunes. Van Buren took the lead. The committees cooperated with Jackson and his coterie at Nashville and also with a local Washington group presided over by General John P. Van Ness who came from Van Buren's home town of Kinderhook, New York, and which included Duff Green, editor of the Jackson-Calhoun organ.

A series of Jacksonian newspapers was established throughout the country. Duff Green was the leading editor with Thomas Ritchie of the Richmond *Enquirer* the second. Up in New Hampshire was Isaac Hill; in Kentucky, Amos Kendall; while in New York, Edwin Croswell held forth in Albany. For this, many thousands of dollars were raised and dispersed by Van Buren, who could draw on a strong Albany bank with New York City connections. Then, too, the senators and congressmen all had the franking privilege, so the taxpayer had to contribute "willy-nilly." Officeholders, those with government contracts for printing and supplies, as well as loyal partisans, were tapped. Electioneering in 1828 was to cost in the neighborhood of $1,000,000.

Likewise, the friends of Jackson had been at work on a unique type of mobilization. They would use the anniversary of the battle of New Orleans, January 8, as a time to rally. They had been at work organizing a nationwide series of meetings on that date in 1828. This mobilization would attract national attention but avoid "centralization" and preserve state individuality. General Jackson himself would go to New Orleans to celebrate on the anniversary of his triumph. The committee formed by the Friends of Jackson in the District of Columbia undertook to arrange such a celebration in the capital city. Other Jackson committees were to be set up in many of the states for the same purpose, and January 8 was quite generally celebrated then and for many years thereafter as Jackson Day.

Typical of the procedure was that in Pennsylvania. Here the meeting not only celebrated the day and Jackson, but it chose a committee of correspondence to begin operations in Philadelphia promoting his candidacy. Similar groups were constituted in other states, and these committees began to communicate with each other and with the committee in Washington, describing their methods and prospects for aiding Jackson's candidacy. This Pennsylvania meeting endorsed the ticket of Jackson and Calhoun proposed by the *Telegraph*, a procedure also followed in Virginia, New Jersey, Ohio, and Kentucky. The rally to Jackson was climaxed on January 31 when the New York Bucktail convention came out for him, even though this act seemed to be following DeWitt Clinton and putting Van Buren in the background. Significantly, the convention did not endorse Calhoun for second place.

The Jackson enthusiasm developed so uniformly that the idea of a national convention was given up. Perhaps its sponsors feared a fight on the proposal to continue John C. Calhoun as Vice President. The Washington committee under Van Ness came to be generally recognized as a national central committee and clearinghouse. Its members worked closely with Duff Green in preparing and distributing campaign material. The editor of the *Telegraph* issued a special edition weekly for use of the different corresponding committees throughout the union which had been appointed for the purpose of "disseminating political truth and refuting slanders" spread by the "corrupt coalition." Much campaign material, which included badges, posters, flags, and copies of the Jackson press, was distributed by these committees. During the summer, mass meetings were organized, militia musters were utilized, barbecues and fish fries were staged as political rallies. Songs were composed. Hickory trees were planted. In the cities Jackson committees were set up by wards. Eaton and Lewis circulated around. They even sought the advice of Aaron Burr. Money became easier to raise, and other newspapers were either converted or created. The story of the hero cheated by the negotiators of a corrupt bargain was taking hold.

It was easy to see that Adams would probably secure New England and Jackson most of the South. The battle was to be in the middle states, in Pennsylvania and New York, and in the West. In Pennsylvania the two main factions were the Family party, the would-be ruling group in the radical new school Jeffersonian faction, and the Amalgams, a group made up of the old school Leib-Duane Independent Republicans and Federalists. They had learned in 1824 how popular Jackson was, and each vied with the other in support of him. Both New York and Pennsylvania were influenced by the new industrialism and had strong desires for a protective tariff. These they shared with New England. Already, as in the matter of the Woolen Bill in 1827, there had been some political maneuvering; now there was going to be a more decisive showdown.

The industrialists were organized, particularly in Pennsylvania where the Pennsylvania Society for the Promotion of Manufactures was active. They realized that not the least of their problems was to get farmers to see that they had as great an interest as the manufacturers in such a tariff. The farmers that raised raw wool needed protection as much as the manufacturers who made woolen cloth. For if woolen cloth were protected, great quantities would be made, and thus the wool of the flocks would be bought in large amounts at good prices. However, if the cloth were not protected, the farmers' wool would have few buyers. These operators therefore organized a convention of manufacturers and farmers to meet in Harrisburg in the summer of 1827 to unite in agreement on an American system which would insure a home market and thus unite urban and rural areas in the East and West in a concentrated demand for protection. This convention agreed on such a program and undertook to launch a propaganda campaign. When the Twentieth Congress met in December 1827, the tariff forces had been mobilized for a tariff of 1828.

The Keystone State was the center of another move indicative of the appearance of what was to be a new force in American politics. The 1820's had witnessed a sporadic series of strikes in the various branches of American industry, breaking out in the northern seaboard cities. This crystallized in Philadelphia where in 1827 there was organized a federation of unions, the first in American history, called the Mechanics Union of Trade Associations. This was followed by the appearance of a weekly labor journal, *The Mechanics' Free Press*, in 1828 and the organization of a Working Man's party, which held city and county conventions and participated in the local elections. They were opposed to chartered monopolies, which forced down wages, denied credit to small businessmen, and kept the men working from sun to sun. They demanded libraries, reading rooms, and a free press, free schools, and opportunities to better themselves. They were opposed to imprisonment for debt and demanded mechanics lien laws to preserve their rights to their wages. These men would not be so much for Jackson, who was enigmatic on their demands, but they were opposed to Adams and those who supported him. These attitudes would incline the new labor vote to Jackson, but it was not large enough to be anything but indicative of the emergence of a new element.

The situation in the Empire State was suddenly altered by the unexpected death of Governor Clinton on February 11. Senator Van Buren moved immediately. He would leave Washington at the end of the session and run for the governorship to save it to his party. He would assume control of his state as now the leading Jacksonian spokesman. Such a campaign would be of great advantage to him. He had had no military career, nor was he as well known to the voters of New York as a leader should be. He had operated largely in Albany in the legislature, where he had twice been elected senator. Clinton's death would give him a chance he needed. As a friend advised him, "Being a candidate at this time would make the justices, constables and all the minor active men in the towns [the Alphas] familiar with your name." But before he undertook this new operation, he had a job to do in Washington.

Van Buren saw capital in the tariff which would enable him to promote Jackson's cause by forging an alliance between East and West. He could seek such various combinations of voters as could be made out of manipulating the tariff rates. He was taking advantage of a practice just commencing which was to have a long life and which was to be pushed in the middle and western states where the battle of 1828 was to be decided.

Congressional legislation was to be a source of subsidy, and a variety of imaginations were being stimulated. Politicians could see advantage if any combination might be able to prove that they could grant the advantage. Some of those "handling" Jackson were aware of this. They believed that the battle would be won or lost in the middle and western states. Adams was conceded New England and Jackson the South. So some shrewd operators went to work to make the most of the tariff. They were going to use the needs of certain raw-material producers in that region plus the iron men and protect such raw materials as wool, hemp, flax, molasses, and iron. This they knew would rouse the opposition of the South, because the costs of their supplies would be kited, and of New England where this raw material protection would hurt their woolen manufacturers, distillers, foreign traders, and shipbuilders. However, they counted on the fact that the South could not vote for Adams, whatever sort of tariff emerged, and Van Buren and the Jackson operators had a couple of fast ones in reserve. They got certain southern leaders to believe that if they kept in these raw-material subsidies, New England would vote against the bill and thus defeat it. This worked; the South voted against all modifying amendments to keep the bill as unpalatable as possible to the manufacturers and thus ensure its defeat. Then, when it came up in the Senate, Van Buren contrived one amendment increasing protection to manufactured woolen cloth to such a degree that enough New Englanders joined to make the bill a law. Thus the Jacksonian operators in Congress manipulated legislation to the advantage of the Hickory campaign.

New England swallowed the pill, and Jackson got whatever advantage could accrue from middle states and western raw-material producers' gratitude. The disgruntled southerners under the leadership of Calhoun could only protest that they had been tricked and then threaten secession, but at this stage they had no one but Jackson to support. Thus the attempt to use an economic issue as an instrument in political maneuvering enters the picture again, in a fashion reminiscent of Hamilton and later the embargo. Pennsylvania, the West, and New York got their tariff, and Martin Van Buren had played a critical role in achieving it. Pennsylvania was probably coming into the Jackson fold, but how about New York?

When Van Buren returned to New York to run for governor, he found his work cut out for him. There were stirrings of unrest. Not only were wage earners becoming politically conscious, particularly in Pennsylvania, but in New York another novel element had to be reckoned with. In 1826 it was noised about that the aristocratic and politically dominant Masonic order, which through their secret oath-bound meetings controlled elections in many New York communities, had murdered a member who was planning to expose their secrets. This rumor fostered by some clever newspapermen like Thurlow Weed was used as a rallying point for those opposed to the Clinton–Bucktail Republican domination. These men had tried the People's party idea of 1824, and they now saw in Antimasonry another possibility to defeat the regency. It had been tried out successfully in western New York in certain local elections in 1827, and now there were plans to organize a state-wide campaign in 1828 to capture the governorship and the legislature. Jackson was a Mason, Adams was not. Van Buren must face the Antimasonic feeling running high in the western counties of the state, and it was obviously to the advantage of the Adams men to nominate a candidate who would attract Antimasonic votes to oppose Van Buren. Thurlow Weed and others wished to nominate Francis Granger, a favorite of the Antimasons, for governor, but they were outvoted by Adams men, and interestingly enough, a sometime friend of Van Buren's, Smith Thompson, was nominated. Granger was given second place. The disappointed Antimasons then nominated a ticket of their own headed by Granger. Granger refused to accept the Antimasonic nomination but kept out of the Adams party. Whereupon the Antimasons, it is alleged with Van Buren's financial help, nominated another ticket. Evidently Jackson was being well served by Van Buren's skill in keeping the Empire State from Adams. It might well be the deciding voice in the election. Presumably during this period, someone close to Jackson, probably Eaton, told Van Buren that if Old Hickory were elected Van Buren would be Secretary of State.

Thus during the complicated months of 1828, this variety of means had been invented, most of them illustrating an ingenuity forecasting a new political era, designed to overthrow the old order which since the beginnings had been the pattern. Statesmen as such were in danger, the star of a popular hero was in the ascendant. But was the old order making no effort to offset this onward march, to build up dikes against this whelming flood?

John Quincy Adams, like all previous Presidents, hoped for two terms, and there was never any doubt but that, like all the rest, he would run again. In February 1828 the Massachusetts legislature presented him. He was likewise recommended by conventions or legislatures in various other states. But though Jackson enthusiasm was mounting, Adams could not bring himself to do anything. The conversations and understandings which preceded his recent election were too vivid in his memory and the charges of corrupt bargaining too stabbing to his conscience, not quite free from reminders, to permit him to act on his own behalf. He removed few officeholders and allowed supporters of his opponents to remain in office, even tolerating a Calhoun Postmaster General. Clay and others tried to remedy his reluctance. Clay got a number of committees organized in various states and Republican Friends of Adams were constituted. A series of committees ranging from a national agency in Washington down to local groups were active. Peter Force edited the Adams organ in Washington, *The National Journal,* and *The National Intelligencer* helped. Adams papers were set up, though Adams himself refused to assist in raising the money. However superficially this organization might resemble that of Jackson's, it had too little of the enthusiasm, loyalty, or efficiency of that of Old Hickory.

One of the Adams organizations, the National General Committee, very regrettably introduced a new note, the smear tactic. Charles Hammond of the Cincinnati *Gazette* became sponsor of the charge that Andrew Jackson was a adulterer, that he had lived with Mrs. Jackson when she was still another man's wife. This story appeared in a widely circulated pamphlet *A View of General Jackson's Domestic Relations*. John Binns of the *Democratic Press* of Philadelphia also sought to injure Jackson by circulating a "Coffin Handbill." This crude woodcut featured six coffins and sought to sustain the charge that during the Florida campaigns the General had hanged six militiamen whom he had charged with desertion. Others sought to associate Jackson with Burr's treason.

The editorial friends of Jackson, Thomas Ritchie of the Richmond *Enquirer*, M. M. Noah of the *National Advocate*, published in New York City, Nathaniel Greene of the Boston *Statesman*, and Isaac Hill of the *New Hampshire Patriot* entered the fray. Not only did they defend Jackson, but they attacked Adams. Jackson had charged that Clay had sought to make a corrupt bargain with him through the agency of James Buchanan, congressman from Pennsylvania. A Senate committee had cited Adams as a corrupter of the civil service. John Randolph and others attacked him as an extravagant waster of public funds, bearing down on the fact that he had bought a billiard table for the White House and thus had used public funds to set up a gaming instrument. Samuel D. Ingham of the Pennsylvania Family party prepared a document which Duff Green circulated; this was *An exposition of the political character and principles of John Quincy Adams showing by historical documents and incontestable facts, that he was educated a monarchist, has always been hostile to popular government, and particularly to its great bulwark, the right of suffrage*. Further, they accused Mrs. Adams of having Tory relatives and Adams of seeking a title, a patent of nobility. The most farfetched charge was a story sired by Isaac Hill that Adams had acted as a pimp and procurer for the czar and had provided a Yankee servant girl for the emperor's pleasure. This canard arose out of the fact that a member of Adams' household was bright and a fascinating purveyor of gossip. So far did her fame spread that the czar asked Adams to bring her to see him. She had a ten-minute audience with the monarch.

So the months of this organized new-style campaigning passed. The contest was clear and sharp between two candidates. There was to be a definite result with none of the uncertainty and confusion of four years earlier. Jackson was decisively elected. He had secured the votes of many Old Republicans and Federalists; this latter group he had on occasion favored. President Adams secured just about what his father had won, and Jackson inherited Jefferson's portion—but he had practically all of the new states besides. Jackson got 83 votes in the South and Adams got 83 from New England, New York, Delaware, and Maryland. The Antimasonic effort in New York had been defeated and Van Buren elected governor. However, the new party did secure 16 of New York's electoral votes for Adams, mainly from the western districts. Old Hickory won because he carried, in addition to the South, all the new western states with their 41 votes and 54 from the East. He won all of Pennsylvania, captured 20 of New York's 36, 5 of Maryland's 11 and one of Maine's 9. Thus it was 178 to 83 and in the popular vote, 647,231 to 509,097. Calhoun fared equally well except that he lost 7 of Georgia's 9; Crawford's resentment was tenacious and was to continue to be venomous.

Thus in 1828 parties with some forms of state and national organization had appeared. No national convention had been attempted, but each party had a sort of national central committee designed for work rather than for direction and a network of some state and local committees of correspondence, in form resembling the committees of correspondence of the Revolution, the fiftieth anniversary of which was in process of somewhat limited celebration. These parties, combinations, or factions, moreover, had no names and no platforms apart from the men whom they supported. Little in the way of difference, principle, or ideology separated them, although there was some effort to conjure up Jefferson. Voters supported Jackson because he was Jackson or because they disliked or distrusted Adams. Others voted for Adams because Jackson opposed him, and they feared Jackson as an irresponsible military chieftain, a *caudillo*, a leader of a rabble.

But there were deeper currents flowing. There was a stirring against old elites. The wage earners were groping toward organization and political action to improve their lot, although here there was no great accretion of support to Jackson. Also, there was a protest against the role of Masonic lodges in politics, and there continued to be sectional implications. The antagonism between North and South was there. Adams was an Adams, while Jackson was a slaveholder. Besides, Jackson was a representative of the new West, a section beginning to demand its place in the political sun. So two new political combinations had appeared, the lengthened shadows of two men: the Republican Friends of Jackson and the Republican Friends of

Adams. In many areas when the returns were printed in the press they were labeled merely Adams and Jackson.

In these new political constructions, as of yore, a relatively small group of operators had been behaving as such men usually did. But there were more of them from ever growing constituencies; there were more men with a sense of power, or a desire for it. They were discovering that the prevailing informality was not enough. Their needs spelled innovation in the direction of organization.

XIX

THE CHIEFTAIN IN POWER

*T*HE PERIOD of so-called Jacksonian political activity is the point in time when the realities of American politics as they are now defined first begin to be discernible. Most of the pre-Jackson political experience differs from, more than it resembles, modern practice. This is especially true because different phases of the long experience have been called by the same names. It is in the so-called Age of Jackson, however, that American party politics came into being. Previously political activity, organizaton, and operation had been relatively simple and if viewed in the perspective of the times not too difficult to understand. But in this epoch complexities appeared. A whole series of factors—personalities and personal relationships, leadership, federal two-level operation, organization complexes, "interests," sectionalism, the rapid increase of a mobile population and the constant creation of new political units, attitudes toward neighboring peoples and the nation's world situation—joined to create new and more intricate patterns. These patterns were further shaped by the fact that the nation was in the throes of indecision regarding self-definition.

In the midst of this, Jackson pre-empted the center of the stage because he was obviously clothed with power and assumed leadership, and besides, he was a most colorful figure. But political leadership is difficult to define and more difficult to understand. Submitting the quality to analysis reveals that it is not a constant. In fact much of the time it does not exist because there is no need for it. Leadership in fact does not waste itself; society is sparing of it. The new United States had had little of it since Washington's day. Whatever Jefferson had contributed was brief in duration and, at that, something of an afterthought. His partisan importance, though large, was more significant at a later epoch when he had become a symbol of great potency.

By the 1830's, leadership was again called for. There were so many people and so many voters that some type of organized mobilization was indicated which could be neither spontaneous nor sporadic if it were to be effective. It must be contrived, and this required a new type of leadership if the necessary regular avenues of communication and persuasion were to be provided. Washington had feared parties. Jefferson could form cabals, but now something new was needed if elites were to be broken down, if the power of rule was to remain fluid and subject to popular choice and rotation, if the concept of frequent change in a growing society, rather than a frozen established order, was to be developed. There was to be a chance from a structured leadership more or less permanent to a constructed one the specifications for which might occasionally be altered. Jackson and his characteristics were to be convenient instruments available for use in achieving this change.

This new pattern was inevitable because of the great changes altering the face of the republic. The thirteen original states and the Northwest and Southwest territories had become twenty-four states and three territories—Michigan, Arkansas, and Florida—together with a large area of unorganized country occupied only by Indians. Of these twenty-four states, nine came from beyond the Appalachians and brought to Washington a new and increasingly powerful interest represented by men of stature, such as Jackson, Clay, and Benton. They were taking a commanding position in the Capitol, and the leadership from the older region had to make place for them in the governing hierarchy. Old combinations do not readily accept new ones. Virginia and South Carolina, ancient and elite states, did not welcome new people, so the coming of any westerner to the Presidency must inevitably raise something of a reorganization conflict.

The rapid growth of the country, marked as it was by the emergence of new communities to the westward and also by the growth of factory towns in the East and commercial centers both East and West, gave encouragement to much enterprise: real estate, communications, industry, banking, and agriculture, both planting and subsistence farming. These growing "interests" were concerned with politics because in the maintenance of public services and in the promotion of new projects the government was in a position to supply, not only authorization, but also material aid. Those who were interested in using public lands, securing subsidies for roads, canals, and railroads, improving rivers and harbors, enjoying the benefits of a protective tariff, or insuring the recharter of the Bank of the United States were bound to press the federal government to enact their measures. This situation was made complex by the size of the nation, which produced sections of varying and at times conflicting interests, and these sections advocated and opposed proposals to the degree that they fitted their self-interest as they understood it. Furthermore, the business of the nation was in that state of undisciplined speculative expansion which meant that business cycles were recurrent, characterized by boom and bust. A deflation and a depression were in the process of evolving, and these conditions were bound to increase confusion.

Then, incidentally, something perhaps of a footnote, Washington "society" was feeling the influx of the new western element. The better established American "society" was conducting itself according to a strictly maintained set of social mores, and conformity was highly valued and rigidly maintained; variations, particularly by so-called new people, were vigorously frowned on. Finally there had been relatively little change in the civil servants in the departments; the civil service had taken on over the years something of a permanent status. Many had grown gray in the employ of the government. Retirement was hanging over them, and age spelled out the fact that many must depart no matter who was President. This did not mean that they would leave the scene gracefully or without providing fuel for political controversy.

Any understanding of the rise of what was to be called an American party system furthermore depends upon as much clarification as can be supplied of the complex relationships of personalities and their behavior in small and large groups and of the reciprocal relationships among these persons and groups with the various larger elements in societies, such as unit communities, states, regions, and the nation. Such an understanding must of necessity reduce Jackson to a figure, spectacular to be sure, but one which was a symbol rather than a directing force. The determinants were much greater than he. Erratic, aging chieftain that he was, he himself can hardly be said to have been dominant except in a few situations. But as a symbol he had a reality that he never achieved as a person. Moreover an organization of sorts had been created to elect him. It had shown its power and its effectiveness. This power would naturally tend to continue to operate.

A second development of the 1830's in the history of American political behavior emphasizing Jackson was a shift in the center of political gravity. The new center was in the White House because for the first time it became a seat of power recognized by even the average citizen. Few of the preceding Presidents had possessed any very tangible influence or power. Washington had achieved the most, but whatever his successors secured depended largely upon their capacity for palace-guard politics, negotiation, and intrigue. Save in foreign affairs, most of them, even Jefferson, had gained little, hardly enough to be a matter of concern to the public. Men of less influence than Madison, Monroe, and John Quincy Adams can hardly be imagined. But now this was changed.

Under Jackson the White House became a seat of power and a party headquarters. Jackson was a general, he had a following which rather fancifully might be said to resemble an army. He was in a sense a *caudillo*, a chieftain with supporters who made the relationship highly personal. You cheered Old Hickory, you were his man. The more sophisticated saw in him either a man of power whom it would be profitable to support or a democratic man of the people who would carry out the people's will, promoting liberty and equality. The Friends of Jackson were in reality not much more than a personal following which might last no longer than the term of Jackson's Presidency. The party of today was not yet nor had been. Parties as now defined were not the creation of Hamilton or Jefferson nor even of Jackson.

The new President because of his personality and temperament, as well as because of the circumstances of his election, was going to function not only as executive of a federal republic but also as a popular leader of an extensive following that had divisions scattered among the twenty-four states. As a general he had had experience with organization, and he was not to forget this experience now. He was also operating in a political organization of sorts which had two factions and two subleaders. How conscious he was of this at the time he became President is not too fully understood. Not only was there Vice President Calhoun, possible heir apparent, but there was another astute lieutenant to be reckoned with, Martin Van Buren of New York. Jackson, old and grief-stricken, believed that Mrs. Jackson, who had died between election and inauguration, had been "murdered" by the slanders of the campaign. He was thereby embittered and had become vengeful. Though expected to serve but one term, he was a leader with a sense of discipline, with a mission to punish evil-doers. With his scattered and complex following, it was quite natural that he should place a premium upon personal loyalty. As old and lonely as he was, it was also natural that he should appreciate friendship and companionship. He was intolerant of opponents among government appointees and demanded loyal political support. On the other hand, he wished to reward those who had worked for him. As a general, it was easy for him to develop the concept that "to the victors belong the spoils." Then, too, he was coming in after a period in which there had been little change in government personnel for years. Change dictated by time was becoming inevitable. As so often in American politics, the passage of time, rather than the determination of men, was dictating new policy and personnel.

Therefore there was a new chief, but there was also to be a new civil service, there was the Jackson political organization and an active Jackson press. There were consequently a swarm of office seekers and, less obvious, a group of very purposeful seekers after government aid, endeavoring to shape policy. There was also the question of who would take over when the sick old man laid down his responsibility. Who would be the powers in Congress, the lawmaking body? In the rising federal organization, who would be first in Rome?

Much was to depend upon the succession which in the winter of 1828–29 was expected to occur more quickly than turned out to be the case. If Calhoun were to be the leader, there would not be much central organization and a great deal of state autonomy. The pattern of the Virginia dynasty would be projected into mid-century. But if Van Buren were in command, skilled in the highly specialized political arts of the Albany regency, there would be a different story to record.

Whatever thoughts Jackson had on this subject when he appointed his Cabinet he kept to himself. His decisions were made hurriedly in a period of grief-stricken confusion and within a few days after he arrived in Washington, February 11, 1829. He relied much on his Tennessee friends, John H. Eaton and Hugh L. White, the two senators, and William B. Lewis, Eaton's brother-in-law, a lesser light from home, and upon James A. Hamilton of New York, son of the great financier and a representative of Van Buren.

Martin Van Buren was to be Secretary of State. He was the Crawford leader who had done much to bring that faction over to Jackson and who had resigned from the Senate in 1828 to run for governor of New York in aid of Jackson. Van Buren had inherited Crawford's dislike of Calhoun. Eaton was to be Secretary of War, and he and Jackson were united in resisting Virginia's pretensions as well as Calhoun's. So they evolved a plan to omit appointing any from Virginia and South Carolina after one Virginian had declined.

John Branch and John M. Berrien were chosen from North Carolina and Georgia for the Navy and Justice posts. Only one Calhoun man was included; the importunity of the Family party secured Samuel D. Ingham of Pennsylvania who was made Secretary of the Treasury over Henry Baldwin of their state whom Jackson probably preferred. John McLean of Ohio preferred the Supreme Court, so William T. Barry of Kentucky, who had been scheduled for the bench, was persuaded to change to the Postmaster Generalship, then raised to Cabinet rank. Neither Van Buren nor Calhoun had been consulted.

Despite Van Buren's seat in the Cabinet, Calhoun started with an initial advantage. He had been Vice President since 1825 and Jackson believed him to be the superior who, as Secretary of War, had upheld Jackson's course in Florida when the General was under attack in Congress. Many thought of Calhoun as the natural heir apparent who would soon succeed Jackson in case of his death or ultimately at the end of his term. But Calhoun's preferred position was not to last for long.

Van Buren did not assume his place as Secretary of State upon inauguration. He himself had just been sworn in as governor of New York, and he wished to wait until he had worked with the New York legislature. However, when he arrived in Washington late in March, he lost no time. He saw that the fiery warrior needed other advice and companionship than he could get from the Tennessee coterie of Eaton, Lewis, and White, so he undertook to be a companion in exercise and relaxation. Jackson and Van Buren began almost daily horseback rides together. The austere Calhoun had no such gift for comradeship.

Jackson and Van Buren had many talks on policy and particularly on appointments, a subject congenial to them both. The President was intent on rewarding certain of his friends. Eaton was in the Cabinet. Lewis was made second auditor of the Treasury. Newspaper supporters like Isaac Hill of the *New Hampshire Patriot* and Amos Kendall of the Frankfort, Kentucky, *Argus* were made second comptroller and fourth auditor. Many others were given jobs. The diplomatic service was reorganized with almost indecent haste. General William Henry Harrison, very recently appointed minister to Colombia, was recalled as soon as he got there. Some superannuates were replaced, an embezzler or two was superseded by men not always more honest. There was a great hue and cry about injustice and hardship. These were blandly answered by the quip that General Jackson as a soldier knew that reality demanded recognition of the fact that "to the victors belong the spoils." Jackson himself announced that democracy and fair play demanded "rotation in office." Many certainly were displaced in the first eighteen months, 919 in fact. Though when it is considered that there were 10,000 officeholders, the proportion does not seem large. This ratio appears to have been maintained during Jackson's Presidency; something of a spoils system was established and not to Calhoun's advantage. He could not compete with the Albany regency.

Calhoun's status as leader was to be further affected by another accident of personality more striking than Van Buren's capacity for companionship, though in a sense similar. The wife of the Secretary of War, John H. Eaton, played a striking part in the drama of leadership. She was the daughter of a Washington publican who kept a political hotel. Here his daughter acted as hostess, and in the long intervals when her husband, a purser in the Navy, was at sea she was particularly active in her role. She was much in the company of her father's financial patron, Senator John H. Eaton, and public opinion generally believed that their relations were adulterous. During the campaign of 1828, her husband had died in a foreign port after at least one unsuccessful attempt to take his life. It was then that various of his friends, Jackson among them, told Eaton that marriage must be solemnized. So they were married shortly before it was announced that Eaton was to be Secretary of War. Mrs. Margaret O'Neill Timberlake Eaton would be one of the Administration ladies.

Washington society, which took its tone from Virginia, South Carolina, and Maryland, states which were not represented in the Cabinet, was all set to be profoundly disturbed by this new western Administration, and the fact that one of its leaders was to be the notorious Mrs. Eaton set off a bombshell. She would not be received, and Mrs. Calhoun, wife of the Vice President, was to be one of the arbiters who decreed her ostracism. Jackson reacted angrily to this decree. His own wife had recently died, "murdered," he maintained by the foul tongue of slander, and he convinced himself that Peggy Eaton was "chaste as a virgin." Today it is difficult to see how he could have been so certain, but Jackson always had a great capacity to believe that which would best fit his purposes. On November 18, 1829, there was a frosty Cabinet dinner marked by the snubbing of Mrs. Eaton by her female associates. Jackson took fire, he ordered his niece and hostess and the members of the Cabinet who had hostesses, Ingham, Branch, and Berrien, to see that Mrs. Eaton was received. In every instance he failed. Only Van Buren, who was a widower, was paying attention to Mrs. Eaton, while Calhoun's wife was her leading critic. Jackson was not one to sympathize with Calhoun's helplessness, and the Vice President had lost a round. Van Buren smiled and cultivated Mrs. Eaton and her boisterous laugh. On December 31, 1829, Jackson wrote to Judge John Overton that he wished Van Buren to succeed him.

The division in Jackson's following and the rivalry which fostered it were further emphasized and exaggerated by the political nature and use made of certain pressures generated by the rapid growth of the population and the national enterprise. These pressures aroused and aggravated personal and regional rivalries. They also involved Andrew Jackson's behavior as a leader in a fashion that makes the whole matter most complex.

It is easy to speak of the needs and pressures for internal improvements at federal expense, for a protective tariff, and for a stabilizing national bank as insistent impersonal pressures. It is also effective to speak of national versus sectional interests and to show that the interests of East, South, and West were pronounced and on occasion conflicting. Soon, however, personality enters into it. Vice President Calhoun had been a nationalist with an eagerness for development, both commercial and industrial. However, it had become apparent that the South, and South Carolina in particular, had come to believe that a protective tariff would build up the North at the expense of the South, so Calhoun had come to oppose the protective measure even to the point of supporting nullification.

The Vice President undertook to make further use of these general pressures and to shape an ideological contest which would determine the pattern of political maneuvering. He was attempting to create a congressional bloc uniting the South and West eventually to defeat protection to industry, centralization, and consolidation. This was to be done, however, by making use of another issue which arose almost by accident. Certain New England interests were disturbed by the migration of important elements of their labor force to the attractive cheap lands of the West. On December 29, 1829, a Connecticut senator, Samuel A. Foot, introduced a resolution asking the Senate to inquire into the expediency of suspending for a time the sales of public lands. This move immediately roused Senator Thomas Hart Benton of Missouri. He protested against this tentative proposal as indicative of a design on the part of eastern interests to circumscribe the development of the West. In a few days he did more than object, he made one of his ponderous speeches and introduced a "graduation" bill to reduce the price of western lands. Calhoun and some of his associates saw in this an opportunity to cement relations with the West. Both wanted cheap lands. These would ensure more agricultural states opposed to protective tariffs. Likewise, if lands were sold cheaply, the Treasury would be deprived of revenues which would otherwise strengthen the spending power of the federal government, a power which would encourage centralizing strength.

Calhoun's colleague, Senator Robert Y. Hayne of South Carolina, joined Benton in this opposition. He too protested against the desire of the East to stifle the nation's growth, particularly in the western ranges. He supported Benton's idea that the national domain should be considered, not as a source of revenue, but as an inducement for western migration and new enterprise. In the course of his remarks he referred to eastern lack of public spirit and even of patriotism; he alluded to their conduct during the War of 1812 and to the shame of the Hartford Convention. These allusions stung New England and the great Webster joined battle. He accused the South, particularly South Carolina, of worse treason in advocating the nullification of law, as it had in 1828. This brought Hayne up again with a defense of southern constitutional theory. The federal government was one of limited power, the rights of the states were supreme. The Constitution was merely a compact, and nullification was the remedy if the compact were violated. This in turn brought Webster to his greatest height of eloquence as he expounded the doctrine of the Constitution as a perpetual grant, subject only to interpretation by the courts. He exalted loose construction and nationalism, liberty and union, one and inseparable, in those mighty last days of January 1830.

Another Calhoun figure now got into the act. Duff Green in the *Telegraph*, still the White House organ, began to lash Webster in his paper, showing how Webster had opposed Jackson's election in 1828, thus trying to rouse Old Hickory's resentment at personal opposition and get him committed to Calhoun's doctrines. Green and other Calhoun supporters sought to clinch this by arranging a banquet on Jefferson's birthday in April. This feast would be a public endorsement of Jefferson, the glorious principles of '98, states' rights, and an assist to Calhoun. Jackson of course was to be the central figure. He accepted, but instead of falling in line with the theme, he came out on the other side, with his famous toast: "Our Union, it must be preserved." The plain truth was that something had happened.

Not only was Jackson incensed at the Calhouns' attitude toward

Mrs. Eaton, but he had recently discovered what others already knew. Jackson's associates had learned before the election that evidence might possibly be had from Crawford that Calhoun had been desirous of censuring Jackson for his conduct in the Florida campaigns during the Monroe Administration. As Calhoun was supporting Jackson in 1828, there was no point in seeking this evidence then, but now in the impending contest over the succession it would be useful. So they had secured it and had showed it to Jackson. He moved vigorously, confounded Calhoun with his nationalistic toast, and demanded explanations. He and Calhoun exchanged several letters, and by May 1830 the angry Chief Magistrate was through with the Vice President.

Jackson had never found his hastily constructed Cabinet very congenial. He seldom met them. Rather he took rides with Van Buren and enjoyed the society of a "kitchen cabinet." This included Eaton, White, and Lewis from Tennessee. There also were Isaac Hill of New Hampshire, second comptroller until the Senate rejected him, and Amos Kendall, fourth auditor, who was something of a ghost writer for the President. Senator Thomas Hart Benton was among his advisers and former Judge John Overton, an old friend who sometimes visited the White House and corresponded with the General from Nashville. These men were the General's intimates, and in this circle he had decided on the Jefferson Day toast and a plan to administer the *coup de grâce* to Calhoun's influence. He was breaking with Duff Green and inviting Francis Preston Blair of Kentucky to come to Washington to set up a new organ, the *Globe*. Blair was ready to undertake this, and the first issue appeared December 7, 1830. The Kentuckian became a leading figure in the kitchen cabinet.

Only one more move seemed needed to complete Calhoun's elimination, and this was suggested by Van Buren. The ladies of the Cabinet and in fact the ladies of Jackson's household had been stubborn about Mrs. Eaton. Only the widower, Van Buren, had paid her any attention or had sought her social recognition. As Secretary of State, he could and did bring pressure upon the foreign embassies, and fair Peggy was not without invitations. In the midst of this "social war" Van Buren played further upon the Old Chief's resentments. He told him that the Cabinet situation was impossible, that Calhoun was calling the tune, and that a reorganization was overdue. Jackson deserved a new Cabinet. He, Van Buren, would resign, perhaps take a foreign mission. Eaton would do likewise, and then Jackson could require the recalcitrants, Ingham, Branch and Berrien, now considered Calhoun followers, to resign. Eaton went first, April 7, 1831; Van Buren, next;

followed by Ingham and Branch immediately and Berrien in June. Edward Livingston of Louisiana became Secretary of State; Louis McLane of Delaware, Secretary of the Treasury; Lewis Cass of Michigan, Secretary of War; Levi Woodbury of New Hampshire, Secretary of the Navy; Roger B. Taney of Maryland, Attorney General. These were a much more distinguished group. Nobody seemed to care about Barry so he stayed on. Jackson's plans to get Eaton back into the Senate went awry, but he sent Van Buren to be minister at London. Later Eaton was to go to Spain.

But Calhoun was not yet through. Van Buren was given a recess appointment and went off to England unconfirmed. When the Senate convened in December 1831, his enemies and Jackson's arranged a tie vote so that Calhoun could have the privilege of casting the vote which would bring Van Buren back home immediately. In doing so, Calhoun remarked, "It will kill him dead, sir, kill him dead, he will never kick."

Van Buren did not have to wait long for the resurrection. On another occasion he is reported to have said that there was "such a thing as killing a man too dead." Jackson's vigorous antipathy to Calhoun had, if that could be possible, become even more deadly. He undertook to exalt Van Buren by using a political instrument recently introduced into partisan use.

Up to this point presidential contests for nominations had been few and haphazard. There had been little plan and less organization. But with a population and a mass of voters increasing at such a great rate and with relatively few politically potent chieftains around, there was need of some innovation in campaigning, particularly in the realm of organization and in propaganda. An epoch-making change was developed in preparation for the campaign of 1832.

As was so often the case, the impulse came from a state situation. And in this instance again it came from the state with the most fertile political soil, the seedbed of so much political innovation, namely New York. Though the death of DeWitt Clinton had made the Albany regency seemingly supreme, there were still the old opposition and a generation of rising young men of great political ingenuity who were restlessly seeking new means of promoting their fortunes. Beginning in 1827 they had snatched at a chance, master opportunists that they were.

This People's party, as they had once called themselves, had taken advantage of the Antimasonic revulsion that had followed the disappearance of William Morgan, presumed to have been about to reveal Masonic secrets. This hostility was spreading to other sections. It had become politically active in Pennsylvania and Ohio in 1828 and was to appear in New England. Had it reached such a proportion that it could be mobilized against the Mason Andrew Jackson? The New York leaders—Thurlow Weed, William H. Seward, and Francis Granger—thought it might be worth a try. It would give them an opportunity to proclaim democracy and attack Jackson as a secret society aristocrat. They would fight the proscriptive order in the name of popular rights and liberty.

They started a plan for national cooperation at the New York Antimasonic Convention in March 1829. The Federalists in 1808 and 1812 had tried the conference idea because there were too few members of Congress of their persuasion to give a congressional caucus any authority. Likwise, there was now too small a number of Antimasonic congressmen for such a move. New York therefore proposed a national conference to meet in Philadelphia on September 11, 1830. Here gathered some budding young politicos, including Thaddeus Stevens of Pennsylvania. Representatives from so few states attended, only nine in fact, that it was decided to try again, and the presidential nomination was then and there referred to another gathering called for Baltimore in September 1831. Each state was invited to send as many delegates as it had members in Congress, thus setting a pattern followed ever since. Thirteen states responded: the nine from New England and the Middle Atlantic region together with two from the South—Delaware and Maryland—and two from the West—Ohio and Indiana.

What proved to be the first national party convention met in Baltimore at the time specified. Its members adopted a statement anticipating a party platform and placed Jefferson on a pedestal as a party leader. From such a pedestal he has never been removed. The Antimasons took the portion of Jefferson's first inaugural in which he outlined the sixteen essential principles of democracy: equality, peace, states rights, preservation of the Constitution, free elections, rule of the majority, militia, supremacy of civil government, economy, payment of debts, encouragement of agriculture with its handmaid commerce, diffusion of information, freedom of religion, freedom of press, privilege of the writ of habeas corpus, and trial by jury. These the members of the convention declared were in mortal danger at the hands of the Freemasons. They then nominated William Wirt of Maryland, a member of Adams' Cabinet, and Amos Ellmaker of Pennsylvania as their candidates for the Presidency and Vice Presidency.

In the meantime opponents other than the Antimasons had been planning to oppose Jackson. Various friends of Henry Clay had been proposing him in legislative and other public meetings. These men, who were generally called National Republicans, had organized in New York City in December 1830. They appointed a committee of seventy to promote the defeat of Jackson. In the meantime informal meetings of anti-Jackson congressmen were held in the lodgings of John W. Taylor, New York congressman, twice speaker and senior anti-Jackson member; these men sought to make as much anti-Jackson capital as possible, particularly from the protective tariff idea. New York continued its leadership by holding a state convention in June 1831 at Albany. Here the National Republicans set up a state committee of correspondence with an office in Buffalo and recommended that county committees be created. By August 1831 the demand for a national convention, which had been set in motion by a Republican convention in Kentucky in December 1830, had become so general that the conservative *National Intelligencer* which had been opposing such a gathering came around and on August 23 urged a conclave. Its task would be to nominate a vice presidential candidate as Clay had in effect been already nominated "by carefully fostered public opinion."

The suggestion of a caucus of the National Republican members of the Maryland legisature that such a gathering meet in Baltimore on the second Monday in December 1831 was accepted. After this time and place were seconded by groups in Pennsylvania, Connecticut, and Maine, it was so arranged. Thus it was ordained that the first national major party nominating convention should function December 12–16 and complete the pattern on a larger scale than the Antimasons. Eighteen states sent delegates, and 156 took their seats; six southern states—South Carolina, Georgia, Alabama, Mississippi, Missouri, and Arkansas—paid no heed. This body under the chairmanship of James Barbour of Virginia, onetime member of John Quincy Adams' Cabinet, unanimously proposed Henry Clay and John Sergeant of Pennsylvania as their ticket. They prescribed a committee organization for each state like that in New York, including correspondence committees in each county. The body endorsed the assembling of a National Republican Convention of Young Men to meet in Washington the next May. The convention itself issued an address and invited each state to go home and issue one of its own.

The address so proclaimed was to be the first major party call to battle. In felicitous phrases the committee spoke of the National Republicans, who had been acting "together in political affairs for some years past," as meeting because "a careful and deliberate survey of the political condition of the country" and of the conduct of the Jackson Administration demonstrated that the "public good imperiously" required "a change." Jackson had pledged himself to suppress party strife and to make removals only for incapacity and corruption. He had failed utterly to keep his pledge. He also had pursued foreign affairs in a fashion "derogatory to the honor of the country, and the dignity of the Government." He had been ambiguous regarding internal improvements and the tariff and openly hostile to the United States Bank, which the address defended. His failure was complete and acknowledged. Despite spoils and a subsidized press, his Cabinet had fallen apart because of blind cupidity and vindictive party spirit. Likewise, pledged to but one term, Jackson had recently announced his candidacy for a second.

A change was imperative and who could better right these wrongs than Henry Clay, one of the principal founders and supporters of the American System? This statesman would develop internal improvements, a protective tariff, and the prosperity of the nation's domestic industry. It called upon the voters to defeat the Jackson Administration which for some time past had "been justly discredited in public opinion." So completely had the Jacksonian party been broken up that the National Republicans were advised that "nothing is wanted but zeal, activity and concert, to ensure success." The congressional caucus continued its meetings during the session of 1831–32, and the "Young Men" duly met in Washington in May to stir up more enthusiasm and to issue another address.

Only one further step was necessary in this unusual campaign. The initial uncertainty as to whether Jackson would run for a second term was dispelled in 1830. The Jackson supporters in the Pennsylvania legislature caucused in March 1830 and presented his name for a second term; this was seconded by a party caucus in Albany in April and by one in New Hampshire in June. In the winter the legislatures of Alabama and Illinois did likewise. The break with Calhoun and Jackson's desire to name Van Buren as his Vice President made it necessary for Jackson to declare himself, so on January 22, 1831, it was announced in the press that he would run if called upon. Thereupon a second Pennsylvania caucus made the call and Jackson in a public letter accepted.

Jackson and his advisers then felt that some authoritative and official demonstration should be made to show that the party approved of his desire to have Van Buren run with him for the Vice Presidency. Calhoun must be formally superseded. Amos Kendall negotiated with Isaac Hill to get the New Hampshire Democrats, in their legislature in midsummer of 1831, to call a convention to meet in Baltimore in May 1832 to select a Vice President. This was done, but there was a good deal of doubt whether the Democrats would take Van Buren. These doubts were removed, however, when the nomination of Van Buren as minister to Great Britain was rejected by the casting vote of Vice President Calhoun.

This action in January 1832 made a martyr of Van Buren, done to death by an unholy coalition of Calhoun, Clay, and Webster. The Jacksonians in various states rallied round him when choosing delegates. Despite general acquiescence by the Jacksonian machine operators in the replacement of Calhoun, this was not to be achieved without opposition. Certain in the South stood out for a southern vice presidential candidate. They did not trust Van Buren on the tariff and other interests affecting their section. The Alabama legislature and certain public meetings in North Carolina and Virginia nominated Philip Barbour of Virginia who had served as chairman of an anti-tariff convention held in Philadelphia in September 1831.

The convention met as scheduled in Baltimore. These delegates, generally styled Democratic-Republicans in contradistinction to the National Republican party which had prescribed Clay, proceeded to organize and make rules to ensure the control of the Jackson managers. In so doing they set precedents to become famous. Each state was assigned as many votes as it had electors. There should be a unit rule, that is the votes of each state should be cast as a unit as a majority of the delegation decided. Two-thirds should be needed to nominate. This latter rule was decided on so that no dissident faction in the party could join with delegates from states which the Jacksonians had no hope of carrying and nominate someone by a simple majority that the leaders of the party did not want. Van Buren was easily nominated, although the disgruntled Virginians and South Carolinians together with the Kentuckians, disappointed by Jackson's opposition to internal improvements, did rally some 75 out of 283 for Barbour and other candidates. The convention contented itself with authorizing its president to appoint a general correspondence committee from each state. No platform was issued, everyone knew that Jackson would be the platform. The chieftain was the issue as he had been in 1828.

Though Jackson's host presented no platform, the needs of the growing nation had brought a number of issues to the fore, and Clay and his supporters in Congress were seeking to use them in their efforts to drive Jackson from the White House. Clay was the author of the American System, designed to supply communication, industrial protection, and banking and credit facilities to those interested in growth of the United States in wealth and power. His followers had attempted not only to enact a series of laws but also to manipulate the process to Jackson's disadvantage. Early in the Administration they had begun to introduce internal improvement bills into the Congress. Jackson and Van Buren discussed this tactic on their afternoon rides, and the President decided on his policy. He was most interested in paying off the national debt, and he realized that if a great deal of money was spent hither and yon on building roads and subsidizing canals, the money for retiring the debt would be frittered away. He would put a stop to it. He and Van Buren selected a bill for a road entirely in Clay's Kentucky. He would veto that with a promise of similar action on others. So on May 27, 1830, he sent in his Maysville Road veto and he was sustained. But had he alienated the West? Time alone would tell.

A second problem with political implications was the Bank of the United States. Its charter would expire in 1836. It was directed by an enterprising Philadelphian, Nicholas Biddle, its third president. He knew that Jackson was believed to be hostile to banks, a fact he had demonstrated in Tennessee. What would his attitude be in Washington? Biddle anticipated problems, so he sought and was sought by such men as Clay and Webster who saw mutual advantage in close association with so great a financial institution. Friends of Jackson were hostile to the Bank, particularly Isaac Hill, the New Hampshire editor. He charged that the Portsmouth, New Hampshire, branch of the Bank was using its money to help Jackson's political foes. Investigation uncovered nothing, so Biddle undertook to see Jackson with a proposal for an arrangement for recharter which would be more to the advantage of the United States Treasury. He had allies, not only in the Cabinet, but in the White House entourage itself. He hoped that his offer would be accepted. Not for a while did Jackson discourage him. Then Biddle's friends sought to aid him and themselves by forcing the issue.

Clay and Webster felt that if the recharter were pushed through before the election of 1832, Jackson might hesitate to veto it for fear of political reprisals from the financial world and the East in General. These two operators therefore went to Biddle and "advised" him to petition for recharter before the election of 1832. They told him they could not answer for recharter after that. Biddle with some hesitation complied; he knew he was playing with fire. Thus Congress, when it met in December 1831, had the Bank issue before it.

Likewise, another tariff battle was impending. In 1828 South Carolina had threatened reprisals if another protective measure were enacted and here was another bill. The friends of the Bank and the friends of protection were in control of Congress, so in July 1832 both bills were passed in the midst of the presidential campaign. What would Jackson do? He had been defied by Calhoun and his South Carolina, but he would not be intimidated. Anything Calhoun disliked, he would sign, and the tariff of 1832 became law. He had likewise been challenged by Biddle, Clay, and Webster by this early petition. He would accept the challenge, and he vetoed the recharter of the Bank. By vetoing the road bill and the Bank bill and by signing the tariff, he had presumably enraged West, East, and South. What had he left but oblivion?

Clay and his associates did their best. They had learned some of the arts of organization. There was a flood of literature, political pamphlets, and press notices. There was a Clay campaign biography extolling his talents and achievements. There were Clay clubs, Clay balls, Clay barbecues, and Clay banquets with their unending toasts. Clay had, likewise, a campaign manager in the person of Josiah S. Johnston, a fellow senator from Louisiana. Clay's campaign literature charged Jackson with being a dictator, a violator of pledges, and an extravagant spender of government money. He had corrupted the civil service, he was attacking the economy by his veto of the Bank bill. He had mishandled foreign affairs and lied about his acts. He had "encouraged a set of bullies to infest the halls of Congress and overawe members in the discharge of their legislative duties," committing disgraceful assaults "with clubs and pistols" on members. He was even putting the Supreme Court to defiance.

Some charges had a very modern ring. During the first Jackson campaign in 1828 it was claimed a fund of $50,000 had been raised for electioneering. A central committee had been set up in Washington to promote the General's election and all but one of them had since been appointed to office. Votes had been bought in New York and the western states for from $5 to $7 apiece, officeholders in Boston were "maced" $5 a month from their salaries for election purposes. Duff Green turned his *Telegraph* against Jackson and called upon the friends of Calhoun to defeat the General. His campaign extra was virulent. This he claimed to be doing without the advice and approbation of Calhoun and his political friends. But it was all to no avail. Whatever the "interests" might think, or however much enterprisers might cherish the American System, Old Hickory was the people's hero and they followed in his train.

Jackson and Van Buren carried sixteen states. The Antimasons succeeded only in Vermont. Clay secured the old Federalist states, Connecticut, Massachusetts, Rhode Island, Delaware, Maryland, and Kentucky, while Calhoun's South Carolina threw her votes away. Pennsylvania would not vote for Van Buren, but he had enough without its support. All states now chose their electors by popular vote save South Carolina; in round numbers, 1,250,000 people voted and Jackson won 687,000 to 563,000 for his opponents. The chieftain reigned because he was a chieftain, and one more commanding than his rival partisan, Clay. Despite the conventions and the committees, it was still *caudillo* politics.

THE OPPOSITION FAILS

*T*HE PROBLEM of defeating a popular chieftain had not been solved by pitting against him another chieftain who, though not so heroic, had glamor and organization and could present the lure of promises of government largesse. At the same time the Jacksonians had gained in experience and would improve in efficiency from the closer association of Martin Van Buren, master of the techniques of the Albany regency. Also state organizations had propelled and been strengthened by Jackson's victory. His popularity to some extent had proved to be transferable. A real American party system was emerging.

Old Hickory, therefore, had not had to meet the fate of the Adamses, father and son, in his quest for a second term. The effort to defeat him had failed, though he himself had seemed to supply his foes with plenty of weapons. He had alienated interests in all parts of the country. He had made enemies in the ranks of his followers, and sections of them were in revolt. His opponents had created an organization, seemingly better knit than his own, and they had endeavored to make full use of the mass media of communication available in that day. To top it all, Jackson had been opposed by the clever, attractive, and widely famed Henry Clay who, together with the National Republican leaders and the rank and file, had worked tirelessly during the campaign, only to be defeated rather ignominiously. Ingenious contriving had not prevailed against a hero. Clay's party fell apart and disappeared as an effective national organization.

The opponents of the Jacksonians must again take up their task of opposition, now made more difficult by this defeat. They must secure more support in the East and South. The solutions of most of their problems were not likely to be found in national conventions or congressional caucuses. They could be discovered only in the states. For the republic was a federal polity and it always presented two levels of political operation. The states and their governments provided twenty-four stages upon which the play of politics, dramatic or otherwise, must be ceaselessly presented. In each one there were local situations and local actors who would recite such lines or write such parts as were deemed effective to meet local conditions. And they were all different. Would these differences permit new efforts to bring to focus any conjunction of forces sufficient to defeat or even threaten the Jacksonian government?

The partisans of Jackson had carried sixteen of the twenty-four states. The one man who seemed best equipped to take the lead against them had just been completely defeated. Was opposition to the regime of President Jackson to be as hopeless as that which had failed to disturb the Jeffersonians more than momentarily? There was no national force or leadership available, or so it seemed. The answer, if any, must be found in the states.

Some hope flourished briefly that a union between the Antimasons and the National Republicans might produce results in some localities. In 1832 such a union had been consummated in New York, but it had failed to keep the state from Jackson and Van Buren. The state elections of 1833 later showed it to be utterly bankrupt. In Pennsylvania there was to be an effort in the legislature of 1833 which would permit the combination to elect the speaker of the house, but it failed to choose a United States senator. The possibility of an anti-Jackson union did not seem very bright on the basis of Antimasonic and Republican cooperation, but a new development opened up another avenue.

Jackson's condemnation of South Carolina's nullification of the tariff, his threat to use the army and navy, and his support of a force bill roused the advocates of states' rights to protest executive coercion; they sometimes called themselves Whigs, reminiscent of their Revolutionary ancestors. Some supporters, like John Tyler of Virginia, were on the road to permanent alienation. Then Old Hickory's removal of the federal deposits from the Bank of the United States in September 1833, designed to hasten its demise, disturbed the financial structure of the nation and called forth the cry of "tyranny." Furthermore, Old Hickory's insistence that Van Buren, who was not glamorous and not popular among southern and western interests, succeed him, stirred up further dissatisfaction.

Revolt spread. Jackson's removal of the deposits caused Biddle to curtail his loans and produced an uncertainty about credit which was upsetting to business. Likewise, the President's policy of caring for government money was disturbing. He ordered the cash placed in a variety of state-chartered banks. These were almost immediately called "pet" banks, and the implication was often that they must be Jacksonian, no others need apply. This was by no means strictly true, but it became a part of the political folklore then current. Added to this was the fact that an economic cycle was about to come to climax, feverish business was inflated almost to the breaking point, and something like psychic apprehension contributed to unsettling politics. Hatred of Jackson and fear gave politicos new opportunities and incentives.

By this time the fact had become more evident than ever that there were still no real national organizations nor much central direction. The National Republican operation of 1832, as well as the Hickory campaign, had been highly personal to Clay and Jackson, and as 1836 approached no one seemed to know how to organize a concentrated opposition to the Jacksonians. Some new form of political crystallization must be attempted in the states, urged on by some impulse from Washington. Congress had always displayed some of the characteristics of a political convention. The congregation of so many political operators from all parts of the land in the hotels and boardinghouses of Washington, as well as in the chambers and committee rooms of Congress, made the capital city a convenient place for political conference and negotiation. Although formal caucus nominations had been given up, there was much informal comparing of notes and exchanges of "understanding."

The sessions of the Twenty-third Congress were used for maneuvers to consolidate an anti-Jackson coalition. Those who opposed Old Hickory's war on the Bank and on nullification, after some complex negotiations, were joining forces. That formidable trio, Clay, Webster, and Calhoun, after burying various hatchets, took charge of the Senate and launched a thunderbolt at Jackson. On March 28, 1834, they engineered a vote censuring him for his financial policies. A little later when a vacancy occurred in the speakership, a combination which included all the anti-Jackson, pro-Bank and states' rights men, together with at least twenty ill-disposed Administration men, on June 2, 1834, elected John Bell of Tennessee over James K. Polk from the same state. This was not so clear an indication of hostility, for both Bell and Jackson maintained that Bell was a Jackson man. Yet the new speaker was a Bank supporter, while Polk had been Jackson's financial floor leader in the House during his destruction of the corporation. In the meantime there had been an increasing amount of anti-Jackson reorganization going on in the states.

This reorganization was as varied as the localities. South Carolina was up in arms because of the nullification fiasco. The leaders in Jackson's home state of Tennessee were in revolt against having that New York machine politician Van Buren foisted upon them. New York City was upset by the Little Panic of 1834 and unemployment, which was rife. Jackson's acts were those of a tyrant. In the Revolution, Patriot Whigs had risen against a tyrannical king. Now it was time for modern Whigs to fight King Andrew the First. They would drive him and his Tory supporters from power. This general emotional appeal could attract National Republicans, Antimasons, Workingmen's parties, Bank Democrats, those who were in business difficulties, those who were out of work, those who feared the economic future.

The name Whig had been much used in South Carolina during the nullification contest of 1832–33, and now it came into more general use in the spring of 1834. It was employed most conspicuously in New York City and other cities in the Empire State, such as Auburn and Syracuse, as well as in Philadelphia and New England. There was a spectacular success in the New York municipal elections in April. In the great metropolis, the new party carried the municipal council, their candidate for mayor was defeated by only 181 votes, and there were Whig victories upstate as well. In neighboring Pennsylvania a state convention was achieved in May, followed by one in New York in August. At this latter gathering William H. Seward was nominated for governor and thereby launched on a long career with his "alter ego," Thurlow Weed, to promote his fortunes. In the South the move was actively pushed, particularly in South Carolina and Georgia where resentment was high at Jackson's tyrannical "disregard" of local rights. These new combinations stood on platforms of states' rights and they smeared the Jacksonians with the "dirty word" Unionists.

In the West, in Ohio, the Antimasons had moved out on the Reserve in 1828 where they had split the opponents of Jackson. In 1832 Jackson had carried the state together with the Democratic candidate for governor, but in 1834 the Whigs carried the legislature and a majority of the congressional seats. Judge McLean of that state began a candidacy for the Presidency which was still active as late as 1860.

In New England the old elite party which had been in control for so many years in Massachusetts was going to assume the title Whig and push Webster for the Presidency. Workingmen's parties and Antimasons appeared in the Bay State later than in the other commonwealths, the former interestingly enough being largely rural. These groups did not run candidates very often but generally endorsed others and by and large were helpful to the Democrats with whom many of them eventually merged on an egalitarian basis. In all sections the political wiseacres were scanning the scattered returns as they found their way into the press or into political correspondence.

When the results of the various state elections scattered over 1834 were tabulated, Whig successes did not bulk too impressively, except in the old National Republican areas of New England, Delaware, and Maryland and in Kentucky. However, the Whigs had won governorships in Indiana, Illinois, and Louisiana and the legislature of Ohio. Their defeats in New York, New Jersey, and Pennsylvania and the loss of the gubernational election in Ohio were discouraging. In 1835 when the elections in the southern states were more generally held, the Whigs got little comfort save in Tennessee, where in Jackson's own state the governorship was gained; in the North Pennsylvania elected a Whig Antimason governor. The Twenty-fourth Congress was again safely Jacksonian in the House. Bell would be defeated for speaker by Polk; and the Senate was going to be less hostile to the President.

But what about 1836? Clay was uncommitted publicly, although privately he was writing that he was not available. McLean and Webster were already announced. More significant was a move originating below the Mason-Dixon line. The southern opponents of Jackson and Van Buren believed that their hope of success in 1836 was to find some southern candidate who could unite the South and New England. A suggestion broached among Old Hickory's Tennessee enemies in his own party as early as 1833 was taken up in various parts of the South on behalf of Tennessee Senator Hugh L. White. He had been gradually frozen out of Jackson's kitchen cabinet, in part by Eaton and Van Buren, and White was resentful. Also, he had recently married an ambitious lady who had dreams of the White House. Southern newspapers launched a demand for White, and in December 1834 a majority of the Tennessee congressional delegation asked him to consent to the use of his name. He replied that the people had a right to choose whom they pleased. The legislature of

Alabama then nominated him, and a newspaper, *The Appeal,* was set up in Washington to promote his fortunes. His candidacy caused a certain amount of confusion because he was a Democrat, and southern supporters were not always too clear in their party designations nor particularly mindful of them.

In the North and West opposition efforts were more distinctively Whig. Webster had done some traveling into the West and in Pennsylvania with little result, and then a new figure appeared. A newspaper in the Keystone commonwealth brought forward the name of a hero and a martyr, General William Henry Harrison of Ohio, victor at the battle of Tippecanoe, whom Jackson had deprived of his diplomatic mission to Colombia almost as soon as he had arrived there. He was proclaimed as the anti-Jackson hope and his candidacy began to take. The Whigs would pit a hero against a hero. In December 1835 Pennsylvania Whigs and Antimasons got up a state convention to endorse him, and while some Antimasons seceded and held another convention, they endorsed no candidate in opposition. A convention in Ohio, his home state, in 1836 put him forth as a favorite son and McLean, also of Ohio, withdrew so as to clear the way for him. Clay at length publicly announced that he was unavailable and gave indications that Harrison was his choice.

Democratic difficulties were to help. In New York State the regency was in trouble. They had seen their Antimasonic opponents wither and the Workingmen's efforts were not gathering impetus as an independent organization, but within the Jacksonian ranks there was a schism developing, the beginning of an historic breach which was to have major repercussions. A radical, hard-money, antimonopoly, anti-Bank faction was growing. Its spokesmen stressed egalitarian doctrines; they were foes of privilege who dubbed themselves advocates of equal rights and who were popularly known as Locofocos because of a curious incident. At a New York City meeting of the Democrats the conservative force seeing itself outnumbered tried to break up the meeting by turning off the gas. The radicals, however, were not deterred. They had a supply of locofoco matches and with them they lighted candles and continued their operations. Thereafter this group were known as Locofoco or Equal Rights Democrats.

The Whigs were further aided by the rise of a nativist group. The increasing number of Irish immigrants and their tendency to join forces with the Democrats roused antiforeign and anti-Catholic prejudices and caused some Democrats to either join nativist local groups or vote Whig. All this encouraged the Whig leaders to stage a state convention in Albany in October 1835 to accept Harrison as their candidate and to suggest New York's Francis Granger as his running mate. In Massachusetts, after Webster had failed to negotiate a Webster-Harrison slate, a convention met and launched a Webster-Granger ticket in the hope of gaining New York support.

The Whig strategy for 1836, if such it can be called, was shaping in the form of having no plan at all. Those opposed to Jackson's wishes returned to the routine of 1824. There would be a multiplicity of state-sponsored candidates with the issue to be settled in the House or by some agreement among the electors that in the event there proved to be an anti-Jackson majority it would unite on whomever received the highest number of votes. The strategists themselves were divided and they never merged their plans. One group included Clay and his lieutenant, John J. Crittenden, who had some communication with Nicholas Biddle, Daniel Webster, and John McLean. In another camp were certain anti-Van Burenites in Tennessee where John Overton, Eaton, and Bell, who had fallen out with Jackson, were supporting White. And then, as so often, by himself, was John C. Calhoun. He would not seek followers, nor would they come to him. Biddle advocated such a bevy of candidates and believed they might bring victory in the House; even the conservative and timid *National Intelligencer* admitted the possibility. Signs of hostility among the White, Harrison, and Calhoun supporters indicated that no concerted leadership was probably possible. It certainly had not paid off in 1832.

White's defection and the appearance of Bank Democrats led the Jackson–Van Buren high command to look to their own organization. It would be well for the Democrats to attempt a rally and to give Van Buren a formal presidential nomination at a national convention, something which the Democratic organization had not hitherto done. Such a move would unite the party and forestall the possibility of the choice of a minority President such as John Quincy Adams had been. At the suggestion of the party leaders in New Jersey, endorsed by a legislative caucus in New York State, a mass convention was called to meet in Baltimore in May 1835, nearly a year and a half in advance of the scheduled presidential election.

This convention was designed not only to nominate Van Buren but also to reach agreement on a vice presidential candidate. The Jacksonians wanted to strengthen the colorless Van Buren by nominating for Vice President a western hero, Colonel Richard Mentor Johnson, who had slain Tecumseh in the War of 1812. He would give strength to the ticket in the West where Van Buren was weak. This proposal of Johnson was to prove unpopular in the South, however, because the slayer of Tecumseh lived with a mulatto slave and sought to introduce their daughters into society.

Some six hundred delegates attended, more than half from Maryland, but each state was assigned only the number of votes which it had in the Electoral College. Speaker Stevenson of Virginia was called to the chair, and the convention followed the precedent of 1832 by adopting the two-thirds and the unit rules. Some of Johnson's opponents, particularly those from Virginia who were supporting Senator W.C. Rives, hoped that the two-thirds provision would defeat the colonel, and it would have, save for a highhanded play. Tennessee had sent no delegates, saying White was her candidate. But the Jacksonian managers found a Tennessean in Baltimore, one Edward Rucker, and prevailed upon him to cast Tennessee's fifteen votes. By this device Van Buren was nominated by the votes of all the states and Johnson barely got the two-thirds necessary. Virginia was wroth and refused to support Tecumseh's slayer, hero though he was.

The Democrats issued an address to the voters. This appeal charged that their opponents were disunionists, trying to sow seeds of strife and doing this by running various candidates in different parts of the country, using one type of propaganda in the South and another in the North, playing upon sectional differences. The Democrats on their part, it was claimed, had attempted to consolidate their ranks by this convention and thus avoid the possibility of a minority President such as might be chosen if the election were thrown into the House. Their opponents, using doubtful constitutional powers, were working to make the rich grow richer and the poor grow poorer by establishing a Bank, exacting exorbitant tariffs, and by taxing one part of the country to build roads and canals in another. The authors of the address pled with the former Republicans who had left the party to return. Bygones would be forgotten, and the recent difference would be considered "a misunderstanding rather than a schism." "Let us promote a spirit of union among ourselves, without which democracy can never triumph."

This compact organization was not followed by the Whigs. Confusion was to be confounded. They ignored the precedents established by Clay, the National Republicans, and the Antimasons. They showed no sense of party, no harmony of leadership. Their most obvious candidate, White, probably thought of himself as a Democrat. Clay, their most prominent statesman, already twice defeated, stayed in the background, though he was presumed to favor General William Henry Harrison, his neighbor across the river, at North Bend, Ohio. Despite lack of formal action, something of the flavor of a campaign was developed at anniversaries of the battle of the Thames and at barbecues and Tippecanoe rallies where Harrison's military exploits were advertised without particular allusions to Van Buren which might offend.

In the end Van Buren won, although not by a wide margin. He secured all of New England, save Massachusetts, which went for Webster and Granger, and Vermont, which supported Harrison and Granger. In the middle states Van Buren carried New York and Pennsylvania, but Harrison and Granger secured New Jersey. White won Tennessee and Georgia; Harrison and Granger, Delaware and Kentucky; while Harrison and Tyler carried Maryland. South Carolina again threw her votes away; the rest of the South, including Virginia, went for Van Buren. Of the West, Harrison and Granger had Ohio and Indiana, leaving only Illinois and Michigan for Van Buren. John Tyler of Virginia, honored for his vote against the force bill in defiance of Jackson, had generally been accepted as Hugh L. White's running mate. He had been specifically designated as such in Maryland, Virginia, and North Carolina and had narrowly missed being nominated for second place in Ohio with Harrison. He received the electoral votes of Georgia and Tennessee on the ticket with White; also those of Maryland, which went for Harrison; and those of South Carolina, which were cast for Willie P. Mangum of North Carolina for first place. Virginia refused to support Richard M. Johnson for the Vice Presidency and voted for William Smith of Alabama. This cut cost Johnson an election in the Electoral College as no one had a majority. The Senate, however, chose him. Van Buren's 762,000 votes topped his opponents by less than 30,000.

Despite this chaotic but widespread variety of opposition effort, large and small, in the various states north, south, and west, the long line of the entrenched succession from Jefferson on down through Jackson, only interrupted—if it was interrupted—by the brief tenure of John Quincy Adams, seemed at the conclusion of the election of 1836 to be as firmly established as ever. The Jacksonians under Van Buren's skillful hand were perfecting their organization in the form of a federation of state organizations working in some kind of quadrennial unison. This increase in organizational skill did not follow any surge of voters. In fact there had been a larger percentage of voter participation in state elections than ever had developed in the Jacksonian contests. In few states had there developed two parties of national significance, so the lack of contest encouraged voter apathy.

But there had as yet appeared no real counterorganization. The various small efforts at injecting issues arising from growing religious and racial popular tensions and the increasing self-consciousness of hitherto submerged groups had accomplished little other than sporadic local success. Nor were there signs of class cleavage, the rich and the poor seemed to be distributed in equal proportions between Jacksonians and their opponents. The campaigns of the Whigs had done no more than continue to register the fact that there were certain areas chronically disaffected and resisting the long-standing Democratic-Republican voting habit. But in 1836 no particularly new pattern of a real two-party nationwide conflict seemed to be emerging. Van Buren and a new Congress were stepping forward March 4, 1837, to continue the Jacksonian persuasion.

The political maneuvering of 1836 had demonstrated a basic principal of politics in a democracy, namely that you cannot beat somebody with nobody. Jackson's machine, now better oiled, had functioned with relative smoothness. His opponents, while numerous and attacking him enthusiastically, were as yet scattered and unorganized on any effective national basis. In most states they had been highly opportunistic. They had made use of local issues, local candidates, and local situations, trying to arrange heterogeneous coalitions of anti-Jackson, Antimason, states' rights, and pro-Bank voters under the faintly marked banner of an ancient symbol, Whiggery, opposing tyrants in the name of liberty. But this lacked the substance of leadership and of effective organization. No national meeting of Whigs seemingly was even thought of. What little direction was tried from Washington was feeble, sporadic, and unstructured. However, a clue to a possible remedy had been turned up. General William Henry Harrison, the hero of Tippecanoe, had proved that he had vote-getting powers. Perhaps it would be possible for a hero to finally vanquish a man who was only a hero's legatee. So far there had been no effective organization. Could the opposition be mobilized?

Underneath the surface during these early and middle thirties there were forces at work which were changing the motivation of those seeking office and the pattern of their politics. There was a new purpose entering into the game of office seeking. Officeholding was gaining new meaning. It was sought not only as a means of satisfying vanity for place and power, but practical interests were developing, arising from growing population and changing habits of human behavior. Men wanted to gain office in order to fill demands made by society. Two basic changes in American living were stirring up these demands.

The population of the republic was pushing out into the western areas, and at the same time larger groups were concentrating in the cities, which were being shaped by the services required by a growing population and the innovations of the industrial revolution. The increasing horde of foreign immigrants was emphasizing these demands. Government and politics were forced to respond, and various legislative and administrative policies were promoted in an atmosphere of increasing controversy. The winds of propaganda were blowing on the voters.

Prior to Jackson's rule there had been no Executive for twenty years with either the power, the capacity, or the inclination to assume any particular administrative responsibility for unusual action, nor had Congress undertaken much in the way of unusual response to the new demands. Jackson himself would act, but the range of his interests was not very wide and he had produced a situation in which partisan conflict largely revolved around his interesting enmities. But there were compulsions rising from the growing class of wage workers, from the immigrant enclaves, from those who were looking toward occupancy, power, and improved status in territories about to be opened up and who were concerned lest human slavery be extended there to block the way. All these urges were to involve government, and the response of government would depend on who controlled it. There would be serious resistance to some demands, and politics would therefore be involved. Often the well-entrenched would be highly negative, and the submerged, those of the outer groups, would be obliged to strive with difficulty against great odds. For the first time, in the late twenties and early thirties, this type of political behavior was evolving—a further step in the pattern of organization.

These moves were designed to strike at certain deeply rooted powers. In both the southern and in the northern states, elites were in practical control. A southern elite had an exaggerated power based upon the undemocratic fact that they owned human beings and could count their chattels as a basis for congressional overrepresentation. In the North other elites were in less secure control because they owned capital and land and held sway over wage workers and tenants or were revered as church leaders. In some instances their domination had appeared to be implemented by a secret order who, behind closed doors in Masonic lodges, made the plans that prevailed over popular will.

So political moves had already begun to appear designed to destroy the power of these elites. Abolitionists were seeking to destroy the slave power. Wage workers were organizing against employers. Tenants would organize, as in the antirent movement in New York, against landlords. Also, the Jacksonians appeared to some to be creating a power by marshaling foreign immigrant hordes in cooperation with the Roman Catholic Church. This alliance called for a counter-nativist organization. Already the two major groups were being found wanting. The Jacksonians, with their concentration on opposition to the Bank and the semi-independence of autonomous and somewhat isolated communities—the rights of states—and the Whigs, with their appeal to the ancient shibboleths of the Revolution and their resistance to executive domination, paid too little heed to these basic uneasinesses. Those distressed and disturbed therefore must have more frequent recourse to that means of organized expression exhibited in the new political mechanism which was appearing in the guise of the special-interest organizations, such as the Antimasons, Native Americans, antislavery, and Equal Rights advocates. The problems of the day were inviting political organization, but the Whigs did not seem to be forming a party and the Jacksonians showed some signs of disintegration. Certainly the power of permanent and efficient central party direction had not yet really materialized.

But a change was at hand, a change which needed more sophisticated analysis than merely to speak of it as the Age of Jackson. Jackson had emotion-rousing significance, but the reason he could arouse emotion was because of the fluid nature of the distribution of people, the changing demography, the constant movement of voters and their preoccupation with the creating of new communities. There were successive concentrations of new people in a succession of new communities with new needs and new demands.

The constant assembling of new people brought strangers with different customs, different speech, and different religions in contact for the first time. These were natural sources of antagonism. The frequent creation of new communities meant the necessity of the organization of new political units which had to be fitted into the power structure. This condition produced inevitable rivalries.

Population was flowing in two directions with serious political implications. Those going out beyond the area of established settlement and those in the less developed regions had demands for cheap money and government aid, particularly in transportation facilities, roads, canals, and railroads. The counterflow into towns and cities, into factory communities, brought demands for protective tariffs and regulated banking, for hard money. The crowding in substandard housing brought new dangers to health and greater prevalence of shared discontent. Racial and religious antagonisms were sharpened. There were demands for control of liquor traffic and for more institutions to aid the unfortunate. All these situations were of political use in the reshuffling of the distribution of power.

The intensity of the emotion and the increase of the numbers involved meant that if self-government were to be carried on, there must be more system and organization; just as there was bigger business, there must be bigger politics. There must be a new structure. As the corporation was becoming more common, so must the organized political party. Politicians in effect must incorporate.

The nature of this incorporation was not to depend so much on Jackson as upon the fact that voters are human and must live in some sort of community relationship. As members of a community they present some sort of an image which is based on the social structure, the mores of that community; and the image can frequently be the product of its evolution, often protracted in time and of long-term growth. This image shapes the pattern of prevailing action and opinion, either positively or negatively.

Individuals either swim with the tide or try to buck it. What they do depends upon the strength and nature of the current—and their own strength and nature, their reaction to water. Are they afraid of it, are they mad at it, do they like it, does it bore them? Voters are swayed by mass behavior. Many like to follow leaders. Others like to be in opposition. Some fewer hope to be leaders themselves. There are times when changes are inevitable, and it is then that people have to make choices between old and new, to decide which trend to follow, to accept change or resist it.

Political behavior therefore depends much on the nature of community structure and the patterns of community behavior. Towns in the same county with different social structures and consequently different behavior patterns, when political organization came to crystallize, could join different parties merely because of habitual difference, independence, prejudice, and antagonism.

In this period of crystallization of what Richard P. McCormick has named "The Second American Party System," Jackson and his emotion-arousing image was but one catalytic agent. But now an even more potent one was in the making, the Panic of 1837.

·•:] XXI [:•·

THE MACHINE DESIGN
TAKES SHAPE

*I*N 1836 the patterns of political behavior produced one of the logical results of their evolving design. Van Buren, the President-elect was a new type. He was neither a statesman nor a member of the Virginia dynasty nor a hero. He was a political manager, a contriver. As chief of the New York Bucktails and director of the Albany regency, he had been one of a group who had undertaken to create a national machine by negotiating an alliance of state machines, in which the chief members were the Richmond Junto in Virginia and his own New York organization. This he liked euphemistically to speak of as an alliance of southern planters and plain northern farmers. This alliance had succeeded, but by a narrow margin, and as a result Van Buren had taken up residence in the White House. A large fraction of Old Hickory's personal following had been willing to support the man whom he had chosen to succeed him.

However, Massachusetts and Vermont had their preferences, and Jackson's own state of Tennessee would have none of this New York spoilsman. Planter-dominated Georgia and South Carolina had voted against him and so had Ohio and Indiana in the West and New Jersey in the East. Of the thousand and more counties in the nation he carried but the barest majority (557 of 1,042). His own Empire State party was showing signs of a schism which were ominous. How long could Old Hickory's strength be transferable? Van Buren's capacity to create popular enthusiasm for himself seemed doubtful even then.

The fact was that Van Buren had gone as far as a political manager could go, and the rest of his effort was to prove one of continuous disaster until the events of the next decade were to consign him to his final oblivion. A man must have more than craft or luck to have a second term in the White House. But on March 4, 1837, with its sunshine and blue sky, little of this was apparent.

What the nature of political behavior or the fortunes of Van Buren might have been had the next few years been a period of normal social and economic development cannot be presumed, for such it was not to be. Those in politics were confronted with a season of disaster which taxed their powers. Two months after Van Buren's inauguration, the nation was engulfed in the Panic of 1837.

This calamity caught the federal government in an impossible situation. For most of the half century of its existence the central organization had specialized in doing as little as possible and particularly so in its last decade. In the name of republican virtue and democratic equalitarianism, it had pursued a financial policy so simple as to be downright naïve. Under such circumstances it was probably too much to expect the federal government to develop any positive remedial action even in the face of such disaster.

On the other hand, the government had probably contributed something to bringing it on. Jackson had been obsessed with a general compulsion to smash his enemies. He had an antipathy for corporations, and he had early come to believe that the Bank of the United States was using its power to encompass the defeat of himself and his friends. Therefore he had decreed the destruction of the Bank and had achieved it in such a way that he put the money supply of the nation in chaos and the government's cash in jeopardy. Likewise, he let himself in for charges of using the pet banks as a part of his spoilsmanship. In order perhaps to restore some reputation for financial respectability to his Administration, he and they retreated to the honesty of hard, real money. There would be no more traffic in rags; the Jackson Administration would support and use only gold and silver coin that had intrinsic value. "Banksters beware." A new mint act had been passed encouraging the coinage of gold. A Specie Circular had likewise been issued which required coin to be proffered in the purchase of public lands. There was unfortunately, however, a basic difficulty: there was not enough coin to do the nation's business. Likewise, in a period of speculative inflation after the destruction of the Bank of the United States, there was no banking structure adequate to produce and regulate the needed fiat paper money.

When the extravagance of speculation reached the point when a crash must come, there was nothing to stop it, no banking strength, no reserve of coin. Firm after firm and countless individuals failed as the banks closed their doors, helpless against the demands of those who sought their deposits.

Despite any lack of precedent for positive federal action on anything, the frightened demanded it, and the whole crisis provided the newly mobilizing Whigs with political ammunition which they proceeded to fire. They had a very specious, though convincing, case. Jackson had been the cause. He had broken the Bank, he had egged on the ruin by wasting the government's funds in a gigantic racket, depositing them in the pet banks run by "deserving Democrats." He had issued the Specie Circular destroying rickety western banks. He had signed a bill distributing the surplus which banks, already shaken, must now produce in response to government demands. Of course this was an oversimplification, today absurd. The causes and circumstances of the Panic were much more intricate and inevitable, but this need not concern us as politics is often little concerned with reality. Rather it deals with symbols and images which may indeed be called another kind of reality.

The Panic was thus to be a liability and an asset. Van Buren and his Administration were on the defensive. The Whigs sensed possible advantage. The President must take action, as the closed banks and declining revenue were threatening the Treasury. Worse, after the debt had been paid off, a surplus revenue had begun to accumulate, and Congress had determined to return it to the states where it would remain on deposit, theoretically at the call of the government. The first payments had been set for 1837 in quarterly installments of some $9,000,000 each. The first two had been made, January and March 1, but shortly the third would be due. There would hardly be funds to pay it and run the government too. There was nothing for Van Buren to do but to call Congress in special session.

When Congress assembled on September 4, Van Buren had made a difficult decision. There had been clamor of various sorts. Its main burden was to abandon hard money, revoke the Specie Circular, and be more helpful to the idea of a sound banking system. The President would have found support for this from a substantial section of his party who were called Conservatives and who flourished in New York and to a lesser extent in Virginia. Likewise, he would have drawn much of the Whig fire. But Van Buren had a certain degree of stubbornness, and he was still confident of his plantation–plain northern farmer Democratic combination. He refused to revoke the Specie Circular, and in his message to the Congress he followed a strict concept of as little government action as possible. He presented no program for relief, no prospect for strengthening banks and business. He merely stated the plight of the Treasury and asked that for the time being it be relieved of certain of its obligations, that suspending banks be put through bankruptcy, that certain commercial supporters in New York be given temporary relief, and that money be borrowed to meet the current obligations. He nailed his flag to the hard-money mast. He further proposed that Congress enact an independent Treasury law. This would divorce the Treasury from any connection with banking whatever. The government would keep its revenues in its own vaults until they were spent. Revenues and expenditures would as far as possible be in hard money or in Treasury drafts payable in hard money. This program brought Calhoun back to the Democratic fold and the various acts required were passed, although the Independent Treasury Act did not become law until July 4, 1840.

Van Buren as party leader had shown no capacity to rally his party against the disadvantages provided by the Panic. In the general malaise, the symptoms of which were popular distress, a rent war in New York, election disputes such as the Buckshot War in Pennsylvania and the Broad Seal War in Congress itself, never once did Van Buren appear out in front offering the panic-suffering people any consolation or cheer. The calamity was bound to cause great distress and dissatisfaction. Van Buren seems to have sensed that it might be harmful to him and his party, but he certainly did nothing to attempt to counteract its baneful effect upon Democratic fortunes.

Signs of these effects were plain enough. Elections began going against the Democrats in the first months of Van Buren's Administration, and so great were Whig gains that they nearly captured the national House in the elections of 1838–39. So close were the lines in that body that a Calhoun Whig, Robert M. T. Hunter of Virginia, now, like his leader, supporting the Independent Treasury, was elected speaker in December 1839 after a protracted fight over credentials which delayed the organization of Congress for almost a fortnight. However, the Democrats seemed to be holding together, despite the disaffection of some Conservatives, and the return of the Calhoun followers was favorable. But the ugly head of slavery was lifted up. With the followers of Calhoun, hope of annexing Texas was not dead—yea, it lived and was to trouble many a northern Democrat. Abolitionist propaganda was increasing in amount, and efforts were made to keep down attacks on slavery and resulting controversy in Congress by refusing to hear petitions as addressed to Congress and by permitting southern postmasters to refuse to distribute abolition literature through the mail. The alliance with Calhoun was disturbing in the North.

Elections in 1837, 1838, and 1839 were in the large very generally encouraging to the Whigs. Calhoun's staunch supporter Duff Green was seeking to promote a ticket of Harrison and Calhoun, which the latter spurned. He was firm in returning to the Democrats. Had he heeded this call, as events turned out, he might have become President. The hopes of Clay and Webster were also stirring. Preparations were being made for 1840. What form should they take?

Up to this point there had been no agreement as to the nature and desirability of national party conventions. The Whigs had never tried one, and the Democrats had been using them merely as a convenient means to carry out the wishes of Jackson and his inner circle of advisers, mainly to promote the fortunes of Van Buren, whom the Jackson junto wished first to make Vice President and then Old Hickory's successor. It was quite obvious that this purpose was to be continued in preparation for 1840 and that the convention was little nearer the "working" stage than before. But with the Whigs, it was to be different.

During the long session of Congress of 1837–38, the Whig members held several caucuses and on May 15, 1838, decided to have their first national convention meet at Harrisburg in November 1839. At the time there seemed to be a trend to Clay, but Webster's pretensions dismayed the Clay men: Harrison was as much interested as he had been in 1836; and where did Calhoun stand? Then there was General Winfield Scott warming up, but for or to whom? The disasters of the Panic of 1837 and the misfortunes of the Van Buren Administration, the sad fate of being in office during the crisis, meant that the Whigs had an excellent chance if they could unite and organize.

The Whigs in Congress began operations. Clay was coy, but he hoped, and he engaged with Calhoun in a forensic duel when the latter attempted to unite a solid block upon the platform of popular toleration of slavery. However, it was not the tactics and leadership of the statesmen but the maneuvers of a series of new powers, state leaders, which were going to shape the event.

The effort to secure a national convention to bring order out of the Whig chaos, heretofore never resolved, was achieved in the assembly finally set for the first Wednesday in December 1839 at Harrisburg, Pennsylvania. This meeting was scheduled at a time and in a place where Clay influence was expected to be paramount, and the move may be considered as designed to aid his candidacy. A series of conventions was first held in most of the states to choose delegations to proceed to Harrisburg. Clay's influence was expected to be strong enough to bring southern delegations unanimous for him, and he was believed to have enough friends in northern states to secure a majority and the nomination.

This convention began a new chapter in the history of American political behavior. Hitherto, the few national gatherings had been held merely to ratify decisions already made. But this Harrisburg convention was one at which a decision had to be worked out in a convention atmosphere. In all probability Clay and his friends had hoped that he could play Jackson and receive a ratification of his own plans. But the task was to be much more complicated. This convention was to be in the hands of a new group of men entering national politics, men who were active organizers and operators on the state level, men who were not particularly moved by desire to hold office or to seek high place but who loved power and sport. They craved the exhilaration of making candidates, of controlling policy, of exercising power obscurely but effectively behind thrones. Two of these were to enjoy long and notorious careers, and their activities in this convention may have been controlling. They were Thurlow Weed of New York and Thaddeus Stevens of Pennsylvania. These men were determined that Henry Clay should not be the man.

Their motives for opposition were probably mixed and perhaps not well understood by themselves. There is not much very conclusive evidence about the personal situations such as unsatisfactory earlier relations, jealousy, uncertainty as to influence in a Clay administration, patronage, power, and the like. It is therefore necessary to consider more general motivations. Thaddeus Stevens was the most prominent representative of the old Antimasonic interest, and he and his associates in this cause were quite naturally opposed to Henry Clay because he was a Mason. More important, however, was a significant situation which quite understandably gave many a northern Whig delegate pause.

Within the preceding four years the slavery issue had come to the fore. The spread of the antislavery movement had produced a flood of literature, much of it designed as highly emotional propaganda. Floods of petitions had also been sent to Congress generally urging the abolition of slavery in the District of Columbia. Violence, rioting, and mob rule had broken out in certain centers. Furthermore, the Texas Revolution had raised the question of annexing a tremendous slave area. All these developments had brought slavery forward, and for the first time it was going to figure in a presidential election. The Jackson Administration had encouraged postmasters to refuse to deliver antislavery literature. The Congress had passed gag resolutions which prevented any discussion of petitions. The question of annexing Texas was so hot that even Jackson refused to handle it, and the erstwhile Mexican province was living a precarious existence as an independent republic. All this had roused bitter antagonism between northern and southern elements in the population. As a result northern Whig politicians with victory perhaps in sight were going to think twice before accepting a southern slaveholder like Clay as their candidate.

In fact, this convention was to emphasize another phase of controlling motivation in democratic behavior, namely expediency. The Panic of 1837 and Van Buren's lack of popular appeal had put opportunity in the path of the Whigs, opportunity such as they had not enjoyed before. What Weed and his more realistic associates wanted above all else was a candidate who could win. They did not want a twice-defeated, shopworn, and tarnished politico, a southern slaveholding Mason with many enemies and many more somewhat tired of his constant striving. Weed and certain of his associates had been busy contriving Clay's defeat. In large part presumably for the reason that they were convinced he could not win.

Weed had been busy at this. He had developed a technique known in those days as "triangular correspondence" which might today bear some resemblance to the "smear" or the "big lie." He would start leaders in three parts of New York State writing to their friends in other sections urging them to work hard for Clay because in their own particular area he had no chance. This spread an atmosphere of defeatism. Weed also sought to get Clay to withdraw until 1844 on the ground that the present was a hopeless time for him to try his luck, particularly because of the antislavery furor. He seems likewise to have negotiated with Webster's backers to get him to withdraw in return for aid in defeating Clay and receiving a commanding interest in the new Whig Administration. Webster did withdraw and later he became Secretary of State in the new Administration. Then Weed appeared to be in favor of General Winfield Scott, who had lately gained popularity by his military assignments on the Canadian border. The indication is that all the time Weed, much impressed by Harrison's unexpected showing in 1836, had been maneuvering to nominate Old Tippecanoe.

He found his task the more difficult because the state conventions had given Clay a plurality of the delegates to the Harrisburg convention. However, such an obstacle would not daunt Weed. He and Webster's backers in New England developed one of the early examples of convention "strategy." When the body organized, a rule was proposed that each state should appoint a consulting committee of three, and these state consultants should meet as a group and exchange views. Next they would return to their state delegations and report. Then the several delegations would make their decisions, and each state would vote as a unit for either Clay, Harrison, or Scott. Virginia's decision was somewhat complicated by the fact that the three candidates had all had Virginia as their place of origin. Among some Virginians with whom Clay was not popular, such as John Tyler, the question was one of a choice between Harrison and Scott. Thaddeus Stevens, who was pushing Harrison, had in his possession a letter which Scott had written in terms designed to woo the antislavery people. This Stevens dropped in a spot where some Virginian would be sure to pick it up. This happened and Stevens' game worked. Virginia turned away from Scott.

All this maneuvering produced a result which Weed may have contrived. An early informal vote of the delegates, each indicating his individual preference, showed Clay the favorite. When the first formal ballot was taken by states, Clay had 103; Harrison, 94; and Scott, 57. At the psychological moment, Weed's New York delegation, which had been marking time for Scott, came over to Harrison with three other delegations—Michigan and Vermont from Scott, and Illinois from Clay—and the prize was Harrison's. As a consolation the Vice Presidency was turned over to Clay's Kentucky delegation. When they refused either to be comforted or to name anyone, the place was offered to Senator John M. Clayton of Delaware, B. Watkins Leigh of Virginia, and Governor Edward B. Dudley of North Carolina. All refused or were withdrawn, so at length it was given to another Virginian, overly ambitious John Tyler, who was in his second round of eagerness, having sought vainly for the prize in 1836. So it was to be Tippecanoe and Tyler too—but without a platform. That convention could never have agreed on any statement of principles, so divided were they between South and North, states' rights and American System.

While the Whigs had undertaken a working convention designed to prepare for the presidential election by some difficult planning, the active program for which was worked out during their deliberations, the Democrats were still going to meet in somewhat haphazard fashion. They still relied on the call of a state convention—again upon New Hampshire—as in the beginning, and no structure had been established to make any particular arrangements. Again, all the states were not sending representatives: Virginia, South Carolina, Illinois, Connecticut, and Delaware were to be unrepresented, and only one delegate appeared from Massachusetts.

When the 248 delegates assembled at Musical Hall in Baltimore on May 4, 1840, there were two jobs to be done. One was to attempt to relieve an embarrassment. The Vice President, Richard M. Johnson, the slayer of Tecumseh, had proved to be one of the most inefficient presiding officers imaginable. He appeared in his famous red vest and spent most of his time sprawled on a sofa. Worse from the southern point of view, he openly consorted with a Negress and attempted to bring mulatto daughters into society. This had been known in 1836, but it had been hoped, though in vain, that the dignity and demands of his office might persuade him to be more discreet. So several state organizations had proposed other candidates to replace him. Senator William R. King of Alabama and the Secretary of State John Forsyth of Georgia had been nominated by their states, and Tennessee had brought forward James K. Polk, who had been speaker of the House. Martin Van Buren himself would express no preference, and so the matter of his running mate must perforce be left to the convention.

The second task was a new departure. Calhoun and his followers had lately withdrawn from their brief fellowship with the Whigs and had returned to Democratic affiliation to support the independent Treasury. However they seemed not to be willing to enter into full communion without making sure of the covenant to which all should subscribe. Therefore it seemed necessary for the Democracy to enter into an agreement, to draft its first formal party platform. The Calhoun faction was determined that there must be a pronouncement for states rights and against a protective tariff, as well as stated opposition to a national bank and internal improvements. Furthermore they must capitalize their greatest asset, their experience with the doctrines of Jefferson and Jackson. They would take out a patent on these which would be their copyrighted trademark. They would thus immortalize tradition for their own benefit, reflect former glory, and keep it vivid so that these reputations of the great might continue to lead them as their persons once had done. They were in effect incorporating a Jefferson-Jackson cult.

Their achievement was the first formal platform, the first full-length statement of principles drafted by an American party. This document had nine sections. Their basic premise was a government of limited powers; hence they were opposed to a federal system of internal improvement directly sponsored or indirectly subsidized by the assumption of state debts contracted for this purpose. They were likewise opposed to a protective tariff and to a United States Bank. There should be rigid economy and a separation of government funds from banking institutions. They were firm believers in states' rights and the control by the states of their domestic institutions, including slavery; abolitionists were condemned. The American Democracy, as they designated themselves, endorsed the liberal principles of the Declaration of Independence which made the United States a refuge for the oppressed of the world. They opposed any attempt to hamper foreigners who wished to come here and become citizens and landowners. The efforts of such hamperers should be resisted in the same spirit that erased the Alien and Sedition Acts from the statute books. This was Jefferson and Jackson made to order à la Calhoun, a treaty between Van Buren and the latter. It was a document designed to resist Henry Clay. It looked backward rather than forward. The two-thirds rule had not been adopted, for there was no need for it.

These two conventions initiated another novelty for the campaign of 1840 which was like nothing ever experienced before in the republic. It set a new fashion. A Young Men's Whig Convention had gathered simultaneously in force at Baltimore from various parts of the country to mock and ridicule the Democrats and hamper their efforts by creating noise and confusion. Regardless of the confusion, the Democrats accomplished their objectives: the treaty was ratified, Van Buren was renominated by acclamation. Richard M. Johnson, the Vice President, was not to have that mark of favor. Johnson was neither renominated nor replaced. A resolution was passed declaring that it was not expedient to choose among the nominees, the decision would be left to their Republican-Democratic fellow citizens in the several states. The efforts of supporters of other candidates, however, bore little fruit, and before the campaign was over practically all Democrats were resigned to "Rumpsey Dumpsey" who had "killed Tecumseh."

Despite the convention meeting, there was still no national attention to campaign organization. Amos Kendall resigned as Postmaster General to help Blair in the field of propaganda. He edited the *Extra Globe*, published throughout the contest. Blair, who was paid $60,-

ooo a year to do the government printing, subsidized the issues. He and Kendall got up a circular on how to organize for the fight. Its recipients were advised how to prepare and distribute propaganda, how to collect funds to pay for it from officeholders and others. Party operators also realized that this was the year when the census marshals were busy counting the population and that they might be used as party workers. Various other papers were set up for the campaign. *The Rough Hewer* at Albany secured 10,000 circulation, and *The Old Hickory* in Illinois, Sam Medary's *Ohio Statesman*, and J. George Harris' Nashville *Union* did yeomen service. Thomas Ritchie of the Richmond *Enquirer* likewise contributed his journalistic and organizational might. He published a special campaign paper, *The Crisis*, and organized the state of Virginia.

While the Democrats were belatedly girding up their loins, the Whigs had already launched a campaign without precedent. Shortly after Harrison's nomination, in December 1839, in fact, the Baltimore *Republican* had disparaged Tippecanoe and sneered that given a pension the hero would be satisfied to remain in his log cabin drinking hard cider. For the rest of his life these facilities would satisfy his ambition. After this slur had been circulated by the New York *Daily Whig*, the *National Intelligencer*, and the Galena, Illinois, *Northwestern Gazette and Galena Advertiser*, it was picked up by two operators in Harrisburg who, in organizing a ratification meeting, prepared a transparency featuring a cabin, with a coonskin nailed to it, a woodpile, and a cider barrel. Over the mountains, in Marysville, Ohio, a log cabin was mounted on wheels and drawn around by four spans of horses. Loyal Whigs followed it with coonskin caps, singing log cabin songs, presumably stirred by hard cider. Songbooks were prepared, supplies of hard cider were mobilized, and on many a village green log cabins were erected where the enthusiastic foregathered to sing, cheer, drink, and listen to the virtues of Whiggery. Horace Greeley, Weed's editor, began to publish the New York *Log Cabin*.

A series of ratification meetings was held, including the Baltimore jollification which disturbed the National Democratic Convention. Another feature was suggested perhaps by the celebration which the Democrats had organized at New Orleans on January 8, 1840, where ailing Old Hickory appeared to lend the magic of his presence to the fortunes of his chosen successor. The Whigs appropriated Washington's birthday and on that date the various state parties held conventions. In imitation of the use of the emotion-rousing battlefield of

New Orleans, the followers of Harrison spent two days on the battlefield of Tippecanoe, May 29–30, and a fortnight later a horde rallied at the site of Tip's victory at Fort Meigs. Here this minor operation was blown up as high as hard cider could inflate it. Finally, the candidate in effect resorted to stump speaking, the first candidate so to do, with the possible exception of John Adams.

It was a frolicsome campaign of song and smear, with seldom an idea or an issue. Not only were there log cabins galore and hogsheads of cider, but other zany devices were achieved. Thomas Hart Benton when he had begun his pressure upon the Senate to expunge their censure resolutions against Jackson, pontifically announced, "I set this ball in motion." Now in 1840 somebody remembered this and sold the idea of constructing huge balls, with a diameter greater than a man's height. Through this a long pole was inserted and a dozen or so shouting men on each end of the pole would roll this "parade ball" through the streets, shouting the slogans painted on the ball and perhaps some others less delicate, as the campaign was marked by a certain obscenity.

The smear element was tried out literally by both sides. The Van Burenites maintained that Harrison was a stuffed soldier of no military capacity who was forced to solicit certificates of bravery from old soldiers. Van Buren was characterized as a perfumed aristocrat in corsets, "Sweet Sandy Whiskers," who lived at ease at public expense in an extravagantly refurnished executive palace. A Pennsylvania congressman, protégé of Thad Stevens, Charles Ogle, entertained the House for three days with a scandalous speech on "The Regal Splendor of the Presidential Palace," in which his gross, mendacious, and salacious descriptive capacities were applied to everything from the "Blue Elliptical Saloon" to the equipment of the President's bathroom and the crockery in his bedchamber. While the poor starved, the President, perfumed with Double Extract of Queen Victoria, dined on massive gold plate and French sterling silver services.

The executive committee of the Whig party labored hard to make the campaign one vast picnic. Efforts were launched to create a central committee in every county. Political leaders like Tom Corwin of Ohio who were talented as public entertainers were much in evidence. Even a buffoon in the person of an Ohio blacksmith, John Bear, was subsidized to tour several states. And minstrels and songbooks were everywhere. Coonskin caps and coon oil, a particularly smooth but potent form of liquor, were much in evidence, together with the better known hard cider. No people wearied and discouraged by a panic and depression were ever so cleverly diverted and rehabilitated than those who entered into the spirit of the "Tippecanoe and Tyler, too," extravaganza. The Democrats worked hard, frowned on drunkenness and appealed to the virtue of the voters but to no avail. Of all Jackson's domain, only Virginia, South Carolina, Alabama, Arkansas, and Missouri in the slave states and New Hampshire and Illinois remained faithful, although as usual, in the popular vote the margin was much narrower: 1,275,000 to 1,128,000.

In the midst of this excitement two new elements were introduced into the pattern of American national political behavior that year and barely noticed. One of these was the greater use of money. It cost to build log cabins and to buy hard cider. Also for the first time there was a party which might appeal to businessmen whose interest in favors might not be negligible. So money was collected, at least by the Whigs. Then, too, there was the slavery issue. During the thirties, the abolitionists had been organized, the Texas issue had emerged, efforts had been made to keep abolitionist literature out of the mails in the South, and Congress had adopted a gag rule related to the receipt of petitions, designed to prevent debate in the national legislature. Also, Great Britain had abolished slavery in the West Indies. The issue was now to be injected into a national campaign. In December 1839 a few delegates from a handful of states gathered in Warsaw, New York, and there established the Liberty party, nominated James G. Birney of Kentucky and Ohio and Thomas Earle of Pennsylvania for President and Vice President, and dedicated their efforts to the extinction of slavery. This party polled only 7,059 votes, the bulk of them from New York, Massachusetts, and Ohio, and these ballots were only 39/100 of one percent of the vote. The obvious incapacity of this party went almost unnoticed, but like the cloud no larger than a man's hand, it indicated a possible storm.

The election of 1840 thus marked another development, another step toward the perfection of the great center of democratic interest, the choice of the Chief Magistrate. Both parties were to continue to experiment, for even yet there had been no final crystallization as to method. The old congressional caucus had been abandoned in so far as it acted directly, for it no longer made nominations, but it was still a factor in that it undertook to arrange that national conventions be held. A second method, that which the makers of the Constitution had had in mind, still influenced certain important leaders. This was a choice by the national House of Representatives from the three top contenders in the Electoral College, the method of 1824. The third method was the national convention arranged by the Administration in power as a convenient mass meeting to perpetuate itself formally in whole or in part. But 1840 had demonstrated that there was still another possibility, a working convention of party managers from the several states actually to decide on nominations, organization machinery, and platform. This curiously operated spasm of political behavior, the log cabin and hard cider campaign of 1840, which no one had planned, quite unwittingly set the stage for the completion of the political mechanism.

The success of the Whigs produced a new situation in the realm of political behavior. For the first time one organized and marshaled party had succeeded in defeating another and was preparing to take over. The situation was different from that of 1829. Then an Administration which had done little or nothing to promote partisan organization had been defeated by a *caudillo*-like heroic figure with an appealing career and a personality strengthened by a grievance. Jackson's triumph had introduced the concept of partisan appointments as a reward for political service, and a somewhat stable, though probably bureaucratic, civil service crystallized by age was in part dispersed and a new, rather definitely political group installed.

Now in 1841 the situation was sufficiently different to be significant. Two organized parties had presented candidates; the Democrats had again nominated an active political operator and technician, Martin Van Buren, whereas the Whig managers had selected a somewhat synthetic leader of diluted Jacksonian proportions, General William Henry Harrison, and now that he had won, these managers expected to reorganize the civil service by replacing Democratic operators with Whig counterparts. A new era was begun, with spoilsmen replacing spoilsmen.

This process, together with certain accidental situations, produced confusion in the ranks of the victors. The new President was old, well past his prime, and he died within a month of his accession. His death produced a new element in the pattern of American political behavior. For the first time a President had left office before the expiration of his term, and for the first time a Vice President had something more to do than preside over the Senate. The first questions raised were: "Is he President or Acting President?" "Does he have full power?"

By common consent, though after some hesitation, he was recognized as President with all the powers thereof. Then another, more subtle question arose. The Whig party was a hodgepodge of Jackson's enemies, and Tyler had been chosen to add strength to Harrison by attracting states' rights devotees in the South. But he himself had no use for Clay's American System. It had never been expected that he would have any power or influence after the election. Now he was in the White House. This was to produce a clash. Clay had been the dominant figure in the brief forty days of Harrison's rule. He had been looking forward to assuming the Whig leadership in the special session of Congress which Harrison had called for early summer.

The new President, sometimes referred to as "His Accidency," had his own ambitons to rule, but he suffered two handicaps. He lacked status in the Whig party, and he was surrounded by a Cabinet in which there were no men of his states' rights view. Besides, Clay was an ambitious, imperious leader who had been thwarted in 1824, 1828, 1832, 1836, and 1840. He did not plan to pay much heed to this "accident." Hardly had Congress assembled in June than Clay announced the legislative program, some of which he knew Tyler opposed, but Tyler was to be pushed aside. Clay proclaimed the old National Republican platform of national bank, protective tariff, and distribution of proceeds of the sales of the public lands among the states. This program also involved the repeal of the independent Treasury. The latter bill went through first and caused no problem; Congress voted it and Tyler signed it.

Then came the Bank proposal. Some deference was paid to Tyler's constitutional scruples but not enough, and on August 16 Tyler vetoed the bill. Then an effort was made to negotiate between Congress and the White House through the cabinet, but this only resulted in another veto and charges of bad faith. All the Cabinet resigned, except Webster, and Clay magisterially summoned a congressional caucus that formally read Tyler out of the party. Tyler's veto of two tariff bills in the regular session caused a select committee of the House to denounce him and the House to ratify this report; an effort was made to start impeachment. "His Accidency" finally accepted the protective tariff act of 1842 but not until he had stopped the distribution of the proceeds of the sale of the public lands. The elections of 1842–43 brought the Democrats back in control of Congress, and Tyler found himself without a party. The Democrats rejoiced in Whig discomfiture and began once more to hope.

A new chapter had been written in the history of the evolution of political machinery. When followers of Jackson had first begun to mobilize, they seemed to be using an old pattern. They appeared to be uniting for a specific, one-shot operation. The supporters of Andrew Jackson had rallied to avenge the wrongs of a popular chieftain, to punish the wickedness of his enemies. So his personal following gathered to their ranks many who were emotionally conditioned to embrace a cause, and Jackson entered the White House. As a general he marshaled his forces to achieve his various ends: to defend Peggy Eaton, to break the Bank, to punish South Carolina's defiance, to pay the debt, to confound Calhoun, and to put Van Buren first into the Vice President's seat and then into the White House.

During the eight years of his Presidency, his foes tried to put forward a popular figure appealing to economic self-interest by advocating the enlargement of the subsidy powers of government under Henry Clay. Such tactics produced no success, so without organization or candidate his enemies fell back on the system of election originally designed by the Constitutional Convention of 1787. They made a variety of attacks upon the Jackson establishment in the several states, using whatever means, issues, or candidates might seem most effective in causing the establishment's overthrow by the defeat of Van Buren, Jackson's chosen successor. This too failed. The process of choosing a President seemed almost as unstructured as it had in the beginning.

But conditions were changing. The nation was in the midst of a great surge of growth. It had just been shaken by the Panic of 1837. There was uncertainty and discontent. Also, Texas had just revolted from Mexico, and there was a demand that it be annexed to the United States, which had renewed sectional hostility. Antislavery excitement appeared in a dangerous form. Antimasons, antiforeign, anti-Catholic, antirent moves were afoot. Labor was striving to organize. There were hostilities on the Canadian border. Had not self-government become too complex? Was there not now too much at stake to permit the choice of the President to be conducted amid such chaos?

The professional politicians in large number, state and national, had again gone to work in earnest. As there had been a sense of something needed in 1787, so it had arisen anew as 1840 approached, and in preparation for that contest the two groups of political operators, the ins and outs, had really begun for the first time to work on machinery for a contest between two organized political forces, which might not be merely fortuitous for a given occasion but part of a permanent and continuous program. But this mechanism was far from complete.

·◦[XXII]◦·

THE STATE OPERATORS TAKE OVER

*T*HE CAMPAIGN of 1844 was to witness a revolution in the management of the Democratic party. The Jacksonians were to experience an internal struggle of unique proportions. Though Harrison was dead and Tyler expelled, the Whigs were rallying quickly, and Clay and his organization were planning to make the Kentuckian their standard-bearer. All Democrats of any consequence knew that Harry would run, and many feared, with reason, that he might at last be elected. Though Tyler was almost completely written off, the Whig situation still provided an element of novelty; Tyler was still the President and he might find some resources for self-assertion.

In the Democratic party the situation at first seemed simple. The election of 1840 had been a temporary aberration. The Van Buren organization had been swamped by mass hysteria and had been sung and drunk to defeat. But now the partisans hoped that the sober second thought of the people would right this erratic variance at the first opportunity, particularly since Tippecanoe was dead and the Whigs distracted by Tyler's insubordination. The Democracy must rally around Van Buren for a third time and present a united front to the voters and defeat Clay again. So the Jacksonian leaders were planning another ratifying convention as early as possible in November 1843 to vindicate Van Buren and to ensure their return to power. State conventions and caucuses began to move, beginning with Missouri's action directed by Benton in 1841. Senator Silas Wright of New York was to be the leader of the Washington-Albany group, and the two editors, F. P. Blair in Washington and Thomas Ritchie in Richmond, were to furnish the propaganda. The aged hero Jackson would deliver his blessing from the Hermitage.

But there were disquieting signs. Calhoun's ambitions were not dead and there were doubts whether Van Buren could beat Clay.

Indeed, Calhoun had come to a decision. The time was ripe for the South Carolinian to achieve his major goal, the Presidency. He saw alarming signs. He feared that Van Buren and the northern Democrats would not maintain the agreement made in 1840 and that the South was again in danger from protection and abolition. There also seemed to be more northern states in the making—Iowa, "Wiskonsan," and even far off Oregon—while for the South there appeared to be only Florida possible. The slave states must see to their own protection. Calhoun would be their leader.

He began to plan to line up the southern states and to enlist support in New England and New York. He formed an organization, money was raised, a newspaper set up in Washington, the *Spectator*, edited by Joseph A. Scoville, later taken over by William A. Harris of Virginia and John Heartt of South Carolina as the *Constitution*, and support secured in free-trading New York City where southern money was banked. Calhoun published his biography and an edition of his speeches. Van Buren was denounced as a northerner and a radical. His support of certain phases of the tariff was condemned, and while he seemed all right on slavery from the southern point of view, growing antislavery sentiment in the North was making the sensitive South apprehensive of northern leadership. Also, northern Democratic votes on the tariff legislation of 1841 further aroused Calhoun. He began to designate lieutenants, to form a central committee, and to build an organization of local committees. His aim was to create a southern bloc which would stop Van Buren and compel either Calhoun's nomination or the selection of a compromise candidate. For the first time a sectional mobilization was projected, though it was hoped with northern support.

The basic motivation was the protection of southern rights and interests against a faster growing North. The alarm of the *Exposition and Protest* of 1828 and the nullification contest of 1832–33 was to be spread beyond South Carolina and appeals made for conservative northern support. Calhoun and his cohorts hoped that Tyler could be attracted and his patronage power secured. He on his part wanted to lead some such move and gain advantage for himself, though in his impossible position it is hard to see what. It was obvious that Calhoun's appeal would be most compelling in the South and that he would rely on growing southern apprehension. The abolition tide was rising, the Liberty party had appeared in the election of 1840.

Van Buren deemed it desirable then, as he had on various occasions before, to go South for conference and fence mending. In the spring of 1842 he visited both Jackson and Clay. He was anxious to emphasize his national interest and if possible to keep sectionalism at a minimum. He and Clay may have agreed on this policy even to the extent of trying to keep any sectional issue out of the campaign which each expected to wage against the other. The state Democratic parties, meantime, seemed generally disposed to support Van Buren. Virginia took the lead in 1843, coming out for an instructed unitary delegation to attend a national convention late that year before the Congress met in December. The Tennessee caucus, presumed organ of Jackson, joined in, and when the New York legislative caucus suggested the fourth Monday in November 1843 as the date, it seemed quite generally acceptable—to most save Calhoun.

Calhoun's campaign for the Presidency was being stepped up. He disliked and distrusted the national convention, which in fact had originally been taken up by his party to eliminate him, and he believed that part of his campaign must be devoted to revising its rules and proceedings. The regency-junto method of operation had been to charge the governing force in each state party with the responsibility for choosing the state delegation or at least the delegates-at-large, for instructing them for whom to vote, and for requiring each state delegation to vote as a unit. This centralized method roused Calhoun's ire, and he and his associates began working for a different system of choice.

Calhoun wanted the voters in each congressional district to hold a species of primary in which the delegation from that district would be chosen. Then at the convention itself the delegates would vote per capita, each delegate voting as he chose or as his district had instructed him. Thus no minorities within state delegations would be suppressed by the will of the majority, and the centralized power of state machines would be limited. This was all in keeping with Calhoun's states' rights, decentralized, minority-conscious views. So he and his associates were endeavoring to postpone the convention until May 1844. They wanted what the Van Burenites wished to avoid, namely the controversy potential of the 1843–44 session of Congress in which to hear what the winds of debate would bring forth.

Van Buren and Calhoun were not to be the only contenders. Colonel Richard M. Johnson, lately Vice President, was put forward by Kentucky and had a vote-getting potential again in the West. Senator James Buchanan of Pennsylvania would probably have the Keystone State behind him, though little else at first. But more significant was to be the American minister to France, General Lewis Cass of Michigan. There were a number of conservative Democrats who disliked Van Buren's radical Locofoco views opposing banks and demanding hard money. They wanted a sound man of wealth, experience, and standing who might not frown on banks, paper currency, and speculation. Cass had been persuaded to resign his post and come home in December 1842 to seek the nomination. His arrival caused a certain amount of attention to be paid him, and certain regionally conscious, anti-Van Buren groups in the Southwest and West found him a convenient candidate. Also, the Tennessee convention had put forward a candidate for Vice President in the person of former Speaker James Knox Polk.

As events were to demonstrate, the most significant development was the appearance of new factions in the Democratic party. Younger men, in all quarters of the land, were tired of Van Buren and uninterested in Calhoun; rather they were ambitious for themselves and fearful of Clay. Active among these was a Mississippi U.S. Senator, Robert J. Walker, Pennsylvania-born and with Pennsylvania connections among the powerful Dallas Family party. These younger men, like the Calhounites, wanted to get the date of the convention changed to May 1844. Like the Calhoun managers, they wanted to listen to what the northern Democrats would say in Congress and to watch their legislative actions. Van Buren would need southern support if he were to be elected, and the hostility of a sizable southern block might be fatal. He also needed a convention of all the states, representing a united party. The Calhounites, joined by Senator Walker and other younger men, began working to persuade the Van Buren managers to postpone the convention. This the managers agreed to do, because the alternative was a series of southern absences, perhaps a union with Tyler and a third, or southern, party supported by his patronage. In fact, Tyler was trying to organize such a party of his own during the summer of 1843, and if the Calhoun men joined it, Clay might well be in.

A correspondence was arranged after a number of southern state conventions, led by South Carolina, had called for a convention on the fourth Monday in May of 1844. The Democratic state central commitee of Indiana wrote to the New York committee citing this widespread disagreement about the date. There had been negotiation in Washington by Walker and Senator Silas Wright of New York, Van Buren's senatorial manager, and on July 4, 1843, the New Yorkers replied that although they preferred November 1843 they were willing to change, "believing that the question ought to be yielded to even a respectable minority." The New York September Democratic convention supported a new date, May 27, 1844, and this it was to be—the alternative would be a stormy congressional caucus and probably a walkout. Besides, what difference did it make? State conventions had already instructed well over a majority of the delegates for Van Buren.

A complicating factor in the Democratic situation was the part which President Tyler was playing. He was in control of the federal patronage and in a vengeful mood. Clay had expelled him from the Whig party and the Democrats had showed no signs of either help or welcome. He was eager to do what he could to block both Van Buren and Clay. He began queer gyrations with the patronage, appointing Democrats of curious vintages. Officeholder gatherings began to call for his re-election, to form committees, and call conventions. Then he made his grandstand play. He had always thought of Texas as a source of political capital, but as long as Webster was Secretary of State and the complex negotiations with Great Britain current, there was little he could do. Webster wouldn't touch Texas and Tyler did not dare to complicate the British settlement. However, at length in the spring of 1843, the Webster-Ashburton Treaty was in effect and Webster had retired. At that point Tyler appointed a Virginia Secretary of State, Abel P. Upshur, who would seek the annexation of Texas. His associates now approached the Calhoun managers with a proposal that Tyler and Calhoun unite on a Texas platform to save the South; they had secured a letter from Old Hickory endorsing the acquisition. In this way the South and the expansionist forces could be united and force the Democrats to cast Van Buren overboard and take Tyler or Calhoun or some other southern sympathizer who would defeat Clay, place the federal government in southern hands, acquire Texas, and ensure the South continued equality within the Union. This understanding was being worked on in the fall of 1843. Calhoun ostentatiously withdrew from the contest, but his mind was afire with new hope of restored southern power. In the meantime, the letter from Jackson was held back from publication, but the southern supporters of Van Buren were tantalized by growing fears. Was Tyler going to take over on the Texas issue?

Despite this southern development, the Van Buren steam roller drove on. The various state Democratic conventions and caucuses continued to pile up Van Buren support, and after the several which met on Jackson Day, January 8, 1844, it looked as though Van Buren, with the endorsement of sixteen of the twenty-six states, had the two-thirds vote necessary. The elections of 1842–43 had been favorable to the Democrats, and they controlled the Congress which assembled in December 1843. But it was the northern Democrats who had won the seats in sufficient number. The efficiency of machines like Van Buren's had done the work, and the new Congress was going to refuse to revise the tariff and would eventually remove the gag on antislavery petitions. Calhoun's original program had failed utterly. Were Texas and Tyler the answers and must his ambitions once more be shelved? It seemed so.

In the meantime Clay's fortunes were advancing. A year before, a Whig congressional caucus on February 18, 1843, had called a national convention for May 1, 1844. No one was opposing Clay, and his nomination was to be purely a formality. At Baltimore on May 1 the plan was carried out smoothly in the fashion of the Democrats. This was not a nominating but a ratifying convention à la Jackson designed to ensure Clay's election. The balloting was merely for Vice President, as in 1832. Senator Theodore Frelinghuysen of New Jersey was ahead from the start, and on the third ballot the Pennsylvania support of John Sergeant, who had run with Clay in 1832, was switched to him, and he defeated "Honest John" Davis of Massachusetts and Millard Fillmore of New York, who was to be heard from again. A neat statement of Henry Clay's American system was adopted as a platform which boasted that "the name of Henry Clay needs no eulogy. The history of the country since his first appearance in public life is his history. Its brightest pages of prosperity and success are identified with the principles which he has upheld, as its darkest and more disastrous pages are with every material departure in our public policy from those principles." A number of Democrats seemed to fear that voters might believe this. Clay was good at organizing, and as before, he had a national party committee of which his Kentucky henchman, Congressman Willis Green, was chairman.

In the meantime fate had intervened. On February 28, 1844, President Tyler, his Cabinet, and guests, together with their ladies, went on an excursion. Captain Stockton was going to try out his great gun "The Peacemaker" on the U.S.S. *Princeton*. There was to be a sail down the Potomac and lunch. Included in the party were David Gardiner of Gardiner's Island and his charming daughter Julia, later to be Mrs. President Tyler. The widower President may have arranged the party to fit into his courtship. The gun was fired several times before lunch, accompanied by the delighted squeals of the ladies. After lunch they must have it again. So the guests trooped up on deck. But not all. Two or three of the fair sex were singing at the piano. This was too much for the susceptible Tyler; to him their warbling was much more attractive than the sullen roar of artillery. He stayed behind with them. On deck Captain Stockton ordered another shot. This time there were shrieks rather than squeals, for the gun burst, killed the Secretary of State and the Secretary of the Navy, and knocked Senator Benton speechless.

Had the President been on deck his mangled body too might have been discerned in the shambles. Then Willie P. Mangum of North Carolina, Henry Clay Whig who had aided so materially in reading Tyler out of the party, as president pro tempore of the Senate, would have become President. Might not the course of events have been altered? Certainly Mangum would not have chosen John C. Calhoun as Secretary of State—and would the annexation of Texas have been dropped? Be that as it may, Tyler and his managers must find a new Secretary of State. Audacity was to be their guide, and an invitation was sent off immediately to Calhoun, it was claimed without Tyler's knowledge, to complete the Texas acquisition. He accepted and hurried to Washington. Texas had agreed, and in fact Upshur had left a treaty ready to be signed; there is some reason to believe that he had received assurance that it would be ratified. On March 16 the *Niles Register* announced "with amazement" the negotiations for the annexation of Texas which, it declared, had been "sprung upon the nation like an explosion, far more formidable than that of the 'Peacemaker.'"

The treaty for the annexation was sent to the Senate at a time when the southern bloc was conscious of what many would call northern "bad faith." The Democratic House had refused assent to a tariff which would restore the Compromise of 1833 and had seemed disposed at one time to repeal the gag rule, thus opening the door to abolition petitions and antislavery debate. Now Texas would kindle an even greater fire of northern opposition. Both Van Buren and Clay saw the danger of such sectional conflict. They knew that in the South there was a mounting sense of minority status, of subjugation by a northern majority unless the balance of population and states were maintained. There was beginning to be a sense of "Annex Texas or else." British prejudices also were injected. Britain had been negotiating, it was believed, with Texas for abolition of slavery in exchange for recognition and financial aid. Duff Green was active in travel and intrigue. In the North there were demands for a more aggressive move to acquire Oregon. A witches' brew was boiling. Whether by understanding or not has never been resolved, but within almost a few hours of each other Van Buren and Clay came out against annexation in letters published April 27, and consequently it was not likely that two-thirds of the Senate could be gotten to vote to ratify the treaty of annexation.

The Democratic forces in Congress, before the publication of the letters of Clay and their leader opposing the annexation of Texas, had been planning a propaganda war exposing the Whig behavior during their congressional control, 1841–43. They had held a caucus on March 5 and appointed an executive committee to arrange for compiling what was to be "The Democratic Text Book," a pamphlet which would provide such an exposé. At the same time another interested congressional group was working on a Texas propaganda. Two Kentucky operators, General William O. Butler and George N. Sanders, invited Senator Robert J. Walker to explain the desirability of securing Texas. He had complied with a long letter dated February 5 which was published in pamphlet form designed to sell the idea in the North as one of paramount national importance. When the Clay and Van Buren letters appeared, Walker's letter became the textbook of the Tyler, Calhoun, and anti-Van Buren operators. At the time, too, Jackson's letter of 1843 favoring the annexation of Texas was produced and published, with, whether by accident or design, the date changed to 1844. The error was quickly corrected but the idea of contemporaneity had been suggested.

The southern Democrats who had been supporting Van Buren were on the spot. They did not want to be forced into an inferior position in the Tyler-Calhoun outfit, nor did they now see how they could carry Van Buren. First they exerted pressure on him to follow Jackson and accept Texas, but this he would not do—he would be handing the North over to Clay. So Thomas Ritchie decided on dramatic action. He called a meeting of the Richmond equivalent of Tammany Hall, the Shockoe Hill Association, on May 1 and there the instructions to the Virginia delegation to support Van Buren were rescinded. The New York–Virginia alliance negotiated by "Little Van" twenty years before on behalf of Crawford was shattered. Now little reliance could be placed on the support of at least six other southern delegations.

A new organization was put into operation in Washington. The annexationists in Congress held a meeting at the Capitol on April 29 with Robert J. Walker in the chair. This group, called the Nocturnals because they held almost nightly meetings, were now with some calculated Buchanan support working for Cass who had recently published a letter advocating annexation. A week after the initial meeting the delegation from Mississippi announced they were no longer bound to Van Buren. They were for Texas and the two-thirds rule, and they were against Van Buren and Calhoun. They designated Walker to cast the state's vote in the convention.

The Van Burenites now must face hard facts. In early March they probably had some 190 delegates instructed for them, enough to cover the two-thirds majority of 177 required. Though Virginia's action had reduced this below the needed level, they still had 173, well over 50 percent. However, a number of these delegates were from the South, they had been instructed long ago, before Texas had become a live issue. There was now not only danger that these southern delegates might repudiate their instructions as Virginia and Mississippi had done, thus reducing the Van Buren votes to less even than 50 percent, but there was also fear of a bolt from the party if Van Buren were nominated. There were portents of 1860 in the air. As it was, South Carolina was not sending a delegation. The party might be split and the White House turned over to Henry Clay.

To many a politician victory is the paramount issue; defeat must be avoided at all cost. Anti-Van Buren operators had been circulating among the supporters of the other candidates the idea that if the two-thirds rule were adopted and Van Buren eliminated, a candidate of their choice might then win. They also worked with some Van Burenites with the idea that some local favorite son—in Pennsylvania, Buchanan; in New England, Levi Woodbury—might be taken as a compromise, and thus they would avoid defeat.

At this point a more significant idea began to germinate. Van Buren's letter against Texas had been a blow to Jackson, who far away in the seclusion of the Hermitage was still keeping his trembling finger on his party's jumping political pulse. The Tennesseans had a candidate for Vice President, James K. Polk, former Jacksonian floor leader in Congress and speaker of the House, onetime governor of the state. Jackson called him in to counsel, and in this conference Polk got the idea that he might be a compromise candidate in case of a deadlock. Jackson himself may have thought so too. At any rate, a small minority of three of Tennessee's delegates—Sam Laughlin, newspaper editor, Cave Johnson, and Gideon J. Pillow, Polk's law partner—caught the vision and went on to talk at Washington and then at Baltimore.

Most significant was Wright's stated preference for Polk as Van Buren's vice presidential candidate which had been intimated early in April.

Despite the growing confusion, the Van Buren managers still believed they could nominate their man. They still had reason to believe that they could muster a majority. They would therefore use that majority to follow the rules of 1840, which had not required a two-thirds vote, and would nominate Little Van in 1844 as they had in 1840, theoretically by the acclaim of the majority. The Nocturnals thereupon bent their efforts to securing the votes necessary to reinstate the two-thirds rule. This they could accomplish only by convincing more of those instructed for Van Buren. Mississippi had joined Virginia; could other southern votes be secured?

Whatever might happen, on the eve of the convention it had become plain that the original idea of a ratifying convention in the tradition of the 1830's was untenable. This gathering must work and work hard. Now the difficulty was to be increased because there was as yet no central party organization, there was no official planning group. The executive committee recently set up by the congressional caucus had been designed solely as a propaganda committee and had confined itself to preparing a campaign textbook. Even the date of the convention had been arranged by the state conventions in correspondence. As there was no central party organization, the convention delegates were converging on Baltimore with no official direction. There was no responsible agency to make arrangements, and the informality of the whole operation invited what happened.

The New York delegation to Baltimore, led by Benjamin F. Butler (not of Massachusetts) under the general guidance of Silas Wright, who, however, was not a delegate and was not going to Baltimore, thought that they would get together with some of the other Jacksonian veterans and choose the officers of the convention. But this the Nocturnals were determined to prevent, for they knew that the officers, particularly the presiding officer, could do much to guide the result. These anti-Van Burenites had found some sympathy in the Pennsylvania delegation, ostensibly for Buchanan and consequently not too interested in Van Buren. So they worked out a fast move of shock troops, a commando raid.

The Nocturnals organized their commandos well. They would take a tall powerful Buchanan man with a booming voice, the veteran Hendrick B. Wright from Wilkes-Barre in the coal regions, former speaker of the Pennsylvania house and familiar with parliamentary law. A bitter enemy of Van Buren, Romulus M. Saunders of North Carolina, rough and strident, was to be the floor operator and steal a march on the Van Burenites, who had just agreed among themselves to put Ike Hill's old New Hampshire associate Henry Hubbard in the chair.

On the appointed Monday, May 27, the delegates began to gather in the Egyptian Saloon, a room in the top story of the Odd Fellows Hall. This building on Gay Street looked much like a miniature of an Egyptian tomb, a fact symbolic, for it was in truth to become a sepulchre. Such meetings customarily began at noon and the crowd was assembling well in advance. Without warning, about 11:30 A.M. Saunders launched the raid. He rose in the midst of the hall and in stentorian tones nominated Wright for chairman, put the question, declared him elected, and called him to the chair. The Van Buren men, caught off base, had no force they could rally, particularly as they did not dare antagonize Pennsylvania at that ticklish point. Saunders then attempted to rush through the two-thirds rule. But here the tidal wave was slowed down, and the issue was debated, the spectacular figures being Benjamin F. Butler of New York, demanding a simple majority, versus Robert J. Walker, contending for the two-thirds rule already used twice, in 1832 and 1835.

Despite the defection of Virginia and Mississippi Van Buren theoretically still had a good majority. He had New England and the middle states; Alabama, Louisiana, Arkansas, and Missouri from the slave states; while Ohio, Illinois, and Michigan were instructed for him from the West. Even if he lost most of the slave-state votes, it would seem that his majority was safe. Would it hold against the two-thirds rule, as the Van Buren managers decreed? The answer was No. Only 116 remained loyal. His southern supporters, 13 from New England, 12 from Pennsylvania, and 54 from the West instructed for him joined others to make the 148 who defeated the loyal 116 and reinstated the two-thirds rule. Then the roll calls on nominations began.

Of the 26 state delegations, 16 had originally been for Van Buren. On the first ballot all his southern support except Missouri—5 states —left him and so did Michigan, but 29 of the 54 deserters on the two-thirds rule returned to their allegiance, and he still commanded a majority, although it was to prove an impotent one. New England, New York, Pennsylvania, Missouri, Ohio, and a majority of Illinois gave him 146 votes, 31 short of the needed two-thirds. The South, with the exception of Kentucky and Alabama, went for Cass who also had his own Michigan and Indiana, but they, with scattering votes, produced only 83. Richard M. Johnson of Kentucky totaled but 24; Commodore Charles Stewart picked up one vote; Levi Woodbury, 2; Buchanan, 4; and Calhoun but 6. All day was consumed in taking 7 ballots. Van Buren slipped down to 99. He had lost New Hampshire, Vermont, and Connecticut, more than half of Pennsylvania, and a few scattering votes, most of which had gone to Cass. Buchanan had never gone above 26, nor could he command his own state. At the end of the day Cass had 123 and the tide seemed to be turning in his direction. Rumor had it that Johnson's men were coming over and that this would start the decisive "trend."

The Cass and Buchanan managers had won to the extent of eliminating Van Buren, but now they must face the defeat of their men. The Van Burenites hated Cass, and they would have none of Buchanan. They still had one hundred delegates, enough strength to defeat anybody. They might have lost Van Buren, but they would choose the nominee. This at first the Cass men seem to have failed to recognize. Despite this misconception, however, it was really up to the Van Burenites to call the tune. Benjamin F. Butler was ready to withdraw Van Buren and substitute Silas Wright with Jackson's protégé, James K. Polk, for Vice President. But the minority of the Tennessee delegation, Gideon Pillow, Cave Johnson, and Sam Laughlin, were thinking that here was a chance for their man as a dark horse to head, rather than tail, the ticket and at the same time a certain New England operator, namely George Bancroft, had picked up the same idea. It was a busy night of negotiation.

There was a fly in the Butler ointment; Wright would not accept. Indeed, he had placed upon Judge John Fine, one of the New York delegation, the responsibility to keep him out of the race and Fine was faithful; he would not yield to Butler's entreaties. Therefore the balloting resumed Wednesday morning with New York still undecided. On the eighth ballot Van Buren regained a few, Cass lost some, but Polk was now tried out and came up with 44—Tennessee, Alabama, and Louisiana from the South; New Hampshire and the majority from Massachusetts. It was then that the Van Buren men yielded, and New York, Pennsylvania, Virginia, and Walker's Mississippi came in. The convention surged to Polk, the first dark horse, naming Silas Wright for Vice President. But again Wright would not; he telegraphed his refusal during the night. Next morning a ballot for Vice President yielded 107 for Senator John Fairfield of Maine, but busy little Senator Robert J. Walker pushed forward his wife's uncle,

George Mifflin Dallas of Pennsylvania, who, despite some objection because he had presented Biddle's petition for the Bank recharter, was swept in on the second tally by 220 votes.

Benjamin F. Butler, chairman of the platform committee, took the old Calhoun bargain platform of 1840 plus the significant planks for reoccupation and reannexation written by Walker. Texas was going to be made to look better in the North by coupling Oregon with it, and it was hoped that all would unite in wrapping up a victory package. If this were true, all would profess to be satisfied and therefore entitled to shares in the spoils.

As its final act the convention advanced a step forward in party organization. It continued the publication committee recently set up "to procure and supervise the publication of a series of political tracts on the leading features of the approaching contest, and earnestly recommending such publications to the democracy of the country," which included S. J. Tilden, J. L. O'Sullivan, and H. G. Langley of New York; Joseph C. Neal of Philadelphia; Thomas Ritchie of Richmond; Sam Medary of Columbus; and Alexander Kayser of St. Louis, but omitted F. P. Blair's name. Even more significantly it established a central committee of fifteen to supervise "an immediate and full organization of the party throughout the Union." Robert J. Walker was chosen chairman. He was to be the first national party chairman designated by a party convention to manage a presidential campaign.

His tasks were significant. In the first place he must deal with Tyler. The President had hoped against hope that he could form some sort of an alliance with the Democrats and at least get an agreement that his fortunes and those of his followers might be in some way advanced. His friends had arranged for a national convention to meet in Baltimore at the same time as the Democratic gathering. No "arrangements" seemed forthcoming despite the juxtaposition, so the Tyler convention nominated him for the Presidency and adjourned. Ratification meetings were held in July.

After an Independence Day rally of the Tylerites in Philadelphia for this purpose, Walker began to move. Some New York and New Jersey Democrats with cold feet were importuning him to get Tyler off the track. So he went to see the President himself and undertook to get Polk and Jackson to work on it. He hoped Old Hickory would approach Tyler. Although Jackson would not move directly, he did write a letter flattering Tyler and urging his withdrawal which he sent to Major Lewis who was authorized to show it to the President. The General also wrote Blair to go easy on Tyler in the columns of the *Globe* and thus make it less difficult for him to step aside. This appeasement worked; on August 20 the President finally withdrew after trying in vain to get an agreement that a goodly share of his appointees would be safe if Polk were elected.

Walker also headed a propaganda effort of his own to supplement the output of the publications committee. He aided in getting Polk to follow his letter of acceptance with his "judicious" Kane letter on the tariff aimed to meet industrial Pennsylvania's needs. The chairman, all told, franked 170,000 campaign documents, including his Texas letter and some of his speeches abridged. He also wrote another phamphlet, "The South in Danger," which depicted Clay as an abolitionist. This rather boomeranged when Willis Green, the Whig national chairman, got the *National Intelligencer* to print 40,000 to be broadcast in the North. For general consumption a campaign newspaper entitled *The Campaign* was circulated from September 7 to November 2.

To aid their cause, the Whigs tried to recall some of the insane rapture of 1840. They got up a songbook, *The Clay Minstrel, or National Songster*. They featured the Clay barbecue and mass meeting, old Clay techniques, and also sought to capitalize the new fad for the waltz. Clay was a lady's man, a hero of the boudoir. Here was this new fashion of embracing ladies publicly to three-quarter time. The Whig operators tried to "dance Harry into the White House" but in vain.

It was to be a hard battle and the contest close. In the end the result may have hinged on certain developments which should have been more arresting than they were. An increasing foreign migration was filling certain seaboard cities like New York and Philadelphia with hordes of newcomers. This roused new phases of nativist, anti-Catholic passion. A "nativist" party had carried the New York City election in the spring of 1844, a move sponsored by Whigs. In the spring and summer of the election year there were serious anti-Catholic riots in Philadelphia started by controversy over reading the Bible in the schools. Catholic churches were burned and troops had to be called out. In one of the riots, in protecting a church, the troops fired, killing and wounding some rioters. As the Democrats worked with foreigners in their political interests, the rising nativist enthusiasm helped the Whigs. This issue was made more explosive when Democratic judges in New York worked hard naturalizing foreigners in time to vote in November 1844. Statistically their efforts could have made it possible for the Polk ticket to carry New York City, over-turning the spring advantage of their opponents.

Then the ugly head of organized fraud raised itself. In Louisiana on Election Day, the Democratic managers organized a scheme whereby they carried the state for Polk. They sent men who had already voted that day by the steamboat load from New Orleans down to Plaquemines Parish. Here they voted them again in such numbers at various strategic polls that the parish and state were carried for Young Hickory. Thus added to the device of "naturalization" was the shadow of "colonization" whereby repeaters were transported in sufficient numbers to vote where they could do the most good.

Finally there was the use of the slavery issue, which hitherto had not figured significantly in a presidential election. Clay's campaign tactics invited the stirring up of sectional antislavery prejudice. The great compromiser thought it to his advantage to retreat on his opposition to Texas and wrote two so-called Alabama letters in July to reassure the South. Also, a flamboyant kinsman of his, Cassius Marcellus Clay, offered to go north and spellbind audiences for his relative. He proceeded to proclaim his chief as an emancipationist, and of course word of this got back to the South. Clay attempted to restrain his cousin's eloquence but too late. Little things might count and they did. The antislavery zealots, who in 1840 had started the Liberty party, had resumed operations when in August 1843 they had met at Buffalo and again nominated James G. Birney for President. If Clay was going to repudiate his opposition to Texas and repudiate C. M. Clay, Harry of the West was a weak reed for opponents of southern power to lean on.

The complete returns showed that Clay had lost the South, Pennsylvania, and New York and had won only Ohio in the West. Polk was therefore elected, 170–105, though chagrined at the loss of his own Tennessee. The fact that 15,000 New York voters cast their ballots for the Liberty party probably accounted for Clay's loss of the Empire State by 5,000 votes. Had he secured these 36 he would have entered the White House. So much for his Texas semantics.

Polk, the first dark horse, had won, and for the first time a national party chairman, and a vigorous one, had contributed appreciably to the success of the ticket. But Robert J. Walker did not become Postmaster General as did certain of his successors in later times. Statesmanlike rather than partisan administrative responsibilities were to be his reward.

THE MACHINE IS COMPLETED

*B*ETWEEN 1844 and 1849 a new and finished pattern of party operation was worked out by those who were building the Democratic machine. Significantly, this was achieved at the same time that the republic was reaching its first continental limits, approaching its "manifest destiny." Since the activities of the Jacksonians, the management of the new party had been White House–oriented. From 1829 to 1841 the leadership had been in the hands of Jackson, Van Buren, and their associates in the kitchen cabinet and the Congress. The journalist Francis P. Blair was ever privy to their counsels. Their chief concern had been the succession to the Presidency. At first this meant the re-election of Jackson and the choice of Van Buren as Vice President, thereafter his election as President. When these goals were achieved, at the expense of Calhoun, the next question was to get Van Buren re-elected in 1840. After that diastrous failure, the goal continued to be in a sense the same. There was no leader of the party in the executive mansion, but the same people were in command at Kinderhook and at the Capitol endeavoring to vindicate Van Buren, return him to the White House, and restore to power the same alliance of leaders, state and congressional, which had controlled the party since its inception.

This was not to be. The White House orientation had been destroyed by those maneuvers of 1844 which had nominated the first dark horse. This *putsch* had been organized by a group of state leaders with some senatorial stimulus. The beneficiary of their crash tactics, James K. Polk, unlike Jackson and Van Buren, was little inclined to undertake party management. His interests were rather in administration. As committee chairman and speaker in Congress and as governor in Tennessee, he had developed an executive bent and while within limits he was an excellent politician, he defined his presidential responsibility as primarily administrative. He had no further political ambition; he announced himself as a one-term President and seems to have devoted himself wholeheartedly to the success and fame of his Administration.

He constructed his Cabinet for work and not for party direction. In fact he was determined to keep the attention of his advisers on the Polk Administration and not on the future. He invited two old friends, John Y. Mason of Virginia, his college classmate and a member of the Tyler Cabinet, together with Cave Johnson, his Tennessee intimate, to join his Administration. He planned to have Senator Walker as Attorney General. These would represent the South. He would not continue Calhoun: he was to be invited to be minister to Great Britain.

The northern representatives would come from New England, Pennsylvania, and New York. Bancroft of Massachusetts, who had played a significant role in his nomination, was a natural choice. The Pennsylvania selection was made in a manner typical of Polk's politics. The Vice President, George M. Dallas, was from Pennsylvania, and Polk, with his curiously jealous mind, did not want the second man to have too much influence, so when the Pennsylvania members of the Electoral College recommended a Cabinet post for Dallas' closest rival, Buchanan, Polk seized the opportunity to have each kill off the other, particularly as he was urged on by Simon Cameron who wanted Buchanan's Senate seat.

New York had demanded the State Department, and Polk offered the Treasury to Silas Wright. Wright had just been elected governor and there is still a question as to whether Polk expected him to accept. At any rate Wright did not. Van Buren in the meantime urged Butler for the State Department. Polk, having offered Wright the Treasury, now offered Butler the War Department, but he would have none of this, to the surprise of many. Butler wanted State or Treasury or nothing. This Polk would not grant nor would he appoint New York's comptroller, the Van Burenite Azariah Flagg, to the finance post. Polk by now was tired of dickering with the Van Burenites, so he invited former governor William L. Marcy to take the War Department, and New York got a reward bitterly resented by the Van Buren management of the Empire State Democracy. As a last resort Polk hoped Van Buren would be mollified by the British mission, which Calhoun had refused. This hope too was vain.

This still left the Treasury vacant. Although Walker had been offered the Attorney Generalship, he and his friends were not satisfied and had built up pressure on Polk to put him in the Treasury.

Walker's friends converged from the South and West. There were also those in the East like Fernando Wood of New York City and the Pennsylvania friends of Walker's uncle, Vice President Dallas. Two Mississippians, well known to Polk, who wanted Walker's seat in the Senate vacated, were very importunate on his behalf; they were William M. Gwin and Jacob Thompson. Though their importunities in Walker's behalf were to be successful, neither got his seat. At the last minute Polk chose Walker for the Treasury, giving Mason the Attorney General's place, and his Cabinet was complete. The main facts, politically speaking, were that the Van Burenites were now further disaffected, Buchanan and Walker were, for the time being, immobilized as far as party leadership was concerned. Calhoun had been to all intents and purposes ignored.

Polk proceeded to concentrate on administration. He was a man of great intensity of will but of limited physical strength. He formulated an executive program of *laissez faire* in domestic matters and of heeding manifest destiny in foreign affairs. He would destroy Whig efforts to enact Clay's American System with its centralization. This he accomplished in the midst of a foriegn war induced by his enthusiasm for this same destiny. He would do his best for reoccupation and reannexation.

Thus he made his choice and he announced immediately that the White House would have no interest in the mechanics of party organization. He would not run again and he exacted a pledge from his Cabinet members that they would not become candidates for the succession. Finally he changed organs, banished Blair, and arranged for Ritchie to take over the propaganda in a new paper, the Washington *Union*, supported by various subsidies, including the government printing and Senator Cameron's Pennsylvania bank. His efforts had produced a working combination designed to labor for the public good and the fame of the Polk Administration. Its interests, politically, were to extend only from 1845 to 1849. The future of the Democratic party leadership was not its concern.

But who then would lead the party and plan for its future? Silas Wright had left the Senate and was fighting a difficult operation in Albany which absorbed all his energies. The "young" hopeful, Walker, was immobilized in the Treasury under Polk's jealous and watchful eye. Calhoun was back in the Senate, but he and the other "statesman," Senator Thomas Hart Benton, never displayed any capacity for practical nationwide party leadership.

The convention of 1844 had done little to look to the future. To date national party conventions had not assumed such responsibility. In that body a combination of state leaders from the Southwest, West, and New England had undertaken to push forward Lewis Cass from Michigan, representative of the new frontier of that day, not unaware of speculative interests. Then at the last minute this new combination, which had defeated Van Buren, was forced by the latter's followers to abandon Cass and accept Polk. The claims of Calhoun as well as those of Van Buren had been overridden. Also, the architects of this new leadership, Walker, Bancroft, and Johnson, were in the Cabinet, with their hands tied serving a President who frowned on party management and speculative interest and who soon was to be engrossed in fighting a war. So the question remained, who would lead the party? As yet no machinery had been devised to answer this question; there was no permanent national party organization unless there was effort from the White House.

The responsibility must fall back on the state leaders; this left Lewis Cass as the man who had the residue of interest. At one time during the convention of 1844 he had secured the support of 16 out of the 25 states, although his numerical strength of 123 delegates had not approached the 177 needed. He was from the Northwest, the first candidate to emerge from that region. He was also a man of wealth who appealed to the growing number in the Democratic party who may have thought *laissez faire* was somewhat overdone, men like Walker who had backed him. Then, too, there were others: former Vice President Richard M. Johnson, old Rumpsey-Dumpsey, was still hopeful; Pennsylvania, despite Buchanan's pledge, was always scheming; and New England began to display ambition for a native son, Judge Levi Woodbury of New Hampshire.

The party had originally been organized around a New York–Virginia alliance contrived by the regency and the junto operators. They had always denied Calhoun's pretensions to leadership and since 1832 had successfully thwarted his ambitions. Although his last efforts in 1841–43 to achieve the Presidency had collapsed, now apparently he was to try again. His plan was to achieve an alliance between the South and the West on the basis of low tariff and western transportation, which would insure the West markets and trade, and low taxes to the South, thus confining the East within a secure minority status of impotence. For a time he seemed on the eve of success, but the events of 1845–47, including Polk's veto of a rivers and harbors bill, the enactment of the Walker "free trade" tariff, the compromise on Oregon, and the Mexican War, destroyed any chance he may have had. He had a small following in the Senate, which led him to try to operate a balance of power minority and dictate legislation to Polk. The climax came when he sought to weaken the President's control of the army and to write the terms of the eventual peace. Polk threw him out of the party in one of his few efforts at party leadership, and Calhoun's hope of a new alliance and the fulfillment of his own ambition was dead.

What Calhoun had feared and fought to prevent was an alliance between the East and the West secured at the price of measures promoting the speedy development of those two sections under government encouragement at the expense of the South. And now this was to come to pass. Polk's feud with Calhoun, which was of Tennessee mountain variety and proportion, was matched by that which developed with the Van Burenites and other elements in the eastern and western wings of the party. It started with the formation of the Cabinet, when Van Buren's followers were left out of any major post in the Administration after negotiations which caused Van Buren and Polk each to doubt the other's good faith. Then Blair was dispensed with as press spokesman. Senator Benton essayed to play Wright's role in the Senate but with worse than no success; Polk tried hard but he and Benton could not remain long on cooperative terms, for Benton as a leader was in many ways impossible. Polk's legislative acts, particularly the Walker tariff which roused so much antagonism in protectionist Pennsylvania and his veto of the rivers and harbors bill which the West had expected to get in return for their votes for the tariff, roused bitterness. The climax came, however, when half of Oregon was sacrificed while the acquisition of all of Texas was achieved and the annexation of a major part of Mexico seemed to be imminent. This great addition, so geographically unbalanced, seemed to indicate but one positive result. New states with southern mores, and therefore politics, were destined to join the Union in larger numbers than those of free-state ordering and completely snow under the predominance in the federal government which an eastern-western alliance might have achieved. The sum total of these grievances prepared the way for a new effort to organize an anti-Polk control of Congress and party. These maneuvers were to result eventually in revolt and civil war.

The first step in this fateful direction was taken in August 1846. Polk asked for money to finance a peace which would include the exacting of an indemnity from Mexico as well as the satisfaction of long-standing claims. Most of this bill was to be satisfied by a great land cession in northwest Mexico. A group of embittered Pennsylvania and Middle Western congressmen, depending on Van Buren allies, planned action. They engineered a move to stop the acquisition of potential slave territory. To that end they formulated a proviso to be added to the appropriation requested by Polk, specifying that no land acquired with the aid of these funds could become slave territory. David Wilmot of Pennsylvania got the floor to present this composite work, and so it bore his name.

The Wilmot Proviso introduced that August day was the formula which would serve as an instrument convenient for the use of those determined to create a new alliance, the eastern and western Democrats, in place of either the old Jacksonian New York and Virginia understanding or Calhoun's abortive South and West agreement. This new group would have unchallenged numerical superiority, for here was where the population was. This regrouping would pay no attention to the equality of the sections nor to the doctrine of states' rights. Some professed at that point to see the handwriting on the wall, the doom of the South and of the Union, if this new aggregation coalesced. The Proviso passed the House on occasion but never the Senate, so it did not become the law of the land. But the flames kindled by this firebrand were to be quenched, if at all, by the bloodletting of the Civil War.

The formula was almost immediately seized upon in several state situations, notably in New York. The Albany regency there had been shaken by faction, and the control of Van Buren had been menaced and weakened. He and his close associates in the troubled days of the panic-ridden thirties had stood for certain "radical" measures designed to stabilize the financial situation and to aid the distressed. These measures, after 1933, seem almost insignificant and meaningless, but a century earlier they filled some people with alarm. A conservative faction opposed to the Van Buren Locofoco, Equal Rights radicals challenged his leadership, and the resultant discord weakened the party. When Polk had found himself unable or unwilling to placate the Van Buren wing by a Cabinet appointment, he had given New York's place, the War Department, to a conservative, William L. Marcy.

Silas Wright, now governor, was unable to heal the breach. Although he was renominated in 1846, he was defeated, and the Whigs won a decisive victory which again gave them control of the state. The Democratic party suffered elsewhere, and it was soon apparent that Polk's second House of Representatives would be hostile to the Democracy. Many people attributed the defeat, in New York at least, to the treachery of the conservative wing of the Democracy to which the Secretary of War, Marcy, belonged. The Van Burenites charged Polk with treachery and the political sacrifice of Silas Wright. When Wright died in August 1847, they accused Polk and the New York "Conservatives" of his murder. A fortnight after Wright's death the New York Democrats met in state convention with the stage set for a bloody battle at which a new precedent was initiated.

The Polk officeholders were in control. Despite this fact, the Van Buren faction endeavored to get the convention to endorse the Wilmot Proviso. They believed that antislavery opposition to the annexation of Texas and the Mexican War, the rankling over the sacrifice of Oregon, and the threat of an enlarged slave power were all uniting to defeat their party unless there was a revolt against the dominance of Polk. When the New York convention, Marcy controlled, rejected the platform, the Van Buren men walked out of the convention and earned their new nickname "Barnburners." They held another convention where they unfurled the Wilmot Proviso banner, although they refrained from nominating candidates. Despite this fact, the Whigs carried the state in 1847, as in 1846. The national conventions were approaching; both factions, the Barnburners and their opponents, now called Hunkers, held separate conventions, and each sent a delegation to the Democratic gathering at Baltimore, each proclaiming itself the legitimate representation of the New York party. Elsewhere in the states the Wilmot Proviso had proved a rallying cry and a point of division but not with the disrupting consequences reached in New York.

Polk and Marcy had done little to attempt to heal the breach. Walker's absorption in the difficult responsibilities of financing the war and his precarious health kept him from attempting to repeat the role of 1844, and Bancroft was out of the country, serving as minister to Great Britain. The party had become what it was generally thereafter to be, a federation of state machines or cliques led by state leaders either in the state or national capitols. The Van Burenites would try to get back their power in 1848. The Pennsylvanians and Buchanan, despite his pledge to Polk, were scheming for the White House. Calhoun was still determined to destroy national convention control and turn power back to what eventually would become local primaries. Father Ritchie was endeavoring to organize a propaganda for party unity without national leadership. The major part of the state machines, as in 1844, was again for Cass.

In the meantime, however, there had been a new dimension added to the republic and to politics, and it was casting its shadow over the elections of 1848. The Mexican War, resulting in the Mexican Cession, and the settlement of the Oregon question with Great Britain meant that the nation had been greatly increased in size. Its boundaries had been carried to the Pacific, a new element had been added to the population, and although it was then realized but dimly, a vast treasure of precious metal in the Rockies and in California awaited new owners. Here were the elements of greater empire which must be ruled and which would give power and reward to the rulers. And the spread in latitude and longitude made the new domain a region which both northern and southern politicos and developers were sure to covet.

The rulers to be chosen in 1848 would have a great responsibility. What would they decree for the new lands and people? The Wilmot Proviso had been the first bid; under it the South was to be excluded from control of the new empire. Calhoun had countered the Wilmot Proviso in February 1847 with a series of resolutions which were to become the doctrine of the South. No citizen of any of the states nor his property could be excluded from the common territories. Buchanan in August tried his hand in a letter advocating the extension of the Missouri Compromise line to the Pacific. Calhoun and Polk were ready to accept this, but the House had defeated such a proposal at the same time that it once again passed the Wilmot Proviso. In 1844 Cass had established his eligibility for the Presidency by coming out for Texas; now in 1847 he was essaying another stroke of penmanship: he would challenge the Wilmot Proviso with a fourth formula. He took an idea which already had some currency, and endorsed it in a letter which he wrote to a Tennessee editor, A.O.P. Nicholson. This Nicholson letter advocated that each territory be permitted to decide for itself whether it would be slave or free. This doctrine was to be known as popular sovereignty or squatter sovereignty. It was designed to remove the slavery issue from Congress and from national politics.

Here was an array of standards, and the delegates being chosen to go to Baltimore in 1848 must select from among them. This situation brought out in such clear relief the fact that 1845–48 had been, from the standpoint of central party leadership, four leaderless years. The party had splintered into its state units, each making a history of its own. The truth was that there seemed little interest in the election of 1848; the Mexican War had been too engrossing, and there had developed no interim party organization on a national level.

The plight of the Democrats and the fortunes of war presented a new opportunity to the Whigs. Their managers, determined that they were through with Clay, began to calculate how best to capitalize on the facts of Democratic schism and the coincidence that the two war heroes were Whigs. Here was a chance to produce an Old Hickory and to repeat the triumph of Tippecanoe. Scott, Old Fuss and Feathers, was eager but hardly equal to Old Rough and Ready, General Zachary Taylor, who appeared made to order. At first he seemed handicapped because he was a man of no political experience, he had never voted, and didn't have any party. He was also headstrong and hard to "advise." Likewise, when he was first thought of after his victories in the spring of 1846 by such political "dodgers" as Thurlow Weed, he would have none of it. Then when the Polk Administration began to push him around, particularly after his great victory at Buena Vista in February 1847, he was more attracted by the idea. However, a political naïveté seemed to assert itself, and he proclaimed he would accept support from any and all parties. Eventually the Whig play proved stronger; he finally was persuaded to sign a letter saying he was a Whig, and he also promised insiders that if elected he would appoint a Whig Cabinet. In the meantime Taylor's earlier lack of interest and seemingly callow nonpartisanship had led some to think of Winfield Scott as the new Jackson. In April 1848 Clay again came back into the running. The Whigs planned to meet in Philadelphia June 7, thus breaking the Baltimore routine. They would first see what the Democrats would do.

The Whigs still were basically unorganized and opportunistic. Whatever organization there was, was dominated and operated by Clay and his supporters. But Clay was old and he bore the onus of a fourth defeat in 1844. It was now almost crystal clear that he could never be President; people were tired of him. Yet it was apparent that he was willing to try again, hoping to take advantage of the growing schism in the ranks of the reigning Democracy.

The course of the Mexican War emphasized Whig opportunity. Zachary Taylor might seem politically inept, but he was proving to be another Jackson, a hero and a martyr. As soon as the signs of this "persecution" became apparent in 1846–47, "smart" Whigs had grasped Taylor's availability, and the defeat of the Democrats in the elections of 1846–47 underlined it. Taylor, was at length goaded by his enemies and flattered by his friends into a growing interest in the Presidency if for no more exalted motive than to confound his enemies.

A skillful congressional junto composed of men like Truman Smith of Connecticut; John J. Crittenden of Kentucky; an obscure, one-term congressman from Illinois, Abe Lincoln; and others took him up. Under their guidance and because of his own naïve precocity, he began to operate, surrounded by a coterie of obscure southern advisers. The objective was to create an Old Hickory–Tippecanoe image in the person of Old Rough and Ready. The idea of a hero and a persecuted hero took hold again. Truman Smith was made head of a promotion committee, Rough and Ready clubs were organized, newspaper support was available. Taylor letters were composed and printed or circulated in manuscript "confidentially." A definite tactic was developed: a southern man of national appeal was promoted to capture southern support because he was a slaveholder, and northern support was invited for a national martyred hero.

The Democrats moved first. At the instance of the congressional party caucus and the state machines, the parties in the states chose delegates at various times and in various fashions. Monday, May 22, 1848, and Baltimore were the day and place accepted by common consent, because it was four years almost to the day from the meeting in May 1844. There was no committee in charge, and the minimum of preparatory work, such as there was, was done by the local Baltimore party leaders. Once again in 1848, as in 1844, the Democratic delegates were approaching Baltimore in confusion.

This time the Universalist Church at Calvert and Pleasant streets was the scene. At noon a delegate otherwise unknown to history, W. D. Latshaw of Illinois, moved that the Honorable J. S. Bryce of Louisiana, likewise uncelebrated, take the chair temporarily, and the committee on organization shortly brought in the names of the permanent officers. They had fixed on a Richmond Junto man, Andrew Stevenson of Virginia, formerly speaker of the U.S. House and minister to England. In the previous decade he had presided over the Democratic National Convention in 1835.

The main question before the convention was not so much the candidate but the organization of the party. Could the delegates handle state situations like that which had developed in New York and which were getting out of hand? The electoral vote of New York was so large that although it was statistically possible to win without it that event was not likely; a split in the Whig vote in New York in 1844 probably had elected Polk. There was now danger that a similar breach in the New York Democracy might cost the party the election in 1848.

The Van Burenites came to Baltimore conscious of the fact that in most of the previous Democratic national conventions they had been the controlling force, their regency had been the agent of winning alliances and the directing element in party management. A faction of the party ostensibly directed from the War Department, if not from the White House, which had thrived on federal patronage, denied these pretensions and threatened to destroy permanently the power of the New York Democracy. The Barnburning Van Burenites on their part were determined to get back their supremacy and demanded that they be recognized as the New York delegation on the ground that they had been defeated in the state convention by men representing speculative interests who were opposed to Democratic *laissez-faire* principles, and they were thus "required" to protest and to protect the purity of Democratic doctrine. To do this they invoked the Wilmot Proviso, restoring government to the people.

Would the convention endorse the Wilmot Proviso and, incidentally, them? The free states had a majority of the convention delegates—would they unite behind the old Van Buren leadership? These pretensions the "regular" Hunker delegates were bound to resist. They endeavored to capitalize certain assets. They would oppose the free-state-oriented Wilmot Proviso formula with one of universal appeal. One of the Hunker leaders, Senator Daniel S. Dickinson, had given some currency to the program taken up by Lewis Cass in his Nicholson letter, that of popular sovereignty. By joining forces with the southern and western supporters of Cass who on the eve of the convention had a majority of the states, the Hunker delegation probably thought they would be accepted despite Barnburner—Van Buren pretensions.

After complex maneuvering, a vote to admit the Hunkers failed. They had the Confederate states-to-be, except Tennessee, Texas, and Alabama, together with Delaware and Missouri of the border, and Michigan, Wisconsin, and eleven of Ohio's twenty-three delegates from the West. The Hunkers got little support from New England, the middle states, where New York could not vote on this issue, or from more than half of the West, from Maryland, or from Kentucky. Of the 254 delegates the Hunkers could not command more than 95.

No recorded test of the Barnburner strength was made, but it could not have been much greater than that of the Hunkers. Those who hoped to heal the breach proposed that both delegations be seated and that each be permitted to cast half the state's vote. The supporters of the Hunkers voted against this, but it carried on a test vote by the closest of margins, 126–124, supported by New England, New Jersey, and Pennsylvania, with a majority of western and some southern votes. This was evidently a move by the Van Burenite friends of the Barnburners, but the latter would have none of it and they walked out. They would have all or nothing. They would not accept crumbs from those who in 1844 had slaughtered Van Buren, even if the Hunkers were willing. A reaffirmation of the two-thirds rule was voted, 176–78, although Cass could count a majority of the 254 votes.

The convention then proceeded to nominate. Lewis Cass, Levi Woodbury of New Hampshire, and James Buchanan were the candidates. Cass had the West and the South with notable exceptions. He lacked North Carolina, South Carolina, Georgia, Alabama, and Florida. His support numbered 125, not quite a majority. Buchanan had Pennsylvania, New Jersey, North Carolina, and Iowa, totaling 55. Woodbury had most of New England, Alabama, and half of Georgia, and at one point he was to have Florida. His strength was 53. During the course of four ballots, Cass picked up Massachusetts and Rhode Island, which he added to Vermont. In the middle states, he carried New Jersey, and in the South, North Carolina, Georgia, South Carolina, and Tennessee, while in the West, Iowa came in. Thus he secured 179, 10 more than the 169 necessary. Woodbury retained Maine, New Hampshire, Connecticut, Florida, and the majority of Alabama's vote and a few scattering for a total of 38, while Buchanan finished with Pennsylvania, the rest of Alabama, and two fractions, totaling 33. Of those who voted on the test to admit both New York delegations, 54 from Texas, Tennessee, Kentucky, Ohio, Indiana, and Illinois voted for Cass on the first ballot; 38 for Woodbury, mostly from New England; and 29, primarily Pennsylvania, for Buchanan; there were three scattering. General William O. Butler of Kentucky defeated his Mexican War comrade General John A. Quitman of Mississippi for the Vice Presidency, and the ticket was complete.

Next in order came the adoption of the party platform. The worn phrases adopted in 1840 were again employed, and others endorsing the Mexican War and the Polk Administration and congratulating the new French Republic were added. Nothing was said about slavery in the territories, and an effort by William L. Yancey of Alabama to get acceptance of the idea that the "doctrine of non-interference with the rights of property either in the States or in the Territories" was the "true republican doctrine" was defeated, 216–36. Only Georgia, Florida, Alabama, Arkansas, and South Carolina's lone delegate would support this. The platform unamended was adopted unanimously on a roll call vote. Nothing was said about the New York walkout or its circumstances except that Barnburners and Hunkers were each permitted to insert a statement of their case in the proceedings of the convention.

But this conclave was to prove the most significant national political gathering to date, probably without any realization of the importance of its final act. From the standpoint of the creation of party machinery the climax of the deliberations of the convention was a decision to provide for permanent organization and for continuing responsibility for party operation by a central committee, national in scope, thus setting a new pattern which was to prove permanent. They set up a national central committee consisting of a member from each state, nominated by its delegation. This committee was organized in Washington on Saturday, May 27, under the chairmanship of Benjamin F. Hallett of Massachusetts. This committee was to carry on after 1848 and was to arrange for the convention in 1852. In the recent convention there had been some mention of raising money to meet the incidental expenses, but the Baltimore hosts had waved this idea aside. However, the new committee was not to forget it when they planned for the next gathering. In such fashion the operators provided that the party management, hitherto haphazard, unstructured, or nonexistent, was now to have national and, as it proved, permanent direction.

A few days after the Democrats adjourned, the Whigs assembled at Philadelphia to open their deliberations on June 7 in the Chinese Museum. The Taylor delegates were the most numerous and probably had enough votes to nominate him on the first ballot. However, prudence dictated that his choice should be achieved in a manner designed to make as few enemies as possible. Slow and persuasive strategy was in order. Clay, Scott, Webster, and Clayton were in due course turned aside by the skillful group of operators who saw in Taylor the best hope of victory. The only real opposition came from northern groups who did not relish a southern slaveholding candidate who was not only noncommittal about slavery but was not too sure he was a Whig.

Taylor's interests had been ably handled by the congressional committee headed by Truman Smith of Connecticut and by a group of unheralded Betas, including Alexander C. Bullitt, Logan Hunton, Balie Peyton, and James Y. Love. A series of Rough and Ready clubs had been functioning effectively in spreading the image. They had also been busy reassuring the doubting that Taylor was really a Whig, not too southern, and the convention went to the unusual length of holding a secret session to promote good will by free discussion. The General prevailed on the fourth ballot over the eternal Clay and Webster, as well as over General Winfield Scott. Millard Fillmore of New York, veteran of 1844 and opponent of Thurlow Weed, was accorded second place over the New England capitalist Abbott Lawrence. As in 1840 there was to be no platform nor any officially designated central organization. Whigs, unlike the Democrats, were not politically inventive.

The campaign was to be complicated by a new chapter in the history of the operation "third party." The Van Buren–Barnburners who had "walked out" of the New York State Democratic convention of 1847 had repeated that maneuver at Baltimore in 1848. Would they support Cass? There was a similar disquiet among the Whigs. The choice of a southern slaveholder who might not be a Whig was a grievous blow to some members of the convention. A group threatened loudly, declaring they would not support Taylor. During the Philadelphia convention Henry Wilson and Charles Allen of Massachusetts walked out, and before it adjourned Wilson called together those who were so dissatisfied that they were ready to renounce the nominee and even the party. Coming back to the Chinese Museum after adjournment, they passed resolutions to that effect and called a national convention to be held in August at Buffalo.

There were in addition several even smaller groups. Before the major conventions a Native American party had convened, but they had contented themselves with naming Taylor. A Liberty League made up of some of the most radical abolitionists had nominated Gerrit Smith, a reform-minded New Yorker of wealth, while the Liberty party had held its third quadrennial convention and put up Senator John P. Hale of New Hampshire, first free-soiler who had been elected to the U.S. Senate. Finally, an incipient labor party had held an Industrial Congress which had endorsed Gerrit Smith.

The significant groups which had to be reckoned with were the

Barnburners, the fewer disgruntled Whigs, and the veterans of the Liberty party. These elements organized a series of state conventions, notably in New York, Ohio, and Massachusetts, to provide delegates and support for the Buffalo meeting set for August. The New York Barnburners anticipated the Buffalo meeting by calling a state convention which assembled on June 22 at Utica and to which they invited delegates from other states; a few came from New England from Massachusetts and Connecticut and from the West from Ohio and Wisconsin. They nominated Van Buren and Henry Dodge of Wisconsin. When Van Buren accepted this nomination, the newly organized Democratic management knew that it was in for trouble.

The antislavery national mass meeting was duly held at Buffalo on August 9. John Quincy Adams' son, Charles Francis, presided. Here the chief task was to get the Liberty party to withdraw Hale and fuse with the new organization. This they resisted, so it was put to a vote between Van Buren and Hale; Van Buren won, 159–129. Hale thereupon withdrew and the Liberty party, such as it was, entered wholeheartedly into the fusion to be called the Free-Soil party. As Dodge remained loyal to Cass, Charles Francis Adams was named candidate for Vice President. The Democrats were in real danger.

Benjamin F. Hallett, first convention-designated national party chairman with more than immediate campaign responsibilities, represented a new figure on the American political stage. He had made his debut on the national political scene as a delegate to the Antimasonic National Convention in 1831. More recently he had worked to bring the Antimasons into the Massachusetts Democratic party in the hope of organizing a combination which could beat the Whigs, so long in the ascendant. He had become the recognized Democratic leader there even though his success in overthrowing the Whigs was not spectacular. Now it was his responsibility to elect Cass.

Hallett and the national committee had to face some hard realities. The expectation that in good democratic fashion the party ranks would close despite the walkout of the Van Burenites had proved fatuous. The Hunker faction was quite obviously willing to return despite their angry declaration and protest in the convention; in fact their leaders had said so. But not the Van Buren faction. They had been had in 1844, and now the same conbination was trying it in '48. At long last the suave Van Buren was mad and his son "Prince John" Van Buren was particularly so. The "Old Man's" wrongs were going to be avenged even if it destroyed the party.

The managers began immediately to organize a propaganda. The editors, Ritchie and Heiss, of the party organ, the Washington *Union,* got up the usual campaign paper, this time called the *Campaign,* and a new departure entitled *The Democratic Text Book being a compendium of principles of the Democratic Party* was compiled by George H. Hickman and published. Efforts were made to heal the breach with Blair and Rives of the former organ, *The Globe,* by giving them some of the campaign printing. The job of projecting a compelling image of Cass was a formidable one.

Whatever Cass may have been as a frontier Indian fighter and administrator during the War of 1812 and as the first governor of Michigan Territory, he was now old and fat and somewhat ludicrous, as a current rhyme proclaimed:

> And he who still for Cass can be
> He is a Cass without the C.

Likewise, he was a millionaire charged with the taint of graft; the "big lie" was known even then. The cloud of the New York defection hung heavily over the party. Then, too, there was so little help from other leaders. Calhoun would lend no aid. Buchanan was contemptuous and disappointed. Polk had little influence. A new figure recently become Senator from Illinois, Stephen A. Douglas, tried some barnstorming in the South. All told it was going to be a formidable job to try to match the image of Old Rough and Ready. Hallett was confronted with a task verging on the impossible, an unhappy augury for the newly perfected machine.

Taylor in fact had all the advantages. The operators who had worked to put him in nomination, well trained to their task, went right on without any official designation. Truman Smith and the congressional committee, together with the Rough and Ready clubs, kept the enthusiasm high. A campaign newspaper called *The Battery* was issued and the minstrels led the singing:

> Then go it boys, strong and steady
> And raise the shout for Rough and Ready.

Some smart moves were made. Crittenden of Kentucky, where Clay and his friends were, to say the least, unenthusiastic, undertook to run for governor to insure Taylor the electoral vote of the Blue Grass State. The General himself sat quietly on his veranda at Baton Rouge, talked to visitors, and signed one or two good letters. Everything in fact was working in his favor.

There was little doubt what was going to happen, and it did. Taylor had an easy victory. This triumph has customarily been attributed to the split in the Democratic party: Van Buren's defection caused the Jacksonians to lose New York and the election. However, this defection worked in reverse. Taylor's southern origin and slaveholding situation probably lost him Ohio's vote because so many Whigs voted for Van Buren's Free-Soil ticket. The real source of Rough and Ready's victory was the fact that he carried Georgia, Louisiana, Florida, and Pennsylvania. Had there been no Van Buren ticket, Cass might have won New York's thirty-six, but he also might have lost Ohio's twenty-three, which Clay had won in 1844. The image of Old Rough and Ready had the same potency as those of Old Hickory and Tippecanoe. This was a romantic age which had inherited little of the rationalism of the founders of the republic.

After the work of the Democratic National Convention of 1848, only one more step was needed to complete the basic pattern of the political machine of the United States, and this was taken during the campaigns of 1852 and 1856. Parties which were growing to such size in such complex times now needed some form of financing. The Democrats took formal account of this necessity in 1852 when the national committee authorized the creation of a party fund. The committee proposed that at least $100 be collected in each of the congressional districts. As there were 233 of them, it was hoped that at least $20,000 could be raised. This money was to be used largely for printing campaign material.

Congress, as usual, was doing its part. It not only supplied its members with printed copies of their speeches, within certain limits, and with tons of government documents, but by supplying them the franking privilege made it possible for them to scatter this printed matter all over the land, to the edification of the voters and their families. Congress also continued to subsidize the Democratic party organ, the Washington *Union*, in a somewhat clumsy fashion. Fundraising did not prove easy for the Democrats, and it was not until August Belmont, the wealthy New York banker, made a substantial contribution that their needs were met. It is doubtful whether their national funds exceeded $50,000. But these were days of small things.

The real enterprise in fund-raising and in shaping an effective pattern for it came not from the Democrats but from the new Republican party, who introduced it in their first national campaign in 1856. The increasingly swift growth of the nation caused by the westward migration of settlers from the East, the Middle West, and foreign shores accelerated the creation of communities between the Mississippi and the Pacific. Slavery could not be carried there, so southern expansion appeared to be stopped. The admission of the flock of free states which seemed imminent would end southern political dominance. The ruling southern group in the federal government sought desperately and for a while with some seeming prospect of success to hold off this destruction of their power. But northern politicos, impatient at this continued frustration, were tireless in their efforts to mobilize northern superior numbers. They followed the design of the Liberty and Free-Soil parties of the 1840's and labored successfully to organize a northern party in 1854–56. They declared that the old Jefferson-Jackson concept of Democratic-Republicanism had been prostituted by making the Democratic party, still sometimes called Democratic-Republican, an agency of the "slave power." Jackson's party, therefore, had forfeited the right to use the word Republican. The northern operators would create a new purified Republican party whose platform would declare that slavery must not be carried into the territories, which henceforth were to be free-soil.

This new organization was consummated in 1856 when the Republican party was finally organized in Philadelphia. Prominent in the move were businessmen from New York, Philadelphia, and Boston, entrepreneurs who were used to organizing in a big way to promote industrial and mercantile enterprises. They placed at the head of their national party committee one of New York's wealthiest businessmen, Edwin D. Morgan. By the end of summer he had worked out a system of raising money for campaign purposes. He held meetings of businessmen, he sent out agents, he set up subscription papers. He also operated a scheme of contingent gifts, subscriptions payable if Frémont won. Newspapers were bought or subsidized, and presumably "understandings" were arrived at, to be honored in the event of victory.

The Republicans undertook responsibilities other than fundraising, including some complicated negotiations. The Whig party had begun disintegrating soon after the campaign of 1852. At the same time the increasing influx of immigrants from Europe and the activity of so many Irish in the Democratic party had stimulated an anti-foreign political organization. Many Whigs were sympathetic with this maneuver and in 1856 a new party was launched that included a goodly number of voters, both northern and southern. It was named the American party. For a time this appeared as a national party and nominated ex-President Fillmore and A. J. Donelson. However, when the party adopted a platform plank sympathetic to southern demands regarding slavery, a considerable northern wing broke away, repudiating the platform and the Fillmore-Donelson ticket. These northern Americans then held a national convention that met after the Republicans had nominated John C. Fremont and William L. Dayton. The northern Americans nominated Fremont but refused to endorse Dayton; instead they put up William F. Johnston of Pennsylvania for the second place. This meant two American parties, with two electoral tickets in various of the several states.

This contretemps would be harmful to Fremont's and Dayton's chances of election so negotiations were undertaken to prevent it. The Republican national committee played its part in persuading the northern American party to withdraw and leave a clear field for Fremont and Dayton. The effort was successful. It required certain negotiators all summer to persuade the Americans to support Dayton. In the course of this campaign the Republican national committee achieved a real operating organization besides collecting a campaign fund possibly amounting to several hundred thousand dollars. The Democrats, probably stimulated by the energy of their new rival, had greater financial success than in the previous campaign; they, like the Republicans, passed the hat in New York City with Belmont again contributing, though much less generously. Although they did not secure as large a fund as their competitors, they used that which they did collect to such advantage that the Democrats gained one more national victory, their last for many a long year.

The design for the political machinery which experience had shown was necessary to implement the program of self-government set up for the people of the United States by the Constitution had thus in most essentials been completed by 1856. Its pattern was that of two political parties, institutionalized and permanently organized, geared to supply and operate the executive and legislative branches of the federal and, to a large extent, the state governments. This was the mechanism used to conduct the elections required by the nation's dedication to the popular choice, periodically, of those operating the instruments of government.

EPILOGUE

𝒯HE POLITICAL machinery required for self-government in the United States was thus completed in general design during the crucial national campaigns of the 1850's, although its operating potential was not fully comprehended by those who were essaying to run it. There were two major elements in the mechanism, the Democratic party and their opponents, the Republicans, who in 1856 had superseded the Whigs. These elements were of almost equal size: they won presidential elections alternately in 1836, 1840, 1844, 1848, and 1852, and the popular vote in 1852 and 1856 indicated clearly how nearly equal were their voting strengths. Their first party platforms,[1] when the Whigs at length contrived one, showed a remarkable degree of consensus as to the nature of the machinery and the pattern of use to which it should be put in carrying on the work of self-government.

These statements announced that they believed in the capacity of the people of the United States for self-government. They supported the Constitution, which they agreed prescribed a government of limited powers which were not too carefully defined. On the basic question of sectional conflict they both agreed to abide by and adhere to or, in the Whig phrase, to "acquiesce in," the Compromise of 1850 as a workable settlement of this vexed question. In effect they were committed to consensus. However, the appearance of such political aggregations as the Liberty, Free-Soil, and in 1856 the American parties had been warnings that this consensus might be premature.

Ever since the thirteen American colonies of Great Britain had begun holding congresses in 1765, there had been evidence of a built-in disunity, determined by ecological and demographic factors. The American communities were united by a common culture, but the

[1] See Appendix B.

different conditions under which they must live their lives were undermining the cultural unity which they instinctively sought. These environmental differences induced different mores, the most spectacular deviation being southern biracial rural society, with its Negro slavery, its lack of centers of enterprise, and its climate, which was more stimulating to romantic emotional motivation than to sustained realistic enterprise. Whenever the question of governing and the exercise of power had arisen, this difference of point of view had had to be reckoned with, from 1774 when the Articles of Association were drafted through 1858. It had always been possible to achieve some sort of consensus until 1860 despite the fact that a third party, the sectional Republicans, had become the second party in 1856 and had pushed the Whigs into the background.

It is significant that this pattern of political organization was completed when it was. The nation had just reached the limits of its immediate continental extent by establishing itself on the shores of the Pacific. Likewise, the institutions of self-government appeared to have achieved a highly commendable degree of stability. The republic had grown in population from 4,000,000 to 31,000,000 and the states from 13 to 34. Basic behavior patterns had been altered and complicated. The industrial revolution had brought in the machine, the factory, and factory town. Various other inventions, such as the mechanical reaper, were beginning to change a significant segment of the prevailing rural environment. But these changes were not distributed uniformly, and the fact that many of them had not entered the life of the South was as significant as the fact that the rapid increase of population was less marked there than in the ranges to the north and northwest. These various factors were inducing greater skill in organization in general, and the growth of party organization may be said to be a part thereof and correlated with it.

In this greatly expanded and fast-growing society significant means of communication had also been achieved. Although by present-day standards there was little through transportation possible, there were seven thousand miles of railroads in operation, and with steamboats on the rivers and the railroads between rivers and connecting the interior with the ports, travel was becoming increasingly expeditious and the networks more complete. The telegraph also was a new factor. These two advances together with mechanical progress in the techniques of printing meant that there were more, better, and larger newspapers with better news coverage. The improvements in transportation also had meant better postal facilities and, consequently, better distribution of journals. Because of these facilities, editors built up much larger exchange lists, and there was much more clipping of exchanges and printing of national news. Communication, information, and organization reached simultaneously a new state of technical proficiency. Would the American people be more closely knit and better able to practice the art of self-government now that their information would be more complete? Would all these advantages produce a better understanding? Could the 4,700,000 voters manage efficiently the great task of governing the 31,000,000?

The political operators had come to realize the need for institutionalizing politics. The nation could no longer afford to rely upon chance or upon personalities. There must be continuity of operation through something like permanent party organization which could be depended upon to function regularly. A real pattern was achieved at this significant time. The design of the operating mechanism of American democracy was this two-party system which had developed permanent organization. In 1848 the Democrats had institutionalized themselves by creating a managing body, the national committee, with continuous existence, and the Republicans made improvements in 1856.

The major parties embraced in this structure were of a size sufficiently equal to ensure close contests and varying success. Except in 1856 and 1860 there was no real ideological difference between them. There was consensus on basic principles, and occasional divergence was but momentarily significant. In fact, the Whigs had been reluctant to make any official platform at all. Both parties had eliminated dominating leadership. The Whigs had abandoned Clay, and Jackson was dead. Both parties were choosing candidates selected on the grounds of expediency and availability. They were only occasionally White House–oriented; indeed, the Whigs had never been. Party organization presented a neater picture among the Democrats than among the Whigs by virtue of the new national committee, but it was still largely under the control of the state leaders who used the national gatherings as trade conventions.

A series of events in the late fifties was producing a confusion which boded ill for stability and once again threatened the permanence of unity when the election of 1856 seemed to demonstrate the inevitability of an eventual Republican victory. When concern over this possibility was accompanied by continued anarchy in Kansas and followed by the Panic of 1857, the religious revival of 1858, John Brown's raid of 1859, and the political overturn in 1860, this series of events seemed to be evidences of a cumulation of tensions and confusions which threatened to be beyond the powers of the system of self-government to reconcile within a viable operative consensus. The consequent breakdown of government was the evidence rather than the cause of the inevitability of a conflict. But neither the Union nor the two-party system was to be destructible.

The Civil War proved to be the final fusing force necessary to produce the permanence of the mechanism of self-government. Hitherto, there had been an underlying distrust and uncertainty about the adequacy of our political institutions. Parties had been formed and feared on the basis of this insecurity. But despite the Civil War this system had survived, the two-party system had continued to operate during the conflict, and the first postwar election of 1868 found its elements battling each other and again closely matched. They were now met on a common ground of confidence in the value and indestructibility of the system which provided for a periodic, organized struggle for power within the narrow limits of basic agreement. The political machine was at length firmly established, designed to emphasize agreement on the nature of the republic and to supply candidates for the recurrent contests who entertained similar views and to ensure issues so narrowly defined that the battles, though exciting, would never be dangerous.

This pattern became standard and with occasional variations is in use today. It is managed by many state and some national operators who either choose one of themselves or some candidate peculiarly available to positions of leadership. Strongly represented in Congress and in the national party conventions and committees, these managers are the real engineers of government. Through politics, which they have made an art, they operate in efficient and reasonably smooth-running fashion a mechanism designed as nearly as possible to solve the problem of perpetual political motion.

A group of political instruments, first projected in the logical years of the Age of Reason in which the republic was born, have ranged from the Constitution to this completed party machine and have included various types of behavioral invention. Only once, and then in an age unfortunately romantic, has this machinery failed to provide the stability which it was designed to ensure. After that failure, it has now been working well for the past century, a product of human ingenuity which it took a millennium of experience on both sides of the Atlantic to invent.

APPENDIX A
PUBLISHED PROCEEDINGS OF THE
NATIONAL POLITICAL CONVENTIONS, 1830-1856

National Anti-Masonic Convention, Philadelphia, 1830

The proceedings of the United States Anti-Masonic Convention, held at Philadelphia, Sept. 11, 1830. Embracing the journal of proceedings, the reports, the debates, and the address to the people. Philadelphia, 1830. 164 pp.

National Republican Convention, Baltimore, 1831

Proceedings of the second United States Anti-Masonic Convention, held at Baltimore, Sept. 26, 1831. Journal and reports, nomination of candidates for President and Vice President of the United States, letters of acceptance, resolutions, and the address of the people. Boston, 1832. 88 pp.

National Republican Convention, Baltimore, 1831

Journal of the National Republican Convention, which assembled in the city of Baltimore, Dec. 12, 1831, for the nomination of candidates to fill the offices of President and Vice President. Published by order of the convention. Washington: National Journal [1831]. 32 pp.

National Republican Convention of Young Men,
Washington, D.C., 1832

Proceedings of the National Republican Convention of Young Men, which assembled in the city of Washington, May 7, 1832. Washington: Gales & Seaton, 1832. 24 pp.

National Republican Convention, Baltimore, 1832

Proceedings of a convention of Republican delegates from the several states in the Union for the purpose of nominating a candidate for the office of Vice President of the United States. Baltimore: S. Harker, 1831 (i.e. 1832). 10 pp.

Summary of the proceedings of a convention of Republican delegates for nominating a candidate for Vice President of the United States; held at Baltimore, 1832. With an address to the Republicans of the state of New York prepared by their delegates. Albany: Packard and Van Benthuysen, 1832. 24 pp.

Proceedings of a convention of delegates appointed by the Democratic Republicans in the several states of the Union, assembled in the city of Baltimore, May 20, 1835, for the purpose of nominating candidates for the offices of President and Vice President of the United States.

The Globe (Washington, D.C.), May 27, 28, Aug. 6, 1835.

National Whig Convention, Harrisburg, 1839

Proceedings of the Democratic Whig National Convention, which assembled at Harrisburg, Pennsylvania, Dec. 4, 1839, for the purpose of nominating candidates for President and Vice President of the United States. Harrisburg: R. S. Elliott & Co., 1839. 42 pp.

National Democratic Convention, Baltimore, 1840

Proceedings of the National Democratic Convention, held in Baltimore, 1840. Embracing resolutions and an address. Baltimore: 1840. 64 pp.

The Proceedings of the Democratic National Convention, May 27-30, 1844

The Daily Globe (Washington, D.C.), June 4-7, 1844
The Sun (Baltimore), May 28-31, 1844
Niles' National Register (Baltimore), June 1, 8, 1844, LXVI, 211-218, 227-228

The Proceedings of the Whig National Convention, May 1, 1844

Niles' National Register (Baltimore), May 4, June 8, 1844, LXVI, 146-148, 236

National Democratic Convention, Baltimore, 1848

The proceedings of the Democratic National Convention, held at

Baltimore, May 22, 1848. Washington: Blair & Rives, 1848. 31 pp.

Proceedings of the National Whig Convention June 7, 8, 9, 1848

Niles' National Register (Philadelphia), Nov. 29, Dec. 6, 1848, LXXIV, 349, 354-358

National Free Soil Party Convention, Buffalo, 1848

Oliver Dyer's phonographic report of the proceedings of the National Free Soil Convention at Buffalo, N.Y., August 9 and 10, 1848. Buffalo: G. H. Derby & Co., 1848. 32 pp.

National Democratic Convention, Baltimore, 1852

Proceedings of the Democratic National Convention, held at Baltimore, June, 1852. Reported and published by William Hincks and F. H. Smith. Washington: Buell & Blanchard, 1852. 44 pp.

Proceedings of the Democratic National Convention, held at Baltimore, June 1-5, 1852, for the nomination of candidates for President and Vice President of the United States. Washington: R. Armstrong, 1852. 78 pp.

Proceedings of the National Whig Convention June 15-19, 21, 1852
New York *Daily Tribune*, June 16-22, 1852

National Democratic Convention, Cincinnati, 1856

Official proceedings of the National Democratic Convention, held in Cincinnati, June 2-6, 1856. Published by order of the convention. Cincinnati: Enquirer Co., 1856. 78 pp.

National Republican Conventions, Pittsburgh and Philadelphia, 1856

Official proceedings of the Republican convention in the city of Pittsburgh, Pennsylvania, on February 22, 1856. Washington: Republican Association of Washington, 1856. 29 pp.

Address of the Republican convention, convened at Pittsburgh on February 22, 1856. Washington: Buell & Blanchard, 1856. 16 pp.

Proceedings of the first three Republican national conventions of 1856, 1860, and 1864, including proceedings of the antecedent national convention held at Pittsburgh in February, 1856, as reported by Horace Greeley. Minneapolis: Harrison & Smith, 1893. 264 pp.

APPENDIX B
DEMOCRATIC PLATFORM—1852

1. *Resolved,* That the American democracy place their trust in the intelligence, the patriotism, and the discriminating justice of the American people.

2. *Resolved,* That we regard this as a distinctive feature of our political creed, which we are proud to maintain before the world, as the great moral element in a form of government springing from and upheld by the popular will; and contrast it with the creed and practice of federalism, under whatever name or form, which seeks to palsy the will of the constituent, and which conceives no imposture too monstrous for the popular credulity.

3. *Resolved,* Therefore, that entertaining these views, the Democratic party of this Union, through the delegates assembled, in general convention of the states, coming together in a spirit of concord, of devotion to the doctrines and faith of a free representative government, and appealing to their fellow-citizens for the rectitude of their intentions, renew and reassert before the American people, the declaration of principles avowed by them on a former occasion, when, in general convention, they presented their candidates for the popular suffrage.

4. *Resolved,* That the Federal government is one of limited powers, derived solely from the constitution, and the grants of power shown therein ought to be strictly construed by all the departments and agents of the government, and that it is inexpedient and dangerous to exercise doubtful constitutional powers.

5. *Resolved,* That the constitution does not confer upon the general government the power to commence and carry on a general system of internal improvements.

6. *Resolved,* That the constitution does not confer authority upon the Federal government, directly or indirectly, to assume the debts of the several states, contracted for local internal improvements or other state purposes; nor would such assumption be just or expedient.

7. *Resolved,* That justice and sound policy forbid the Federal government to foster one branch of industry to the detriment of another, or to cherish the interests of one portion to the injury of another portion of our common country—that every citizen and every section of the country has a right to demand and insist upon an equality of rights and privileges, and to complete an ample protection of persons and property from domestic violence or foreign aggression.

8. *Resolved,* That it is the duty of every branch of the government to enforce and practice the most rigid economy in conducting our public affairs, and that no more revenue ought to be raised than is required to defray the necessary expenses of the government, and for the gradual but certain extinction of the public debt.

9. *Resolved,* That Congress has no power to charter a National Bank; that we believe such an institution one of deadly hostility to the best interests of the country, dangerous to our republican institutions and the liberties of the people, and calculated to place the business of the country within the control of a concentrated money power, and that above the laws and will of the people; and that the results of Democratic legislation, in this and all other financial measures, upon which issues have been made between the two political parties of the country; have demonstrated to candid and practical men of all parties, their soundness, safety, and utility, in all business pursuits.

10. *Resolved,* That the separation of the moneys of the government from banking institutions is indispensable for the safety of the funds of the government and the rights of the people.

11. *Resolved,* That the liberal principles embodied by Jefferson in the Declaration of Independence, and sanctioned in the constitution, which makes ours the land of liberty and the asylum of the oppressed of every nation, have ever been cardinal principles in the Democratic faith; and every attempt to abridge the privilege of becoming citizens and the owners of the soil among us, ought to be resisted with the same spirit that swept the alien and sedition laws from our statute books.

12. *Resolved,* That Congress has no power under the constitution to interfere with, or control, the domestic institutions of the several states, and that such states are the sole and proper judges of everything appertaining to their own affairs, not prohibited by the constitution; that all efforts of the Abolitionists or others, made to induce Congress to interfere with questions of slavery, or to take incipient steps in relation thereto, are calculated to lead to the most alarming and dangerous consequences; and that all such efforts have an inevita-

ble tendency to diminish the happiness of the people, and endanger the stability and permanency of the Union, and ought not to be countenanced by any friend of our political institutions.

13. *Resolved*, That the foregoing proposition covers, and is intended to embrace, the whole subject of slavery agitation in Congress; and therefore the Democratic party of the Union, standing on this national platform, will abide by, and adhere to, a faithful execution of the acts known as the Compromise measures settled by the last Congress, "the act for reclaiming fugitives from service labor" included; which act, being designed to carry out an express provision of the constitution, can not, with fidelity thereto, be repealed, nor so changed as to destroy or impair its efficiency.

14. *Resolved*, That the Democratic party will resist all attempts at renewing in Congress, or out of it, the agitation of the slavery question, under whatever shape or color the attempt may be made.

15. *Resolved*, That the proceeds of the public lands ought to be sacredly applied to the national objects specified in the constitution; and that we are opposed to any law for the distribution of such proceeds among the states as alike inexpedient in policy and repugnant to the constitution.

16. *Resolved*, That we are decidedly opposed to taking from the President the qualified veto power, by which he is enabled, under restrictions and responsibilities amply sufficient to guard the public interests, to suspend the passage of a bill whose merits can not secure the approval of two-thirds of the Senate and House of Representatives, until the judgment of the people can be obtained thereon, and which has saved the American people from the corrupt and tyrannical domination of the bank of the United States, and from a corrupting system of general internal improvements.

17. *Resolved*, That the Democratic party will faithfully abide by and uphold the principles laid down in the Kentucky and Virginia resolutions of 1797 and 1798, and in the report of Mr. Madison to the Virginia Legislature in 1799; that it adopts these principles as constituting one of the main foundations of its political creed, and is resolved to carry them out in their obvious meaning and import.

18. *Resolved*, That the war with Mexico, upon all the principles of patriotism and the law of nations, was a just and necessary war on our part, in which no American citizen should have shown himself opposed to his country, and neither morally nor physically, by word or deed, given aid and comfort to the enemy.

19. *Resolved*, That we rejoice at the restoration of friendly rela-

tions with our sister Republic of Mexico, and earnestly desire for her all the blessings and prosperity which we enjoy under republican institutions, and we congratulate the American people on the results of that war which have so manifestly justified the policy and conduct of the Democratic party, and insured to the United States indemnity for the past and security for the future.

20. *Resolved*, That, in view of the condition of popular institutions in the old world, a high and sacred duty is devolved with increased responsibility upon the Democracy of this country, as the party of the people, to uphold and maintain the rights of every state, and thereby the union of states, and to sustain and advance among them constitutional liberty, by continuing to resist all monopolies and exclusive legislation for the benefit of the few at the expense of the many and by a vigilant and constant adherence of those principles and compromises of the constitution which are broad enough and strong enough to embrace and uphold the Union as it is, and the Union as it would be, in the full expansion of the energies and capacity of this great and progressive people.

WHIG PLATFORM—1852

The Whigs of the United States, in convention assembled, adhering to the great conservative principles by which they are controlled and governed, and now, as ever, relying upon the intelligence of the American people, with an abiding confidence in their capacity for self-government, and their devotion to the Constitution and the Union, do proclaim the following as the political sentiments and determination for the establishment and maintenance of which their national organization as a party was effected:

First. The Government of the United States is of a limited character, and it is confined to the exercise of powers expressly granted by the Constitution, and such as may be necessary and proper for carrying the granted powers into full execution, and that powers not granted or necessarily implied are reserved to the States respectively and to the people.

Second. The State governments should be held secure to their reserved rights, and the General Government sustained on its constitutional powers, and that the Union should be revered and watched over as the palladium of our liberties.

Third. That while struggling freedom everywhere enlists the warmest sympathy of the Whig party, we still adhere to the doctrines of the Father of his Country, as announced in his Farewell Address, of keeping ourselves free from all entangling alliances with foreign countries, and of never quitting our own to stand upon foreign ground; that our mission as a republic is not to propagate our opinions, or impose on other countries our forms of government by artifice or force; but to teach by example, and show by our success, moderation and justice, the blessings of self-government and the advantage of free institutions.

Fourth. That, as the people make and control the Government, they should obey its Constitution, laws, and treaties, as they would retain their self-respect and the respect which they claim and will enforce from foreign powers.

Fifth. That the Government should be conducted on principles of the strictest economy; and revenue sufficient for the expenses thereof, in time of peace, ought to be mainly derived from a duty on imports, and not from direct taxes; and in laying such duties sound policy requires a just discrimination, and protection from fraud by specific duties, when practicable, whereby suitable encouragement may be afforded to American industry, equally to all classes and to all portions of the country.

Sixth. The Constitution vests in Congress the power to open and repair harbors, and remove obstructions from navigable rivers, whenever such improvements are necessary for the common defence and for the protection and facility of commerce with foreign nations or among the States—said improvements being in every instance national and general in their character.

Seventh. The Federal and State governments are parts of one system, alike necessary for the common prosperity, peace and security, and ought to be regarded alike with a cordial, habitual, and immovable attachment. Respect for the authority of each, and acquiescence in the just constitutional measures of each, are duties required by the plainest considerations of national, State and individual welfare.

Eighth. That the series of acts of the Thirty-second Congress, the act known as the Fugitive Slave law included, are received and acquiesced in by the Whig party of the United States as a settlement in principle and substance of the dangerous and exciting questions which they embrace; and, so far as they are concerned, we will maintain them, and insist upon their strict enforcement, until time and experience shall demonstrate the necessity of further legislation to guard against the evasion of the laws on the one hand and the abuse of their powers on the other, not impairing their present efficiency; and we deprecate all further agitation of the question thus settled, as dangerous to our peace, and will discountenance all efforts to continue or renew such agitation, whenever, wherever, or however the attempt may be made; and we will maintain this system as essential to the nationality of the Whig party and the integrity of the Union.

BIBLIOGRAPHICAL NOTES

I began the study of political behavior as a graduate student at Columbia when I undertook to analyze the situation in the Democratic party in the 1850's with the secondary objective of discovering what part it played in the outbreak of the Civil War. In the course of time I wrote three books: *The Democratic Machine 1850–1854; Franklin Pierce, Young Hickory of the Granite Hills;* and *The Disruption of American Democracy.* In the course of this study, 1919–48, I was lecturing to graduate students on the general theme of the evolution of American political behavior. In the 1930's I concluded that the basic patterns of this behavior were both ancient and not indigenous to the United States, so I undertook to explore their origin in time and place. The result was this book. This work, covering as it does not a decade, 1850–60, but in a somewhat fanciful sense something short of two millennia, 55 B.C. to A.D. 1856, could not be worked out on the basis of so detailed an exploration of the sources as had marked the research of the first three books.

I therefore had to substitute selectivity for complete coverage, secondary works for sources. Fortunately I was working in the midst of a changing climate of historical interest. I began at a time when scholarship was in revolt against a traditional concept of history as political and constitutional. New waves of doctrine, economic and social, were carrying the seminars by storm, and I seemed at times to be one of the "passing race." However, during the course of recent decades the waves, happily, have subsided and new tides have set in. There has been a veritable renascence of interest in political behavior in which political and social scientists, statisticians, and other analysts have contributed significantly. A new generation of vigorous minds and perceptive analysts have poured forth a series of studies. So-called political history, albeit in a behavioral guise, has come into its own.

In the following pages I present chapter by chapter, some lists of books which may be useful to those wishing to corroborate what I have written, to confound it or to carry it further.

CHAPTER I

Evolution of English political institutions: *The Anglo-Saxon Chronicle. A Revised Translation,* ed., Dorothy Wheelock with David C. Douglas and Susie I. Tucker, 1961; S. B. Chrimes, *English Constitutional Ideas in the Fifteenth Century,* 1936; George L. Haskins, *Growth of English Representative Government,* 1948; C. Warren Hollister, *Military Organization of Norman England,* 1965; Ernest Frazier Jacob, *Oxford History of England, Fifteenth Century,*

1399–1485, VI, 1961; J. E. A. Joliffe, *Constitutional History of Medieval England*, 1937; M. M. Knappen, *Constitutional and Legal History of England*, 1942; William Dunkel, *William Lambarde, Elizabethan Jurist 1536–1601*, 1965; E. M. Leonard, *The Early History of English Poor Relief*, 1900; William E. Lunt, *History of England*, 3rd edition, 1946; May McKisack, *Oxford History of England, Fourteenth Century, 1307–1399*, V, 1959, and *Representation of English Borough in the Middle Ages*, 1932; J. E. Neale, *Elizabethan House of Commons*, 1949, *Elizabeth I and Her Parliaments*, 1953–57, *Essays in Elizabethan History*, 1956; J. R. Pole, *Political Representation in England and the Origins of the American Republic*, 1966; Wallace E. Notestein, *The English People on the Eve of Colonization*, 1954; Austin L. Poole, *Oxford History of England, from Domesday Book to Magna Carta*, III, 1955; *New Cambridge Modern History, The Renaissance, 1493–1520*, I, George R. Potter, ed., 1957; Frederick M. Powicke, *Oxford History of England, The Thirteenth Century*, IV, 1953; H. G. Richardson and G. O. Sayles, *The Governance of Medieval England from the Conquest to Magna Carta*, 1963; Frank M. Stenton, *Oxford History of England, Anglo-Saxon England*, II, 1947; George M. Trevelyan, *England in the Age of Wyclif*, 1909; Eleanor Trotter, *Seventeenth Century Life in the Country Parish*, 1919; Albert B. White, *Self Government at the King's Command*, 1933.

English religious influences: John W. Allen, *A History of Political Thought in the Sixteenth Century*, 1928, and *English Political Thought, 1603–1660*, 1938; *New Cambridge Modern History, The Reformation, 1520–1559*, II, Geoffrey R. Elton, ed., 1958; Christina H. Garrett, *The Marian Exiles*, 1938, 1966; Thomas C. Hall, *Religious Background of American Culture*, 1930; William Haller, *Rise of Protestantism*, 1938; Albert Peel, *The First Congregational Churches*, 1920; Frederick M. Powicke, *The Reformation in England*, 1941, and *Cambridge Platonists*, 1926.

English commercial venturing: Mildred Campbell, *English Yeoman under Elizabeth and the Early Stuarts*, 1942; William E. Lingelbach, *Merchant Adventurers of England*, 1902; David B. Quinn, *Raleigh and the British Empire*, 1949; A. L. Rowse, *The Elizabethans and America*, 1959; William R. Scott, *Constitution and Finance of English, Scottish and Irish Joint Stock Companies to 1720*, 1910–12; Louis B. Wright, *Religion and the Empire . . . 1558–1625*, 1943.

CHAPTER II

Charles M. Andrews, *The Colonial Period of American History*, I, 1934; Bernard Bailyn, "Politics and Social Structures in Virginia" in *Seventeenth Century America*, James Morton Smith, ed., 1959; Alexander Brown, *The First Republic in America*, 1898; Charles Campbell, *History of the Colony and Ancient Dominion of Virginia*, 1847; Wesley Frank Craven, *Dissolution of the Virginia Colony*, 1932; *The Southern Colonies in the Seventeenth Century*, Vol. I of *History of the South*, Wendell H. Stephenson and E. Merton Coulter, eds., 1949; Richard L. Morton, *Colonial Virginia*, 1960; *Travels and Works of Captain John Smith*, Edward Smith and A. G. Bradley, eds., 1910; William Stith, *History of Virginia*, 1747; Thomas J. Wertenbaker, *The Shaping of Colonial Virginia*, 1958; Louis B. Wright, *The First Gentlemen of Virginia*, 1940; *Records of the Virginia Company of London*, Susan M. Kingsbury, ed., 1933.

Chapter III

Testimony of the founders: William Bradford, *Of Plymouth Plantation,* Samuel E. Morison, ed., 1952; John Winthrop, *Journal,* James Savage, ed., 1853. Findings of the scholars: James T. Adams, *The Founding of New England,* 1921; Charles M. Andrews, *The Colonial Period of American History,* I, II, 1934; Bernard Bailyn, *The New England Merchants in the Seventeenth Century,* 1950; Emery Battis, *Saints and Sectaries: Anne Hutchinson and the Antinomian Controversy,* 1962; Daniel J. Boorstin, *The Americans: The Colonial Experience,* 1958; Samuel H. Brockunier, *The Irrepressible Democrat Roger Williams,* 1940; Isabel M. Calder, *The New Haven Colony,* 1937; Richard S. Dunn, *Puritans and Yankees—The Winthrop Dynasty of New England, 1630–1717,* 1962; William Haller, Jr., *The Puritan Frontier Town Planning . . . 1630–1660,* 1951; George L. Haskins, *Law and Authority in Early Massachusetts,* 1960; Edmund S. Morgan, *The Puritan Dilemma: The Story of John Winthrop,* 1958; Samuel E. Morison, *The Builders of the Bay State,* 1930; Sumner Chilton Powell, *Puritan Village: The Formation of a New England Town,* 1963; Darrell B. Rutman, *Winthrop's Boston: Portrait of a Puritan Town, 1630–1649,* 1965; Alan Simpson, *Puritanism in Old and New England,* 1955; *Seventeenth Century America: Essays in Colonial History,* James M. Smith, ed., 1957; Harry M. Ward, *The United Colonies of New England, 1643–1690,* 1961; Ola E. Winslow, *Master Roger Williams,* 1957.

Chapter IV

The First Proprietors: Frank B. Sanborn, *New Hampshire,* 1904; Richard A. Preston, *Gorges of Plymouth Fort,* 1953; Newton D. Mereness, *Maryland as a Proprietary Province,* 1901; Elizabeth Baer, *Seventeenth Century Maryland,* 1949.

The Proprietors of the Middle Colonies: *History of the State of New York,* I-III, C. C. Flick, ed., 1933; Morton Pennypacker, *The Dukes Laws,* 1944; Wesley Frank Craven, *New Jersey & the English Colonization of America,* 1964; Richard P. McCormick, *New Jersey from Colony to State,* 1964; John E. Pomfret, *The Province of West New Jersey,* 1952, *The Province of East New Jersey,* 1956, *The New Jersey Proprietors and Their Lands,* 1964; Edwin B. Bronner, *William Penn's Holy Experiment,* 1962; Frederick B. Tolles, *Meeting House and Counting House: Quaker Merchants of Colonial Philadelphia,* 1948.

The Southern Proprietors: R. D. W. Connor, et al, *History of North Carolina,* 1919; Hugh T. Lefler and A. Ray Newsome, *North Carolina, the History of a Southern State,* 1954; David D. Wallace, *History of South Carolina,* 1934, and *South Carolina: A Short History,* 1951; M. Eugene Sirmans, *Colonial South Carolina: A Political History 1663–1763,* 1966; Verner W. Crane, *Southern Frontier,* 1928; A. A. Ettinger, *James Edward Oglethorpe,* 1936; Trevor Richard Reese, *Colonial Georgia,* 1963.

Chapter V

W. W. Abbot, *Royal Governor of Georgia,* 1940; Viola Barnes, *The Dominion of New England,* 1923; C. L. Becker, *History of Political Parties in the Province of New York,* 1909; Cortland F. Bishop, *History of Elections in the American Colonies,* 1955; Carl Bridenbaugh, *Cities in Revolt,* 1955; Richard

M. Brown, *South Carolina Regulators*, 1963; Robert E. and B. Katherine Brown, *Virginia, 1705–1786: Democracy or Aristocracy*, 1964; Mary Patterson Clarke, *Parliamentary Privilege in the American Colonies*, 1943; Leonidas Dodson, *Alexander Spottswood*, 1932; Percy S. Flippin, *The Royal Government of Virginia, 1624–1775*, 1919; Douglas S. Freeman, *George Washington*, (7 vols.), 1948–1954; William H. Fry, *New Hampshire as a Royal Province*, 1908; Lawrence H. Gipson, *British Empire before the American Revolution*, (12 vols.), 1936–1967; Jack P. Greene, *The Quest for Power: Lower Houses of Assembly in the Southern Royal Colonies, 1689–1776*, 1963; Michael G. Hall, *Edward Randolph and the American Colonies, 1676–1703*, 1960; Bernard Knollenberg, *George Washington: The Virginia Period*, 1964; Leonard W. Labaree, *Royal Government in America*, 1930; Leonard W. Levy, *Legacy of Suppression: Freedom of Speech and Press in Early American History*, 1960; Irving Mark, *Agrarian Conflicts in Colonial New York, 1711–1775*, 1940; A. E. McKinley, *Suffrage Franchise in the English Colonies*, 1905; Perry Miller, *From Colony to Province*, 1953; T. F. Moran, *Rise and Development of the Bicameral System in America*, 1895; Robert Munford, *The Candidates or the Humours of a Virginia Election*, 1948; Herbert L. Osgood, *The American Colonies in the Eighteenth Century*, 1924; Jerome R. Reich, *Jacob Leisler's Rebellion*, 1953; Dietmar Rothermund, *The Layman's Progress: Religious and Political Experience in Colonial Pennsylvania, 1740–1770*, c 1961; W. Roy Smith, *South Carolina as a Royal Province*, 1903; Theodore Thayer, *Pennsylvania Politics and the Growth of Democracy*, 1953; Wilcomb Washburn, *The Governor and the Rebel*, 1957; Thomas J. Wertenbaker, *Torchbearer of the Revolution*, 1940.

CHAPTERS VI–VIII

James T. Adams, *Revolutionary New England, 1691–1776*, 1923; John R. Alden, *The American Revolution*, 1951, and *The South in the Revolution*, 1957; Clarence W. Alvord, *The Mississippi Valley in British Politics*, 1916; Edith A. Bailey, *Influence Toward Radicalism in Connecticut, 1754–1775*, 1920; Charles A. Barker, *Background of the Revolution in Maryland*, 1940; Daniel Boorstin, *The Genius of American Politics*, 1953, and *The Americans: the Colonial Experience*, 1958; Julian P. Boyd, *Anglo-American Union*, 1941; Carl Bridenbaugh, *Mitre and Sceptre . . . 1689–1775*, 1962; Robert E. Brown, *Middle Class Democracy and the Revolution in Massachusetts, 1691–1780*, 1955; Kenneth Coleman, *The American Revolution in Georgia, 1763–1789*, c 1958; Philip A. Crowl, *Maryland During and After the Revolution*, 1943; Philip Davidson, *Propaganda and the American Revolution*, 1941; Bernard Donoughue, *British Politics and the American Revolution*, 1964; O. M. Dickerson, *The Navigation Acts and the American Revolution*, 1951; Elisha P. Douglass, *Rebels and Democrats*, c 1955; L. H. Gipson, *The Coming of the Revolution, 1763–1775*, 1954; E. B. Greene, *The Revolutionary Generation, 1763–1790*, 1943; William S. Hanna, *Benjamin Franklin and Pennsylvania Politics*, 1964; L. A. Harper, *English Navigation Laws*, 1939; David Hawke, *In the Midst of Revolution*, 1961; J. F. Jameson, *The American Revolution Considered as a Social Movement*, 1940; Donald L. Kemmerer, *Path of Freedom* [New Jersey], 1940; Bernhard Knollenberg, *Origin of the American Revolution, 1759–1766*, 1960; David S. Lovejoy, *Rhode Island Politics and the American Revolution, 1760–*

1776, 1958; Leonard Lundin, *Cockpit of the Revolution* [New Jersey], 1940; Jackson Turner Main, *The Social Structure of Revolutionary America*, 1965; Joseph J. Malone, *Pine Trees and Politics . . . 1691–1775*, c 1964; David J. May, *Edmund Pendleton*, 1952; Charles H. McIlwain, *The American Revolution: a Constitutional Interpretation*, 1923; J. C. Miller, *Sam Adams: Pioneer in Propaganda*, 1936, 1960, *Origins of the American Revolution*, 1943, 1960, *Triumph of Freedom*, *1775–1783*, 1948; Edmund S. Morgan, *The Birth of the Republic*, *1763–1769*, 1956; Edmund S. and Helen Morgan, *The Stamp Act Crisis*, 1953; L. B. Namier, *The Structure of Politics at the Accession of George III*, 1958; L. B. Namier and John Brooke, *Charles Townshend*, 1964; C. P. Nettels, *George Washington and American Independence*, 1951; Allan Nevins, *American States During and After the Revolution*, 1924; Lee Nathaniel Newcomer, *The Embattled Farmers: Massachusetts*, 1953; Robert R. Palmer, *The Age of the Democratic Revolution: A Political History of Europe and America*, *1760–1800*, 1959, 1964; Richard Pares, *King George III and the Politicians*, 1957; C. R. Ritcheson, *British Politics and the American Revolution*, 1954; Clinton Rossiter, *Seed-Time of the Republic*, 1953; Max Savelle, *Seeds of Liberty*, 1948; A. M. Schlesinger, Sr., *The Colonial Merchants and the American Revolution*, 1918: Robert L. Schuyler, *Parliament and the British Empire*, 1929; Jack M. Sosin, *Whitehall and the Wilderness*, 1961, and *Agents and Merchants: British Colonial Policy and the Origins of the American Revolution*, 1965; Charles S. Sydnor, *Gentlemen Freeholders: Political Practices in Washington's Virginia*, 1952; Robert J. Taylor, *Western Massachusetts in the Revolution*, 1954; Carl Ubbelohde, *The Vice Admiralty Courts and the American Revolution*, 1960; Richard Walsh, *Charleston's Sons of Liberty: A Study of Artisans*, *1763–1789*, 1959; J. Steven Watson, *The Reign of George III*, 1962; Esmond Wright, *Fabric of Freedom*, 1961; Oscar Zeichner, *Connecticut's Years of Controversy*, *1750–1776*, 1950.

CHAPTERS IX–X

Merrill Jensen, *Articles of Confederation*, 1948, and *The New Nation*, 1950; Charles A. Beard, *An Economic Interpretation of the Constitution*, 1913; Catherine Drinker Bowen, *Miracle at Philadelphia*, 1966; William Crosskey, *Politics and the Constitution in the History of the United States*, 1953; Burton J. Hendrick, *Bulwark of the Republic*, 1937; Cecilia M. Kenyon, *The Antifederalists*, 1965; Forrest McDonald, *We the People: The Economic Origins of the Constitution*, 1958, and *E Pluribus Unum, The Formation of the American Republic*, *1776–1790*, 1965; Jackson Turner Main, *The Antifederalists*, *1781–1788*, 1961; Francis S. Philbrick, *The Rise of the West*, *1754–1830*, 1965; Fred Rodell, *Fifty-five Men*, 1936; Frank F. Stephens, *Transitional Period*, *1788–1789*, 1909; Charles Warren, *The Making of the Constitution*, 1937; Chilton Williamson, *American Suffrage from Property to Democracy*, *1760–1860*, 1960; Benjamin F. Wright, *Consensus and Continuity*, *1776–1787*, 1958; James T. Adams, *New England in the Republic*, 1926; S. B. Harding, *Contest over Ratification in Massachusetts*, 1896; R. J. Purcell, *Connecticut in Transition*, 1918; Thomas Cochran, *New York and the Confederation*, 1932; Richard P. McCormick, *Experiment in Independence: New Jersey in the Critical Period*, 1950; Robert L. Brunhouse, *Counter Revolution in Pennsylvania*, 1942;

L. I. Trenholme, *Ratification of the Federal Constitution in North Carolina*, 1932.

CHAPTERS XI–XIII

Thomas P. Abernethy, *The South in the New Nation, 1789–1819*, 1961; Leland D. Baldwin, *Whiskey Rebels*, 1939; Charles A. Beard, *Economic Origins of Jeffersonian Democracy*, 1915; Stuart G. Brown, *The First Republicans*, 1954; Joseph Charles, *The Origins of the American Party System*, 1956; Noble E. Cunningham, Jr., *Jeffersonian Republicans: Formation of Party Organization, 1789–1801*, 1957, and *Jeffersonian Republicans in Power*, 1963; F. W. Dallinger, *Nominations for Elective Office*, 1897; Manning J. Dauer, *The Adams Federalists*, 1953; Alexander Deconde, *Entangling Alliance: Politics and Diplomacy Under George Washington*, 1958; Russell J. Ferguson, *Early Western Pennsylvania*, 1938; David Hackett Fischer, *The Revolution of American Conservatives*, 1965; *Memoirs of the Administration of Washington and John Adams*, George Gibbs, ed., 1846; Paul Goodman, *The Democratic Republicans of Massachusetts*, 1964; Rufus W. Griswold, *The Republican Court; or Society in the Days of Washington*, 1855; Bray Hammond, *Banks and Politics in America, 1776–1861*, 1957; James Hart, *The American Presidency in Action in 1789*, 1948; Louis Hartz, *Liberal Tradition in America*, 1955; Stephen G. Kurtz, *The Presidency of John Adams: The Collapse of Federalism*, 1957; George D. Leutscher, *Early Political Machinery in the United States*, 1903; Eugene P. Link, *Democratic Republican Societies, 1790–1800*, 1942; Shaw Livermore, *Twilight of Federalism*, 1962; John C. Miller, *The Federalist Era, 1789–1801*, 1960; John A. Munroe, *Federalist Delaware, 1775–1815*, 1954; Lloyd M. Short, *Development of National Administrative Organization*, 1923; James M. Smith, *Freedom's Fetters: The Alien and Sedition Laws and American Civil Liberties*, 1956; Harry M. Tinkcom, *Republicans and Federalists in Pennsylvania, 1790–1801*, 1950; Frank van der Linden, *The Turning Point: Jefferson's Battle for the Presidency*, 1962; Raymond Walters, Jr., *Albert Gallatin*, 1957; Leonard White, *The Federalists*, 1948; Page Smith, *John Adams*, 1962; Winfred E. A. Bernhard, *Fisher Ames*, 1965; Morton Borden, *Federalism of James Bayard*, 1955; William H. Masterson, *William Blount*, 1954; John C. Miller, *Alexander Hamilton*, 1959; Broadus Mitchell, *Alexander Hamilton* (2 vols.), 1957–1962; Nathan Schachner, *Alexander Hamilton*, 1946; Frank Monaghan, *John Jay*, 1935; Dumas Malone, *Thomas Jefferson*, (3 vols.), 1943–1962; Nathan Schachner, *Thomas Jefferson*, 1951; George Dangerfield, *Chancellor Robert R. Livingston of New York*, 1960; Richard E. Welch, Jr., *Theodore Sedgwick, Federalist*, 1965; Douglas S. Freeman, *George Washington*, (7 vols.), 1948–1954; Nathaniel W. Stephenson and Waldo H. Dunn, *George Washington*, (2 vols.), 1940.

CHAPTERS XIV–XVI

Henry Adams, *History of the United States, 1801–1817*, (9 vols.), 1889–1891; James T. Adams, *The Living Jefferson*, 1936; Claude Bowers, *Jefferson in Power*, 1936; Irving Brant, *James Madison*, (6 vols.), 1941–1961; Roger H. Brown, *The Republic in Peril: 1812*, 1964 ; W. C. Bruce, *John Randolph of Roanoke*, 1922; R. Carlyle Buley, *The Old Northwest: Pioneer Period, 1815–1840*, 1950; Albert Z. Carr, *The Coming of War . . . 1812*, 1960; W. P. Cresson, *James Monroe*, 1946; George Dangerfield, *The Awakening of American Nationalism, 1815–1828*, 1965, and *The Era of Good Feelings*, 1952; D. R. Fox, *Decline of Aristocracy in the Politics of New York*, 1919; Reginald Horsman, *Causes of the War of 1812*, 1962; J. A. Krout and D. R. Fox, *Completion of Independence*, 1944; Bradford Perkins, *Prologue to War . . . 1805–1812*, 1961; Arthur Styron, *Last of the Cocked Hats: Monroe*, 1945; Patrick C. T. White, *A Nation on Trial: America and the War of 1812*, 1965; Louis Hartz, *Economic Policy and Democratic Thought: Pennsylvania, 1776–1860*, 1948; Sanford W. Higginbotham, *The Keystone in the Democratic Arch: Pennsylvania Politics, 1800–1816*, 1952; Gustavus Myers, *The History of Tammany Hall*, 1917; J. W. Pratt, *Expansionists of 1812*, 1949; Norman K. Risjord, *The Old Republicans*, 1965; Leonard D. White, *The Jeffersonians: A Study in Administration History, 1801–1829*, 1951; James Sterling Young, *The Washington Community, 1800–1828*, 1966.

CHAPTERS XVII–XVIII

D. S. Alexander, *Political History of New York*, 1906; J. S. Bassett, *Andrew Jackson*, 1925; Samuel F. Bemis, *John Quincy Adams*, 1956; George Dangerfield, *Era of Good Feelings*, 1952; C. R. Fish, *Rise of Common Man*, 1937; Marquis James, *Andrew Jackson*, 1933–1937; Alvin Kass, *Politics in New York State*, 1965; James A. Kehl, *Ill Feeling in the Era of Good Feeling: Western Pennsylvania Political Battles, 1815–1825*, 1956; Philip S. Klein, *Pennsylvania Politics, 1817–1832*, 1940; Glover Moore, *The Missouri Compromise, 1819–1821*, 1953; Francis S. Philbrick, *The Rise of the West, 1754–1830*, 1965; Harry R. Stevens, *Early Jackson Party in Ohio*, 1957; C. S. Sydnor, *The Development of Southern Sectionalism, 1819–48*, 1948; G. G. Van Deusen, *Henry Clay*, 1937, and *Thurlow Weed*, 1947; Florence Weston, *Presidential Election of 1828*, 1938; Lonnie J. White, *Politics on Southwestern Frontier, 1819–1836*, 1964; Charles M. Wiltse, *John C. Calhoun*, (3 vols.), 1944–1951, and *The New Nation*, 1961.

CHAPTERS XIX–XX

A. M. Schlesinger, Jr., *Age of Jackson*, 1945; Lee Benson, *The Concept of Jacksonian Democracy, New York as a Test Case*, 1961; C. S. Boucher, *Nullification Controversy in South Carolina*, 1916; E. Malcolm Carroll, *Origins of the Whig Party*, 1925; A. C. Cole, *Whig Party in the South*, 1913; C. R. Fish, *Civil Service and Patronage*, 1904; Hugh R. Fraser, *Democracy in the Making*, 1938; William W. Freehling, *Prelude to Civil War: Nullification Controversy in South Carolina, 1816–1836*, 1966; Samuel R. Gammon, *Presidential Campaign of 1832*, 1922; Richard P. McCormick, *The Second American Party System*, 1966; Robert V. Remini, *The Election of Andrew Jackson*, 1963, and *Martin Van Buren and the Making of the Democratic Party*, 1959; Leonard D. White, *The Jacksonians*, 1954; William N. Chambers, *Old Bullion Benton*, 1956; Elbert B. Smith, *Magnificent Missourian: Thomas Hart Benton*, 1958; Thomas P. Govan, *Nicholas Biddle*, 1959; W. C. Smith, *The Blair Family in Politics*, 1933.

CHAPTERS XXI–XXIV

F. J. Turner, *The United States, 1830–1850*, 1935; Glyndon G. Van Deusen, *The Jacksonian Era, 1828–1848*, 1959; Ray A. Billington, *The Protestant Cru-*

sade, 1938; H. D. A. Donovan, *The Barnburners*, 1925; Robert G. Gunderson, *The Log-Cabin Campaign*, 1957; O. D. Lambert, *Presidential Politics in the U. S.*, *1841–1844*, 1936; Frederick Merk, *Manifest Destiny and Mission*, 1963; Marvin Meyers, *Jacksonian Persuasion*, 1957; James C. N. Paul, *Rift in the Democracy*, 1951; R. R. Russel, *Improvement of Communication with the Pacific Coast as an Issue in American Politics, 1783–1864*, 1948; Charles McCool Snyder, *The Jacksonian Heritage: Pennsylvania Politics, 1833–1848*, 1958; E. G. Bourne, *History of the Surplus Revenue of 1837*, 1885; Stanley M. Elkins, *Slavery*, 1963; David Kinley, *The Independent Treasury of the U. S.*, 1910; R. McGrane, *Panic of 1837*, 1924; Russel B. Nye, *Cultural Life of the New Nation*, 1960; Kenneth M. Stampp, *The Peculiar Institution: Slavery*, 1956; Richard C. Wade, *Slavery in the Cities*, 1964; G. M. Barnes, *Anti-Slavery Impulse 1830–1844*, 1933; D. L. Dumond, *Anti-Slavery: The Crusade for Freedom in America*, 1961; John Hope Franklin, *From Slavery to Freedom*, 1956; J. A. Krout, *Origins of Prohibition*, 1925; Arthur Y. Lloyd, *Slavery Controversy 1831–1860*, 1939; Alice F. Tyler, *Freedom's Ferment*, 1944; Russell B. Nye, *George Bancroft*, 1945; Philip S. Klein, *President James Buchanan* (early years), 1962; G. R. Poage, *Henry Clay and the Whig Party*, 1936; G. G. Van Deusen, *Henry Clay*, 1937; D. B. Goebel, *William Henry Harrison*, 1926; Leland W. Meyer, *Life and Times of Col. R. M. Johnson*, 1932; James A. Rawley, *Edwin D. Morgan*, 1955; R. F. Nichols, *Franklin Pierce*, 2nd edition, 1958; E. I. McCormac, *James K. Polk*, 1922; Charles G. Sellers, Jr., *James K. Polk, 1795–1846*, 1957, 1966; Charles H. Ambler, *Thomas Ritchie*, 1913; Holman Hamilton, *Zachary Taylor*, 1941, 1951; Robert Seager, *And Tyler Too*, 1963; Holmes Alexander, *Martin Van Buren*, 1935; James P. Shenton, *Robert J. Walker*, 1961; Richard N. Current, *Daniel Webster and the Rise of National Conservatism*, 1955; C. M. Fuess, *Daniel Webster* (2 vols.), 1930; Charles Buxton Going, *David Wilmot*, 1924; John A. Garraty, *Silas Wright*, 1949.

INDEX

A

H

I

J